The Contentious Crown

To my parents
Jean and Peter Williams

The Contentious Crown

Public Discussion of the British Monarchy in the Reign of Queen Victoria

RICHARD WILLIAMS

Ashgate

Published by
Ashgate Publishing Limited
Gower House
Croft Road
Aldershot
Hants GU11 3HR
England

Ashgate Publishing Company
Old Post Road
Brookfield
Vermont 05036–9704
USA

British Library Cataloguing-in-Publication data.

Williams, Richard
   The contentious crown : public discussion of the British
monarchy in the reign of Queen Victoria.
   1. Monarchy—Great Britain—Public opinion—History
   2. Republicanism—Great Britain—History   3. Great Britain—
Politics and government—1837–1901
   I. Title
   941'.081

Library of Congress Cataloging-in-Publication data.

Williams, Richard
     The contentious crown : public discussion of the British monarchy
   in the reign of Queen Victoria / Richard Williams.
     Enlargement of author's thesis (Ph.D.)—Cambridge University,
   1989, originally presented under the title: Public discussion of the
   British monarchy, 1837–87.
     Includes index.
     ISBN 1-85928-106-0 (hb : acid-free paper)
     1. Great Britian—Politics and government—1837–1901.   2. Public
   opinion—Great Britain—History—19th century.   3. Monarchy—Great
   Britain—Public opinion.   4. Victoria, Queen of Great Britain,
   1819–1901.   I. Title.
   DA550.W73   1997
   320.941'09'034—dc21   96-51681
                                                             CIP

ISBN 1 85928 106 0

Printed on acid free paper

Typeset in Sabon by Manton Typesetters, 5–7 Eastfield Road, Louth, Lincolnshire and printed in Great Britain by the Ipswich Book Company, Suffolk.

Contents

Preface

This book is an expansion and updating of my 1989 Cambridge PhD thesis, 'Public discussion of the British monarchy 1837–87'. I would like to thank Professor David Cannadine, who first excited my interest in the subject when I was an undergraduate, supervised my thesis and renewed his advice and encouragement during preparation of the book. I would also like to thank Professor Derek Beales who was my initial PhD supervisor when David Cannadine was on sabbatical.

I am grateful to several people for the fact that the thesis has now become a book. Dr Miles Taylor encouraged me to return to the subject three years ago. Alec McAulay at Scolar Press has shown the patience necessary to obtain a book from someone working outside the higher education system. I could not have carried out the extra research without the help of the Fellows of Churchill College, Cambridge who elected me to a Schoolteacher By-Fellowship in Easter Term, 1994, and my then employers, Gorseinon College, who gave me leave of absence to take it up. Mary, my wife, has generously put up with three book-dominated Summer 'holidays'.

My most long-standing debts are acknowledged in the dedication.

Richard Williams

CHAPTER ONE

Introduction

Until recently nineteenth-century history was written mainly in terms of the 'rise of the middle class' and the 'making of the working class', while what might be called 'the survival of the 'upper class' – the monarchy and aristocracy – was neglected. The work of F.M.L Thompson began to redress the balance as far as the aristocracy is concerned[1] and the 1980s were marked by a reaction, possibly not unconnected with political developments, against the 'history from below' which dominated the 1960s and 1970s and the substitution of a revisionist 'history from above'. That the aristocracy survived and prospered in the nineteenth century has been demonstrated by David Cannadine, W.D. Rubinstein, Lawrence Stone and J.V. Beckett.[2]

Yet a major study of the institution and caste at the very apex of Victorian society – the monarchy and Royal Family – has yet to be produced, despite the new historical interest in the monarchy resulting from the renewal of debate about the institution in the 1990s.[3] Biographies of Queen Victoria abound but they have not on the whole been written by professional historians concerned with the relationship of the Crown and royalty to the wider Victorian world while one that does purport to do this[4] was not, as the author acknowledges, a work of fresh research. Such contextualized work as has been produced has either focused narrowly on one event[5] or, in bold, broad exploratory essays, has of necessity been too superficial and schematic.[6] This book is not an internal study of the Queen and court but an analysis of attitudes to the monarchy. What did Victorians make of the archaic, hereditary institution which stood atop a society priding itself on progress, political reform, middle-class energy and self-made success? Until now we have known of Victorian attitudes to work, religion, sex and drink, but not of attitudes to the institution whose incumbent gave to the society and epoch their name. My key sources are not the Queen's own letters and journals but contemporary writings – in newspapers, journals, pamphlets and popular ballads – and parliamentary and public debates on the monarchy. There are already accounts, based on the Queen's private writings, of her relations with ministers and of her political and social outlook:[7] here I am less concerned with what Victoria did and what sort of Queen she was than with what people thought she did and what sort of Queen they thought she was.

I cannot pretend to be making an analysis of national public opinion, except in so far as newspapers and speech-makers reflect and shape the opinions of their readers and audiences. Readers' letters to newspapers, figures of attendance at republican meetings or of participation in celebrations of royal events hint, in descending degrees of certainty, at popular attitudes, but, while a sociologist undertaking a study of attitudes to the current monarchy and Royal Family would make a mass observation survey, the historian cannot interview the dead. Local studies, ransacking surviving diaries and other such sources, will be needed before anything more precise can be deduced about the opinions of the silent majority.

What I can provide, however, is a view over the shoulder of the makers of public discourse in Victorian England as they observe and comment on the monarchy. I have largely confined myself to public rather than private writings as I feel that the former are more important in that they show how much public discussion of the monarchy there was and how rigorous and varied was that discussion. The private diaries and letters of important people were read by only one or two contemporaries, even if the writer had an eye on posterity, but newspaper articles, speeches and pamphlets were read and intended to be read by large numbers of people – and therefore it is these sources that are so significant in reconstructing how those in the informed, literary and political society presented the monarchy to the sections of the public whose opinion they believed they reflected and moulded. W.R. Fox Bourne, erstwhile editor of the *Examiner*, wrote in 1887 of the interaction between newspapers and opinion – only in the past few years had the increase in the intelligence of the readership of newspapers definitely tipped the balance and made the leading article less the stentorian director of opinion than its mirror.[8]

This was pre-eminently a literate society, a 'print-culture' in which the vehicle of public debate was the written word.[9] Politicians and their literary propagandists attempted to influence opinion on the great issues through the reproduction in print of speeches, through the publication of pamphlets and, above all, through the newspapers. For much of the period under my examination editors such as Fox Bourne felt justified in regarding their newspapers as 'thrones and altars' from which 'to control and reform the world'.[10] Popular movements needed newspapers to propagate their beliefs. Chartism, the greatest working-class movement of this period, had the *Northern Star* as its organ. A particular concern of mine, republicanism, a school of thought in the late 1840s and 1850s and an organized movement in the early 1870s, spoke through newspapers – a series of short-lived, specifically republican ones in the former period, and through established weeklies, the *National Reformer* and *Reynolds's Newspaper*, in the latter.[11] A recent historian of the Victorian press, Lucy Brown has written, 'In the second half of the nineteenth century the newspaper became established as part of the normal furniture of life for all classes'.[12]

The newspapers that I have read can be divided into different categories which illuminate the views of the monarchy being received by different sections of society. The London dailies were read by the better-off middle class in the capital and, thanks to the railways and the enterprise of newsagents such as W.H. Smith, in the provinces. Before the removal of stamp duties in 1855 the cost of a daily paper was prohibitive and circulation was low, with *The Times*' figure of 50,000 in the early 1850s putting it ahead of the others such as the *Standard*, *Morning Post*, *Morning Herald*, *Globe*, *Morning Chronicle* and *Morning Advertiser*.[13] Provincial weeklies and bi-weeklies were bought by the same people who took the dailies from the capital – the *Leeds Mercury* had a circulation of 9,000 in 1845.[14] With the removal of duties and of the paper tax in 1861, *The Times*' circulation rose to around 68,000 in 1871 and 100,000 by 1882 but it was outstripped by the newer, cheaper dailies, the *Daily News* which reached 150,000 by 1871 and the *Daily Telegraph*, which, starting in 1855, sold a daily average of 200,000 in 1870 and 250,000 in 1882 – these two papers put most of the other London dailies out of business.[15] The repeal of the stamp prompted many provincial papers to publish daily – the *Manchester Guardian* had attained sales of 30,000 by 1880.[16] While the London and provincial dailies must, through the public newsrooms, have reached a broader readership, their purchasers remained middle class.[17]

Until the advent of cheap dailies in the late 1880s and 1890s, the working class and lower middle class could only afford to buy cheap weekly newspapers.[18] *Lloyd's Weekly Newspaper* had the largest circulation, rising from 90,000 in the early 1850s to 600,000 by 1890, with a predominantly metropolitan, old artisanate and lower middle class, small shopkeeping clientele, and also with readers among women working in the clothing industry. *Reynolds's Newspaper*, with a mainly artisanate readership extending from the capital to the industrial areas of the North and Midlands, had a circulation of 50,000 on the eve of the removal of the stamp and maintained a steady 300,000 from the 1860s on.[19] During the pre-repeal, Chartist years, the *Northern Star* had easily undersold its bourgeois rivals such as the *Leeds Mercury* and *Manchester Guardian* and had a circulation variously reported at between 35,000 and 60,000 in the late 1830s.[20] The 'new journalism' of the late 1880s/1890s brought new popular dailies such the radical *Star*, whose largely working-class circulation was 300,000 in 1893[21] and the conservative *Daily Mail*, founded in 1896, which built up a mainly lower middle-class readership of around a million by 1900.[22]

There were also weeklies catering for the middle class. The *Illustrated London News* enjoyed great success because of its pictorial representation of events, boasting a circulation of 41,000 in 1843 rising to 123,000 on the removal of stamp duty;[23] while the *Sunday Times* and *Observer* were at the smaller, more 'respectable' end of the Sunday market, dominated by *Lloyd's* and *Reynolds's*.[24] *Punch*, having begun in 1841 as a somewhat disreputable lower middle-class comic print moved up-market throughout the 1840s and 1850s, its circulation at around 40,000, as its humour became less ribald and critical.[25] Sophisticated political weeklies such as the *Spectator*, *Saturday Review*, *Examiner* and *Pall Mall Gazette* and periodicals such as the *Fortnightly Review*, *Quarterly Review*, *Edinburgh Review*, *Westminster Review* and *Nineteenth Century* were the preserve of well-informed political and intellectual milieux.[26]

As well as examining these and other national and provincial newspapers and periodicals, I have looked at the special newspapers of various bodies and movements – the trade unions' journal the *Bee-Hive*, the *Free Press*, the mouthpiece of the Foreign Affairs Committees of David Urquhart, and, of course, the republican newspapers of the late 1840s and 1850s and of the 1880s and Charles Bradlaugh's secularist organ, the *National Reformer*, which was the main vehicle of the republican movement of the early 1870s. All these, together with parliamentary debates, political pamphlets, books on the Queen and Royal Family and the popular ballads printed and hawked around London streets,[27] enable me to furnish the first concrete, detailed and multi-layered study of Victorian attitudes to the monarchy as displayed in public discourse upon it.

Victoria's reign can be seen as a turning-point in the history of the modern British monarchy in that throughout it two basic strands of discussion of the monarchy, one reverential, the other critical, coexisted, with the latter superseding the former conclusively – at least for the time being – by the end of the reign.

This statement begs an explanation of how my work represents an advance on the exploratory essays on the Victorian monarchy referred to earlier. In a pioneering historical account of attitudes to the Crown, Kingsley Martin postulated a linear progression of royal popularity. In the first half of Victoria's reign, the Crown was held in low esteem, being regarded as anachronistic, costly, unEnglish and as interfering unconstitutionally and partisanly in politics. By the end of the reign the picture had been transformed: the monarch was elevated above the arena of political and social conflict and was venerated as the emblem of the English nation and of the empire.[28] Subsequent historians have made similar observations when alluding to the monarchy[29] and David

Cannadine's work on ceremonial interprets the staging of major royal events in Victoria's reign within this framework. Early ceremonies are seen as low-key and ill-managed affairs because of a prevalent utilitarian spirit and because a monarchy which was still actively and contentiously involved in politics, and which enjoyed at best only equivocal popularity could not be ceremonially glorified. The later ceremonies were by contrast magnificent – the Crown, now above party, politics and society, was grandly feted as the symbol of national and imperial self-esteem at a time of increasing taste for the elaborate, irrational and 'magical' in public affairs.[30]

What I have done is excavated in depth where other historians have only surveyed the terrain, and in doing so have gone beyond generalities and discovered what diverse sections of people thought at different times about the monarchy in all its aspects. The result is a complex one in which the linear, chronological scale of development hitherto employed is considerably modified. It is true that one has only to read the despairing editorials of and letters to George Standring's newspaper, the *Republican* in the late 1870s and 1880s, lamenting the 'sickly "loyalty" of the age'[31] to see that the critics of the monarchy had been overwhelmed by its supporters by the later stages of the reign. (The *Republican* finally hoisted the flag of surrender in 1886 by changing its name to the *Radical* in an effort to boost circulation.)[32] But veneration for Victoria as the Queen and as a woman, and sentimental or, as radicals dismissed it, 'gush' writing on the Royal Family had existed in profusion from the outset of the reign, alongside the criticism of the monarchy and royalty, which, on the other hand, had by no means died out by 1901.

Linda Colley has shown that George III, during the war with France, became the first British monarch since 1688 to be exulted in the prose and in grandiose ceremonial as the virtuous father of his people and the patriotic figurehead of the nation.[33] Such enthusiasm for the Crown came to the fore again with the accession of a young, virgin Queen in 1837.[34] But Victoria also inherited the anti-monarchical feelings that had bedevilled the reigns of all her Hanoverian ancestors and which were to bedevil hers – and, if by 1901 the Crown was commonly seen as a guarantee of constitutionalism, a national figurehead, a ceremonial cynosure and an icon of domestic respectability, such a vision had crystallized only recently and there were still dissentient voices questioning the validity and importance of its claims to these roles. In order to demonstrate the richness and variety of contemporary debate on the monarchy the book proceeds thematically, analysing the discussions on the very existence of the monarchy, its cost, its political and ceremonial functions and its patriotism, as well as the reverential literature that steadily built up throughout the reign.

The first two chapters look at the most outspoken criticisms of the Crown, radical and republican, of the institution of the monarchy itself – the iniquity of hereditary rule, the costliness of royalty, and the class critique of working-class radicalism. The first of these chapters discusses Chartism and middle-class radicalism in the period 1837–61 and explains the emergence of republicanism in the late 1840s. The following chapter has as its main theme the development and subsequent decline of the republican movement over the period 1861–87 but at the same time the persistence of serious criticism of the monarchy, some of it republican, right to the end of the reign.

Crucial to the national consensus believed to be embodied in the celebrations of 1887 and 1897 and mourning in 1901 was the transformation in the perceptions of the Crown's political role and of its patriotism, and the next three chapters will examine these perceptions. Chapters 4 and 5 show that between 1837 and 1887 opinions moved gradually towards the reassuring picture of the Crown as politically neutral and virtually insignificant but that this movement of opinion was subjected to severe crises at various times – even in the late 1870s there was a rigorous debate over the royal prerogative – while in the final phase of the reign there was a growing awareness of the Queen's Conservative bias, even if there was less concern that this could be used to interfere with democratic politics.

The Crown's identification with national pride and with empire in the Jubilee celebrations is to be contrasted with the frequent depiction of it as German and treacherous to English interests during the first half of the reign, especially because of Prince Albert's alleged interference in national policy. This shift can be linked with Hugh Cunningham's thesis about the appropriation by the right and by the state of the 'language of patriotism' in the last quarter of the nineteenth century.[35] However, this will require serious qualifications. Republicans continued to stigmatize the Queen, Royal Family and court as German after Albert's death – *Reynolds's Newspaper* was still doing so at the end of this period – and radicals and republicans who opposed special grants to the Queen's children on their weddings in the 1870s and 1880s characterized their opposition as 'patriotic'. Conversely, Linda Colley has argued that the 'language of patriotism' became the possession of the King and state during the Napoleonic wars, when George III replaced Wilkes as 'the patriot'.[36] In chapter 6 I shall argue that while there was no conclusive appropriation of the 'language of patriotism' in this period – radicals and conservatives, republicans and loyalists continued to employ it according to their peculiar interpretations – the monarchy after Albert's death was better equipped to become the symbol of the new assertive British nationalism and imperialism coming to the fore at the end of the period.

Next, an analysis is made of enthusiastic, loyal writing on the monarchy – of the 'gush' in the press and books on the Queen and Royal Family bemoaned by royalty's critics. This traces the veneration of the Queen as the exemplar of the monarchy and of womanhood in its successive stages – as virgin Queen, as wife, as widow and always from the late 1840s on as mother – the projection of the Queen and Royal Family as the icons of English domestic virtues; and the all-embracing interest in the Royal Family, presented at the same time as fairy-tale figures and as an ordinary middle-class family – the publication of trivia encouraged the belief that everyone could identify with them and know them intimately, yet the romantic haze through which they were depicted made them ultimately unknowable and fascinating.

Finally, the chapter on ceremonial shows that as the Crown's political importance declined its role was seen increasingly to lie in the performance of ceremonial duties. Radicals continued to criticize royal pageants on rational and utilitarian grounds throughout the reign, but there was always a current of opinion in favour of frequent and spectacular pageantry. It was the organizers of ceremonials and the Queen herself – especially during her seclusion after Albert's death – who were slow in responding to continued calls for staging royal events as splendid, public affairs.

I have referred to this period as a turning-point in the history of the British monarchy, and themes dealt with in the separate chapters should link together to highlight this. In this period there persisted from the lampoons on the eighteenth- century monarchy and from the era of the Stuarts, a critical, questioning attitude to the monarchy that was not revived until the 1990s. At the same time existed a veneration of the monarchy, similar in tone and content to that associated with the last years of the reign and with the British Royal Family for most of the twentieth century, promoting Queen Victoria as the universally popular emblem of national consensus. That in reality she could never be, but the balance in the perception of the monarchy had moved decisively in this direction by 1901.

Notes

1. F.M.L. Thompson, *English Landed Society in the Nineteenth Century* (London, 1963).
2. David Cannadine, *Lords and Landlords: The Aristocracy and the Towns, 1774–1967* (Leicester, 1980); idem, *The Decline and Fall of the British Aristocracy, 1880–1980* (New Haven and London, 1990); W.D. Rubinstein, *Men of Property: The Very Wealthy in Britain Since the Industrial Revolution* (London, 1984); Lawrence Stone and Jeanne C. Fawtier Stone, *An*

Open Elite?: England 1540–1880 (Oxford, 1984); J.V. Beckett, *The Aristocracy in England, 1660–1914* (Oxford, 1986). The same tendency in eighteenth-century historiography can be observed in J.C.D. Clark's *English Society, 1688–1832: Ideology, Social Structure and Political Practice During the Ancien Regime* (Cambridge, 1985).

3. Philip Hall, *Royal Fortune: Tax, Money and the Monarchy* (London, 1991); Vernon Bogdanor, *The Monarchy and the Constitution* (Oxford, 1995); Frank Prochaska, Royal Bounty. *The Making of a Welfare Monarchy* (New Haven and London, 1995).

4. Dorothy Thompson, *Queen Victoria. Gender and Power* (London, 1990). In chapter 5 I show that some contemporary commentators, including leaders of the suffragist movement, did use Victoria's political role as an argument for female participation in politics – lack of primary research meant that Dorothy Thompson could only speculate (p. 145) that ' the presence of a woman at the head of the state worked at a deeper level to weaken prejudice and make change more possible in the century following her reign'.

5. The Jubilees are examined in J.L. Lant, *Insubstantial Pageant. Ceremony and Confusion at Queen Victoria's Court* (London, 1979) and P. S. Baker's, 'The Social and Ideological Role of the Monarchy in late Victorian Britain' (unpub. MA, Lancaster, 1978); the Thanksgiving for the recovery of the Prince of Wales in 1872 in Freda Harcourt, 'Gladstone, Monarchism and the "New Imperialism", 1868–74', *Journal of Imperial and Commonwealth History*, vol. 14, no. 1 (October 1985), pp. 20–51 and William M. Kuhn, 'Ceremony and Politics: the British Monarchy, 1871–1872', *Journal of British Studies*, vol. 26, no. 2 (April 1987), pp. 133–62; and the visits of the Sultan and Viceroy of Egypt in 1867 in Freda Harcourt, 'The Queen, the Sultan of Turkey and the Viceroy: A Victorian State Occasion', *London Journal*, vol. 5, no. 1 (May 1979), pp. 35–56.

6. Kingsley Martin, *The Magic of Monarchy* (London, 1937); idem, *The Crown and the Establishment* (London, 1962); David Cannadine, 'The Context, Performance and Meaning of Ritual: the British Monarchy and "The Invention of Tradition" c. 1820–1977' in Eric Hobsbawm and Terence Ranger eds, *The Invention of Tradition* (Cambridge, 1983), pp. 101–64.

7. In the numerous biographies of Victoria, the best of which is Elizabeth Longford's *Victoria R.I.* (London, 1983 edn); and in Frank Hardie, *The Political Influence of Queen Victoria, 1861–1901* (Oxford, 1935).

8. H.R. Fox Bourne, *English Newspapers. Chapters in the History of Journalism*, 2 vols (London, 1887), vol. 2, pp. 387–8.

9. See Richard D. Altick, *The English Common Reader. A Social History of the Mass Reading Public 1800–1900* (Chicago, 1957); Lewis James ed., *Print and the People 1819–1851* (London, 1978 edn).

10. Bourne, *English Newspapers*, vol. 2, pp. 387–90.

11. See below, chapters 2 and 3.

12. Lucy Brown, *Victorian News and Newspapers* (Oxford, 1985), p. 273.

13. Ibid., p. 31; Altick, *The English Common Reader*, p. 394; Stephen Koss, *The Rise and Fall of the Political Press in Britain. Vol. One: The Nineteenth Century* (London, 1981), p. 60

14. Koss, *The Rise and Fall of the Political Press . . . Vol. One*, pp. 60–1.

15. Altick, *The English Common Reader*, p. 394; Brown, *Victorian News and*

Newspapers, p. 52; Koss, *The Rise and Fall of the Political Press . . . Vol. One*, p. 94.

16. Koss, *The Rise and Fall of the Political Press ... Vol. One*, p. 121; Brown, *Victorian News and Newspapers*, p. 53.

17. Koss, *The Rise and Fall of the Political Press ... Vol. One*, p. 60; Altick, *The English Common Reader*, p. 355.

18. Altick, *The English Common Reader*, p. 355.

19. V.S. Berridge, 'Popular Journalism and the Working Class Attitudes 1854–86: A study of *Reynolds's Newspaper, Lloyd's Weekly Newspaper* and the *Weekly Times*' (unpub. PhD, London, 1976), pp. 39–41, 99, 119, 123.

20. Koss, *The Rise and Fall of the Political Press ... Vol. One*, pp. 60–1; Altick, *The Common Reader*, p. 393.

21. Henry Schalck, 'Fleet Street in the 1880s' in Joel H. Wiener ed., *Papers for the Millions; the New Journalism in England, 1850s to 1914* (New York, 1986), pp. 82–3.

22. Joel H. Wiener, 'How new was the new journalism' in idem, ed. *Papers for the Millions*, p. 56.

23. Bourne, *English Newspapers*, vol. 2, p. 227; Altick, *The English Common Reader*, p. 394.

24. Altick, *The English Common Reader*, p. 355.

25. Ibid., p 394; R.G.G. Price, *A History of Punch* (London, 1957), pp. 31, 46–113.

26. *Bourne, English Newspapers*, vol. 2, p. 291; Brown, *Victorian News and Newspapers*, p. 100; Altick, *The English Common Reader*, pp. 359–60.

27. See John Ashton, *Modern Street Ballads* (London, 1888); T. Fontane, *Journeys to England in Victoria's Early Days* (transl. Dorothy Harrison, London, 1939), pp. 100–6.

28. Martin, *The Magic of Monarchy*, pp. 25–45; idem, *The Crown and the Establishment*, pp. 20–65.

29. Ross McKibbin in 'Why was there no Marxism in Great Britain?', *English Historical Review*, vol. 99 (1984), pp. 311–12. Tom Nairn, 'The glamour of backwardness', *Times Higher Education Supplement*, no. 636 (11 January 1985), p. 13; idem, *The Enchanted Glass. Britain and its Monarchy* (London, 1988), pp. 271, 282–5, 349; John M. MacKenzie, *Propaganda and Empire. The Manipulation of British Public Opinion, 1880–1960* (Manchester, 1984) pp. 3–4.

30. Cannadine, 'The Context, Performance and Meaning of Ritual', pp. 101–64.

31. *Republican*, vol. 5, no. 4 (July 1879), p. 125 cols 1–2.

32. Ibid., vol 12, no. 6 (August 1886), p. 36 cols 1–2.

33. Linda Colley, 'The Apotheosis of George III: Loyalty, Royalty and the British Nation, 1760–1820', *Past and Present*, no. 102 (1984), pp. 94–129.

34. Recognized by John Cannon, 'The Survival of the British Monarchy', *Royal Historical Society Transactions*, 5th ser. no. 36 (1986) pp. 143–64.

35. Hugh Cunningham, 'The Language of Patriotism 1750–1914', *History Workshop*, issue 12 (Autumn 1981), pp. 8–33.

36. Colley, 'The Apotheosis of George III', pp. 102, 127–9.

CHAPTER TWO

Radical and Republican Criticism of the Monarchy, 1837–61

This study of public discussion of the Victorian monarchy begins with the most outspoken, fundamental criticisms – those of the very institution of monarchy on the grounds of its irrationality, its costliness and luxury; criticisms which at times assumed a republican form. While the next chapter shows an English republican movement developing specifically in reaction to the peculiar circumstances of the British monarchy after Albert's death, this chapter on 1837–61 shows such criticisms of the monarchy being made as part of the broader philosophic and political outlooks of the groups which set the tone of intellectual and popular radicalism in this period – the utilitarians, the Chartists and the idealistic republicans inspired by the 1848 revolutions on the Continent.

Beginning in 1837, we see an ambivalent England. On the one hand, the accession of a young, virgin Queen occasioned, as I shall demonstrate later, a renewed enthusiasm for the throne[1] which had fallen back into ill repute during the reigns of the debauched and latterly reclusive George IV and the uninspiring William IV, himself the father of seven well-rewarded bastards.[2] On the other hand, there was a well-entrenched tradition of criticism of the Crown and Royal Family, and the nation which celebrated the anachronistic ceremonial of the coronation of the latest in its venerable line of hereditary monarchs was also the nation characterized by industrialization and a spirit of political reform which had threatened revolution when checked in 1831–2. The 1830s and 1840s were the decades of utilitarianism and Chartism, creeds with programmes to carry improvement and reform to what they saw as their logical and just climaxes. What did radical England think of the institution which more than any other embodied old England? The Benthamite radicals and Chartists have been written about by many historians but their attitudes to the monarchy have escaped attention.

The chapter looks in turn at middle- and working-class radicalism. In the sections on middle-class radicalism, parliamentary and journalistic, we see how intellectual criticisms of the Crown were based on the utilitarian principles that government should be rational and economical. Benthamite MPs such as Joseph Hume and middle-class publications such as *Punch* were also concerned at the selfishness of royalty in burdening an already overtaxed people with extra charges for royal annuities. Such rhetoric was shared by the Chartists and it is important to remember, as Gareth Stedman Jones has argued, that the Chartists continued to identify as their chief enemy that of all radicals since the 1760s – the oppressive state.[3] The section on Chartism shows that, while it professed loyalty to the Queen, the great working-class movement wished the Crown to identify with the people and not, as it currently did, with the narrow, oppressive governing class. The final section analyses the emergence, content and failure of the republicanism inspired in some prominent Chartists by the European republicans, especially Mazzini, in 1848.

Middle-class radicalism

Intellectual and parliamentary

In an open letter to the new Queen on the state of the monarchy, Lord Brougham warned, 'Royalty has never been exposed to so severe a trial'. He pointed out that monarchy, once accepted without question by an ignorant multitude, now stood at odds with the belief in the 'imprescriptible right of men to govern themselves' arising from 'the rapid improvement of all classes in knowledge'. and that the lottery of hereditary government was now highlighted by the crowns of Spain and England's descent to mere girls: men must surely question whether 'some more rational form of polity were not more fitted for rational beings'.

Brougham's themes and language were those of Benthamite radicalism – in an age of reason and of the 'march of the mind', the constituent elements of government were to be judged by their rationality and their utility; accordingly men were prone to dwell on the 'anomalies of kingly government', on its 'blind chance' and to see it as one of the 'fictions in which the law delights'[4] – a 'fiction' was Bentham's term for an irrational and unnecessary law or institution. We see a similar view in the *Spectator*, a mouthpiece of Benthamism at this time, which in 1840 likened the monarchy's role in government to that of the ceremonies prescribed to be performed when drinking from a health-bringing spring – 'an accidental concomitant, not an essential agent', of dubious utility.[5]

Hand in hand with the principle of rationality went that of political economy – the cost of government and thus taxation should be kept to a minimum and expenditure on otiose items should cease. So, wrote Brougham, the tendency of the modern age towards the Crown was to 'count its cost'. He reminded the Queen of the contemporary call for 'cheap government' and of Paine's dictum that 'an able-bodied man might easily be got to do the work of king for five hundred pounds a year'. His letter was ultimately a call for a further extension of the franchise: monarchical government needed a 'popular foundation'; in the meantime unbridled royal affluence and the consequent burden of taxation could only antagonize the unenfranchised masses.[6]

The Benthamite radicals in parliament, led by Joseph Hume, regularly opposed or sought to reduce grants to the Royal Family, citing the need for economy, the weight of taxation and the condition of the labouring classes. In 1837 Hume moved that the proposed Civil List for the new reign of £385,000 per annum be fixed instead at £335,000. He pointed out that the ministry's calculations were based on the Civil List assigned in 1816 at a time of runaway inflation and that all other departments of state other than the Royal household had had their expenditure corrected subsequently. The classes outside parliament should be taken into account, 'instead of wringing from them the utmost extent of money which the aristocracy in that House might be disposed to grant'. People would, he warned, contrast expenditure on Britain's monarchical government with that on 'the simple forms of Republican Government' in the United States, which he estimated at a twenty-fifth, at most, of the total cost of the Royal Family.

Hume's supporters agreed that, in Bulmer's words, 'the proposed civil list was constituted on a scale wholly unsuited to the age'. Grote pointed out that this was the first Civil List which had been brought forward since the Reform Act, and that, as a necessary result of that improvement, the people expected and had a right to expect greater economy, and more strictness in the administration of public money. Nineteen MPs voted with Hume.[7]

In 1840 Hume called for a reduction of £30,000 in the grant of £50,000 per annum proposed for the establishment of Prince Albert. William Williams, seconding Hume, condemned the proposal as 'an extreme waste of the public money', especially given 'the distress which prevailed throughout the country'. The radicals were in a minority of 38 but in the end found themselves in the winning lobby when the Tory opposition, in the wake of the Bedchamber crisis, as a protest against the blatant Whig bias of the court,[8] voted for a reduction of £20,000.[9]

In 1843, 57 MPs voted with Hume in opposing the Tory government's grant to Princess Augusta, the Duke of Cambridge's daughter, as her marriage settlement. Hume had protested that there was no principle under which the country was called on to provide for the children of cadet branches of the Royal Family and that 'the ample allowance from the public revenue which has been so long enjoyed by his Royal Highness the Duke of Cambridge, should have enabled him to make provision for his own children'.[10]

The family of the Duke of Cambridge was again the source of contention in 1850 when, on the Duke's death, yearly annuities of £12,000 and £3,000 respectively were settled on his heir and his unmarried daughter Mary. Hume, whose proposal to reduce the new duke's grant to £8,000 received 53 votes, argued that 'In a time of peace, like the present, the House ought to study economy', particularly 'whilst there was so much want and poverty in other circles'.[11] *The Times* concurred: in an age of reason, 'an inquisitive and a calculating age', 'blind adoration' could not be relied upon – the 'rational loyalty' which had replaced such adoration, must surely baulk at 'unnecessary expenditure' such as that on a junior branch of the Royal Family.[12]

Two other parliamentary debates of the 1850s – on the savings on the Civil List in 1850 and on the marriage settlement of the Princess Royal in 1857 – contained the seeds of the major controversies over the expenses of the Crown of the 1870s. In August 1850 Brougham unsuccessfully demanded a return relative to the savings on the Civil List, which amounted to nearly £40,000 for the previous year. He pointed out that the danger he cited in 1837 of fixing the Civil List for the duration of the whole reign was now becoming clear – the allocation was proving to be too great and the Crown was accumulating an embarrassing superfluity: 'It was not in conformity with the genius of the constitution that the Sovereign of this country should have the means of acquiring wealth'.[13] The Queen's virtual retirement after 1861 was to make the savings on the Civil List a matter of considerable speculation and enabled the writer of the highly influential pamphlet *What does she do with it?* to raise Brougham's questions with even greater force.[14]

The grant to the Princess Royal was the first of nine that were to be made to the Queen's children on their marriages. That the Princess was the first of a long line was paramount in the considerations of Roebuck in his opposition to the proposed annual grant to the Princess of £8,000 – the acknowledgement of a duty to support the Queen's children after their marriages would set a costly precedent. Roebuck was not opposed to the single payment of a dowry, and he finally withdrew his motion opposing the grant[15] – but by the 1870s, as royal marriages followed fast on each others' heels, radical and republican opposition to any form of annuity was much sterner.[16]

Criticisms in Punch *and other weekly papers*

As Susan and Asa Briggs have noted, while historians have ransacked *Punch* for cartoons to embellish an argument, 'The verse and prose in *Punch* have tended to be neglected'. This verse and prose represented middle-class radicalism, and of an increasingly watered down, respectable kind as the 1840s and 1850s proceeded – E.P. Thompson wrote of the parting of the ways of working-class and middle-class radical journalism in the 1830s, 'One way led to political Owenism and Chartism and the other to *Punch*'. In its initial years in the early 1840s, with Henry Mayhew, who had written for the *Poor Man's Guardian*, a moving spirit and a readership more lower middle class than it later became,[17] its radicalism was more outspoken and a principal target was the monarchy – its cost, its burden on the common people, and its apparent indifference to the poverty which blighted the nation.

Punch wanted the Queen to be popular but stressed that she would only be so if she were sensitive to the world outside the court – and this was the sentiment voiced in other papers of *Punch*'s genre.[18] On the Prince of Wales in 1842 *Punch* drew a contrast between the condition of the royal baby and pauper baby: only if the Queen would reflect on this and say, 'God bless the poor!', would *Punch* join in the rejoicings at the birth.[19] Other royal events were greeted with similar qualifications. *Punch* wrote of the marriage of Princess Augusta in 1843, 'Reader, when you listen to the bells merrily ringing the birth of a Prince or Princess, what changes do they sound? – Merely the changes of £. s. d.'. Its illustration depicted a lavish bridal procession proceeding up an aisle surrounded by starving wretches.[20]

The cost of royalty and its extreme affluence made *Punch* especially sensitive to loyal claims of royal selflessness and benevolence. The Queen's offer to pay the new income tax in 1842 gave rise to such effusions – for example, *The Times* described the Queen's action as 'munificent . . . of inestimable advantage in refuting those who are ever anxious to prove our political and social constitution to be a mere juggling machinery for enabling the rich and great to plunder the poor and feeble'.[21] *Punch* ridiculed such an argument, ironically citing 'the many, keen privations' which the Queen would undergo when deprived of her seven pence in the pound – such as the decline of the royal steeds, despite their previous grant of £70,000 for proper shelter, which had been voted at the same time as the £10,000 grant to the voluntary societies 'for the education of the people; thereby proving to a royal horse that he was of seven times the value of any English spinner or peasant'.[22]

Rather than benevolence, radicals saw in the monarchy selfishness, meanness and insensitivity to the distressed state of the country. The *Sunday Times*, a radical newspaper at this time, in 1843 pointed to the Queen's neglect of her duties in spending so little time in London – the Civil List was granted for the 'munificence and hospitality' of the court, not for the Queen to enjoy 'the rights and privileges' of her birth at

Windsor without undertaking any of its obligations. The Queen's absence moreover had an adverse effect on 'the trading interests of the west end of the Metropolis'.[23] The following year, the *Sunday Times* highlighted the elaborate and costly funeral which had been given to one of the Queen's dogs, a disgrace, 'whilst so many starved creatures are literally flung into pauper graves'.[24] In 1846 the *London Pioneer* drew a pointed contrast between parliament's readiness to make a grant for 'improvements' in the royal residences and its unwillingness to aid the totally destitute.[25] The flunkeyism displayed at the opening of the Coal Exchange in 1849 was, *Punch* felt, tasteless: the Queen was surrounded by members of the Corporation of the City, who presented her with a diamond. In an illustration, 'Opening . . . As Mr. Punch hoped it would have been', a blackened collier presented a delighted Queen with 'a Magnificent Black Diamond' – a huge lump of coal.[26] The message was clearly that the Crown and people needed to be brought closer together.

As one of its historians has observed, *Punch* rose with its middle-class readership,[27] and in the 1850s its criticisms of the monarchy were no longer made from the perspective of the helpless poor but from that of an ambitious middle class wanting a meritocratic society in place of one where aristocratic birth secured office and reward. Accordingly it concentrated its fire on the privileges and sinecures of the Royal Family, especially on Albert's Field Marshalship at the time of the Crimean War, when failure was seen to stem from untalented aristocrats holding such positions. Albert should set an example and resign the baton of that office:

> Then rose a cry among us for a Government of worth,
> We said, 'Away with empty Rank, and down with stupid Birth; . . .
>
> On the altar of his country the good Prince that baton threw;
> And thus he spoke, 'O public and soldiers! I resign
> The title with the token that ought not be mine . . .'
>
> Then every Lord incapable and every booby Duke,
> Accepted at their Prince's hands a lesson and rebuke;
> They cast away their offices; their places up they threw,
> And England's Oak revived again and England throve anew.[28]

The Prince of Wales' automatic entrance into the Universities contrasted with the struggle of ordinary people to attain any sort of education and a *Punch* illustration showed him walking into Cambridge in 1857 through an aisle of fawning dons, with the caption reading, 'The Royal Road to Learning'.[29]

In considering the attitude of middle-class radicalism to the monarchy in this period we have seen a utilitarian critique of the irrationality and

costliness of the institution and a broader concern with the social inequalities which its costliness highlighted. It is noticeable that middle-
class radicals were at their most concerned about the latter in the 1830s
and 1840s at a time of economic distress and Chartist unrest. The repeal
of the Corn Laws in 1846, the failure of the Continental revolutions to
reproduce themselves in Britain in 1848 and the comparative prosperity
of the 1850s directed middle-class radicals away from such social issues.
In this decade criticisms of the Crown were more narrow and specific –
the savings on the Civil List, the future provisions for the Queen's children – and more peculiar to middle-class ambitions – the need for a
thoroughly meritocratic system in which privileged birth would not guarantee success; and these issues were to be the principal concerns of the
middle-class leadership of the republican movement in the early 1870s.

Working-class radicalism, 1837–48: the Chartists

Historians of Chartism have not examined Chartist attitudes to the
monarchy,[30] probably because Chartism was not republican. Dorothy
Thompson makes a fleeting observation that the accession of a new
monarch in 1837 was one of the grounds for optimism about a popular
movement's prospects of success: 'A new reign was beginning, one
which represented a change in generations, which seemed to move away
from the corruption and cynicism of the monarchy thus far in the
century'.[31] However, she does not examine the disillusionment of the
Chartists with the Crown – while not espousing republicanism, Chartism was a bitter critic of the monarchy and royalty as they currently
existed in Britain. Patricia Hollis has shown that in the 1830s the
radical discourse became a mixture of the 'old and new analyses' – the
old Cobbetite picture of the 'Old Corruption' bearing down in the
shape of heavy taxation on the people, had been supplemented though
not superseded by a class analysis where labour was the victim of
capital.[32] We see this dual analysis in Chartist references to the monarchy – sometimes it is seen as part of the 'Old Corruption' of aristocracy,
landlords and Church taxing the people to the hilt; at others it is a
symbol of the dominance over the labouring classes of property –
landed and industrial; though, as Gareth Stedman Jones has pointed
out, this 'new analysis' was in some ways merely an extension of the old
in that the dominance was seen to be political, the middle class, after
the 1832 Reform Act, having joined the aristocracy in controlling the
oppressive machinery of the state.[33]

Commenting on the coronation, the *Northern Star*, the official organ
of Chartism, declared, 'We love the Queen ... None can desire more

ardently than we do the happiness of the Throne; but it can only rest securely on the universal happiness of the people.' At present, the monarchy was the prisoner of a narrow, selfish clique imposing class legislation – especially the Poor Law Amendment Act – on those excluded by property qualifications from the franchise.[34] The previous week *The Times* had published a protest from the Trades Councils of Manchester and Salford urging working men to abstain from celebrating the coronation. It was, they said, an abomination to expect workers to participate in the costly festivities when so many of their fellows were unemployed and underfed, and when their brothers of Dorchester had been deported by the Queen's government – the Queen stood at the head of an unjust political system whose consequence was the 'tyranny of capitalism, whom the laws allow to ride roughshod over prostrate labour, and drive the labour to associate for common protection, since the law allows them none'.[35] There was working-class counter-ceremonial on coronation day – a Chartist meeting at Newcastle led by Feargus O'Connor, at which one speaker asserted, 'if it [the monarchy] did not reign for the good of millions, it should not reign at all'. The account of the meeting in the *Northern Star* consciously echoes descriptions of the coronation in the middle-class press, which typically depicted events in London as the greatest ever display, in sheer weight of numbers, of national pageantry, loyalty and unity – the *Northern Star* called the Newcastle meeting 'the most splendid display of the working classes ever witnessed in England ... The pomp of coronation festivals could not seduce the people from their allegiance to the principles of liberty.' Thus the coronation was seen as a ruling-class and not a truly national celebration.[36]

This feeling characterized even more strongly the Chartist attitude to the Queen's wedding in 1840, as concurrent with its celebration was the sentencing of the Chartists of Newport for their alleged treason. Again the *Northern Star* proclaimed the loyalty of the Chartists but warned that the Crown would be in jeopardy if it continued to identify with an oppressive governing class whose indifference to working-class deprivation had occasioned the Newport rising, and if such lavish expenditure on royal weddings continued: 'It is the province of a Sovereign to feel for all the people's ills the anxiety and yearning of a parent'. This was manifestly not so in reality, when the Queen's allowance was £1,000 a day and the allowance for a working man's family seven shillings a week. The Queen in receipt of all this money 'certainly is not at all necessary for the nation's welfare' and 'does nothing for the public service'.

Moreover, a further £1,000 a week was now to be exacted from 'her "famishing people" ... to keep her husband supplied with slippers, pocket handkerchiefs, and night-caps!' These could not be the actions of a 'Christian Queen' – 'Think you', the newspaper asked, 'that loyalty, the bastard of tyranny will always be permitted to usurp the place of justice?' It poured scorn on the view fostered in the London pro-ministerial press that the wedding was an occasion of national consensus – it was rather a celebration exclusively of the ruling classes, who, through the sentences on Frost and his fellow Chartists, had 'sought to introduce the fatal and bloody gallows between the people and her royal nuptials'.

The filling of the London press with trivia relating to the wedding represented a deliberate diversion of attention from the serious, class issues which were agitating the country. Similar to the counter-ceremonial of coronation day, Chartist meetings were organized for the wedding day throughout the industrial north to get up addresses to the Queen for the pardon of Frost and the others. Britain, the *Northern Star* asserted, could become a truly popular monarchy only when Victoria, a 'kind-hearted being (for so we are disposed to believe her)' was freed from 'the foul array of the iniquitous Few opposed to the injured and enlightened many'.[37] *The Royal Wedding Jester*, a collection of satirical ribaldries, contained a bitter poem which expressed the complete alienation of the lower classes from the court celebrations, by contrasting the Whigs' provisions for Albert, 'the German pauper', with their provisions for the British pauper under the new Poor Law:

> Oh, a time shall come, . . .
> When the royal blots on the nation's page
>   Shall be swept with a mighty arm away;
> When Britannia's cry shall be raised on high
>   And the curse of her writhing poor
> Shall thunder at last, like a tempest blast,
>   At the haughty oppressor's door.[38]

Such anger at the obscene luxury of the monarchy marked Chartist treatment of royal events in the 'hungry forties'. The birth of the Princess Royal in 1840 prompted the *Northern Star* to observe that the Queen had not been a tender mother of her country since her accession.[39] The following year it commemorated the birth of the Prince of Wales by setting two *Times* reports of 10 November alongside each other – one the account of the birth of the Prince in opulent surroundings and with thorough medical attention; the other a report of the death in her accouchement of one of three women to be delivered in the same bed in a room where two other women were confined.[40] *A New Song on the Birth of the Prince of Wales* lamented the increase in taxation which the sundry accoutrements of the Prince would entail.[41]

Of the coincidence of the death of the Duke of Sussex and the birth of Princess Alice in 1843, the *Northern Star* commented, 'One has left us, and left £21,000 a year!! and another has come to fill up the niche'.[42] Sussex had been the most liberal in politics of the Royal Family and was deemed popular for this reason – the *Spectator*'s obituary declared, 'Such men are the oil poured over the tempest-tossed surface of society to make the waves abate . . . the Duke of Sussex formed a link between the people and his Family, rendering its power more stable'.[43] The *Northern Star* regarded this as nonsense: 'We hear much fulsomeness about his "virtue" and his "patriotism". None of them ever taught him that it was his duty to earn his own living! He was an incumbrance, from the first moment he drew breath.' Much had been made of his wish to be buried like a commoner in Kensal Green Cemetery – the only allusion to this made by the *Northern Star* was that he would rest alongside the republican writer Richard Carlile, a 'better man, because more useful to his kind'.[44]

The monarchy was never seen to serve the interests of the people but rather to be part of an aristocratic and middle-class constitution's obstruction of these interests. The *Northern Star* derided the 'admirable and delicate sensibility' which had moved an outraged parliament to suspend its sitting after the assassination attempt on the Queen in 1842 when it should have been debating the new tariff 'to lower the price of provisions for the people'.[45] The supreme example of royal meanness was Prince Albert's attempted evasion of the payment of the poor rate for his Windsor farm. The *Northern Star* compared the Prince with the paupers whom he refused to help support: 'Both are wholly dependent upon public charity, with this sole distinction, that many of the Union paupers have at some time or other contributed to the burthens of the state'. Such continued insensitivity would endanger the existence of the monarchy as it contravened social justice. The Royal Family should remember that an alternative executive head of government was possible – a president would cost the country £5,000 a year, a Duke would need no payment.[46]

An examination of Chartist attitudes to the monarchy shows that the new reign was seen by working-class radicals as having altered nothing. The Crown was still a cynical part of the 'Old Corruption' and was roundly criticized as such. While these criticisms stopped short of republicanism, they spelled out a clear warning that a republic would be seen as an alternative if the monarchy continued to be selfish and to ignore the needs of the people. The 1848 revolutions were to enkindle a republican conviction in some Chartists and it is to the effect of events on the Continent that we must now turn.

Working-class radicalism, 1848–61: republicanism

It was cynically observed that the philanthropy of the British Royal Family took a sudden upsurge as a result of the 1848 revolutions when brother monarchs were toppled from their thrones. *Punch*'s article 'Prince Hal and Prince Al' compared the indolence, hitherto, of Prince Albert, with the prodigal behaviour of that 'madcap Prince of Wales' and observed that suddenly Albert had sprung into action as a patron of the working classes, especially in the Society for Improving the Condition of the Labouring Classes.[47] That Albert's activities were calculated to present royalty in a favourable light is shown by the coverage in the respectable press – *The Times* wrote that 'every loyal subject' would take satisfaction in Albert's chairing the Society's meeting 'at a time when it is much easier for Royal personages to lose popularity than to win confidence'.[48]

The 1848 revolutions had indeed produced an effect on working-class radicals in Britain. The republicanism of Europe, and especially of Mazzini and Italy, came as an inspiration to leading radicals disillusioned with the increasingly apparent failure of Chartism. It made final the growing rift between Feargus O'Connor, who deplored foreign influences on the Chartist movement, and G. Julian Harney, his editor at the *Northern Star*, who saw such influences as the new blood needed to be pumped into the flagging movement. In March 1849 O'Connor's weekly address to the readers of his newspaper denounced those by whom 'the cry of Republicanism is attempted to be raised – certainly without much support from the Chartist ranks'. He warned that championing the revolutionists of the Continent and calling for the abolition of the British monarchy would wreck their chances of obtaining the Charter, as it would put an end to the Chartists' new alliance with the parliamentary radicals and instead bring upon them 'the persecution of all classes'. O'Connor denied the superiority of a republican to a monarchical form of government, 'provided the power behind the throne was greater than the throne itself' – the system of representation was the key, together with laws providing for the free transfer of land. Belgium, an elective monarchy, where 'the Labour Field is open; the transfer of land is facilitated', was a juster state than the republics of Switzerland or the United States, where 'there is as much class distinction, national suffering, and popular discontent as in any Monarchy in the world'. O'Connor preferred a monarch ruling for life to a president whose election every few years was a source of instability and corruption. Working-class radicals in Britain must, he concluded, keep their attention focused exclusively on the Charter.[49]

But the rallying cry of the British republicans was 'The Charter and Something More'.[50] By June, Harney had left the *Northern Star* to start his own republican newspaper the *Democratic Review*, the first of several short-lived publications with small circulations which he owned and edited in these years – the *Red Republican*, *Friend of the People*, *Notes to the People*, *Star of Freedom* and *Vanguard* followed in quick succession between 1850 and 1853. The other prominent English republican of this period was W.J. Linton, another former Chartist, who between 1851 and 1855 produced the *English Republic* and, with Joseph Cowen, the *Northern Tribune*.[51] A lesser-known radical, George Harding, began this spate of republican journals with the *Republican* in 1848. The prolific publisher G.W.M. Reynolds advocated republicanism in several of his diverse publications, the most important of which was the weekly *Reynolds's Newspaper*.

W.E. Adams, who assisted Linton and Cowen, stressed in his memoirs the way in which European republicanism gave to those disillusioned with Chartism a renewed sense of mission. 'Chartism was not satisfying. The Charter, as a declaration of rights, was excellent. It covered the whole ground of political demand. But popular power proclaimed – what then? ... Some of us were Democrats, pledged to afford material help and sympathy to the struggling peoples of the Continent.' Harney, in breaking from Chartism, embraced the 'red republicanism' of Louis Blanc and the French socialists, his newspapers proclaiming, 'Vive la république démocratique et sociale'.[52] Political freedom, he emphasized, was useless without social freedom.[53] Still, wrote Adams, 'we longed for something better. We had found a programme, but we wanted a religion.' This came from Italy, from Mazzini, 'the greatest teacher since Christ', whose apostle in England was Linton. The key text in the new republican faith was Mazzini's 'Republican principles' issued by the Central European Democratic Committee and translated and explained by Linton in the first number of the *English Republic*. The central theme was that only in a republic could all the people feel a sense of citizenship and of duty. It was the idea of duty which held such appeal to Mazzini's disciples, wrote Adams, where Chartism and other radical movements had spoken of rights.[54] Moreover, Mazzini's vision of citizenship transcended the narrow class consciousness of Chartism – all would patriotically serve their state: republicans constituted, wrote Linton, 'a party, not of one class only, but of all classes' united in a 'notion ... of patriotism, of duty'.[55]

The foreign inspiration was clear from the numerous pages of all the republican newspapers devoted to continental news, articles on foreign radicals, including those political refugees who had fled from the counter-revolution to London, where they were in close contact with English republicans.[56] However, as the title of Linton's journal indicates, English republicans located their creed in an English tradition. Linton wrote that while England should not be parochial but receptive to the ideas of the great European republicans, 'our Republicanism' would be 'of English growth, characteristic of the genius of our people'.[57] His newspapers, and those of Harney, contained frequent celebrations of Cromwell and the Commonwealth, and the poetry of Milton and of later republicans Byron and Shelley. Readers were reminded that the English republican tradition had been carried on by Paine in the late eighteenth century and by Richard Carlile in the 1820s and early 1830s.

The criticisms of the monarchy made by these republicans were the staples of the radical analysis that we have already encountered – that the monarchy was an irrational, anachronistic obstacle to the sovereignty of the people and that in its luxury, provided by the taxation of a poor people, it both symbolized and reinforced the gross inequalities between classes in an unjust political and social system. Harding's *Republican* was billed as 'A Magazine, Advocating the Sovereignty of the People'. Hereditary government had 'sprung from ignorance and infidelity to the dictates of reason', the goal for the modern age should be 'a government of the People created by themselves, existing only for their interests.[58] Linton and Cowen's *Northern Tribune* defined republicanism as the 'Sovereignty of the people, untrammelled by birthright'.[59] Harney contrasted 'the worn-out faith . . . in the right divine of kings and nobles', a relic of the 'non-age' of man, with the living faith in a 'greater *Majesty* . . . the *Majesty of labour; the Sovereignty of the People*'.[60]

On the one hand, the argument for the abolition of the monarchy was that political reforms, made in increasing acknowledgement of the sovereignty of the people, had rendered it politically negligible – constitutional monarchy was thus a 'miserable compromise'.[61] On the other hand, the continued interference by the Queen and especially her husband in politics was used to demonstrate the dangers to popular sovereignty which the monarchy still posed. The crisis of unpopularity experienced by Albert in 1853–4 as a result of revelations (and some false reports) of his role in government highlighted these dangers;[62] and suspicion of royal interference in the conduct of the Crimean War provoked the *Northern Tribune* to call for a truly popular war-government – a Committee of Public Safety on the French revolutionary model to take over the government.[63] *Reynolds's Newspaper* reacted angrily to Albert's Trinity House speech of 1855, which seemed to envy the secrecy enjoyed by the despotic Russian government in time of war: Albert's sentiments showed that Britain's much-vaunted constitutional monarchy was 'an enormous sham'; but 'the Prince is silly in supposing that there is no other alternative than despotism. We beg to remind him that there is such a thing as republicanism.'[64] The military and administrative failures of the War showed the ineptness of a system in which aristocratic birth counted for so much – the *Northern Tribune* wrote, that the Queen was 'the tinselled puppet of a selfish oligarchy'.[65]

This embodied the familiar complaint of working-class radicalism – that the Crown was not of the people, but part of the narrow ruling class which oppressed them. In republican critiques we again find a mixture of the old and new class analyses. The cost of the Crown and its contribution to the weight of taxation was one theme. The *Republican* enumerated the burdens of the Civil List and the Pension List:[66] 'a few facts showing the manner in which the people of this country are robbed, under the pretence of rewarding the servants of Royalty for past services'. Harney and Linton pointed to the profligacy of keeping in 'barbaric' splendour an institution of no practical political function, particularly 'while millions starve'.[67] The settlement on the Duke of Cambridge's family in 1850 could only confirm the people in the view fostered by the political economists that 'considering the return he gets for his money, John Bull pays dear for his whistle'.[68] Queen Adelaide's funeral was a rare and creditable example of royal parsimony, but what of the 'immense haul of *one hundred thousand pounds yearly* from the pocket of John Bull' which she had enjoyed during her life?[69]

The 'Old Corruption' with the Crown at its centre was still at times presented as the source of the people's oppression. Harney referred to 'the humbug of Queen, Lords and Commons – the rule of landlords and usurers'.[70] Reynolds' *Mysteries of the Court of London* were lurid tales of royal and aristocratic depravity designed to expose the vices of the upper classes.[71] In his *Political Instructor* Reynolds chided the crowds who had cheered the royal opening of the Coal Exchange in 1849 – the meaning of the ceremony was royalty's blessing to the monopolists of the Corporation of the City who taxed every ton of coal entering the port.[72] In 1858 those who had cheered in great numbers the wedding procession of the Princess Royal were faulted by *Reynolds's Newspaper* for failing to identify their real enemies: 'The indigence, squalor, and destitution to which tens of thousands of the working classes are just now exposed, are the natural and inevitable result of the superfluity, extravagance, and profligacy which characterizes the Court and aristocracy of England . . . the authors of their misery'.[73]

At the same time the Crown featured in the 'new analysis' of capital as the enemy, sharing power with the aristocracy. Harney described the monarchy as 'a puppet in the hands of a ruthless oligarchy of landlords and capitalists'.[74] The royal inauguration of the Great Exhibition was significant in this respect, as the Exhibition was a celebration of manufacturing industry and of its gospel, Free Trade. Linton saw the royal blessing as being given to man's ability 'to organize theft'.[75] Harney pointed to the exclusion of the working class from the royal opening ceremony of what should have been a festival of labour's achievements; instead, 'it wanted all that was needed to make it really national' – such a celebration could take place only when Britain had 'substituted for the rule of the masters, and the royalty of a degenerate monarchy, – "the Supremacy of Labour, and the Sovereignty of the Nation"'.[76] Linton wrote that only a republic could put an end to 'class-government'.[77] Albert's patronage of the Society of Arts, which espoused free trade and condemned workers' association was seen by *Reynolds's Newspaper* as an example of royalty's upholding 'the tyranny of Capital'.[78]

Above all, the monarchy's privilege and wealth stood as an affront to the helplessness and pathetic poverty of the multitude. Harney contrasted the lavish accoutrements of the new royal baby, Prince Arthur, in 1850, with a stark picture of the starving needlewoman and her child.[79] Harney argued that 'the elevation of the multitude generally is impossible so long as the monarchy exists' not only because of the privileges of the hereditary principle and class government which it embodied and perpetuated but because 'the ignorant and unthinking, too prone to self-abasement, will never learn self-respect until all that pertains to a throne is annihilated. There are people who are so unreflecting that they will honour anything that proclaims their own shame – even a palace flunkey.'

To elevate the people was the task of the republicans as the multitude were 'incompetent to save themselves, and must be saved in spite of themselves'.[80] Harney has been described as an advocate of violent revolution in the continental manner,[81] but in fact he acknowledged that the immediate task of republicans was to educate the British people into seeing that the republican form of government was the best: 'the people of England are not quite prepared for that form, much as they are animated with its spirit'; republicans must not be 'impatient' but in the meantime 'animate the people, with the spirit to sweep away the barbarous institutions founded in ages of ignorance and tyranny'.[82] Harney doubted even that the time was ripe for republican organizations, when there were so many other radical associations, many of which were struggling to survive.

Linton, however, saw organization as essential to the promulgating of republicanism – he too saw teaching as his main role as an English republican. He suggested a model, based on Mazzini's 'Young Italy', for republican associations, with a republican catechism, based on Mazzini's 'Republican principles', as essential learning for members. The first such body formed in Bethnal Green called itself the Republican Propagandist Society. It was followed by similar associations in Cambridge,

Liverpool, Cheltenham, Newcastle, Sunderland, Glasgow and Stockton. However, the initial impetus was difficult to maintain. Letters to the *English Republic* complained that the time was not ripe for English republicanism and that there was 'so much else to take up attention'. By 1852 little organization was taking place and Linton denounced 'public apathy' over republicanism. The *English Republic* folded in 1855 through lack of sufficient subscribers and Linton wrote of 'the disappointment of a propagandist'.[83] He continued his work in Newcastle, with Cowen, who formed the Republican Brotherhood – a Mazzinian title – as a new form of republican association, with the *Republican Record* as its organ.[84] But by the end of the 1850s this too had died out and English republicanism was to lie dormant for a decade.[85]

There was an undercurrent of antipathy to royalty for republicanism to cultivate – Mayhew's *London Labour and the London Poor*, which came out in 1851, recorded of the inmates of one lodging house for tramps in Seven Dials, 'They hate the aristocracy. Whenever there is a rumour or an announcement of an addition to the Royal Family, and the news reaches the padding-ken, the kitchen, for half-an-hour, becomes the scene of uproar – "another expense coming on the b-y country"'.[86] Popular ballads and music hall songs attacked the cost of the Crown and often depicted the Royal Family in an imaginary state of destitution – the Queen and Albert should experience the poverty of many of their subjects.[87] The Queen's windfall legacy – of anything between £250,000 and £500,000[88] – from 'Miser' Neild's will in 1852 was unpopular. *Lloyd's Weekly Newspaper* referred to 'that lunatic Neild' as 'a dangerous maniac' whose action would bring the problem of emulation. It cited more needy causes that Neild could have benefited and predicted incorrectly that the Queen would not touch 'one coin of the dirty 300000' but give it all to charity.[89]

However, there was also, as Linton noted, a great deal of apathy – and the group of which Mayhew was writing could not be expected to become involved in the highly intellectual movement which the *English Republic* was seeking to create. Harney, as we have noted above, regarded cowed deference resulting from the downtrodden condition of the people as a major obstacle to republicanism. This he saw as especially evident in the crowds who cheered the Queen on her way to open the Great Exhibition. *Punch's* celebration of the event showed the loyalty of the magazine, despite its satirical criticisms of flunkeyism, sycophancy and royal extravagance. Parodying wild rumours that the day would be undermined by the plots of exiled, foreign revolutionaries and their English, republican friends, its illustration of the Queen and family surrounded by happy and loyal subjects was ironically entitled, 'Her Majesty as She Appeared on the First of May, Surrounded by "Horrible

Conspirators and Assassins"', and an article described the British revolution occurring instead of the opening ceremony.[90] It was Britain's uniqueness in 1848 which made the great impression on most political commentators – Harney, Linton and their colleagues were alone after 1848 in seeing the revolutions on the Continent as the harbinger of what would follow in Britain. In 1849 *The Times* was able to assert confidently of an attempted assassination of the Queen, '. . . there is not the smallest reason for concluding that the revolting outrage was suggested by any motives more substantial than the vain folly of an idiot, or the meaningless desperation of a ruffian'.[91]

Republicans could only despair at the loyalty demonstrated at successive royal events: Reynolds fulminated at the cheers that greeted the Queen and Albert on opening the Coal Exchange in 1849,[92] and the Princess Royal and her husband in 1858 – 'Can it be possible that the hardworking people of England, should gladly see so much of the nation's wealth squandered to gratify the pride and vanity . . . and to sustain in laziness and luxury of a couple of idle, useless, and freedom-hating human beings, while thousands of the workers of England, with their wives and children, are deprived of the necessities of existence'.[93]

Traditional Chartism had, as we have seen, abjured republicanism, but its final organ, the *People's Paper*, continued to criticize the monarchy for its extravagance and lack of concern for the people during the 1850s. Its attitude to the Princess Royal's wedding in 1858 was expressed in 'A Royal Marriage Ode' which juxtaposed the wedding celebrations and the scandalous workhouse burials discovered to have been taking place in Lambeth, where paupers' bodies were disposed of in sham funerals. Britain was depicted as a savage, tyrannical state like Prussia, whither the Princess Royal was bound.

The paper carried a report of the town council meeting at Northampton, where a resolution, supported mainly by shopkeeping councillors, that the town should honour the wedding as a public holiday, was defeated. Councillor John Bates pointed to the marked absence of working-class signatures on the petition requesting a holiday and said that to declare one would be to approve of the profligate expenditure of £50,000 on the wedding and the grant of £8,000 per annum to be paid to the Princess Royal henceforth and to rob a working man of another day's wages for it. His amendment, which was passed, encapsulated the attitude of popular radicalism to the monarchy in this period – noticeably couched not in republican terms but in those of loyal criticism:

> That while this meeting wishes to express a feeling of respect towards the Queen and her family, it is of opinion that, especially as the government has decided that the labour of this country shall be taxed to support the Princess, whilst the labourer must support

his wife and family at home, it is wrong that the wealth of any class should be squandered on such occasion, when the distress of their fellow-creatures needs anything they have to spare of that wealth.[94]

Conclusion

At the outset of this chapter I juxtaposed the two contradictory Englands – that of the hereditary monarchy and that of radicalism. Having assessed the way in which the latter reacted to the former, we can see that while radicalism was not on the whole republican, it did raise fundamental questions about the compatibility of the institution of monarchy with the modern age. The Benthamite preoccupation with rationality in government pervaded middle-class radicals' discussion of the Crown and also entered into working-class discourse, with allusions to the utility – or lack of it – of the Crown and Royal Family. Both middle- and working-class critics attacked the cost of the Crown and the selfishness of royalty in the face of poverty, but with working-class radicals this led to a more bitter class critique of royalty. Both classes of radicals saw the monarchy as an obstacle in some way – the middle class wanted an end to the privileges of birth and a fully meritocratic society; Chartists and republicans saw the Crown as embodying the frustration of the sovereignty of the people by the narrow political class whose power rested on property and wealth.

Republicanism was only stimulated by foreign influence and then only as the preserve of a small group of former Chartists, whose short-lived newspapers were read by a closed circle of adherents. Yet the criticisms of the Crown which were the content of this idealistic republican form were common to the wider world of English radicalism, which under certain circumstances could furnish a broader support for republicanism. The 1860s brought a signal failure of the English Royal Family to discharge their duties. Albert, for all the unpopularity of his foreign birth and political interference,[95] had at least been tireless in keeping royalty before the country and fastidious in presenting the Royal Family as paragons of domestic virtue. There had been occasional complaints in the 1840s and 1850s about the Queen's absence from London, and about hoarding of the Civil List, and these were to take on real significance and become the motor of the organized republican movement after the Prince Consort's death. While the period 1837–61 did not give rise to a specific English republican movement, it showed the monarchy to be the object of intense criticism from the important radicals of an epoch characterized by rigorous questioning of established forms and practices.

Notes

1. In chapter 7.
2. See Christopher Hibbert, *George IV* (London, 1976 edn) and Philip Ziegler, *William IV* (London, 1971).
3. Gareth Stedman Jones, 'The Language of Chartism' in James Epstein and Dorothy Thompson, eds, *The Chartist Experience* (London, 1982), pp. 3–52.
4. *Letter to the Queen on the State of the Monarchy*. By a Friend of the People (London, 1838), pp. 5–14, 23.
5. *Spectator*, 28 November 1840, p. 1140; see H.R. Fox Bourne on the *Spectator* in *English Newspapers. Chapters in the History of Journalism*, 2 vols (London, 1887), vol. 2, pp. 45–7.
6. *Letter to The Queen on the State of the Monarchy*, pp. 39–40.
7. *Hansard*, 3rd ser., vol. 39, cols 137–85, 843–937, 945–8, 1119–60, 1186–90, 1279–331, 1337–72. (All subsequent *Hansard* references, in this and other chapters, 3rd ser., unless otherwise stated.)
8. See below, chapter 4.
9. *Hansard*, vol. 51, cols 583–633.
10. Ibid., vol. 69, cols 1527–48.
11. Ibid., vol. 113, cols 18–29.
12. *The Times*, 30 July 1850, p. 5.
13. *Hansard*, vol. 113, cols 685–97.
14. See below, chapter 3.
15. *Hansard*, vol. 145, cols 720–48.
16. See below, chapter 3.
17. Susan and Asa Briggs eds, *Cap and Bell. Punch's Chronicle of English History in the Making, 1841–61* (London, 1972), xxvi; R.G.G. Price, *A History of Punch* (London, 1957), pp. 19–31.
18. For example, *Figaro in London*, 27 May 1837, pp. 81–2; *London Pioneer*, vol. 1 (1846), passim.
19. *Punch*, vol. 1 (1842), p. 209.
20. Ibid, vol. 4 (1843), pp. 256–7.
21. *The Times*, 17 March, p. 4.
22. *Punch*, vol. 2 (1842), p. 128.
23. *Sunday Times*, 30 April 1843, p. 4.
24. Ibid., 11 August 1844, p. 4.
25. *London Pioneer*, 3 September 1846, p. 303.
26. *Punch*, vol. 17 (1849), p. 177.
27. Price, *A History of Punch*, p. 31.
28. *Punch*, vol. 28 (1855), pp. 197–9
29. Ibid., vol. 37 (1857), p. 177.
30. For example, there is silence on the subject in James Epstein and Dorothy Thompson eds, *The Chartist Experience* (London, 1982); David Goodway, *London Chartism 1838–1848* (Cambridge, 1982); and James Epstein, *The Lion of Freedom. Feargus O'Connor and the Chartist Movement, 1832–1842* (London, 1982).
31. Dorothy Thompson, *The Chartists* (London, 1984), p. 6.
32. Patricia Hollis, *The Pauper Press. A Study in Working Class Radicalism of the 1830s* (Oxford, 1970).
33. Stedman Jones, 'The Language of Chartism', pp. 3–52.

34. *Northern Star*, 30 June 1838, p. 4. Tom Nairn is incorrect in asserting in *The Enchanted Glass. Britain and its Monarchy* (London, 1988) pp. 284, 326 that the 'mass opposition of Chartism was automatically republican'. As we shall see, some Chartists embraced republicanism in the late 1840s and early 1850s, inspired by European example, when the Chartist movement was in decline and fragmentation but, in the years when it was a 'mass opposition', Chartism did not view the monarchy as the first element of the 'Old Corruption' to be stripped away, but hoped to detach it from that 'Old Corruption'.

35. *The Times*, 23 June 1838, p. 5.

36. *Northern Star*, 30 June 1838, p. 4; R.G. Gammage, *History of the Chartist Movement 1837–1854* (1st pub. 1850, 2nd edn, 1894; new impression London, 1969 with an introduction by John Saville), p. 25.

37. *Northern Star*, 15 February 1840, pp. 4–8; 25 January 1840, p. 4.

38. *The Royal Wedding Jester or Nuptial Interlude. A Collection of the Wedding Facetiae displayed on this joyful event.* The whole collected and arranged by Rigdum Funnidos (London, 1840), pp. 12–13.

39. *Northern Star*, 28 November 1840, p. 3.

40. Ibid., 13 November 1840, p. 4.

41. John Ashton, *Modern Street Ballads*, (London, 1888), pp. 279–80.

42. *Northern Star*, 6 May 1843, p. 5.

43. *Spectator*, 29 April 1843, p. 395.

44. *Northern Star*, 6 May 1843, p. 5.

45. Ibid., 4 June 1842, p. 4.

46. Ibid., 16 May 1846, p. 3.

47. *Punch*, vol. 14, (1848), p. 228. See Frank Prochaska, *Royal Bounty. The Making of a Welfare Monarchy* (New Haven, 1995), pp. 80–3 for the connection between royal charitable activities and threats to the monarchy.

48. *The Times*, 19 March 1848, p. 4.

49. *Northern Star*, 3 March 1849, p. 1.

50. The motto of the *Red Republican*; and W.E. Adams, *Memoirs of a Social Atom*, 2 vols (London, 1903), vol. 1, p. 261, recalls 'We were Chartists and something more'.

51. For Harney and Linton, see A.R. Schoyen, *The Chartist Challenge. A Portrait of George Julian Harney* (London, 1958); F.B. Smith, *Radical Artisan. William James Linton 1812–97* (Manchester, 1973); Miles Taylor, *The Decline of British Radicalism 1847–1860* (Oxford, 1995); Margot Finn, *After Chartism. Class and Nation in English Radical Politics 1848–1874* (Cambridge, 1993).

52. *Democratic Review*, vol. 2 (September 1850), p. 156.

53. *Red Republican*, 22 June 1850, p. 1.

54. Adams, *Memoirs of a Social Atom*, vol. 1, pp. 261–5; *English Republic*, vol. 1 (1851), pp. 16–34.

55. *English Republic*, vol. 3 (1854), pp. 1–2.

56. See Bernard Porter, *The Refugee Question in Mid-Victorian politics* (Cambridge, 1979).

57. *English Republic*, vol. 1 (1851), p. 251.

58. *Republican*, (1848), pp. 22–3, 158–9.

59. *Northern Tribune*, vol. 2 (1855), pp. 116–17.

60. *Red Republican*, 24 August 1850, p. 77; *Democratic Review*, vol. 1 (July 1850), p. 70.

61. *Red Republican*, 22 June 1850, p. 4 under new title, *Friend of the People*, 15 February 1851, p. 74 ; *English Republic*, vol. 1, (1851) p. 70.
62. *English Republic*, vol. 3 (1854), p. 77 and see chapters 4 and 6.
63. *Northern Tribune*, vol. 1 (1851), p. 281; vol. 2, (1855), p. 64.
64. *Reynolds's Newspaper*, 17 June, 1855, pp. 8–9.
65. *Northern Tribune*, vol. 2(1855), pp. 64, 78.
66. *Republican* (1848), pp. 131–3, 145–6.
67. *Red Republican*, 22 June 1850, p. 4; *English Republic*, vol. 1 (1851), p. 70.
68. *Red Republican*, February 1850, passim, 3 August 1850, pp. 52–3, 10 August 1850, pp. 61–2; as *Friend of the People* 15 February 1851, p. 74.
69. *Democratic Review*, vol. 1 (January 1850), p. 319.
70. *Red Republican*, vol. 1, no. 8 (10 August 1850), p. 59 .
71. G.W.M. Reynolds, *The Mysteries of the Court of London* 8 vols, (London, 1849–56), vol. 1, p. 339; postscript to vols 3–4.
72. *Reynolds's Political Instructor*, 4 November 1849, pp. 17–18.
73. *Reynolds's Newspaper*, 4 May, 1851 p. 7; 31 January 1858, p. 1.
74. *Friend of the People*, 26 July 1851, p. 277.
75. *English Republic*, vol. 1 (1851), p. 193.
76. *Friend of the People*, 10 May 1851, pp. 189–90.
77. *English Republic*, vol. 2 (1852–3), p. 396.
78. *Reynolds's Newspaper*, 15 January 1854, p. 1.
79. *Democratic Review*, vol. 1 (February 1850), pp. 347–8.
80. *Friend of the People*, 26 July 1851, p. 278.
81. By Norbert J. Gossman, 'Republicanism in nineteenth century England', *International Review of Social History*, vol. 7 (1962), pp. 48–50.
82. *Red Republican*, 10 August 1850, p. 62.
83. *Friend of the People*, 1 March 1851, p. 91; 15 March 1851, pp. 109–110; *English Republic*, vol. 1 (1851), pp. 54–60, 125–6, 158, 250–1, 255, 351–2; vol. 2 (1852), pp. 81–3; vol. 4 (1855). p. 107.
84. *Northern Tribune*, vol. 2 (1855), pp. 105–6.
85. Adams, *Memoirs of a Social Atom*, vol. 2, p. 329.
86. Henry Mayhew, *London Labour and the London Poor* (1st pub. 1851; 2 vols, London, 1967 edn), vol. 1, p. 249.
87. Ashton, *Modern Street Ballads*, pp. 210–13, 281–3, 287–9; Peter Davidson, *Songs of the British Music Hall* (London 1971), p. 66
88. Philip Hall, *Royal Fortune: Tax, Money and the Monarchy* (London, 1992), pp. 11–13, 255.
89. *Lloyd's Weekly Newspaper*, 12 September 1852, p. 6. In fact Victoria and Albert used some of the money to help build a new castle at Balmoral and to carry out work at Osborne but most was saved to form 'the basis for Victoria's personal capital.' (Hall, *Royal Fortune: Tax, Money and the Monarchy*, p. 15).
90. *Punch*, vol. 20 (1851), pp. 192–5.
91. *The Times*, 21 May 1849, p. 4.
92. *Reynolds's Political Instructor*, 24 November 1849, p. 17.
93. *Reynolds's Newspaper*, 31 January 1858, p. 1.
94. *People's Paper*, 30 January 1858, p. 5.
95. See chapters 4, 6.

CHAPTER THREE

The Rise and Fall of the British Republican Movement, 1861–1901

We have seen that there was considerable radical criticism of the monarchy in the first twenty-five years of the Queen's reign. Such criticism, including the republicanism kindled in 1848, was the by-product of wider outlooks – utilitarian, Chartist and Mazzinian. In the period 1861–87 we find a specific republican movement which made the abolition of the British monarchy its aim – the first reform necessary before others could be contemplated. As in 1848, inspiration from abroad – the collapse of the Empire and foundation of the Third Republic in France in 1870 – prompted English republicanism but this time as an organized movement because of the intensification of the economic critique of the Crown that had taken place since 1861 due to the Queen's virtual retirement from public life since Albert's death. These economic criticisms persisted after the decline of organized republicanism in the mid-1870s and it is important to remember that in this period there were other non-republican criticisms of the monarchy – of its political and ceremonial roles – which will be discussed in later chapters.

There are accounts of the republican movement of the early 1870s in broader works on radicalism[1] or the monarchy[2] and in individual articles.[3] On the whole these accounts tend to be superficial or partial in that they are concerned with republicanism as part of Bradlaugh's career, as part of English freethought or as a stepping-stone in the movement of popular politics towards socialism. My discussion is a fuller one and is set in the wider context of radical criticisms of the monarchy from Victoria's accession so that it should furnish a more detailed and coherent account.

Historians have written of divisions within the republican movement of the early 1870s.[4] In fact two distinct republicanisms existed, having sprung from different sources in the 1860s and 1870. More prominent at the time and historically, is the mainstream republicanism of Bradlaugh's *National Reformer*, embodied in the National Republican League. This was the republicanism of a section of the respectable Reform Union alliance of middle-class radicals and artisans who were made potentially republican by the Queen's retirement and the Prince of Wales' unpopularity in the 1860s and inspired by France in 1870 but who organized into a republican movement in early 1871 only as a result of the agitation against Princess Louise's dowry. A sans-culotte alliance of a section of the middle classes and artisans against the 'Old Corruption', its prime concerns were the need for a meritocracy to replace aristocratic privilege, and the excessive cost of the Crown.

The other republicanism, proletarian and socialist, was that of the *Republican* newspaper, then embodied in the National Republican Brotherhood. Its origins lay in the small socialist groups of the late 1860s, such as the Poor People's Union and the Land and Labour League, and the most advanced branches of the Reform League. In the 1860s these were tending towards republicanism as the inevitable corollary of their social programmes – in this respect more reminiscent of the criticisms we have described in the 1840s and 1850s. Their republicanism was thus an endogenous growth, not dependent on the unpopularity of the Royal Family: events in France in 1870 prompted their open declaration of republicanism; the inspiration did not need the mediation of the anti-dowry agitation. The ideology of these groups represented a definite, socialist break with the old analysis – capital, not privilege, was the real enemy.

The chapter traces the rise and fall of republicanism by looking at the way in which criticism intensified into virtual republicanism in the 1860s; describing the formation, activity and ideology of the organized movement in the early 1870s; and examining the decline of the movement and the persistence of critiques of the cost of the Crown from 1874 to 1901, including the continuation of republicanism in *Reynolds's Newspaper*.[5]

The 1860s – from criticism to republicanism

Many of the former Chartists were subsumed in the 'respectable' Reform agitation of the 1860s organized by middle-class radicals such as John Bright, in the Reform Union. This movement remained loyal. At its height in 1867, in a crowded meeting in St James' Hall, one radical MP, Ayrton, criticized the Queen for her widowed seclusion, only to be rebuked by Bright, the chairman of the meeting, whose speech of sympathy with the Queen's six-year-old bereavement was received with cheers, and the meeting dispersed singing, 'God Save the Queen'.[6] However, during the decade the economic critique of the Crown intensified as the Queen in retired seclusion was seen to be performing none of the functions for which royalty was kept in such expensive state, while the Prince of Wales seemed to be embarking on the same prodigal career as his immediate predecessor, George. America, on which attention was focused by the Civil War, provided an alternative model of government – and the replacement of the French Empire with the Third Republic in 1870 was to add political inspiration to the complaints about the cost of the Crown, to turn, via the dowry agitation, part of this Reform alliance into a republican movement.

The readership of *Reynolds's Newspaper* was mainly of the skilled artisan class[7] from which the republican movement was to recruit its membership and, throughout the 1860s, this newspaper closely scrutinized the British Royal Family, making the criticisms we have found to be familiar ones of popular radicalism. Six months after Albert's death it complained that the Queen's continued absence in mourning from London was injuring the industrial classes – in which it included the small tradesmen whose conditions of work and life were not dissimilar from the artisans and who were allied with them in Reform politics-dependent on the custom and stimulus to trade of the court's presence. The wedding of Princess Alice should, the paper argued, signal the Queen's resumption of her duties, particularly as the marriage necessitated a further 'bleeding of the people on account of royalty'.[8] The following year, the enthusiasm displayed by the crowds at the Prince of Wales' wedding and the concurrent distress of textile workers because of the American 'cotton famine', prompted *Reynolds's* to observe, 'A portion of the people has been trampled, and a portion has grovelled in the dirt'. Only future lives of devotion to the people's needs on the part of the royal couple could excuse 'the contrast between the profusion and splendour of this royal wedding, and the destitution and squalor to which millions of our fellow-subjects are now exposed'.[9]

The paper wrote in 1864, that the British Crown was now reputed to be the meanest in Europe, with the Queen in obstinate retirement hoarding the Civil List money which, it argued in a class critique of the monarchy, 'was taken out of the pockets of the working classes, without their consent being either asked or obtained, by those whose political tool and convenience the emasculated monarchy of England is'.[10] Far from there being a reduction in the money paid to the Royal Family, there were constant additions as the Queen's children grew up. In 1866 grants were made to Princess Helena on her marriage and Prince Alfred on his coming of age, and 'Gracchus', *Reynolds's* regular columnist, at the end of the year, 'foresaw incessant repetitions of those demands for dowers to princesses, and settlements for princes, that impoverish the country, and by their frequency have become intolerable nuisances' – while all the Princes did was to shoot game 'from morn till night' and the Queen's doings were a mystery to everyone.[11]

The Royal Family was alleged to be indulging itself not only in luxurious indolence but in immorality. The Queen's attachment to her

Balmoral servant John Brown gave rise to rumours that Brown was her lover or morganatic husband. *Reynolds's Newspaper* in 1866 reported the *Gazette de Lausanne*'s assertion that the Queen was carrying Brown's child;[12] and the popular press contained thinly veiled allusions to the Queen's infatuation. In July 1866 *Punch* published a mock Court Circular:

> Mr. John Brown walked on the Slopes. He subsequently partook of
> a haggis.
> In the evening Mr. John Brown was pleased to listen to a bagpipe.
> Mr. John Brown retired early.[13]

The more scurrilous and short-lived satirical paper, *Tomahawk* in August 1867 printed a cartoon entitled 'A Brown Study' showing the British lion, its crown resting under a glass case, lunging towards a kilted Highlander with pipe in hand.[14] In October 1868 *Tinsley's Magazine* contained an article by an American visitor who professed himself to be shocked by 'constant references to and jokes about "Mrs Brown" . . . an English synonym for the Queen . . . I have been told that the Queen was insane, and John Brown was her keeper; that the Queen was a spiritualist, and John Brown was her medium'.[15]

The Prince of Wales was considered to divide his time between blood sports, gambling, smoking, the racecourse and, it was alleged in some quarters, womanizing. The example of George IV when he was Prince of Wales was frequently cited by diverse observers with obvious yet unstated contemporary allusions. In 1869 the Prince was at the centre of the 'Warwickshire scandal' when the *Royal Leamington Chronicle* attributed to him the seduction and consequent derangement of a local girl.[16] The nadir of his popularity came when in early 1870 he was cited as a co-respondent in the Mordaunt divorce case. 'Gracchus' in *Reynolds's Newspaper* denounced 'Gutter Royalty' and asserted, 'The middle and humbler orders are the power of the nation and they have spoken out. They have said – "No more such filthy fellows as George the IV shall ever sit upon the throne of England"'.[17] Bradlaugh's secularist journal the *National Reformer* began to turn its attention in earnest to the Royal Family at this time, with articles on 'The Life of George, Prince of Wales. With recent contradictions and coincidences' – the present Prince of Wales' income was, Bradlaugh wrote, disproportionate to his abilities and his morals.[18] The *National Reformer*'s circulation of 3,000 in 1867 had doubled by 1872[19] and this perhaps reflects its becoming the organ of the republican movement in these years.

Gladstone, during the 1860s became increasingly concerned at what he called the 'royalty question' – the problem being, as he wrote to Granville in 1870, that 'the Queen is invisible and the Prince of Wales is not respected'.[20] In 1864 *The Times* had admitted that 'the rationale of

hereditary monarchy' must be questioned in the modern age and that a
newly established state, without tradition, would probably choose a
different form of government.[21] America's was seen as the government
of the modern age and the Civil War thrust this example more promi-
nently before British radicals. The organ of the trade unions, the *Bee-
Hive* predicted that the victory of the North, led by a 'working man
raised by universal suffrage' to the presidency, would give 'a vast impetus . . . to Republican sentiments in England' which would soon have
to be reckoned with.[22] Following the annuities to Alfred and Helen,
Reynolds's Newspaper looked enviously across the Atlantic, 'The Amer-
icans do not expend nearly a million per annum in the support of
royalty.[23]

With the Reform agitation and the distress of the country, *Reynolds's*
tone became increasingly hostile to the Royal Family and tinged with
republicanism. In January 1867 an article entitled 'Wholesale Starva-
tion of the London Poor' approved of placards appearing in the capital
denouncing the superfluity of the rich while the poor starved, and
compared these with the placards that appeared in Paris just before the
1789 Revolution – the Royal Family, the paper alleged, were the worst
offenders. *Reynolds's* detected a republican spirit in the great Reform
demonstration of February in London – loud cheers went up as the
procession passed the American embassy and 'the mottoes on the ban-
ners' included not 'one loyal allusion to royalty', the red flag was
carried and caps of liberty worn. In October 1868 *Reynolds's* contained
an article on 'Monarchical Failures and Republican Successes', concluding that 'With a very few exceptions it must be confessed that monarchy
is a failure everywhere, and that whatever good government there is, is
produced and goes on in spite of it, rather than in consequence of it'.
The anomalies produced by the English monarchy were an example of
this: labour representation was prevented by non-payment of MPs, but
a hundred MPs could be paid with the additional sum that parliament
was prepared to vote to the Prince of Wales; and until there were such
labour representation 'the British constitution is reduced to the pro-
spectus of a joint-stock company in which royalty holds the debenture
stock, aristocracy preference shares, and plutocracy a lien upon income'.[24]

The republican ensignia noticed at the Reform rally of 1867 were
symptomatic of the move towards republicanism in the most socialistic
quarters of the Reform League, which was the proletarian association
for Reform, unassimilated into the middle class led Reform Union. In
May 1869 George Howell, a moderate trade unionist in the Reform
League's leadership, was complaining about those who 'seem determined to convert the League to ultra-Republicanism'.[25] In July the

International Republican Association was formed by the fusion of the Holborn branch of the League with the Poor People's Union, a democratic and socialist body. Within a week the Association had changed its title from 'Republican' to 'Democratic', 'in order to steer as clear as possible from the law', but it was soon debating whether 'to agitate for a Republic'. Such a republic would be a social one to uphold the right of labour and to nationalize the land.[26]

By the end of the 1860s not only popular radicals were seeing similarities in Britain with France on the eve of the Revolution. *The Times* in August 1869 commented on the drab closing of parliament, which the Queen again declined to open in person, and likened it to the appearance of Roland with strings in his shoes at Versailles. It warned that 'the time may yet come when the only formula repeated at the closing of parliamentary sessions' would be 'a reminder that the Acts they have passed will be found in due course in the Statute Book'.[27]

Organized republicanism 1870–3

The collapse of the French Empire and its replacement by a republic in September 1870 was the catalyst in producing a professed republicanism in Britain. The republic received the support of all elements of the broad British left, which held demonstrations of solidarity with the new regime. These demonstrations in turn further inspired the republican sentiments we have seen developing in the 1860s. There was an immediate embracing of republicanism as the framework of their programme by the small proletarian, socialist bodies formed in the late 1860s. However, it was the anti-dowry agitation of late 1870 to early 1871 which gave birth to the first of the Republican Clubs which soon came under the aegis of Bradlaugh's *National Reformer* and which represented the old-middle class/artisan radical alliance. I shall proceed by looking at the effect of the French upheaval on the British left in general and on the socialist left in particular; showing how the mainstream republican movement emerged finally from the anti-dowry agitation; examining the arguments and aims of this republicanism – and its differences with social republicanism; and finally analysing the decline and failure of the organized movement.

The Commune was to highlight the divisions in British radicalism but the initial establishment of the republic was met with unanimous approval; and large demonstrations in London and other parts of the country expressed support of the new French government in its defence against the Prussian invasion. Middle-class radicals such as Bradlaugh, trade unionists and labour politicians like Howell and George Odger, as well as the more militant like John Johnson and G.E. Harris of the International Democratic Association could unite in these demonstrations.[28] On 18 September, the day of the first of these mass meetings in Hyde Park, Bradlaugh printed in the *National Reformer* a mock report of a 'Commission of Inquiry as to Complaints against Royalty', the 'complaints' arising from the Queen's seclusion. The conclusion was that as 'it is considered by very many and seems proved by the experience of the last nine or ten years that the country can do quite well without a monarchy, and may therefore save the extra expense of monarchy', the monarchy be replaced by a 'Dogeship' filled yearly by a succession of dukes.[29] Bradlaugh travelled the country in the autumn lecturing on the debts of the Prince of Wales and the benefits of republicanism over monarchy.[30]

However, it was the Land and Labour League which became the first espouser of republicanism in Britain for over a decade. The League, formed in October 1869, stood for nationalization of the land and held an anti-capitalist analysis influenced by Marx.[31] The first number of its newspaper published in September 1870 bore the title *Republican*; its editor was G.E. Harris, also of the International Democratic Association.[32] The title was a salute to the French republicans but also showed a belief that only a social republic could fulfil the rights and needs of the working class. The second number of the *Republican* cast a sceptical eye on those middle-class radicals such as Bradlaugh who toured the country hailing the French republic: 'Let the working classes ask themselves whether it is reasonable to expect that the middle classes of this country are disposed to pay for Halls and Noisy Orators, to advocate true principles that will lead to the establishment of a Republican form of Government, based upon equitable principles'. Only 'social justice' could found a republic and only the principles of the Land and Labour League provided this through land nationalization and replacement of the capitalist cash nexus by the 'exchange medium for our productions' – all 'social republicans' should adhere to this programme.[33] This recalled Harney's 'Vive la république, démocratique et sociale', and the *Republican* claimed his *Red Republican* of 1850–1 as a forerunner, having former contributors to the latter among its writers.[34] Like Harney, the *Republican* in bitter and emotive language, depicted monarchy as a selfish part of an oppressive class government which cared nothing for the poor.[35] A republic, it was argued, must come in Britain as the workers would see that their material conditions would be so much better than under a monarchy.[36]

While the republicanism of the Land and Labour League was expressed directly on the downfall of the Empire in France, the artisanate republican movement, organized by middle-class radicals sympathetic with French republicanism, did not begin to take shape until early 1871, the mediating event being the agitation against the dowry of Princess Louise who was getting married to the Marquis of Lorne. *The Times*, commenting on English republicanism a few months later, observed that it originated with 'those who opposed Princess Louise's dowry'.[37] Thomas Wright, the 'journeyman engineer', writing in *Fraser's Magazine* on the republicanism prevalent among his class by mid-1871, also saw the grant to the Princess as the turning-point in working-class resentment of annuities to members of the Royal Family, when 'it broke out in bitter protest and reviling, and assumed the shape of an organized movement'.[38]

The annuity to Princess Louise was so provocative because of the Queen's decade-long retirement, the straitened economic conditions of the country and the impulse to republican sentiment given by the demonstrations in favour of France. Following on the annuities to the Prince of Wales, the Princess Royal, Princess Alice, Prince Alfred and Princess Helena in the late 1850s and 1860s, it was a further reminder that every member of the Queen's large family was going to be provided for by the tax-payer. Wright noted, 'This matter of semi-royalty is the sorest point of all with the Republicans'. He ridiculed *The Times'* editorial on the marriage which had presented the nation as regarding 'their' daughter as marrying a commoner, 'one of themselves':

> By the working-class section of 'the people', the Princess was not held to be in any sense their daughter, but rather the daughter of the horse leech . . . and they certainly look upon her husband more in the light of a vampyre fastened upon them than as one of themselves.[39]

The *National Reformer* printed a satirical song about Lorne's sending the begging-bowl around, the immense wealth of his father, the Duke of Argyll, who was in the cabinet which proposed the grant, not being enough to keep his bride. It also carried reports of anti-dowry meetings – one at Nottingham warned the borough MPs that working men would henceforth withhold their support if they voted for the grant.[40] *Reynolds's Newspaper*, with its artisanate readership, greeted the news of the engagement in October 1870 with the classic radical picture of John Bull being bled dry by the 'Old Corruption'. Of the grant passed by parliament, *Reynolds's* predicted that 'another similar demand would shake the throne to its foundations'.[41] Peter Taylor, one of three radical MPs (Fawcett and Dilke being the others) who voted against the grant, warned that opinion out-of-doors was at variance with the House's: 'large masses' disapproved with 'bitter feeling'.[42]

It was in the midst of the anti-dowry agitation that C. Charles Cattell, a Birmingham radical of lower middle-class background,[43] placed an advertisement in the *National Reformer* inviting all friends to attend a meeting to inaugurate a republican club in Birmingham.[44] The first meeting was held on 14 February 1871 and reported in the *National Reformer* which commended it as a model for other towns and cities to follow.[45] The following issues contained reports of numerous such clubs coming into existence and, from late March, a special 'Republican Club Department' with accounts of meetings and new clubs was a regular feature of the newspaper.[46] For the next two and a half years the *National Reformer* was the organ of the republican movement and Bradlaugh, president of the London Republican Club, its leader and coordinator, organizing in May 1873 the National Republican Conference at Birmingham.[47] In all, 85 Republican Clubs were founded in Britain between 1871 and 1874;[48] it has been estimated that there was a total only of 5,000 to 6,000 paid-up members of these clubs[49] but it must be remembered that there were greater attendances than this at individual meetings and events organized by them.[50]

The aim of the movement was, as Bradlaugh stressed, a legal and constitutional, not a revolutionary one – the parliamentary repeal, on the Queen's decease, of the Act of Settlement whereby the House of Brunswick reigned as monarchs in Britain and the establishment of a republic.[51] No similarities were to be allowed with the violence and disorder which the Terror and now the Commune had associated with French republicanism: the committee of the London Republican Club reproved those who had worn caps of liberty and waved red flags at a republican meeting convened by Odger in March 1871.[52] The grievances which had given rise to the movement were enumerated as 'the monopoly of land by the aristocracy, the frightful increase of imperial taxation, the expensiveness and uselessness of the monarchy, the immoral example of the present heir-apparent to the throne, and the utterly obstructive character of the House of Lords'. Only under a republic could radical policies of abolishing the House of Lords, and the standing army and initiating free, compulsory, non-sectarian education be accomplished.[53] The republican movement thus represented an attempt by certain advanced radicals to focus on a single aim – the abolition of the monarchy – which, as Feargus D'Arcy has written, would serve to 'carry the cause of social and political progress further'.[54]

The anti-monarchical ideology of the movement was essentially a utilitarian one, combining the meritocratic outlook of its middle-class leadership with an appeal based on the cost of the Crown to its predominantly artisanate support. The Crown was irrational, useless and expensive and served to perpetuate the monopoly on land and position of a hereditary aristocracy, however talentless. A republic, a rational, efficient, cheap form of government in keeping with the democratic spirit of the age, should replace the 'Old Corruption' of incompetent monarchs, princes, sinecurists and aristocrats which weighed down upon the taxpayer and thwarted the legislative hopes of the people. These arguments of republicanism can be found in articles and reports of meetings in the *National Reformer* and in *Reynolds's Newspaper* which supported the movement. An analysis of the republicanism of the early 1870s should also draw upon the speeches of Sir Charles Dilke and writings of Frederic Harrison. Dilke, though he never joined a republican club, became associated in the public mind with the movement, and an influence on it, through his touring speeches on the cost of the Crown and his questions on the Civil List in parliament; while Harrison in the *Fortnightly Review* was a cogent theoretician of republicanism. Having examined the ideology of the mainstream republican movement, I shall show how it clashed with the social republicanism of the *Republican* and of the National Republican Brotherhood which certain northern republican clubs established in defiance of Bradlaugh in 1873.

The republican ethos was eminently a meritocratic one. Cattell in his inaugural address to the Birmingham Republic Club, said: 'Useless people must be replaced by useful people'. A republic would destroy the hereditary principle of an effete aristocracy and install the open competition for office and honour in which self-made middle-class talent would rise to the top.[55] Dilke's speech on royalty at Newcastle on 6 November 1871 attacked, among other abuses, the key positions in the armed services, including at present Commander-in-Chief of the army, given to members of the Royal Family regardless of their inability and inexperience.[56] The *Pall Mall Gazette* derisively described Dilke as the 'fugleman of the middle-classes',[57] his speech having concluded '. . . if you can show me a fair chance that a republic here will be free from the political corruption that hangs about the monarchy, I say, for my part – and I believe the middle classes in general will say – let it come'.[58] The *Spectator*, read by the intellectual middle class, approved of Dilke's sentiments: the journal professed itself republican in principle and commented, 'Under a Commonwealth men are more free, careers more open, aspirations more lofty, capacities more unfettered, classes more united; the nation more alive to its responsibilities than under a monarchy'.[59] Harrison in the *Fortnightly Review*, the journal of advanced liberalism, put a utilitarian, rationalist case for republicanism. The tendency of modern civilization was the triumph of reason and rational government was to be exercised by a meritocracy, where 'Power . . . rests on "fitness to rule"'.[60]

A major plank in Bradlaugh's republican platform was the demonstration of the House of Brunswick's unfitness to rule. Just as Thackeray in the 1850s had lectured and written a book on the evils of the four Georges, Bradlaugh toured with lectures, 'The Impeachment of the House of Brunswick', printed in the *National Reformer* and as a book. The crimes of and misuse of power by British monarchs from George I's line were turned into a case against their continued rule and for the repeal of the Act of Settlement.[61] The final lecture, on the Queen and her family, condemned the interference in politics of the German Prince Consort, the Queen's neglect of her duties, the sinecure positions in the army and navy given to incompetent princes and the immorality of the Prince of Wales.[62]

The Prince of Wales was a special target for republicans. Bradlaugh expressed the hope that he would never so dishonour the country as by becoming its king[63] and it was the prospect of his accession that fired much republican propaganda about the lottery and dangers of the hereditary principle. When the Prince lay near death through typhoid in December 1871 and *Reynolds's Newspaper* put to press in the belief that he would have expired by the time it was read, it printed this damning obituary:

> It would be flunkeyish to assert and foolish to argue, that the Prince of Wales has ever displayed the slightest capacity for filling the high position of ruler of this mighty empire . . . his life would appear for the last fourteen years to have been an incessant round of frivolous amusement.[64]

The potential descent of the crown to the Prince highlighted the irrationality of hereditary kingship which thus stood in conflict with the modern age's belief in what Brougham had called at the outset of the reign, the 'imprescriptable right of men to govern themselves'.[65] Charles Watts, one of the *National Reformer's* most prolific republican propagandists, wrote that hereditary monarchy defied 'the spirit of the age', the acknowledgement that 'the foundation of true government is the will of the people'.[66] Another, Austin Holyoake, pointed out that local government showed the fitness of the people for republican self-government unencumbered by a hereditary executive.[67] Dilke was convinced that progress, political and intellectual, had fitted England for a republic: 'Have we not the republican spirit? Have we not the practice of self-government? Are we not gaining a general education?'[68]

Like the republicans of the 1850s, those of the 1870s on the one hand pointed to the waning political power of the Crown as proof of the inevitable rationalization of government and passage of power to the people, and on the other cited the continued exercise of royal influence as evidence of the dangers of arbitrary hereditary rule. Harrison argued that Britain was, as Bagehot had described it, a 'disguised republic'[69] – in his own words, 'a republic, though a most imperfect republic ... an aristocratic republic, with a democratic machinery and a hereditary grand master of ceremonies'. The Crown's political power had diminished to such an extent – a process accelerated by Victoria's seclusion – that the effective wielder of executive power was the Prime Minister, an office continually changing hands and whose occupant was embroiled in the party warfare of the legislative chamber.[70] Bradlaugh said that the country was 'a nominal monarchy', that the Crown was 'the tarnished gilded drapery', that it was 'fictitious' – Bentham's term for all that was irrational and useless in government and law.[71]

However, another article in his newspaper warned that, 'Under the most limited Monarchy the sovereign has the prerogative of over-ruling the entire community'.[72] A pseudonymous pamphlet – in fact by G.O. Trevelyan – entitled *What does she do with it?* warned of the unconstitutional political implications of a sovereign's accumulating a vast reserve of personal wealth as was happening through the enormous savings being made on the Civil List since the Queen's retirement.[73] Dilke's Newcastle speech referred to this pamphlet and to Disraeli's recent statement that the Queen signed nothing of which she did not approve – 'what does the Emperor of Russia do more than that?!' he asked.[74] The *Spectator* commented that the divergence between the self-governing instincts of the British people and their actual constitutional circumstances was 'a permanent source of weakness'.[75]

Complete self-government, possible only under a republic, would bring to an end the selfish dominance of the aristocratic oligarchy of which the monarchy was the figurehead. A meeting of the Maidstone Working Men's Club resolved 'that a Republican form of Government is decidedly more calculated to secure a favourable representation to the lower and middle classes than is to be secured under a Monarchical form of Government'.[76] The belief in the power of political representation as a universal panacea was a hallmark of popular radicalism stretching back through Chartism and Cobbett to Paine, and it was shared by the republican movement: the Doncaster Republican Club, after hearing Watts lecture on pauperism, resolved that 'the sooner we had a Government which had a fair representation the earlier would all the evils cease'.[77] The enemy by whom power was currently abused was identified as that same 'Old Corruption' Cobbett had attacked. W.D. Rubinstein has written of 'the end of the "Old Corruption" in Britain' in the period 1780–1860[78] but acknowledges that it remained part of the rhetoric of popular radicalism even in the late nineteenth century,[79] and my examination of radical writing on the monarchy reinforces this, showing that even at this late date the costly Crown was viewed as a significantly pernicious institution. *Reynolds's Newspaper*, decrying 'the great epidemic of typhoid loyalty' which accompanied the Prince of Wales' recovery, hoped that in future Englishmen would 'comprehend the facts of corruption in monarchy, aristocracy, Church, Exchange and trade; when they see how their fathers die by the typhoid created by the landlords of fetid courts and dismal alleys'.[80] Bradlaugh in his opening speech to the London Republican Club spoke of the

> oligarchy, consisting of a few aristocratic families, who have, since the time of Sir Robert Walpole until now, kept up the expensive pageant of a king or queen, while they have wielded the entire sovereign power, monopolized the land, gorged greedily on the fruits of labour, and thrown the gross and ever-swelling burden of taxation on the shoulders of a much-enduring people.[81]

It was the expense of the Crown and Royal Family and the consequent burden on the taxpayer that attracted the large artisanate support enjoyed by the republican movement.[82] Thomas Wright, analysing the republicanism of his own class, wrote, 'Republicanism as it now exists in England is founded less on pure admiration of its own professed principles than upon the cry "Take away the baubles" . . . '

> Indeed Republicanism is scarcely the proper name for it. Utilitarianism would be more accurately expressive of its meaning. They (working men) know that in many respects our constitution is as beneficial to the country as any Republic could be, and they would not care what the government was called provided it was purged of the (costly) fictional and hereditary elements.[83]

W.E. Adams, who in the 1850s had assisted Linton in propagating the idealistic republicanism of Mazzini, wrote that he and republicans of his generation 'had little or no sympathy' with those of the 1870s because their republican convictions:

> were based on no principle and informed by no elevated ideas . . . What . . . was the worth of that paltry cry about the Cost of the Crown, raised by Sir Charles Dilke . . . ?[84]

The *Spectator*, republican on principle, shared this view of Dilke's emphasis on the cost of the Crown but acknowledged that it was this 'argument which seems for the moment so attractive to the masses of the North'.[85] We have seen how the Louise dowry was decisive in producing the 1871 organized movement and another grant – to Prince Arthur in July – prompted further mass agitation but in the ensuing months republican activity was slack partly because, said the London Club's committee, there had been no galvanizing event since the grant to Arthur.[86]

Complaints about the cost of the Crown centred on the Queen's retirement and failure to discharge the duties which the Civil List was designed to pay for; and the recurrent demands for additional annuities to her children as they came of age or were married. Harrison wrote that the Crown would be judged on its 'public utility'[87] and, argued Wright, it was found to be 'worse than useless'[88] and therefore an utter waste of expenditure. It no longer fulfilled a political role and its ceremonial duties had fallen into desuetude. Bradlaugh drew forth great cheers when, in his inaugural speech to the London Republican Club, he said that 'the enormous sum paid for the support of royalty was vastly more than an equivalent for the services performed in return, that three-quarters of a million per annum was far too high a payment for the display of state robes across the back of a chair once a year'.[89]

The manifest non-application of the Civil List money to the duties of state occasioned the 1871 pamphlet *What does she do with it?* which Dilke took as the text for the main theme of his Newcastle speech and for his questions on the Civil List in parliament. In 1850 Brougham had raised the matter of the savings being made on the Civil List expenditure in parliament[90] and the author of *What does she do with it?* was at pains to point out that such savings had now assumed massive proportions as a result of the Queen's retirement since 1861. The point had been reached where the sovereign was accumulating a vast reserve of personal wealth and where additional requests for annuities for her children were quite superfluous as she could easily provide for them out of her own unspent income. Republicanism would only be arrested by parliament's legislating to ensure that in future the Civil List money was spent for its expressed purpose while the surplus hitherto accumulated should be used to provide for future marriage settlements of and annuities to the Queen's children.[91]

While the author's purpose was professedly loyal, the pamphlet provided republicans with further ammunition. Dilke at Newcastle created a sensation when, using the evidence contained in it, he effectively accused the Queen of a misappropriation of public money. His subsequent tour with the speech drew audiences of around 5,000 at Leeds, Middlesborough, Bristol, Birmingham and Bolton; bellicose royalists attended to disrupt the meetings and in one of the brawls provoked a member of the Bolton Republican Club was killed.[92] There were rowdy scenes in the House of Commons in March 1872 when Dilke demanded a public enquiry into the expenditure of the Civil List. Tory backbenchers howled down the speech of his seconder, Herbert, and his motion was defeated by 276 votes to 2. In the debate, Fawcett, a republican on principle, disassociated himself from Dilke, in 'protest against the question of Republicanism being raised upon a miserable haggle over a few pounds . . . degraded to a huckstering and quibbling over the cost of the Queen's household'.[93]

Yet, as others who were idealistic republicans regretted, this was the prime motive force of the movement, and the Republican Clubs' greatest bursts of activity were in protest against the grants made to Prince Arthur on his majority in 1871 and to Prince Alfred, Duke of Edinburgh, on his marriage in 1873. Republican Clubs throughout the country organized protest meetings against the grant to Arthur made in July 1871[94] – Watts in the *National Reformer* wrote that the vote of parliament of £15,000 p.a. to the Prince was 'a cruel injustice to a heavily taxed nation'.[95]

In the debate in the Commons Peter Taylor asked how parliament could possibly 'twice in the same session make additional grants to Royalty, which in the opinion of a large portion of the people of this country, are already excessive and extravagant'. Dixon protested that 'the pomp, the pageantry and the hospitality of the Crown ... had materially diminished since the death of the Prince Consort' without a commensurate diminution of the financial demands made on its behalf from the people. The result 'among the working people' had been 'a large amount of Republicanism' which was 'increasing'. Eleven MPs voted against the grant.[96] Gladstone, in trying to persuade the Queen to close the session in person, told her that many Liberal MPs had voted for the grant against the wishes of their working-class constituents.[97]

Bradlaugh organized a republican rally in Hyde Park against the 1873 annuity to the Duke of Edinburgh – reports of attendance varied from 1,500 to 10,000 – and Republican Clubs held similar meetings in their various towns.[98] In parliament opposition was again led by Taylor. Dilke supported him, saying that until this reign there was no precedent for a grant on a royal marriage except where the heir to the throne was involved. Seventeen MPs voted against the £10,000 annuity.[99]

The republican movement had clear negative political objectives – the abolition of the monarchy and ridding the country of the burden of taxation attendant on it. These objectives embraced the ending of aristocratic government, but the republicanism of Bradlaugh, Cattell and other leaders of the National Republican League lacked a social programme, aside from breaking the aristocratic monopoly on land. In summoning Republican Clubs to the National Conference of 1873 Bradlaugh specifically stated that there should be no discussion of 'those vexed economical or purely social questions which so greatly divide even avowed Republicans'.[100] The analysis of Bradlaugh and of *Reynolds's Newspaper* still identified the aristocracy as the enemy of progress, political and social, but they were outflanked on the left by the 'social republicanism' of a number of small and generally short-lived organizations and newspapers – the Land and Labour League and the *Republican*, the Universal Republican League, the National Republican Brotherhood, the English section of the International Working Men's Association, and the *International Herald*.

While Bradlaugh attacked the monopoly of the aristocracy, he remained an orthodox political economist, whereas all these groups were anti-capitalist and saw a republic as the vehicle of social and economic reorganization rather than as the apotheosis of the ideals of political radicalism. Bradlaugh's anti-aristocratic land policy consisted in making the land market free like the labour market, but the Land and Labour League stood for nationalization of land.[101] Bradlaugh refused publication in the *National Reformer* to an article on the Franco-Prussian War declaring that the next war would be between capital and labour, and the article appeared in the *Republican*.[102] He opposed the Commune as associating republicanism with anarchy and socialism and left the General Council of the I.W.M.A. when it adopted Marx's *Civil War in France* as its statement on the situation in Paris;[103] the *Republican* hailed the Commune with the headline, 'Paris Today, London Tomorrow'.[104] The Commune shattered the broad left consensus shown in meetings of support for the French Republic in late 1870. Respectable leaders of labour, including Odger, the most prominent involved in the republican movement, withheld their support from the Communards, but the more militant were inspired by their struggle to form the Universal Republican League for the propagation of democratic and social republicanism in May 1871.[105] The same month the Republican criticized Odger and his supporters for seeing a republic merely in terms of the removal of hereditary, aristocratic privilege: 'We have two aristocracies – one of birth and one of money, and this latter never seems to attract the attention it deserves'.[106]

The divergence of the two republicanisms was embodied in late 1872 to 1873 in the formation of two would-be national organizations – the National Republican Brotherhood and the National Republican League. The Brotherhood was formed in November 1872 without the blessing of Bradlaugh. Twenty-two Republican Clubs were represented at its conference in Sheffield and a further twelve promised support. The *National Reformer* disapproved of its title, 'Brotherhood' having the revolutionary resonance of underground continental movements, its technically seditious display of republican flags and the advocacy of violence by its eccentric leader the self-styled 'Professor de' Morgan. Bradlaugh asserted that the republican movement must be a thoroughly legal organization which pursued its ends constitutionally. Morgan for his part used the circulars of his Sheffield Republican Club and the pages of the *International Herald* to chastise the bourgeois moderation of the main republican and labour leaders.[107] Many of the clubs affiliated to the Brotherhood boycotted the Birmingham conference which launched the National Republican League in May 1873, feeling slighted by its very existence and disagreeing with its moderate standpoint and lack of a social programme.[108] Forty-eight clubs were represented at Birmingham.[109]

Within a few months, both national bodies had fallen into obsolescence and by the end of the year organized republicanism had lost all momentum and contracted markedly, ever fewer entries being recorded in the 'Republican Club Department' of the *National Reformer*.[110] This trend continued during 1874, the section being omitted for long periods and discontinued altogether after October.[111] Henceforth, while continuing to criticize the Royal Family, the journal's attention was once more concentrated almost exclusively on the freethought cause. Symptomatic was the London Republic Club's giving up its meeting place to the Secular Club in December 1874 – with the injunction to its members to 'show more interest in the welfare of the club' henceforth.[112] Watts' New Year message to the *National Reformer*'s readers contained only a brief reference to republicanism – 'I feel sure that the Republic will come at latest as soon as the people are in general fit for it' – and expressed satisfaction that G.W. Foote, erstwhile Secretary of London Republican Club and of the National Republican League, was giving 'evidence of his ability as a Freethought propagandist'. Previous New Year's messages had promised to strive in the interests of secularism and republicanism, but Watts this time concluded '. . . my constant desire has been – and ever will be, I hope – to serve the Freethought cause with earnest and conscious devotion to its principles'.[113] In April 1875 in the first number of George Standring's *Republican Chronicle* which, designed to resuscitate the movement, in fact became the swansong of English republicanism, Cattell wrote of the failure of the Republican Clubs.[114] By the end of the decade Standring acknowledged 'the almost total collapse of propagandist work by means of Republican clubs and kindred bodies'.[115]

Republicanism had little or no chance of achieving its ultimate aim in the early 1870s. The *Spectator* pointed out that only a regency could have raised the constitutional discussions necessary to make republicanism a serious issue – and while the illnesses in quick succession of the Queen and Prince of Wales in 1871 provoked much excitement in republican ranks, the recovery of the Prince put an end to all immediate hopes of debating the Act of Settlement in parliament.[116] There was no serious revolutionary spirit in English republicanism, as Wright's analysis of working-class attitudes stressed.[117] More serious than the short-term failure of republicanism was its failure to turn itself into and sustain itself as a mass popular movement. It only represented a strand of popular radicalism and only mobilized large-scale support in temporary agitation against annuities to the Royal Family – there was no thorough, popular, republican conviction to sustain the movement between such agitations.

The foremost difficulty was the belief held by the great body of liberals and radicals that all desirable reforms could be attained under Britain's constitutional monarchy, as this appeared to be the lesson of an era of peaceful reform. *Lloyd's Weekly Newspaper*, with its large circulation representative of respectable lower middle-class and old artisanate radicalism, disapproved of the excesses of the French revolutionary spirit displayed in the horrors of the Commune and, contrasting these with the concurrent celebration of Princess Louise's wedding, reflected, '. . . if we are of slower blood and slacker fibre than our neighbours, . . . we are steadier and more reasonable in our aims'.[118] *Lloyd's* reaction to the Thanksgiving for the recovery of the Prince of Wales in 1872 showed how the paper combined radicalism and loyalty – the enthusiasm of the crowds demonstrated, it argued, not the sycophancy of the masses but 'the wisdom, the moderation, and the sound heart' which merited their enfranchisement – 'full political rights' under the monarchy which they so clearly supported.[119] A critical correspondent to the *National Reformer* cited John Bright's great reform speeches of 1858 which had respected the monarchy – 'I am not one of those who believe you cannot be free and happy under a monarchy such as ours'.[120] Bright himself dealt a blow to the republican movement when he declined to preside at the National Conference in Birmingham, instead sending a letter which declared:

> For forty years past in this country we have seen a course of improvement in our laws and administration equal, perhaps superior, to anything which has been witnessed in any other nation. This gives me hope and faith that we can establish a civil government so good as to attract to its support the respect and love of all the intelligent among our people, and this without bringing upon us the troubles which I believe are inseparable from the uprooting of an ancient Monarchy. I have no sympathy with the object which gives its name to your Club.[121]

This being the view of a majority of their party, the advanced Liberals such as Dilke and his friend Joseph Chamberlain quickly distanced themselves from the republican movement with which they had become identified. By late 1872 Dilke was acknowledging that the country saw progress and reform as compatible with a constitutional monarchy.[122]

The trade unions were opposed to the republican movement as an unnecessary distraction from the questions that should interest labour. Andrew Boa, president of the Scottish trades council, said that his native trade unionists looked on the Queen as an exemplary constitutional monarch and that the identification of the republican movement with Bradlaugh's atheism made it even less attractive.[123] (The overlap of personnel and media between the republican and freethought movements was a constant source of embarrassment;[124] and Standring was to state expressly in the first edition of the *Republican Chronicle* that it would not be propagating the secularist cause.[125]) The official organ of trade unionism, the *Bee-Hive*, described the sovereign as 'the key-stone of the arch which joins and binds us together'[126] and argued that until remaining political and social reforms had been achieved there was no point in discussing the form of government.[127] All that was needed to prevent any abuse under the present form was a simple addition to the constitution – a guarantee that the monarch had to abide by the wishes of the people, expressed through the House of Commons, in the choice of ministry.[128] Professor Edward Beesly's leading article in June 1871 attacked the republican movement as a partial interest group, prematurely diverting working-class energies from the key goal of organizing effective trade combinations.[129] A similar denunciation of the agitation against Louise's dowry came from the Labour Representative League, the trade unions' organization for the key purpose of securing a better representation of their members in the Commons.[130] In 1872 the *Bee-Hive* saw the Thanksgiving ceremony for the recovery of the Prince of Wales as an 'all-classes' celebration, showing the nation to be 'united in sentiment . . . one in heart' in its loyalty to the throne.[131]

The republicans were acutely aware of the obstacles in their way. The *Republican* complained of the refusal of newsagents to sell the paper because of its title[132] and of the low sales which forced it to cease publication in February 1872 after only twenty-six numbers.[133] Sycophancy and flunkeyism were identified as English diseases checking republicanism: the Englishman 'has two idols; one is gold; the other is rank. If there is some limitation to his idolatry of gold, to his idolatry of rank there is none.'[134] Bradlaugh spoke of the need to educate the English people into republicanism[135] – at his most optimistic he felt that four to five years of such education were necessary.[136] The rowdy royalist mobs – reminiscent of the old 'Church and King' mobs – who disrupted Dilke's meetings and attacked Odger, showed that the working class was by no means uniformly antipathetic to the throne and Royal Family.[137]

It was above all the celebration of royal events which disillusioned republicans and eventually convinced them that their cause was a premature one. Bradlaugh observed '"royal fever" . . . at its height' in Scotland at the time of the wedding of Louise and Lorne.[138] The 'fearful storm of loyalty' that attended the Prince of Wales' recovery was viewed in many quarters as the death-blow to republicanism. The Thanksgiving service at St Paul's was designed by Gladstone to overwhelm republicanism.[139] Bradlaugh observed that apart from those who had heard him lecture on Thanksgiving Day at the New Hall of Science, 'London is thanksgiving mad while we write, and the huge crowds on Monday night, gazing at the tawdry decorations in Fleet Street and Strand, showed how little at present Republicanism had permeated the general population'.[140]

Reynolds's Newspaper derided 'the great epidemic of typhoid loyalty' and described the Thanksgiving celebrations as a 'sickening display of hypocrisy, sycophancy, idolatry, idiocy and buffoonery'.[141] *Punch* marked the Thanksgiving by an engraving of a working man in the guise of Bottom having his ass's head marked 'Republicanism' removed by Mr Punch. His republican dream had proved bottomless.[142] In July 1872 an article in the *National Reformer* on the hysteria into which towns were sent by royal visits reflected:

> The *cultus* of Royalty has been carried on too long in England to be abandoned all at once ... how just is the remark often made by leaders of the Republican party in this country, that if in the present condition of the people, they were able to found a Republic, they would not do it. The ideal Republic cannot be yet. The common, the dull, the ignorant, the depraved will do for a Monarchy; the Republic demands the best.[143]

Republicanism like other radical causes suffered from the loss of momentum of Liberalism in the last years of Gladstone's ministry and the resurgence of the Conservative party crowned by its election victory in 1874. In September 1872 Normanby Republican Club felt that the 'Liberalism of the people' was 'dormant'.[144] At the same time Disraeli had begun his attack on Gladstonian Liberalism as a dangerous, alien and revolutionary creed encouraging contempt for the institutions upon which British greatness was founded and of which his party was the defender. At Manchester in April 1872 he said that he stood as champion of the throne, when 'the banner of republicanism is unfurled'.[145] He again rebutted republicanism at the Crystal Palace in June. The enthusiastic reception of the Duke of Edinburgh and his bride in London in March 1874, coming in the wake of the Conservatives' return to power prompted G.W. Foote to write:

> Taken in conjunction with the Conservative Reaction the late Royal Farce may perhaps signify that the people are desirous of a temporary political calm. All the vested interests of the country have conspired to produce a Tory reaction, and it may be considered that the loyal shouts of a London mob at the pageantry of kingship are indeed the climax of popular rejection of extreme principles ... the wheels of progress ... clogged by the forces of reaction.[146]

A further sign of the times was Joseph Arch's request to the Prince of Wales to be the patron of his agricultural workers' union, when the labourers on the Queen's Osborne estate were known to be in a state of destitution.[147]

Bradlaugh in November 1873 said that a republic in England was not an immediate prospect as the 'people were not yet ready for it'.[148] In fact English republicanism had touched its highest point. In Bradlaugh's official biography, John M. Robertson attributed the brevity of the movement's life to the 'vivid recollection of the horrors of the Commune', the 'want of unity of motive and purpose' among republicans, the rise in the Prince of Wales' popularity and the weakening of the economic case against the Crown as the cost and corruption of republican government in America and elsewhere became better known. Bradlaugh had found that he 'could make little headway against the vast forces of habit and prejudice which buttress the Throne'. Henceforth, 'his political work went mainly to reforms within the lines of Constitution'[149] – as did that of most other radicals.

1874–87: the last vestiges of organized republicanism; continued radical criticisms

H.A.L. Fisher described British republicanism as 'an eddy rather than a current'[150] and this period marked the disappearance even of this 'eddy' as an organized movement. It had effectively collapsed in 1873–4 and Standring's newspaper the *Republican Chronicle* (entitled the *Republican* after 1879, ostensibly as a more assertive name,[151] but, one would presume, because there was very little republicanism to chronicle) was the dying voice of republicanism as a distinct creed. It divided its pages between propounding the old republican arguments and lamenting the lack of public support for these arguments. As we shall see in subsequent chapters, these were the years in which the monarchy, after the controversy in the late 1870s over the prerogative, was moving outside the realm of political contention and in which its role as a national and ceremonial figurehead became less equivocal than earlier in the reign; these developments being accompanied by an increasing glorification of the ageing Queen as the venerable mother of her own, national and imperial families. In 1886 Standring finally hoisted the flag of surrender, changing his newspaper's title to the *Radical*, as the old name had 'always been a stumbling-block in the path'.[152]

The extinction of the republican movement does not, however, signify that the Crown had become a universally popular institution by the time of the Golden Jubilee in 1887. During the years 1874 to 1887, and indeed to the end of the reign, the economic and class critiques we have encountered from the accession persisted in parliament and in the radical press, often occasioned as in previous decades by demands for annuities to members of the Royal Family, and reinforced by the dissentient voices of Irish MPs angered by the neglect and coercion of their country during the reign of a Queen who was supposed to have brought progress and freedom to her subjects.

Standring's newspaper reaffirmed the arguments of the early 1870s and of previous decades in favour of the republican form of government as the only one which could be a true expression of the sovereignty of the people; it would dispense with the cost of the Crown and of royalty; and would be the vehicle of social reform. In the modern age, it was asserted, 'real faith in the Crown' was untenable and those who professed it and yet made any claim to being intelligent, rational beings bore 'a strong resemblance to those modern Christians who struggle to reconcile the teachings of science with their own interpretation of the tenets of Christianity'. Here was the utilitarian view that political science developed alongside natural science towards a rational ordering of the world.[153] Disraeli's frequent recourse to the royal prerogative, obtaining the consent of the parliamentary representatives of the people only retrospectively,[154] strengthened the argument that a republic was needed 'for a "Government *of* the People, *by* the People, *for* the People"'; under the monarchy Britain was in danger of becoming 'the home of Imperialism and of tyranny'.[155] The old targets of the Civil List, the Pension List and their contribution to the National Debt were regularly attacked,[156] as were 'the frequent exhibitions of Royal avarice' given in the parliamentary votes of annuities to the Queen's children on their marriages.[157] The need for the republican programme to have a social content was seen as an omission of the movement of the early 1870s and it was determined that hitherto republicanism 'should be the name to cover the whole ground of Political and Social reform'.[158]

Yet Standring realized that he was not articulating the programme of an extant republican party. At the outset, in mid-1875, he believed that a latent republican spirit existed but that it was 'too apathetic to combine and organize'.[159] Only a handful of the clubs founded in the early 1870s survived[160] and these had folded by the end of the decade. In 1881 Standring formed a new Republican League but it had branches only in Hipperholme, Southampton, Edinburgh, Halifax and South Shields,[161] which all collapsed by May 1885, when Standring wrote, 'We do not at this moment know of a single Republican organization in the United Kingdom'.[162]

The failure of the attempt to resurrect the organized movement dented Standring's belief in the immanent republicanism of the country. A correspondent in his paper lamented 'the sickly "loyalty" of the age'[163] and editorials began to complain of British flunkeyism[164] and of the 'journalistic servility' to the Royal Family which encouraged such flunkeyism.[165] In April 1884 Standring acknowledged that the 'results of our work have, so far, not been of a nature to call for excessive congratulation. The Republican propaganda in this country cannot, we think, ever hope to excite much public support and enthusiasm.' The main reason for this, he felt, was that 'the power and influence of the royal and hereditary elements in the "Constitution" has gradually diminished, as the democratic element has advanced in intelligence and organization', thus avoiding the sort of collision between royal prerogative and the popular will which would shake the throne's foundations, and indeed convincing the people that self-government was not incompatible with a limited monarchy.[166] In early 1886 the Marseillaise was hissed at a musical evening of a London radical club, while another such club passed a resolution thanking the Queen for opening in person the first parliament 'in which the labouring classes are fully represented'.[167] In one of the *Republican*'s last issues Standring wrote that he had been driven 'mad' by what Marxians would now call the 'false consciousness' of loyal working men: 'The Winter of our discontent is made glorious Summer by the reappearance of the Queen, and the old superstition of royalty flourishes like a green bay-tree'.[168] The dropping of the title *Republican* in an effort to boost sales was the conclusive admission of defeat.[169]

While republicanism faded, there was no slackening in the economic criticisms of royalty by radical MPs and newspapers. The thrust of such criticism was the familiar argument that in a state with such glaring inequalities in wealth it was immoral to ask the people to subsidize the extravagant, leisured lives and useless pomp of the Royal Family. To radicals the Prince of Wales remained the embodiment of otiose royal prodigality. In 1874 Taylor wrote a public letter to his constituents about the Prince's debts, which, he alleged, amounted to £600,000, mainly through gambling – the Prince had, he said, asked Gladstone and would ask Disraeli to go to parliament to pay them off.[170] No such demand was made of parliament but in 1875 it was requested that £42,850 be voted to pay for the Prince's visit to India. The radical MP MacDonald said that the working class did not want any money to be voted; and twelve members voted against it. MacDonald's colleague Burtt regretted members' blanket assertions in the debate about working-class opinion being either for or against the grant: 'The working classes are very much like other folk – they differed in their opinions on the subject. Some of them, he dared say, were in favour of that Vote. A very large number of them had a very strong objection to it; but the great mass, he believed, were indifferent to it'.[171]

The popular radical press took a class-oriented view of royal wedding celebrations: the working class could have no cause for celebration as they were called upon to foot the bill for the junketing of the 'upper ten thousand'. *Reynolds's Newspaper* in 1874, as Chartist newspapers had done in the past,[172] emotively juxtaposed the lavish royal marriage proceedings with an appalling contemporary case of destitution: the Duke of Edinburgh's entry into London with his newly wedded Russian princess was contrasted with the inquest held in a single room tenanted by six people on a 'poor woman who died of heart disease', the inquest being held there because the parish of Clerkenwell had no mortuary since the Marquis of Northampton, owner of most of the land in the parish, had ordered its pulling down.[173]

In an attempt to prevent any further charges on the nation, Annie Besant, Bradlaugh's close companion in the freethought movement, launched in 1875 a monster petition against future grants to the Royal Family until a full declaration of its existing finances had been made public.[174] MacDonald and Burtt presented it, with its 102,937 signatures, to the Commons on 16 June 1876 but it was greeted with laughter.[175]

Burtt alluded to this petition in 1878 when opposing the annuity to be made to Prince Arthur, Duke of Connaught, on his marriage, and pointed to new petitions against the present proposal. MacDonald concurred that 'there was no question which was so freely and thoroughly discussed by the working classes as that of the continual demands which were made upon the country to maintain the members of the Royal Family apart from the Civil List of her Majesty'. Earp felt that opposition was not confined to the working class: he pointed out that the country's economy was not in the buoyant state of ten or so years earlier; not only had pauperism increased but 'the struggling middle classes' had become a familiar phrase. In this context the apparent indolence of Connaught and the other princes made the grant especially objectionable. Plimsoll, in moving the annuity bill for its third reading, said that he had had to defend his vote against 'a portion of constituents, who preferred, in the abstract, a Republican form of government to any other', particularly in the light of the recent use of the royal prerogative. Forster too criticized this late phenomenon but made the telling observation that 'there could scarcely be any greater presumption than a man getting up and saying that he spoke on behalf of the working classes' – though he proceeded to do this, saying that like the rest of the community they wished the monarchy to be maintained in style; an argument also put forward by Tory MPs for working-class constituencies. The bill was passed by 151 votes to 13.[176] *Reynolds's Newspaper* viewed the wedding celebrations as 'an attempt to distract public attention' from the Zulu War and as an affront to the grief of the widows and bereaved mothers of ordinary soldiers. Connaught's military position was that of a sinecurist: he was a 'featherbed, counterfeit soldier'.[177]

The utility and cost of the Royal Family was soon under further radical examination with the marriage of the Queen's last son, Prince Leopold, Duke of Albany, in 1882. The Liberals were now back in power with several men connected with the republican movement of the early 1870s holding government positions. In the debates on the annuity proposed, Labouchere created a stir when he said that were they to adhere to their true principles, four members of the government – Chamberlain, Dilke, Fawcett and Trevelyan – would all follow him in opposing the grant. (In the event Dilke abstained, to the fury of the Queen.[178]) Labouchere maintained that the Civil List was an adequate provision for the whole Royal Family. He delivered a petition on the day of the bill's introduction from around 14,000 working men protesting against additional and 'excessive demands for the maintenance of the Royal Family'.

Forty-two MPs voted with Labouchere. One, Storey, took an extreme 'self-help' stance in his opposition to the grant: 'he felt that the House of Commons had no business to apply the public money in order to keep any persons in the state in a condition of titled idleness'. And he spoke of the moral degeneration of the poor as a result of charity. He would therefore vote against the grant in order to save Prince Leopold's moral character. He then launched an attack on honorary military commands being granted to utterly inexperienced and incompetent princes, while the veterans of fifty fights enjoyed no such sinecures. The money wasted on courts and courtiers should be spent on providing free schooling or pensions for 'decent old couples' – 'he recognized no distinctions between Royal personages and common personages'.[179]

An equally iconoclastic attitude to the wedding was taken by *Reynolds's Newspaper*, which saw it as 'ghastly and grotesque' – the sickly Leopold could not live long and the marriage was merely a device to pension his bride Princess Helen of Waldeck, 'the penniless daughter' of a 'beggarly family'. The false sentimentality in which the loyal press wallowed was exposed with savage irony – it was said that the Princess was 'singularly suited' to Leopold; presumably she 'has also a chronic affliction of sores? But perhaps it means that, having prepared herself for marriage by studying the art of healing, she will be enabled to poultice and plaster those of her husband'. The attention being lavished on the wedding was symptomatic of the way in which 'we hold the drone in the highest honour', so that the 'Old Corruption' could still rule and 'plunder' the nation: 'We start badly in England. We have a Crown and an aristocracy, and these constitute two sources of mischief'.[180] Leopold's death within two years confirmed *Reynolds's* in its view of the marriage and occasioned a damning obituary. The Prince, allegedly the intellectual of the Royal Family, had been pretentious, self-satisfied and ignorant, as had his frequent and much-praised public speeches. For example, at Liverpool he had condemned outdoor relief for what he termed in easy rhetoric the lazy, thriftless poor – when in fact he and his family were the main recipients of such relief and chief burdens on the community.[181]

The last of the Queen's children, Princess Beatrice, was married in 1885 and it was noticeable that in introducing the resulting annuity bill Gladstone stressed that this would be the final occasion on which parliament would be requested to assign public money to the Queen's children. Labouchere again led the opposition, arguing that 'those who oppose this vote are far stronger friends of the Monarchy than those who support it. The real danger to the monarchy at the present time is that many persons come to the conclusion that the advantages derived from it are counterbalanced by the costs if these grants are to be continually voted'.

Among the 38 MPs who voted against the grant were several Irish MPs. O'Brien, in the debate, had reminded the House that his countrymen had no reason to feel loyalty to the Queen. As far as the Royal Family was concerned, 'their lives are something worse than a blank. We never see them in Ireland at all'. The recent visit of the Prince of Wales was mere political propaganda.[182] O'Brien was supported by Redmond who stated that the abiding impression of royalty left in Ireland by the visit was of 'something we must take our hats off to and cheer, whether we like it or not, on pain of having our heads broken by a policeman and being turned out of our own railway stations'. The Royal Family thus embodied the English attitude towards Ireland – it was best ignored and better coerced than properly governed. Redmond did not see why royalty should be any more popular in England when the government did its utmost 'to feed and pamper royal personages' while 'you see the streets of your capital filled with unfortunate wretches who are starving' and large numbers of people were unemployed. Surely the common people of England did 'not care the snuff of a candle about Royalty' and there would be a revolution if the government continued 'robbing the people' on its behalf.[183] *Reynolds's Newspaper* while not prophesying revolution, expressed similar sentiments: 'How long will the British public endure?' – the sovereign was a 'phantom' still in effective retirement while the cost of the Crown remained real.[184]

Beatrice's wedding brought yet another burden and Gladstone's assertion that this was the last request rang hollow.[185]

Yet all these attacks on the expensive and inequitable luxury of the Crown and Royal Family were not refracted into a consistent and significant critique of the institution of monarchy. The unpopularity of the House of Lords in 1884 for its obstruction of the Reform Bill did not produce a corresponding sentiment against the other hereditary branch of the constitution. The reception at this time of the Prince of Wales in radical Newcastle was taken by *The Times* as proof that while the Lords was currently in disrepute, 'the Crown is, on the contrary an eminently and universally popular institution'.[186] Chamberlain's *Radical Programme* for the 1885 election excluded the Crown from the abuses needing reform: 'so long as the functions of royalty are recognized as being ornamental and consultative, the Throne has nothing to fear from Radicalism. Radicals have something better to do than to break butterflies on wheels.'[187] Standring acknowledged the prevalence of this opinion, however mistaken: republicanism was to 'a very large number of Radicals' an academic study of comparatively little importance.[188]

Yet on the eve of the Golden Jubilee, the dissentient voice of radical protest against the monarchy could still be heard, and *The Times'* description of the latter as a 'universally popular institution' could not hold true. Commenting on the debate on the allocation of £7,000 for the celebrations, the newspaper regretted the persistence of 'a certain residuum of obscure and random politicians who are stimulated by a pestilent desire to achieve notoriety by carping sometimes at the Royal Family, and sometimes at monarchical institutions'.[189] The opposition – 84 MPs voted for Labouchere's proposed reduction to £2,000 – represented the continuation of radical and Irish protest against the annuities to the Queen's children over the past twenty-five years. Pease, the MP for Barnard Castle, pointed out that the wages of working men had fallen dramatically in the previous fifteen years and that the grant would be an intolerable burden on them. T.P. O'Connor dismissed the government speakers' presentation of the Jubilee as a classless, national event. 'The Upper ten thousand' only, he said, would be represented in Westminster Abbey, perhaps with a few token working men. What, he asked, had the reign done for Ireland? Jubilee Day should be marked there as one of 'humiliation and general sorrow at the amount of destruction and desolation brought about by famine and by plague, and emigration and eviction in Ireland during this half century' in a 'reign more disastrous . . . than the blood-stained and horrible reign of Elizabeth'. Redmond told the House that the Jubilee was 'an English not an Irish subject'. Another Irish MP, Arthur O'Connor, wondered 'what earthly good this vote will do to the poor people of Great Britain or of Ireland'.

The most outspoken criticism came from Conybeare, the MP for Camborne, who said that only the denizens of the Strand would rejoice, while the working classes 'do not care two-pence halfpenny about the whole business'. The working class, not the Queen, was responsible for the progress of the past fifty years – the Royal Family was a 'burden' on the nation. The only possible good that might come of the Jubilee would be to make people see the useless, parasitical nature of 'some of the institutions we are told to respect and venerate'. He hoped that thus it would prove the last ever Jubilee celebration: 'I sincerely hope that before another century has passed this nation will be a Republic and not a Monarchy'. The government had stated that the whole nation would be represented in the Abbey – if that were the case the starving and destitute should be included in the congregation and a choir of Irish MPs should sing a hymn of thanksgiving for the 86 Coercion Acts passed during the reign.[190]

1887–1901: the persistence of criticism

The last phase of Victoria's reign has generally been viewed as the apotheosis of the nineteenth-century monarchy, including the spectacularly successful Jubilee celebrations and the solemn grandeur of Victoria's funeral and the accompanying eulogistic obituaries. These features are described in later chapters but here the persistence of radical criticism of the monarchy is discussed. While there was no longer a republican movement or a newspaper expressly devoted to that cause, republicanism continued to be espoused by *Reynolds's Newspaper* and by individual MPs, including the first Labour MP, Keir Hardie, who propagated the doctrine in parliament and in the *Labour Leader*, the official organ of the Independent Labour Party which he and others founded in 1893. As before, the old radical analysis of the 'Old Corruption' was present, together with a class critique of monarchy, while concerns about the cost of the Crown, the constitutional implications of its private fortune and the personal fitness or otherwise of the Prince of Wales were expressed by republicans and non-republican reformers.

The Golden Jubilee 1887

J.L. Lant has described how arrangements for the Golden Jubilee did not proceed entirely smoothly, partly because of economic distress and the perception in some quarters that the Queen was taking an unduly selfish view of the celebrations.[191] The *Spectator* commented on a wide-spread feeling that the Queen ought to distribute largesse, something which she had no intention of doing, and remarked that people 'had never forgotten Mr Neild's legacy'.[192] When the Queen opened the People's Palace in the East End in May there was booing, her advisers putting it down to socialists and 'the worst Irish'.[193] Lant points out that H.M. Hyndman, leader of the Marxian Social Democratic Federation, and other perceived extremists were imprisoned as a preventative measure during the Jubilee festivities.[194] The *Daily News* displayed its meritocratic brand of radical liberalism in scoffing that the Duke of Connaught's controversial leave from his command to attend the main ceremonial only showed how little he was needed at his post.[195] Describing the Jubilee day procession, the newspaper opined that instead of titled courtiers it should have been made up 'of pure merit' such as the fireman who had saved a life the previous day and Miss Ramsay of Girton College, Cambridge who had come top of the Classical Tripos.[196]

To *Reynolds's Newspaper*, the *Daily News*'s own account of Jubilee day was a 'flunkey' one because of its overall praise of the Queen and of the monarchy. *Reynolds's* identified itself as the sole 'Republican journal' in Britain, alone able to declare that the 'British monarchy is, perhaps, the most colossal fraud and farce that ever existed in this world'. It denounced the monarchy as anti-democratic, grasping, functionless and contrary to the teachings of Christ, who, were he in Britain in 1887, would be locked up together with Hyndman and his colleagues 'as a Social Democrat'. The English people had, unlike their Celtic fellow subjects, embraced the Norman yoke – a persistent image of radicalism – and now displayed their servility in an 'odious sycophancy'. In a nation of many faiths the monarchy's role as 'Defender of the Faith' was meaningless, especially as a Catholic (Matthews) was Home Secretary and an atheist (Bradlaugh) was a possible member of a future Liberal government.[197] Deriding the much trumpeted argument that the Queen's example had lifted the moral tone of the monarchy and the country, the newspaper commented that if the Queen's 'alleged purity' was indeed a fact it had 'not been contagious' as aristocratic 'Society' was as debased in its morality as the most depraved epochs of Roman history.

Reynolds's scorn was especially directed at the hereditary principle. Victoria had 'no discoverable qualifications for Queenship', her only only achievement being that 'she took the trouble to be born in a certain family'. Her own situation gave her an 'aversion to real merit' which 'amounts to a mania' so that she jobbed her family regardless of 'qualifications, or rather positive disqualifications'. All the males in her family had military titles yet 'not one of them has brains enough for any responsible command of any kind'. This hereditary privilege had a degrading effect on the British people who were taught to worship meritless grandeur.

The 'robbery and jobbery'[198] practised by the Royal Family was presented as part of the 'Old Corruption' still weighing down on the British people: 'Royalty, aristocracy and the Church are today just as troublesome as they ever were'.[199] The Jubilee represented the triumph over the 'masses' who worked for their income of the non-producing 'classes', who comprised 'all manner of thieves, pickpockets, peers of parliament, their families and menials; all, or nearly all, the 600 and odd scoundrels of the House of Commons; the 20000 State parsons ... '[200] It was the middle class – the 'suburban snobocracy' – which perpetuated this situation through its desire to be identified with 'Society': 'Middle-class vulgarity gathered in full force to worship royalty'. Nine out of ten working men, the newspaper claimed, agreed with its description of the Jubilee as a 'costly and needless pageant', especially at a time when 'hospitals are in sore need of immediate and substantial succour ... many of them ... compelled to close wards and beds'. The trade union representatives attending the Jubilee service in Westminster Abbey, Potter and Drummond, were as representative of their class as the 'louse' of the 'lion'.[201] *Reynolds's* printed an address from a group of Bristol working men, a critique of monarchy in which the more proletarian, 'new analysis' of the struggle of labour against capital and *laissez-faire* complemented the older attack on aristocratic privilege. The address decried the involvement of trade unions and friendly societies in the ceremonial as 'an organized attempt by the aristocratic and middle classes', attacked the House of Lords and citing the 12-month strike of the chainmakers of South Staffordshire and East Worcestershire noted that the Queen had never expressed sympathy with workers in their battles against the ruthless strictures of political economy.

The cost of the Crown was an abiding theme. The Queen was accused of 'the plunder of her people' in accumulating a vast Privy Purse and securing abundant grants and sinecures for her family. *Reynolds's* quoted from Carnegie's *Triumph of Democracy* in which the author demonstrated that more was spent on the royal yachts than on the combined salaries of the President, Vice President, Cabinet officers and Supreme Court judges of the USA.

References to the royal fortune occasioned bitter personal criticism of the Queen. She was described as an 'incorrigible usurer', who 'grinds the faces of the poor like a very *Shylock*', while never giving in charity 'a single farthing'.[202] The language used about the Queen was not just irreverent but vicious.[203] She was termed an 'ugly parsimonious German *frau*' and 'a fat old lady of sullen visage and sordid mind'. She was said to take delight in showing her power 'in the meanest and cruellest manner', especially in her off-hand treatment of her ministers, notably Gladstone, in summoning them to her remote hideaways rather than remaining in London. (We shall see in chapter 5 how Liberal and radical newspapers became increasingly aware and restive about the Queen's political bias in the latter part of her reign.) Of her absence from London and infrequent public appearances, the newspaper remarked, 'Her selfishness is simply unbounded and her neglect of her public duties absolutely scandalous'. The Queen's shortcomings and those of the 'idiot princes' to whom she was mother were scarcely surprising given their lineage from a 'pack of rapacious thieves, murderers, and filthy adulterers whom the British people delight to honour'.[204] *Reynolds's* conclusion on the 'Jubilee Calamity' was that the people must 'agitate, agitate' to change the whole political and social order.[205]

1888–1896

W.T. Stead's editorial article on the Golden Jubilee in the *Pall Mall Gazette* was entitled, 'How long will it last?' His conjecture was 'as long as the Queen lasts' for certain, but he could not be so sure that the 'fat little bald man in red', as he termed the Prince of Wales, would rule. Stead's argument was based more on doubts about the continued utility of monarchy in a democratic age than on the issue of the heir apparent's personal fitness,[206] but the latter did cast a shadow over the monarchy and provide fuel for its critics as Victoria's death became a more imminent prospect.

The first issue in this period to provoke renewed debate on the monarchy involved not the Prince but his children and their financial provision. The forthcoming marriage of his daughter Louise and the impending coming of age of the rest of his offspring resulted in 1889 in the setting up of the select parliamentary committee on royal grants promised by Gladstone's government in 1885, at the time of the last grant to one of the Queen's children, and demanded of the Salisbury government by radicals on numerous occasions since.[207] The government initially proposed to the committee a set of individual grants to the children totalling £49,000 per annum (£27,000 until the sons were married) with additional capital sums totalling £30,000 to the daughters on their marriages. Gladstone and the Liberals opposed this and, to ensure his support when the grant reached the floor of the House and avoid the first Commons dispute between party leaders over royal grants since the one over Albert's, the government members of the committee proposed that the Prince of Wales should be given a quarterly sum of £10,000 out of which he would make provision for his children. Gladstone managed to get this reduced to £9,000. He also got inserted in the committee's proposal as a *sine qua non* of his support a waiver from the Queen of claims on parliament for her other grand-children. This was justified by the means at the Queen's disposal: the preamble to the grant proposals in the committee's report included a statement of the increase in the financial yield of the Crown lands and the committee was shown that savings on the Civil List were £824,025.[208] When the proposals reached the Commons, there were votes of 116 and 134 respectively for amendments of Bradlaugh's and Morley's opposing the grants[209] – the largest votes cast against such grants in the whole reign with the exception of Albert's when the Tories' opposition was party-political rather than over the principle of the grant. The *Pall Mall Gazette* described the support for Morley's amendment as 'the most Radical vote ever recorded in the House of Commons'.[210]

William Kuhn has made much of the 1889 financial settlement as part of his argument that the Queen's solvency, enabling her to fund the other grandchildren, and the openness of discussion of her finances – 'daylight . . . let in' – were important in consolidating the public image of the monarchy. He contends that the very establishment of a commit-tee in mid-reign, with powers to investigate the savings made on the Civil List, was an unprecedented example of the greater parliamentary control over the Victorian monarchy which was essential to its popular-ity.[211] This interpretation of the events of 1889 is not sustainable when one examines the reception of the proposals in parliament and in the radical press. Kuhn acknowledges that the opposition even of some front-bench Liberals like Morley and the significant size of the hostile vote showed that 'the Queen's private fortune could breed resentment against the royal family'[212] but he does not realize that this resentment was as much on constitutional grounds as social ones. (The constitu-tional probity of the sovereign having private wealth had been queried by Brougham in 1850[213] and growing radical concern about this, cli-maxing in the 1889 debates is discussed in chapter 5.) Moreover, many contemporaries felt that far from 'daylight' being let in the government had practised subterfuge; and there was dispute, not mentioned in Kuhn's article, over the precise nature of the Queen's waiver of a claim for her other grandchildren.

In the debates on the grant, John E. Ellis, the Liberal MP for Notting-ham Rushcliffe, said that there was still 'great mystery about these money matters'.[214] The House as a whole was not informed of how the savings on the Civil List had been spent or invested so that it had no real idea of the total size of the Queen's fortune. Bradlaugh, now MP for Northampton, spoke of the government's evasiveness on this matter – 'half-confidences and half-denials and evasive statements instead of dealing frankly with the house'.[215] Besides, he argued, the full cost of the Royal Family was hidden as money over and above the Civil List and personal annuities were buried in the civil service, army and navy estimates – royal palaces and royal yachts were expensive examples of this.[216] MacNeil was answered in the negative when he asked W.H. Smith, the leader of the Commons, whether the committee's scope would extend to 'the secrecy which now exclusively attaches to the last wills and testaments of Royal personages?'[217] Gladstone tried to broaden the committee's remit when he proposed that in view of the increased revenue of the Duchy of Lancaster an investigation could be made into the possibilities of economies in the Civil List.[218] The *Star*, the popular new radical evening newspaper edited by T.P. O'Connor, felt that the accumulation of an imprecisely known private fortune together with 'the repeal of the Acts which forbade the Monarchy to hold property in land' and 'the refusal to disclose the Royal will' constituted 'a system of secrecy unparalleled in the history of our dealings with the Crown'.[219]

Thus contemporaries were far less impressed by the committee's existence than Dr Kuhn is. Labouchere saw it as 'a sort of sop to make grants more palatable to the House'.[220] Scoffing at the government's unwillingness to broaden the debate to the Civil List on the grounds that the latter was a compact made at the beginning of the reign, G.O. Trevelyan commented that 'in the reign of George III, after he had been reigning 20 years, the Civil List was re-opened, reviewed, revised, and reformed altogether in the great measure of Mr Burke'.[221] Kuhn himself refers to this fundamental reappraisal of the Civil List but later in his article states that the 1885 promise of a select committee effected in 1889 was 'an important surrender on the part of the royal family' as it meant that 'Henceforth, parliament could appoint an inquiry into the Crown's finances, not only at the beginning of the reign, but at virtually any time it wanted'.[222] In fact, Gladstone, in the debates on the Crown Private Estates Bill in 1873, had observed that the Queen's reign was an unusually long one and that parliament had become accustomed through the close accessions of George IV, William IV and Victoria to frequent opportunities of 'considering the position of the Sovereign with respect to the private estates'[223] – this seemed to prefigure the possibility of the appointment of a committee at some point during the reign.

Dr Kuhn emphasizes the Queen's promise not to press claims on parliament for her other grandchildren. However, the government's refusal to clarify whether this meant a waiver for the present or for the whole reign was a source of dissatisfaction, especially to John Morley, who made this and his dislike of the acknowledgement of the Queen's right to such a claim the grounds for his amendment opposing the grant.[224] While such grants were not as it subsequently turned out claimed, the Queen's correspondence with Smith in July 1889 shows that Morley's misgivings were justified. The Queen telegraphed during the debates to impress on Smith that 'the non-pressing of such claims is only for the present. I do not relinquish the right of claiming grants for my grandchildren'.[225]

The Commons debates on the 1889 grants are the most lengthy ones on the monarchy in the whole reign and show how even at this time the institution was a centre of discussion. The leading radical newspapers were in no doubt that the Crown remained a key concern of modern radicalism. The *Star* declared, 'It is the great battleground of Radicalism'.[226] It argued that while 'there are worse things no doubt than these royal grants' they were one example of the way in which the labouring classes were being 'cheated' – 'The giant Labor is stretching his limbs and asking for a share of the wealth he creates'. This language of the new radicalism was again complemented by the old image of 'the most costly monarchy in the world' bearing down on 'the shoulders of an overburdened people'.[227] Parliamentary opposition to the grant was welcomed by the paper as a revival of radicalism until now submerged in the moderation of the broad Liberal party: '. . . hitherto the old Radical tradition had been too much merged in the general interests of Liberal politics'.[228] Morley's stand against the grant marked him out as 'the rising hope of the stern and unbending Radical' and had stamped him as 'the leader of the advanced section', greatly increasing his popularity with the *sans culotte* rank and file – 'wage earners' and 'small traders'. The 134 votes cast for his amendment represented 'the high-water mark of Radicalism'.[229] Gladstone, in contrast in his speech supporting the grant, had professed undemocratic sentiments in saying that statesmen were servants of the Crown as well as of the people.[230] *Reynolds's Newspaper* observed that he had not moved with the times.[231]

In the parliamentary debates themselves no MP declared himself in favour of the immediate abolition of the British monarchy but several made clear a very unreverential, conditional acceptance of its existence, a theoretical preference for republicanism or a desire to modernize the institution. Labouchere pointed out that while the supporters of the grant argued that the Royal Family was the model family, '. . . my own idea of a family is that the head of it keeps its own children'.[232] Storey argued that no further money could be voted when so much was already wasted on superfluous, honorific courtiers and that an end must be put to a situation where princes received money for doing nothing and princesses were rewarded out of the public purse for marrying already wealthy noblemen. He said that the Queen had a vast private fortune of £3,000,000 and referred to the interest accumulated on Neild's legacy which had been 'singularly infelicitously bequeathed'.[233]

Labouchere went into detail on the Household salaries and argued that people saw such useless 'tinsel and gilding' as 'a relic and a survival of savagedom'. Loyalty to the throne consisted purely 'decent respect for the living symbol and emblem of the laws which they themselves have made'. Storey made a similar argument. Monarchy could be 'useful and advantageous' as the representative of the law and as preserving it avoided the 'trouble, cost and possibly bloodshed' of a change. The Royal Family were 'relics of the past' but he had 'no objection to [them] remaining a little longer on the earth if it is convenient to the majority'. However, there was an intolerable disparity between on the one hand the wealth of the monarchy and court and on the other the poverty of other state pensioners such as soldiers and the widows of scientists and literary men and the refusal of public assistance for the poor when he had called for it in parliament. The Prince of Wales should not be given more money by parliament but encouraged to lead a simple life which would serve as a better example than conspicuous consumption.[234] Pickersgill, MP for Bethnall Green, refuted accusations of disloyalty against opponents of the grant but said that 'if the times should ever come when it is necessary to choose between loyalty to the Crown and loyalty to the people, there are those . . . in this quarter of the House who will not hesitate for a moment which side to espouse'.[235] William Abraham (Mabon), MP for the Rhondda, Welsh miners' leader and the first Welsh working man elected to parliament, ridiculed the description in the *Daily News* of the following schedule as 'a hard day's work' by the Prince of Wales – a levée, the unveiling of a statue, dinner with the Lord Mayor and attendance at part of *The Marriage of Figaro*. His mining constituents had a different notion of hard work and would willingly swap. Like Labouchere and Cremer Mabon pointed to the paucity of visible public duties undertaken by the Queen as another reason for resisting any further additions to royal income.[236] The notion that the monarchy gave the nation a moral lead was discounted by Lawson (Cumberland, Cockermouth): '. . . it is the morality of the country which has made the Court moral, not the morality of the Court which has made the country moral'.[237]

The idea of a slimmed-down, modernized monarchy was apparent in the ideas of several MPs. Cossham (Bristol East) inferred that if the country was devising a constitution in the abstract it would not have a monarchy but said that one concrete problem which could be addressed was the 'parasite' aristocrats who accounted for much of the income given to the monarchy through their ceremonial sinecures.[238] Cremer contrasted superfluous public expenditure on the Civil List in Britain with the equivalent payment only of functioning government officials in the USA.[239] Brown agreed that the problem lay with payments to such as the Hereditary Grand Falconer, the Master of the Buckhounds and the Mistresses of the Robe – 'Down with the parasites who cluster round the Throne'.[240] Picton argued that veneration for the monarchy was part attributable to its antiquity but also conditional on its 'impersonating the living characteristics of this country in each age and in each generation through which we pass'. He therefore referred to 'the modernizing process that must affect all the most venerable institutions of our country – the Crown as well as the Church'. He pointed out that as far as its political, legal and military roles were concerned, 'We have modernized the Crown in successive generations'. It was now time to do so with its cost.[241] Morley felt that one aspect of this modernization should be for the junior princes to work for their living as 'other men' instead of 'bearing titles which have no meaning' and were 'an embarrassment to themselves and an embarrassment to the community'.[242]

Throughout the debates MPs made references to the support or hostility of their constituents towards the grant. Picton even claimed that his reformist views were seen as conservative in Leicester where at a public meeting he had addressed 6,000 of the 7,000 present were republicans.[243] The *Star* organized what it hoped would be a mass meeting against the grant at Hyde Park but only 5–6,000 attended, though the paper claimed this as a relative triumph given the storms on the day.[244] Even the leading ministerial newspaper, *The Times*, while disputing the confidence with which MPs claimed to speak for the people – 'Nothing is more difficult than to get at their opinions' – declared, 'There is no use in attempting to disguise the fact that these Royal grants are unpopular with a large portion of the working classes'.[245] The *Spectator* loftily wrote of the prevalence among opposition MPs and their constituents of 'a spurious Republicanism of the pocket', a 'rather vulgar feeling of democratic dislike to paying for royalty, as distinguished from genuine Republican preference for social equality'.[246]

One objection raised to the grant, in the *Star*, was that the Prince of Wales was reputed to be a heavy gambler and that the money could be designed to offset debts of the table – it cited baccarat as his particular pastime.[247] It was the public revelation of the Prince's devotion to this illegal game which caused a royal crisis in 1891, when, as in the Mordaunt divorce case, the heir apparent had to appear in court as a witness in an action arising from an accusation of cheating at a baccarat game at Tranby Croft in which the Prince, staying in the house as a guest (while he attended the Doncaster races!), had taken part.[248] The loyal, mainstream daily newspapers were in no doubt that damage had been done to the reputation of the monarchy. *The Times* wrote that next to the Queen the Prince was 'the most visible embodiment of the Monarchical principle; and any personal default of his gives a shock to the principle which in these democratic days is mischievous, even dangerous'.[249] The *Daily News* warned, 'Woe to the Monarchy when it can no longer perform what may fairly be called its last surviving use' – providing a moral lead.[250] The popular, pro-monarchy *Lloyd's Weekly Newspaper*, like the rest of the press, lamented the Prince's addiction to the game as revealed in his carrying the equipment around with him, and cited the 'monstrous inequality of the law in dealing with the gambling of rich and poor' – baccarat players were arrested in raids on gaming houses.[251] The Nonconformist conscience was outraged. The *Nonconformist* referred to the Prince's 'evil propensities', revealed in his initiating a low game disapproved of by his host, and advised 'all classes, Nonconformists included, ' to end 'abject adulation and worship of royalty'. The Queen had proved herself worthy of devotion but recent events provoked 'increasing apprehensiveness to what will happen when Her Majesty ceases to reign'.[252] *Reynolds's Newspaper* had a field day, denouncing the 'black character of English Society, led by the Prince of Wales' and declaring, 'Monarchy in this country is snapped to its foundations'. The events proved the folly of the 1889 fund as the Prince had doubtless gambled himself into debt through 'Doncaster by day, baccarat by night'.[253]

Reynolds's continued in the 1890s to offer a republican critique of the monarchy. In 1892 when the Queen was believed to have prevented Labouchere's appointment to the cabinet, the newspaper observed that the Queen was 'keeping back the hands on the dial plate of progress. And this when all is said and done is what our monarchy exists for'. It argued that the time was ripe for a new political party, a democratic one, rather than a narrow, class-based labour one, which would include abolition of the monarchy as a key principle.[254] (Constitutional criticism of the Queen's action is considered in chapter 5.) *Reynolds's* provided a hard, raucous counterpoint to the rapturous, sentimental accounts of the royal events of this period found in the other newspapers and described in chapter 7. When Albert Victor, Duke of Clarence, the eldest son of the Prince of Wales, died in 1892 and eulogies to the supposed virtues of the lost future king appeared elsewhere, *Reynolds's* printed a far more accurate summation, writing that his 'mental faculties were extremely limited' and that he cut the 'poorest possible appearance' when he had fulfilled public duties.[255] Just over a year later, Mary of Teck, originally betrothed to Clarence, was betrothed to his younger brother, George, Duke of York and there was the usual effusion over a 'love match'. *Reynolds's* pointed out that the original betrothal had been greeted in the same way. Such talk was 'sickening' when it was an 'arranged marriage' with the 'official sanction of the young man's granny'. Of the forthcoming wedding it asked, 'Is this a love match too? If so she has managed to transfer her affections pretty quickly. Or is she in love with the Crown, irrespective of whose head wears it?'[256] *Reynolds's* argued that the working classes had no interest in the wedding celebrations and that they did not express hostility to the monarchy primarily because landlordism and capitalism were perceived as greater evils. The newspaper felt that this was a mistake as the monarchy was 'a buttress to these institutions' and an evil in itself. It contrasted the lack of republican fighting spirit in Britain with what it saw as the first step towards a republic in Australia – South Australia had done away with the Governorship.[257] The accruel of wedding presents worth £250,000 was described as greedy at a time of depression and the paper criticized the way in which its contemporaries extolled the supposed beauty of the participants and attributed non-existent intellectual qualities to the members of the Royal Family: 'With the solitary exception of the Princess of Wales, who contrives by artificial means to prolong the beauty with which nature endowed her there is not a good-looking person in the whole lot'. A handsomer young man than the groom could easily be found playing cricket in Victoria or Battersea Park and any Oxford Street young lady assistant was betterlooking than the bride. *Reynolds's* went to the other extreme by asserting that one 'could not have got together an uglier gathering' and that members of the Royal Family 'have no personal characteristics to be admired or loved by any human being'.[258]

The birth of the Duke and Duchess of York's first child, the future Edward VIII, in 1894 occasioned the most outspoken words against the Royal Family uttered in parliament in Victoria's reign – from James Keir Hardie, who in 1892 had been returned as the first Labour MP and who had founded the ILP in 1893. Speaking against the Liberal government's moving of an address of congratulation to the couple, Keir Hardie declared, 'I owe no allegiance to any hereditary ruler' and said that the government 'seeks to elevate to an importance which it does not deserve an event of everyday occurrence'. He irreverently remarked that it was of little concern to him whether 'the first ruler of the nation be the genuine article or a spurious one' and mockingly observed that the only blessing conferred on the nation by the Royal Family was the Queen's noninterference in its affairs so lauded at the time of the Jubilee. 'I do not know', he continued, 'anything in the career or the life of the Prince of Wales which commends him especially to me'. He referred to his gambling and, a particular concern of Keir Hardie, the existence of 'some of the vilest slums in London' on the Prince's Duchy of Cornwall lands. He wondered why the Liberals who were so critical of 'the hereditary element in another place [i.e. the House of Lords] should be so willing to endorse it' as far as the monarchy was concerned. It was equally bad in both cases. He predicted that the new prince would be 'surrounded by sycophants and flatterers' and would 'be sent on a world tour' after which there would be 'rumours of a morganatic alliance'. Keir Hardie further objected to the government's refusal to make time for an address of condolence to the relatives of the 251 men and boys killed in the week's pit explosion at Cilfynydd.[259] Elaborating on his position in the *Labour Leader*, he wrote, 'The life of one Welsh miner is of greater commercial and moral value to the British nation, than the whole Royal Crowd put together, from the Royal Great Grand-mama down to this puling Royal Great Grand-Child'.[260]

The Diamond Jubilee

The radical response to the second Jubilee of the reign was similar to that of 1887. *Reynolds's Newspaper* described it as a celebration by the wealthy[261] and denounced the whole corrupt system of aristocracy, title and unproductive wealth, which 'depends on the monarchical' – 'so do all the titles of greater toadies and tuft-hunters, the brewers, . . . the gamblers on the Stock Exchange . . . the State priesthood . . .' This Jubilee was again presented as a middle-class celebration and the trumpeting in the rest of the press of the event as a commemoration of the progress of the past 60 years was grimly satirized in the newspaper's suggestion of an alternative procession of paupers – led by the largest dependants on public charity, the Royal Family, prostitutes, criminals, drunks, the destitute and hungry and the ghosts of starved Irish people and natives of lands conquered in the expansion of Empire. (The strongly Imperialist character of the Diamond Jubilee is discussed in chapter 6.) Personal criticism of the Queen persisted – she was described as a civil servant who refused, in her absence from the public eye, to face her employers, despite the fact that the normal retirement age had been waived for her.[262] Summing up the Jubilee, *Reynolds's* described 'insolent wealth . . . parading itself . . . in the sight of hopeless poverty'. The so-called working men's representatives participating represented no one but themselves. The paper pointed out that monarchy had cost the people £60,000,000 during the reign. It linked monarchy with the radical preoccupation with land reform: monarchy was to be equated with aristocracy and hence with land monopoly. Once rid of monarchy, 'we should have the land. Our people festering in large towns would be scattered over it.' Other privileges would disappear – the public schools would once more become truly public, the Universities would be open to the people, funds appropriated in tithes and trade guild funds would be restored, the 'army and navy would not be officered by the favourites of the Throne' and the legal system would be purified.[263]

Keir Hardie, writing in the *Labour Leader*, showed that socialism shared with radicalism a political critique of hereditary monarchy – 'democracy and monarchy are an unthinkable connection' – and a flair for knockabout invective against individual members of the Royal Family – the Queen was 'an old lady of very commonplace aspect' and the Prince of Wales 'a fat, bald-headed nonentity'. In language similar to that of *Reynolds's*, he wrote that the monarchy was the centre, if not the source, of the corrupting influences which constitute Society'. At the same time, however, the socialist perspective dictated that the capitalist system rather than monarchy was the root of the nation's problems. Keir Hardie pointed to the plutocracy of republican America to warn that the abolition of the monarchy alone would not suffice: 'until the system of wealth production be changed it is not worth while exchanging a queen for a president. The robbery of the poor would go on equally under the one as the other.'[264]

Thus while the abolition of the monarchy was an aim of Keir Hardie's socialist agenda it was not a priority, and it was a short step from this position to the lack of concern about the monarchy in other sections of the socialist movement – the position which was to become the characteristic of the Labour party in the twentieth century. Robert Blatchford's *Clarion* was the highest circulation socialist newspaper, with an informal style of the 'new journalism' type. It criticized the Jubilee as a 'big national raree show' puffed by 'jerry-built millionaires who have bought newspapers and are fishing for peerages' but it disassociated itself from the republicanism of the ILP. *Nunquam* wrote that while he had been a republican, 'of a mild kind', he was 'now simply neutral . . . the question of the abolition of the monarchy does not concern me. It seems a trivial matter compared to such greater questions as the health, the security, the happiness and the daily bread of the people.'[265]

Radicals and socialists at the end of the reign

By the time of the Queen's death this tone of indifference towards the monarchy or at least defeatism in the face of its popularity had largely overtaken the *Labour Leader* and *Reynolds's Newspaper*. Keir Hardie's articles in the former and his speeches in the Commons were more concerned with attacking the militarism of the funeral in order to criticize the Boer War than with attacking the institution of monarchy itself.[266] He wrote of 'the loss to Britain of Queen Victoria' in order to accuse the government of murdering her through putting her frailty through pro-War propaganda parades. Keir Hardie did show his disapproval of the blanket coverage of the Queen's death and the fulsome obituaries by beginning his column in the week of Victoria's death with a tribute to a deceased Liverpudlian member of the ILP: 'The unstinted sympathy of the Socialist movement will go out to John Edwards in his great bereavement . . . [Mrs Edwards] was the most kindly and unselfish creature that ever trod upon this earth[267] . . .' *Labour Leader* also contained articles by *Marxian*, who pointed to the proclamation of an unelected king by an unelected Privy Council as a 'curious comment on the sort of "democracy" at present existing' and who predicted that the 'personal popularity which attached to Queen Victoria' would not necessarily be transferred to her successor. He predicted 'a revival of Republican activity' in the 'near future' as 'all unconsciously, we have outgrown *kingship*'.[268]

Reynolds's Newspaper, however, which had long beaten the republican drum, and which in 1897 had written, 'The time is surely at hand for the formation of a Republican party in this country',[269] had now come to the conclusion that 'the Republican ideal, so strong half a century ago, is now slumbering and we do not wish for a Republic without the Republican virtues, which alone can keep it from decaying'. It predicted, regretfully, that the new King was likely to 'popularize the monarchy' still further because of his common touch and reputedly advanced politics (though at the same time it noted that any scandal or serious trade depression would damage the Crown and that it was difficult for a male sovereign to be as popular as a female one).[270] *Reynolds's* obituary, though containing measured praise for the Queen's generally constitutional conduct, differed from the mass of tributes in the rest of the press, in criticizing her appearance, political prejudices and rapacity.[271] A socialist columnist in the newspaper proclaimed, 'Long live the British Republic, Federal, Socialist and Democratic'.[272]

Meanwhile, one socialist newspaper, the *Clarion*, was, with a few exceptional features, covering the Queen's death in a similar manner to the mainstream Conservative and Liberal press. The exceptions were a criticism of the excesses of grief and sentimentality in the latter,[273] an outspoken condemnation of political intervention by Victoria and a concern with reports that the new Civil List might be greater than the old one.[274] Its obituary was highly respectful (though the praise for her political forbearance was retracted in the next issue after the intervening week brought revelations of Victoria's activities – a matter discussed in chapter 5) and observed that a line of sovereigns like Victoria would ensure the maintenance of the monarchy as it was 'as convenient, cheap, and effective a figure-head as human wisdom has yet discovered: it is not exactly logical, but it serves better than some that are more so'.[275] Its columnist Julia Dawson wrote approvingly of the new King and Queen because of their apparent concern for the poor. In an unconscious contradiction of the paper's disapproval of the late Queen's political activities, Dawson was pleased to note the 'flat Clarionese' spoken by Edward on the housing problem. She also applauded the new King's patronage of the arts. Reporting on the funeral, the *Clarion*'s correspondent described Edward as a modest, sympathetic man, a 'jolly good fellow' in the terms of the crowd – 'I shall be surprised if he does not prove the most popular representative of the monarchy that England has yet had'.[276]

Conclusion

This chapter has addressed the origins, nature and decline of the organized republicanism that appeared in England in the early 1870s and the persistence of republican and critical radical opinions right to the end of the reign. It has demonstrated that there were two distinct republican movements – the larger, mainstream one led by Charles Bradlaugh, the old *sans-culotte* alliance with middle-class leadership and artisante support; the other more proletarian and socialistic, existing in the more militant circles of London radicalism and in some parts of the industrial north. Both republicanisms were fostered at a time of trade depression and disillusionment with the effects of the 1867 Reform Act and under the inspiration of the new French republic, but Bradlaugh's, though broader in support, was narrower in its focus – without the social content of working-class republicanism, its ideology was the meritocratic one of its middle-class leadership, directed against hereditary privilege, and its artisanate support was based on an attack on the cost of the Crown when the Queen, in her widowed seclusion, was fulfilling none of her public duties. Whereas the social republicanism of the Land and Labour League and the International Republican League evolved as part of a wider critique of the status quo and manifested itself immediately upon the downfall of the Imperial regime in France, the mainstream republican movement needed the additional stimulus of the grant to the Princess Louise; its organization grew out of the anti-dowry agitation. Its rhetoric was still that of the 'Old Corruption' – Bradlaugh and his colleagues were criticized by the advanced social republicans for eschewing attacks on capital.

Republican clubs were able to mobilize widespread support only in campaigns against royal grants and stagnated between times: pure republicanism remained the conviction of a small minority and the movement had collapsed by the mid-1870s. Republicanism could not in nineteenth-century Britain be the vital and powerful creed it had become on the Continent: in Britain the Crown did not surmount an 'ancien regime' but a liberal constitution. The foreign inspiration of

1848 had touched a comparatively small number of idealists among British radicals; and that of 1870 resulted in an organized republic movement only because of the concurrent economic discontent and the Prince of Wales's unpopularity.

But if organized republicanism was an 'eddy' appearing only briefly and without real strength, there was from the accession to the Jubilees a strong current of radical criticism of the Crown. We shall see below how major obstacles to the monarchy's popularity – its political interference, its alleged 'Germanism' – had been more or less removed by the end of the reign. But in a country of wide class divisions and including a nation, Ireland, which had suffered economic devastation, not progress, and had the much-vaunted political liberties of the mainland periodically suspended, the monarchy could not stand always and for the whole nation as an unequivocally popular and unifying institution. This accounts for the persistence late in the reign of economic and class criticism of the Crown as fierce as had been made in 1837.

Notes

1. The best setting of the republican movement in the wider context of post-Chartist radicalism comes in Margot Finn, *After Chartism. Class and Nation in English Radical Politics 1848–74* (Cambridge, 1993). See also H.A.L. Fisher, *The Republican Tradition in Europe* (London, 1911), E.G. Collieu, 'The Radical Attitude towards the Monarchy and the House of Lords, 1868–85' (unpublished BLit, Oxford, 1936), Roydon Harrison, *Before the Socialists. Studies in Labour and Politics* (London, 1965), Edward Royle, *Radicals, Secularists and Republicans. Popular Freethought in Britain, 1866–1915* (Manchester, 1980).
2. Martin, *The Crown and the Establishment*, pp. 44–50.
3. Norbert J. Gossman, 'Republicanism in nineteenth century England', *International Review of Social History*, vol. 7 (1962), pp. 51–5, 58–9, Feargus A. D'Arcy, 'Charles Bradlaugh and the English Republican Movement, 1868–78', *Historical Journal*, vol. 25 no. 2 (1982), pp. 367–83.
4. D'Arcy, 'Bradlaugh and the English Republican Movement', p. 369.
5. Antony Taylor, '*Reynolds's Newspaper*, Opposition to Monarchy and the Radical Anti-Jubilee; Britain's Anti-Monarchist Tradition Reconsidered', *Historical Research*, vol. 68 (1995), pp. 318–37 provides a useful summary of some of the themes of criticism in the 1880s and 1890s in an article which appeared while this book was in preparation.
6. G.M. Trevelyan, *The Life of John Bright* (London, 1913), pp. 398–9.
7. V.S. Berridge, 'Popular Journalism and Working Class Attitudes 1854–86: A Study of *Reynolds's Newspaper*, *Lloyd's Weekly Newspaper* and the *Weekly Times* (unpublished PhD, London, 1976), pp. 2, 39.
8. *Reynolds's Newspaper*, 6 July 1862, p. 1.
9. Ibid., 15 March 1863, p. 1.
10. Ibid , 25 December 1864, p. 1.

11. Ibid., 30 December 1866, p. 3.
12. See Tom Cullen, *The Empress Brown. The Story of a Royal Friendship* (London, 1969).
13. *Punch*, 7 July 1866, p. 4.
14. Elizabeth Longford, *Victoria R.I.* (London, 1983 edn), pp. 412–13.
15. *Tinsley's Magazine*, vol. 3 (October 1868), p. 354 cols, 1–2. The Queen's obsessive widowhood and preoccupation with Brown provoked widespread speculation about her mental state, which was seriously discussed by the cabinet. John Vincent ed., *Derby, Disraeli and the Conservative Party. Journals and Memoirs of Edward Henry, Lord Stanley 1849–1869* (Sussex, 1978), p. 313.
16. Collieu, 'The Radical Attitude towards the Monarchy', pp. 62–3.
17. *Reynolds's Newspaper*, 6 March 1870, p. 2.
18. *National Reformer*, 10 April 1870, pp. 225–7; 7 April 1870, p. 241.
19. Royle, *Radicals, Secularists and Atheists*, p. 7.
20. Philip Magnus, *Gladstone. A Biography* (London, 1954), p. 207.
21. *The Times*, 11 March 1864, p. 8.
22. *Bee-Hive*, 29 April 1865, p. 4.
23. *Reynolds's Newspaper*, 16 December 1866, p. 3.
24. Ibid., 20 January 1867, p. 1; 17 February 1867, p. 4; 27 October 1867, p. 4; 18 October 1868, p. 1; 25 October 1868, p. 1; 11 July 1869, p. 4.
25. Harrison, *Before the Socialists*, p. 212.
26. Ibid., pp. 214–15; *National Reformer*, 20 June 1869, pp. 397–8; 4 July 1869, p. 14; no. 2 (11 July 1869), p. 29; 3 October 1869, p. 222; D'Arcy, 'Bradlaugh and the English Republican Movement', pp. 368–70.
27. *The Times*, 12 August 1869, p. 6.
28. D'Arcy, 'Bradlaugh and the English Republican Movement', p. 374; Martin, *The Crown and the Establishment*, p. 44.
29. *National Reformer*, 18 September 1870, pp. 177–9.
30. Ibid., 30 October 1870, p. 282; 6 November 1870, p. 294.
31. Harrison, *Before the Socialists*, p. 214.
32. D'Arcy, 'Bradlaugh and the English Republican Movement', p. 374.
33. *Republican*, no. 2 (October 1870), p. 5.
34. Ibid., no. 6 (February 1871), p. 5 .
35. Ibid., no. 16 (1 August 1871), p. 2; no. 14 (1 July 1871), p. 4.
36. Ibid., no. 7 (March 1871), p. 8.
37. *The Times*, 27 March 1871, p. 9.
38. *Fraser's Magazine*, vol. 83 (June 1871) p. 753.
39. Ibid, vol. 83 (June 1871), pp. 753–9.
40. *National Reformer*, 18 December 1870, p. 39; 5 February 1871, p. 88.
41. *Reynolds's Newspaper*, 23 October 1870, p. 4; 26 March 1871, p. 4.
42. *Hansard*, vol. 204, cols 156–8, 359–62.
43. Collieu, 'The Radical Attitude towards the Monarchy', p. 36.
44. *National Reformer*, 22 January 1871, p. 61.
45. Ibid., 26 February 1871, pp. 136–9.
46. Ibid., 9 March 1871, p. 1185.
47. Ibid, 2 April 1871, pp. 222–3; 8 May 1873, pp. 306–13.
48. Collieu, 'The Radical Attitude towards the Monarchy', p. 148 lists them.
49. Gossman, 'Republicanism in nineteenth century England', pp. 58–9.

50. And notably at Dilke's speeches on the cost of the Crown (see below).
51. *National Reformer*, vol. 17, no. 9 (26 February 1871), p. 137.
52. Ibid., 2 April 1871, p. 223; 16 April 1871, p. 255.
53. Ibid., 16 April 1871, p. 255; 18 May 1873.
54. D'Arcy, 'Bradlaugh and the English Republican Movement', p. 372
55. *National Reformer*, 12 March 1871, p. 171; 19 March 1871, p. 186; 21 May 1871, p. 322.
56. Charles Dilke, *On the Cost of the Crown*, (London, 1871), pp. 21–2.
57. *Pall Mall Gazette*, 9 November 1871, p. 1.
58. Dilke, *On the Cost of the Crown*, pp 22–3.
59. *Spectator*, 11 November 1871, p. 1356.
60. *Fortnightly Review*, vol. 11, (June 1872), p. 615.
61. *National Reformer*, 23 July 1871, pp. 49–50.
62. Ibid., 1 September 1872, pp. 130–1. Disraeli in September 1871 unintentionally provided Bradlaugh with further ammunition when, in a speech defending the Queen against criticisms of her retirement from public duties, he described her as 'physically and morally incapacitated' from performing them. *National Reformer*, 1 October 1871, pp. 217–18.
63. Ibid., 22 October 1871, p. 258.
64. *Reynolds's Newspaper*, 10 December 1871, pp. 4–5.
65. See above, chapter 2.
66. *National Reformer*, 2 April 1871, pp. 210–11.
67. Ibid., 17 December 1871, p. 387.
68. Dilke, *On the Cost of the Crown*, pp. 22–3.
69. For Bagehot's views on the political role of the monarchy, see chapter 5.
70. *Fortnightly Review*, vol. 1, (June 1872), pp. 615, 637–8.
71. *National Reformer*, 21 May 1871, pp. 321–2.
72. Ibid., 20 April 1873, p. 251.
73. *What does she do with it? Tracts for the Times, no. 1* by Solomon Temple, Builder (London, 1871), pp. 36–7.
74. Dilke, *On the Cost of the Crown*, pp. 19–20.
75. *Spectator*, no. 2, 263 (11 November 1871), p. 1356.
76. *National Reformer*, 7 May 1871, p. 303.
77. Ibid., 6 April 1873, p. 215.
78. W.D. Rubinstein, 'The End of "Old Corruption" in Britain, 1780–1860', *Past and Present*, no. 101 (November 1983), pp. 55–86.
79. Ibid., pp. 81–2.
80. *Reynolds's Newspaper*, 17 December 1871, p. 1.
81. *National Reformer*, 21 May 1871, p. 321.
82. Bradlaugh told an American interviewer that the movement was strongest among 'the artisans and mechanics of Birmingham, Sheffield and Nottingham, and the operatives of Manchester, of the Rochdale cotton district, of the Bacup Valley, together with the mines of Northumberland and Durham' (*National Reformer*, 12 October 1873, p. 227).
83. *Fraser's Magazine*, vol. 83 (June 1871), pp. 752–3.
84. W.E. Adams, *Memoirs of a Social Atom* 2 vols, (London, 1903), vol. 2, pp. 329–30.
85. *Spectator*, 11 November 1871, p. 1356.
86. *National Reformer*, 8 October 1871, p. 238 .
87. *Fortnightly Review*, vol. 11, (June 1872), p. 617.
88. *Fraser's Magazine*, vol. 83 (June 1871), pp. 752–3.

89. *National Reformer,* 2 April 1871, p. 222 .
90. See above, chapter 2.
91. *What does she do with it?,* pp 3–47.
92. S. Gwynn and G.M. Tuckwell, *The Life of the Right Hon. Sir Charles Dilke,* 2 vols, (London 1917), vol. 1. pp. 139–44; *National Reformer,* 3 December 1871, p. 367; 10 December 1871, p. 376.
93. *Hansard,* vol. 210, cols 251–317; *The Times,* 26 March 1872, p. 9.
94. *National Reformer,* 30 July 1871, p. 74; 13 August 1871, p. 111; 20 August 1871, p. 127.
95. Ibid., 20 August 1871, p. 111.
96. *Hansard,* vo1.208, cols 570–90.
97. Philip Guedalla, *The Queen and Mr. Gladstone vol. 1, 1845–1879* (London, 1933), pp. 297–304.
98. *National Reformer,* 3 August 1873, pp. 71–3; 10 August 1873, pp. 81–2.
99. *Hansard,* vol. 217, cols 1180–7, 1337–48, 1440–5.
100. *National Reformer,* 16 March 1873, p. 164.
101. Harrison, *Before the Socialists,* pp. 212–14.
102. D'Arcy, 'Bradlaugh and the English Republican Movement', pp. 301–2.
103. Ibid., pp. 374–5.
104. *Republican,* no. 10 (1 May 1871), p. 1.
105. Ibid., no. 10 (1 May 1871), pp. 5–6; Martin, *The Crown and the Establishment,* p. 44; Harrison, *Before the Socialists,* p. 237.
106. *Republican,* no. 11 (15 May 1871), p. 7.
107. *National Reformer,* 3 November 1872, p. 287; 8 December 1872, pp. 366–7; 15 December 1872, pp. 373, 378.
108. *National Reformer,* 4 May 1873) pp. 276–7.
109. Ibid., 18 May 1873, p. 306; 25 May 1873, p. 329.
110. *National Reformer,* 24 August–28 December 1873, passim.
111. Last entry, *National Reformer,* 18 October 1874, p. 255.
112. Ibid., 13 December 1874 p. 383.
113. Ibid., 3 January 1875 pp. 9–10.
114. *Republican Chronicle,* no. 1 (April 1875), pp. 1–2.
115. *Republican* (continuation of *Republican Chronicle*), vol. 5 (January 1880), p. 169.
116. *Spectator,* 2 March 1872, pp. 270–1; *National Reformer,* 22 October 1871, pp. 257–8.
117. *Fraser's Magazine,* vol. 83 (June 1871), p. 758.
118. *Lloyd's Weekly Newspaper,* 26 March 1876.
119. Ibid., 3 March 1872.
120. *National Reformer,* vol. 20, no. 7 (18 August 1872), p. 98.
121. Ibid., 8 May 1873, p. 307.
122. *The Times,* 2 October 1872, p. 9. For Chamberlain see J.L. Garvin, *The Life of Joseph Chamberlain, vol. 1 (1836–1885),* (London, 1932), pp. 152–4.
123. David Tribe, *President Charles Bradlaugh, MP* (London, 1971), p. 155.
124. For example, the *National Reformer,* 4 May 1873.
125. *Republican Chronicle,* no. 1, (April 1875), p. 1.
126. *Bee-Hive,* 13 November, p. 4.
127. Ibid., 25 November 1871, p. 3.
128. Ibid., 11 November 1871, p. 2.

129. Ibid., 24 June 1871, p. 1.
130. Collieu, 'The Radical Attitude to the Monarchy', p. 139.
131. *Bee-Hive*, 2 March 1872, p. 9.
132. *Republican*, no. 8, (April 1871), p. 7; no. 12, (1 June 1871), p. 5.
133. Ibid, no. 14, (1 July 1871), p. 5; no. 17, (5 August 1871), p. 7; no. 26 (1 February 1872), p. 5.
134. Ibid., no. 16, 1 August 1871, p. 2.
135. *National Reformer*, 21 May 1871, p. 323.
136. Ibid., 22 October 1871, p. 258.
137. Ibid., 16 February 1873, p. 101.
138. Ibid., vol. 17, no. 17 (23 April 1871), p. 267.
139. Ibid, vol. 19, no. 3 (21 January 1872), p. 42; Freda Harcourt, 'Gladstone, Monarchism and the "New Imperialism"', *Journal of Imperial and Commonwealth History*, vol. 14 no. 1 (October 1985), p. 28.
140. *National Reformer*, 25 February 1872, pp. 124, 138.
141. *Reynolds's Newspaper* 17 December 1871, p. 1; 25 February 1872, p. 2.
142. *Punch*, 9 March 1872, pp. 102–5.
143. *National Reformer*, 14 July 1872) p. 1.
144. Ibid, 8 September 1872, p. 151.
145. T.E. Kebbel, ed., *Selected Speeches of the Late Right Hon. the Earl of Beaconsfield*, 2 vols (London, 1882), vol. 2, pp. 491–6, 525–6.
146. *National Reformer*, 22 March 1874, p. 179.
147. Ibid., 21 June 1874, p. 394.
148. Ibid., 2 November 1873, p. 274.
149. Hypatia Bradlaugh Bonner, *Charles Bradlaugh. A Record of His Life and Work by his Daughter.* (With an account of his political struggles, politics and teachings by John M. Robertson), (2nd edn, 2 vols, London, 1895) vol. 2, pp. 166–7. Bradlaugh's political opponents continued to use his republicanism against him, however. In the 1880 debates on the admittance as an MP– see *Hansard*, vol. 152, cols 190–1, 334–9 and Roland Quinault 'The Fourth Party and the Conservative opposition to Bradlaugh 1880–1888', *English Historical Review*, vol. 91 (1976), pp. 352–7.
150. Fisher, *The Republican Tradition*, p. 256.
151. *Republican*, vol. 4 (January 1879), p. 73.
152. Ibid., vol. 12 (August 1886), p. 36.
153. Ibid, vol. 6 (May 1880), pp. 206–7.
154. See below, chapter 5.
155. *Republican Chronicle*, vol. 1, May 1875, p. 12; *Republican*, vol. 4 (January 1879), p. 73.
156. For example, *Republican*, vol. 4 (February 1879); vol. 5 (May, December 1879), pp. 109, 164–5; and a reprint of an old Bradlaugh lecture on the Civil List, vol. 5 (February 1880), pp. 177, 180.
157. *Republican Chronicle*, vol. 1, (April 1875), p. 7.
158. Ibid., vol. 1 (April 1875), pp. 1–2.
159. Ibid, vol. 1 (May 1875), pp. 1–2.
160. Ibid., vol. 1 (May 1875), p. 22.
161. Royle, *Radicals, Secularists and Republicans*, pp. 204–5.
162. *Republican*, vol. 11 (May 1885), pp. 12–13.
163. Ibid., vol. 5 (July 1879), p. 125.
164. Ibid., vol. 5 (September 1879), p. 136.

165. Ibid., vol. 12 (April 1886), pp. 96–7.
166. Ibid., vol. 10 (April 1864), p. 4.
167. Ibid., vol. 11 (February 1886), p. 85.
168. Ibid., vol. 12 (April 1886), pp. 96–7.
169. Ibid., vol. 12 (August 1886), p. 36.
170. G.E. Buckle, ed., *The Letters of Queen Victoria*, (2nd ser. 3 vols, London, 1926–8), vol. 2, p. 352.
171. *Hansard*, vol. 225, cols 1487–525.
172. See above, chapter 2.
173. *Reynolds's Newspaper*, 15 March 1874, p. 4.
174. *Republican Chronicle*, vol. 1 (May, June 1875), pp. 12, 23.
175. *National Reformer*, 25 June 1876, pp. 410–12.
176. *Hansard*, vol. 242, cols 231–61, 779–804.
177. *Reynolds's Newspaper*, 16 March 1879, pp. 3, 5.
178. Buckle, ed., *Letters of Queen Victoria* (2nd ser.), vol. 3, pp. 298–9.
179. *Hansard*, vol. 267, cols 1678–704.
180. *Reynolds's Newspaper*, 30 April 1882, pp. 1, 4.
181. Ibid., 30 March 1884, p. 4.
182. Cf. Samuel Kydd writing in Harney's *Democratic Review*, vol. 1 (September 1849), pp. 137–9, of the Queen's visit in the wake of the Famine – 'the latest move is to pacify the naked Celt with a royal visit'.
183. *Hansard*, vol. 298, cols 492–511.
184. *Reynolds's Newspaper*, 14 June 1885, p. 4.
185. Ibid., 26 July 1885, p. 4.
186. *The Times*, 21 August 1884, p. 1. The Queen was in fact anxious that the Lords should cease its obstruction of the Reform Bill and tried to take an active part in the resolution of the crisis – see C.C. Weston, 'The Royal Mediation in 1884', *English Historical Review*, vol. 82 (1967), pp. 296–332.
187. Joseph Chamberlain, *The Radical Programme* (London, 1885), pp. 38–40.
188. *Republican*, vol. 12 (August 1886), p. 36.
189. *The Times*, 14 May 1887, p. 13.
190. *Hansard*, vol. 314, cols 1770–98.
191. J.L. Lant, *Insubstantial Pageant; Ceremony and Confusion at Queen Victoria's Court* (New York, 1980), pp. 134–8.
192. *Spectator*, 18 June 1887, pp. 825–7.
193. Longford, *Victoria R.I.*, p. 625.
194. Lant, *Insubstantial Pageant*, pp. 158–9.
195. Lant, ibid., p. 46.
196. *Daily News*, 21 June 1887, p. 4 .
197. *Reynolds's Newspaper*, 26 June 1887, p. 1.
198. *Reynolds's Newspaper*, 19 June 1887, p. 1.
199. Ibid., 12 June 1887, p. 4.
200. Ibid., 19 June, p. 1.
201. Ibid., 26 June 1887, p. 4; 19 June 1887, p. 4.
202. Ibid., 19 June 1887, pp. 1, 4. Antony Taylor, '*Reynolds's Newspaper*, Opposition to the Monarchy', p. 327 notes an anti-semitic side to popular anti-royalism.
203. *Pace* Anne Humphreys, 'Political narrative and political discourse in *Reynolds's Weekly Newspaper*' in Laurel Brake, Aled Jones and Lionel

Madden, eds, *Investigating Victorian Journalism* (London, 1990), pp. 33–47. She argues that personal attacks on Victoria were eschewed by the newspaper, probably because she was a woman.
204. *Reynolds's Newspaper*, 19 June 1887, p. 1.
205. Ibid., 26 June 1887, p. 4.
206. *Pall Mall Gazette*, 22 June 1887.
207. *Hansard*, vol. 337, cols 1466–70.
208. *Parliamentary Papers*, 1889, vol. IX, *Reports from the Select Committee on Grants to Members of the Royal Family*, passim.
209. *Hansard*, vol. 338, cols 1534, 1684.
210. *Pall Mall Gazette*, 25 July 1889, p. 2.
211. William Kuhn, 'Queen Victoria's Civil List: what did she do with it?', *Historical Journal*, vol. 36, no. 3 (1993), pp. 645–65.
212. Ibid., p. 660.
213. See above, chapter 2.
214. *Hansard*, vol. 338, col. 1651.
215. Ibid., vol. 338, col. 1447.
216. Ibid., cols 1439–43.
217. Ibid., vol. 337, col. 1465.
218. *Select Committee on Grants*, p. 12.
219. *Star*, 27 July 1889, p. 1.
220. *Hansard*, vol. 337, col. 1473.
221. Ibid., vol. 338, cols 1673–4.
222. Kuhn, 'Queen Victoria's Civil List', pp. 648, 661.
223. *Hansard*, vol. 217, col. 697.
224. *Hansard*, vol. 338, cols 1353–4, 1533, 1679–82.
225. G.E. Buckle ed., *The Letters of Queen Victoria*, 3rd ser., vol. 1 (London, 1931), p. 517.
226. *Star*, 9 July 1889, p. 1.
227. Ibid., 5 July 1889, p. 1; 4 July 1889, p. 1.
228. Ibid., 10 July 1889, p. 1.
229. Ibid., 27 July 1887, p. 1; 30 July 1889, p. 1; 23 July 1887.
230. Ibid., 26 July 1889, p. 1.
231. *Reynolds's Newspaper*, 28 July, p. 4.
232. *Hansard*, vol. 337, col. 1472.
233. Ibid., cols 1479–80; vol. 338, col. 1305.
234. Ibid., vol. 338, cols 1294–310.
235. Ibid., col. 1329.
236. Ibid., cols 1288, 1336–8, 1475–6.
237. Ibid., col. 1522–3.
238. Ibid., cols 1340–2.
239. Ibid., col. 1478.
240. Ibid., col. 1488.
241. Ibid., cols 1501–4.
242. Ibid., col. 1595.
243. Ibid., cols 1503–4.
244. *Star*, 21 July 1889, p. 1.
245. *The Times*, 5 July 1889, p. 9; 27 July 1889, p. 11.
246. *Spectator*, 27 July 1889, pp. 100–1; 3 August 1889, pp. 129, 134–5.
247. *Star*, 19 July 1889, p. 1.

248. For a full account of the Tranby Croft affair, see Philip Magnus, *King Edward the Seventh* (Harmondsworth, 1967 edn), pp. 279–89.
249. *The Times*, 10 June 1891, p. 9.
250. *Daily News*, 10 June 1891, p. 4.
251. *Lloyd's Weekly Newspaper*, 14 June 1891, p. 8.
252. *Nonconformist*, 12 June 1891, p. 428.
253. *Reynolds's Newspaper*, 7 June 1891.
254. Ibid., 21 August 1892, p. 4; 4 September 1889, p. 1.
255. Ibid., 17 January 1892, p. 4.
256. Ibid., 7 May 1893, p. 4.
257. Ibid., 2 July 1893, p. 4.
258. Ibid., 9 July 193, p. 4.
259. *Hansard*, 4th ser., vol. 26, cols 462–3. There had been rumours of secret marriages involving various princes – see Elizabeth Longford, *Victoria R.I.*, p. 654.
260. *Labour Leader*, 30 June 1894, p. 8.
261. *Reynolds's Newspaper*, 13 June 1897, p. 1.
262. Ibid., 20 June 1897, p. 1.
263. Ibid., 27 June 1897, p. 1.
264. *Labour Leader*, 19 June 1897, p. 203.
265. *Clarion*, 19 June 1897, p. 196. Ross McKibbin, 'Why was there no Marxism in Great Britain', *English Historical Review*, vol. 99 (1984), pp. 296–332 argues that the Labour movement as it gained representation in parliament began to see the Crown not as a class enemy but as a benificent, neutral umpire.
266. *Labour Leader*, 9 February 1901, p. 43; *Hansard*, 4th ser., vol. 91, cols 1204–6.
267. *Labour Leader* 26 January 1901, p. 27.
268. Ibid., 2 February 1901, p. 1; 9 February 1901, p. 43.
269. *Reynolds's Newspaper*, 27 June 1897, p. 1.
270. Ibid., 27 January 1901, p. 1.
271. Ibid., p. 5.
272. Ibid., 5 February 1901, p. 4.
273. *Clarion*, 2 February 1901, p. 33; 9 February 1901, p. 45.
274. Ibid., 2 February 1901, p. 33.
275. Ibid., 26 January 1901, p. 28.
276. Ibid., 9 February 1901, pp. 34, 44.

CHAPTER FOUR

Perceptions of Political Power and Partisanship, 1837–61

Constitutional history has hitherto concentrated on the correspondence of sovereign and ministers and has not considered contemporary perceptions of royal power. Yet these perceptions are of vital importance – the popular belief that the political power of the Crown had declined to nothing was identified by George Standring in 1884 as the main reason for the failure of British republicanism.[1] In an era of reform no more direct monarchical collision with the 'spirit of the age' could be imagined than through the arbitrary exercise of political power by a hereditary sovereign. That a collision with results calamitous to the throne was avoided has led general historians of the nineteenth century to present too straightforward a picture of public consensus as to the limited, constitutional nature of the Victorian monarchy. According to this interpretation, William IV's failure to impose the ministry of his choice on parliament in 1834–5 signalled the death of the old, interfering Hanoverian monarchy and Victoria, after an initial, childish infatuation with Melbourne and the Whigs, quickly settled, under Albert's tutelage, into being the first thorough exponent of constitutional monarchy.[2]

In fact no such consensus as to the Crown's political role existed. Standring was correct in asserting that the 'whole tendency of politics in this country during the last sixty years' was such that 'the power and influence of the royal and hereditary elements in the "Constitution" have gradually diminished, as the democratic element has advanced in intelligence and organization'.[3] But the movement in this direction was by no means a smooth one and was temporarily checked and even reversed by crises over royal partisanship and royal interference.

There was not only a lack of consensus about what the Crown did politically but about what it *should* do. All constitutional history has been 'Whig' history in that it is written from the perspective that the reduction of royal influence is right and desirable. We must not overlook that there were Victorian champions of the royal prerogative, especially David Urquhart and his followers; and that in the 1860s some observers including *The Times* expressed fears that the Queen's seclusion would so reduce royal involvement in government as to unbalance the constitution. On Victoria's death Conservative ministers praised the active role the Queen had played, causing some dismay in the liberal and radical press.

These two chapters on the perception of the Crown's political role examine how Victorians envisaged this role and how far they saw Victoria herself as discharging this role. By the 1880s the Queen, in many ways despite herself, could stand as a symbol of national unity – above party, above politics; a position occupied by all subsequent British monarchs. But this position had only recently been fully attained – for much of her reign she wore the politically contentious Crown bequeathed by her predecessors, and in the final years there was a renewed awareness of Victoria's partisanship, even if it now seemed not to threaten parliamentary authority.

This chapter challenges the prevalent historical interpretation of the period 1837–61. According to this interpretation Victoria was guided by Albert away from her girlish Whig prejudices to an impartiality and thorough constitutionalism, which conclusively lifted the British monarchy above party and political controversy. By looking at what contemporaries said and wrote about the monarchy we find that Albert's advent brought no such decisive break. While he ended the overt partisanship of the Queen, this was part of his conception of a more powerful monarchy, standing above factious parties so as to control policy better according to (what it saw as) the national interest. The mistake made by nearly all those who set Albert on a constitutional pedestal is the conflation of impartial monarchy with limited monarchy.

The period 1837–61 is a cohesive one in which political controversy surrounded the Crown – controversy not ended by the arrival of Albert but intensified by it. The tendency has been to see the Queen's Whig prejudices and the resulting Bedchamber crisis of 1839 as a ripple on the surface of modern constitutionalism. Norman Gash has written that the Bedchamber crisis was 'considerably more significant than later commentators have sometimes allowed', and has observed that 'whereas William IV in 1834 acted constitutionally but unsuccessfully, Victoria in 1839 acted successfully but unconstitutionally'. Yet he too sees it as girlish obstinacy, soon to be allayed by Albert – 'whereas William IV had at least till 1835 some recognizable policy, Victoria merely had predilections. She came as Palmerston is reported to have said, "from the nursery to the throne" and could not therefore uphold royal authority in the face of the Cabinet.'[4] In fact Victoria was a determined upholder of her prerogatives and Albert's arrival stiffened royal resolve. The first section of this chapter looks at the attitudes to royal power at Victoria's accession and contains the first study of contemporary attitudes to the Queen's partisanship as shown in particular in the Bedchamber crisis. The second section demonstrates what Albert's impact really was.

1837–40: 'Queen of the Whigs'

The Crown which Victoria inherited in 1837 had yet to rise above the partisan strife of the two political parties but it was widely acknowledged to be a limited, constitutional one – though the degree to which it was and should be limited was a matter of dispute. The removal of the Stuarts in the Glorious Revolution of 1688 was hailed by Whig historians and constitutionalists as the moment at which England rid itself of despotic government; while a romantic Tory such as the young Disraeli, whose early writings yearned for a revival of royal power, lamented that since that date England had possessed a 'Venetian constitution' with the once-proud monarch cast in the role of an impotent Doge, the puppet of the magnificoes – the aristocratic oligarchy which dominated parliament.[5] George III was regarded as having attempted to reassert the royal prerogative[6] but, unsuccessful, had abandoned this policy[7] and subsequently the Crown had been forced onto the retreat in politics. G.H.L. Le May has described George IV's acceptance of Wellington's ultimatum over Catholic Emancipation, an anathema to the King, in March 1829 as a landmark in the development of ministerial authority.[8] George, for all his Tory prejudices was described by the Whig lawyer, Campbell, as 'the model of a constitutional King of England . . . He has stood by and let the country govern itself.'[9] 'The passing of the first Reform Bill in 1832', wrote Frank Hardie, was 'the decisive date at which the Crown, ceasing to be powerful, becomes influential',[10] as the Bill tipped the balance of the constitution in favour of the branch of the legislative elected by the people. William IV, the monarch eventually coerced by his government into using his influence to get the Bill passed, found out its effects in 1834–5 when he had to bow to the Commons majority against the Conservative ministry and recall the Whig government which he had dismissed.[11]

The comments prompted by the accession of Victoria affirmed the tendency away from personal government. The radical *Westminster Review* while acknowledging the continued influence of the Crown, wrote that 'the ultimate triumph of liberal principles is certain' and that 'the fate of our country is mainly in its own hands, and its future weal and woe depends on the wisdom and energy of its people'.[12] From a different perspective, 'an octogenarian' Tory formed the same conclusion, arguing that this drift should be halted and the prerogatives of the Crown defended against the 'encroachments' of 'the popular part of the constitution', which had gained a disproportionate power through the Reform Act: 'The glory and advantages of our constitution consist in the combination of three independent powers, who are a check upon each other'.[13] Coronation ballads celebrated the freedom of the British people under a constitutional monarchy.[14]

Yet the *Westminster Review* recognized that 'it would be absurd indeed to suppose that Her Majesty's personal feelings will not before long exercise some influence'.[15] The monarchy was still very much a part of the battle between Whigs and Tories. The Tory Bolingbroke's *The Idea of a Patriot King* had depicted the ideal monarch as above faction[16] and liberals such as Brougham saw the neutrality of the Crown as a necessity concomitant with its abstention from arbitrary interference;[17] but in practice a non-partisan monarch had yet to be known and Whig and Tory politicians looked to the advantages that would accrue to them from a sympathetic sovereign – the Crown after all still appointed the ministry; the name of the monarch was used in elections behind his favoured party; and was used to sway the votes of the remaining independent members in the Commons; while to have the sovereign's ear was to secure place and preferment for one's political clients.

The obituaries to the deceased King and the reception of the new Queen highlighted the way in which the Crown was embroiled in party warfare. William IV had shown himself antipathetic to reform and to his Whig ministers after his short-lived support for the Reform Bill, and the fulsome death-bed praise of *The Times*, the chief Tory organ, reflected the opposition's loss of its most influential political ally.[18] Ministerial newspapers in their obituaries emphasized the liberal reforms instituted during the reign, one, the *Examiner*, regretting that William 'sank, accordantly with the natural gravitation of Royalty into the swamp of Toryism'.[19] The new Queen's mother, the Duchess of Kent was, however, known to be a liberal and it was thought that Victoria, whose household was dominated by Whig politicians or sympathizers and their wives,[20] had been educated to favour Whiggism. The *Westminster Review* forecast that the change of sovereign would 'probably give the present ministry a considerable accession of strength', as it would no longer encounter the resistance of the sovereign in framing its legislation and could now hold the threat of a mass peerage creation over the heads of the opposition which was using its majority in the Lords to obstruct bills.[21] Each party used the sovereign's name in the 1837 election, the Tories having as their constant refrain the need to free the Queen from her Whig ministers. When *The Times* implored Victoria to abjure faction, it meant Whig faction – it had no compunction in stating, 'Her Majesty is a Conservative'.[22] Whig newspapers presented the Queen's Address, with its pledge to continue to ameliorate the laws and institutions of the nation, as proof of her attachment to liberal principles.[23] Though the coronation was supposed to be a day on which political discussion was set aside, *The Times* and other opposition publications used their editorials to make party political points. The coronation was depicted as a Whig ruse, rushed on to distract attention from their parliamentary difficulties – *The Times* presented a list of 69 bills still in the process of going through parliament – and to occasion a creation of rabble peers to ease these difficulties. It pointed out that Wellington received a far greater ovation in the procession than any of the government ministers.[24]

The first years of the reign presented the strange spectacle of the Tories, for so long the party of government and of the Crown, in opposition and constantly at odds with the court; while the Whigs, accustomed to opposition and to criticizing the Crown and court, were in government and maintained there, increasingly, by royal favour. The Tories resented this situation. They saw themselves as the friends of the Crown and if they used the argument that the Crown should not be factious it was because, after Bolingbroke, they regarded the Whigs as a faction and themselves as the patriotic party.[25]

The Bedchamber crisis of May 1839 and the newspaper debate which followed highlighted the incongruity of the parties' respective positions. The Tories, traditionally the upholders of the royal prerogative were effectively prevented from taking office by an assertion of that prerogative and the Whigs, one of whose salient principles was the curtailment of prerogative, found themselves kept in power by it, when the Queen refused to accede to Peel's request that to show her confidence in the incoming Conservative ministry she make some changes in her female household, removing the wives of prominent Whig politicians – and Peel as a result felt unable to take office. *The Times* pointed out that if the parties' roles had been reversed the Whigs would have been quick to condemn royal interference with parliamentary government.[26]

The Queen's household had from the beginning of the reign been a target of Conservative criticism. One of the party's organs, the *Quarterly Review* had remarked on 'the decided political basis, and the marked political position, of some of the ladies selected' – some were the wives of Whig cabinet ministers – 'it must never be forgotten' that the Queen 'is not the sovereign of one party but of *all*', and it foresaw the constitutional difficulties that might ensue.[27] Tory animosity to the household was manifested and sharpened during the Lady Flora Hastings scandal, in early 1839. Lady Flora, one of the ladies of the bedchamber, was the victim of court slanders[28] that she was pregnant.[29] The Tory press took up the cause of Lady Flora, criticizing what it saw as Melbourne's peremptory replies to her family's letters. Some Tory newspapers connected the Bedchamber crisis with the Lady Flora scandal – the *Morning Post* conjectured that the ladies had persuaded the

Queen to refuse to part with their services by intriguing the royal ear 'with some new tale of lasciviousness and corruption';[30] and the *Morning Herald* suggested that Peel's proposed changes were motivated by the opportunity of 'purifying the household'.[31]

The Bedchamber crisis in intensifying the identification of the Crown with the Whigs was all the more galling to the Conservatives, who objected especially to the government's campaign promoted in the Whig press of getting up addresses to the Queen, whom they portrayed as acting in their interests against the opposition. The *Sunday Times* stated that the Queen was 'evidently at present a Liberal in politics' and could not give Peel the confidence he required as she did not feel any in him or his party;[32] the *Morning Chronicle* wrote that the Queen had 'done her duty' by her ministers;[33] and the *Leeds Mercury* argued that the Queen should be supported as she had used her prerogative in the interests of liberty.[34] Tory horror at such statements was expressed in the *Standard* which quoted Bolingbroke – 'To espouse no party, but to govern like the common father of his people is so essential in the character of a patriot King'. To assert, as the ministerial newspapers did, that the Queen hated the Conservative body was unconstitutional: looking somewhat idealistically at recent history the *Standard* declared, 'It has been ever the wisdom of the British constitution, and the practice of all by whom our constitution has been reverenced, to withdraw the *person* of the Sovereign from party disputes'.[35]

The crisis itself turned on the respective rights of the sovereign and Prime Minister to designate the composition of the royal household. The Conservatives protested that Peel's request was reasonable and constitutional, while the Whigs upheld the Queen's insistence that Peel could exercise no such control. Greater weight attached itself to the Tories' arguments – in 1841 Melbourne was to admit to Anson, Prince Albert's secretary, that the Whig government was able to support the Queen in the crisis only because of the forbearance of the Conservative leaders, Wellington and Peel.[36] The Tory newspapers, however, continued to press Peel's initial point that the household of a queen regnant unlike that of a queen consort, was a public and state, not a private, institution.[37] Besides, there was the precedent of the Whigs' altering Queen Adelaide's household at the time of the Reform Bill.[38] Peel, it was argued, could not hope to govern while the wives and sisters of his political opponents remained in such numbers around the sovereign, who, in moments of human frailty, was bound to divulge worries of state to those assigned to be her bosom companions. The danger was of a petticoat 'camarilla' as existed in Portugal and Spain – where there were also young female monarchs – and as had existed in England in the reign of Queen Anne.[39]

Moreover, with the Tories in a minority in the House of Commons and the Queen so openly sympathetic to the outgoing ministry, a Conservative Prime Minister would need the concession of some changes in the household as a mark of royal confidence. To withhold such confidence and to insist on preserving intact a partisan court, which could exercise a secret and irresponsible influence, was in the eyes of the Tory press, unconstitutional.[40] Most papers stopped short of personal criticism of Victoria, though all alluded to her youth, inexperience and female weakness, which, it was alleged, the Whigs had exploited in staging 'mock resignations' – in the knowledge that a dispute over the household would arise.[41] The *Liverpool Mail*, however, stated bluntly, 'To tell the truth, the Queen has evinced no mental authority worthy of a British sovereign. She is not ripe for nobleness.'[42]

As Melbourne's admission of 1841 would imply, the Whig defence was fought on rather precarious ground. Much was made of the 'dastardly' attempt by the Tories to impose unfamiliar companions on the young Queen in place of the 'friends of her youth'[43] – a quite spurious charge, as the ladies to whom Peel objected had been placed in the household by Melbourne only one and a half years earlier.[44] The Whigs denied the distinction between a queen regnant and a queen consort and cited 1812 as an example of an incoming (Whig) ministry being denied changes in the household. *The Times* countered that the circumstances of 1812 were exceptional, Lord Moira, who was negotiating for the palace, deeming it expedient that, in the light of allegations of corruption and immorality in the Prince Regent's retinue, the *customary* changes requested by a new government should be eschewed, lest their significance be misconstrued.[45] The *Spectator*, disinterestedly, supported Peel's stance: 'The Household appointments are State appointments, for State purposes, and for them the *Minister is held responsible* ... The accident of the Sovereign being a female does not alter the case'. It surmised that had the Queen acceded to Peel's request there would have been no Whig outcry.[46]

Another Whig argument was to say that it was Peel who was politicizing the court by seeking to pack it with Tory ladies, but the blatantly partisan character of the household chosen by Melbourne in 1837 gave the lie to this contention. An independent observer, Brougham, dismissed all Whig explanations as rank hypocrisy, flying in the face of the acknowledged constitutional convention on which the Whigs themselves had taken their stand in 1812.[47]

The far-reaching effect of Victoria's refusal to countenance Peel's proposals – the failure of the Conservatives to take office – raised a larger question; that of whether parliament or the sovereign should have the decisive say in the formation of the government. The Queen's personal predilection for the Melbourne ministry had interrupted the course of parliamentary politics.[48] The crisis threw into relief all the doubts about the rationality of hereditary government that had accompanied the accession of a very young woman. Favouritism in such a girl queen in the choice of government must be dangerous to the monarchy warned Brougham in his open letter to the Queen at the time of the coronation.[49] In the parliamentary debate on the explanations of the Bedchamber crisis, he said that it was a matter of grave concern that 'Sir Robert Peel's attempt to form an administration was defeated by two ladies of the bedchamber' and that the Commons vote of 7 May which had induced the Whig resignation had meant nothing and the Queen's refusal of 10 May everything.[50]

Indeed, the consensus of non-partisan opinion was that the Queen had exceeded royal power in a way damaging to the principle of monarchical government. An anonymous 'Councillor of the Crown' in an open letter to the Queen professed himself a radical and no friend in politics to Wellington or Peel but deemed it essential to the workings of the constitution that the Conservative leaders should have been enabled to form a government: the Queen's actions 'cannot be reconciled to any principle of our limited Monarchy'. The result was to set 'Your Majesty at variance with your Parliament and your people', which would encourage those who wished 'to pare down the powers of the Executive and of the Aristocracy to some standard of a republican kind'.[51] The *Spectator* agreed that the Queen had set herself against the tendency of the constitution away from executive government. The journal had criticized her predecessor for hindering his ministers through his background machinations against them[52] and now it feared that Victoria was following an even more overt and perilous course: 'These are not times for stretching the Royal prerogative; and the disposition to exercise questionable powers does not promise a happy reign'.[53]

Even Tory newspapers, infuriated by the denial of office to their party, began to use language described by the ministerial *Globe* as 'republican'[54] – and Wellington, Greville noted, declined a parliamentary attack on the constitutional propriety of the Bedchamber proceedings because he really feared that the monarchy might come into danger.[55] The opposition press pointed out that the Whigs had resigned because by their own admission they no longer enjoyed the confidence of parliament – how could they justify resuming power? Whence sprang any new confidence in them? *The Times* reflected that is was only from 'the increased proof of their ascendancy over the Royal Household! Verily this throws fresh light on the lot of Empires and on the fortunes of the human race.'[56] The local Tory press was more outspoken. *Berrow's Worcester Journal* described the episode as 'a flagrant act of atrocity . . .

perpetuated in opposition to ... the calm opinion and feeling of the British people expressed in the House of Commons';[57] and the *Kentish Herald* lamented:

> Oh, the political absurdities that flow from the noblest theories. We reverence, for its abstract wisdom, the principle of hereditary government, but when we see the destinies of a mighty Empire ... all depend on the nod of an amiable little girl of nineteen ... we confess ourselves staggered and filled with apprehensiveness.[58]

The pro-government press defended the Queen's and Whigs' actions in several, often contradictory, ways. The *Northampton Mercury* criticized Peel for trying to expose and exacerbate the weakness of the sovereign when compared with the power of parliament:

> the tendency of all that has passed since the Revolution of 1688 ... has been to increase the power of the popular branch of our constitution, at the expense of the monarchical. Two centuries ago it was the duty of the patriot to protect the people against the tyranny of the Crown; it is now no less his duty to protect the Crown against the encroachment of the people.[59]

The *Globe*, however, admitted the pernicious effect of 'backstairs' influence which Peel feared and, though it declared Peel's demands unreasonable, virtually confessed that all that distinguished 1839 from 1812 was that 'The sun is on the Whig side of the hedge now'.[60] Like the government newspapers cited earlier, this implied that the Queen's use of the prerogative should be supported because it served liberal interests.

The *Globe* and other ministerial publications also took the line that Peel, by trying to substitute royal confidence for a parliamentary majority, was the man trying to undermine the popular branch of the constitution[61] – Peel could not command a majority in the Commons; the government's resignation having been caused by a collapse of the majority Whig-radical-Irish coalition which sustained it. The Chartists seemed to agree with this in crying 'a plague on both your houses' – the *Northern Star* viewed the crisis, with Whigs and Tories both lacking parliamentary support and vying for royal favour as proof that the will of the whole people could be the only true and effective source of confidence for a ministry.[62]

The animated public debate provoked by the Bedchamber crisis has been overlooked by historians who have viewed the crisis only from the 'inside' perspective of the Queen's relations with Melbourne and Peel. Gash has written that the Queen acted 'successfully',[63] but her success – the retention of the Melbourne ministry – was a very narrow and ephemeral one, at the expense of the wider reputation of the Crown and its long-term security. If Peel had been at the head of a large majority after an election, the Bedchamber crisis would surely have had greater public reverberations, for there was a widespread feeling that, to quote Greville, the Queen had exceeded 'the exact limits of her constitutional priority' and that the Whigs 'ought to have been impressed with the paramount obligation of instructing her in the nature and scope of her constitutional obligations and duties, . . . and to have advised her what she ought to do, instead of upholding her in doing that which was agreeable to her taste and inclination'.[64] This was to be the lesson of the crisis applied after the Conservative election win in 1841.[65]

Immediately, however, the effect of the crisis was to exacerbate the hostility between the court and the Conservatives. In January 1840 the *Spectator* commented, 'George the Third would as soon have sent spontaneously for Charles James Fox, as Victoria the First for Sir Robert Peel'.[66] Tories now openly admitted the Queen's antipathy towards them.[67] The Tory press had in fact adopted the pro-Conservative Dowager Queen Adelaide as an alternative figure of veneration, always contrasting her popularity with the unpopularity of the court.[68]

A widening of the division between opposition and court resulted from the speeches of ultra-Protestant Tory orators denouncing the Queen for countenancing what they saw as the pro-Catholic policies of her ministry – the Revd Mr Gregg speaking at Manchester on 5 November 1839 said that 'were the Queen a Christian' a military force 'would be sent with Protestant missionaries throughout Ireland'.[69] The Whig newspapers saw the implication of such speeches as a desire to replace the Queen with her uncle, the reactionary Ernest, King of Hanover (the Duke of Cumberland and heir presumptive)[70] and these newspapers hailed the announcement of the Queen's marriage as an insurance that, with the hoped for appearance of an heir apparent, the succession would be secured and not 'devolve upon a line', whose 'accession to the throne of England would not be favourable to public liberty or to the continued union of Great Britain and Ireland'.[71]

The events surrounding Prince Albert's arrival and the wedding reflected and accentuated the rift between Crown and the Conservatives. The opposition press reported that the announcement of the marriage to the Privy Council was more an occasion for a demonstration against the Whig ministers than an event of national celebration, the assembled crowd booing them as they arrived for the meeting.[72] The declaration itself became a point of party contention, Conservatives in the newspapers[73] and then in parliament protesting at the omission of the formula used in the announcement of George III's marriage – that the spouse came from a line firm in the Protestant faith. They saw this as another example of the government's pandering to Catholics and contended that, in view of the Catholic marriage alliances of some of Albert's family, an assurance should have been given of the Prince's Protestant credentials. Wellington used the Conservative majority in the House of Lords to amend the marriage address to include the epithet 'Protestant' – Melbourne expressed his regret that the marriage of the sovereign could not have been free of such factious debate.[74]

The Tories in a spirit of revenge for the Bedchamber crisis delivered a double rebuff to the government, court and newly arrived Prince by allying with the radicals in the Commons to reduce Albert's proposed annuity from £50,000 p.a. to £30,000 p.a. and by refusing to pass through the Lords the precedence clause in his Naturalization Bill which would have given Albert precedence above all but the sovereign for his lifetime. In the debate on the grant, Lord John Russell said that 'no Sovereign of this country has ever been insulted in such a manner as her present Majesty has been';[75] and the *Morning Chronicle* wrote that, as Peel had disavowed 'economical' reasons in urging the reduction, it was 'virtually a fine upon the Queen and her Consort for not bearing allegiance to the Tory party'.[76] Conservatives denied this, saying that the grant was extravagant and as such detrimental to royal popularity and that the proposal was further evidence of Whig sycophancy, the cultivation of favour at court being the only prop of the government.[77] Over the precedence question, the opposition baulked at the subordination of the Blood Royal, especially as the King of Hanover had not given his consent to such a move. In the face of the government's insistence that it was the Queen's *urgent* wish that her husband have this precedence, *The Times* protested that the House's 'independence was at stake' and congratulated the peers on staying 'firm'.[78]

Unsurprisingly, the Tory leaders, with the exception of Wellington and Liverpool, were excluded from the wedding, and this drew forth renewed protests from the party's organs and *The Times* made a point of remarking that Wellington was 'most warmly cheered'.[79] Apart from the most ardent supporters of the ministry, observers saw the partisanship of the Queen, so blatantly manifested in the narrow character of the wedding celebration, as degrading the Crown of England: the *Spectator* felt that 'it is unfortunate that on such an occasion the Queen should be so exclusively surrounded as to countenance the charge that her Majesty's advisers contrive to make her the Sovereign of a faction instead of a united people'.[80]

The Tories trusted that the wedding would prove to be a turning-point – the introduction of an important new personage at court gave a ray of hope to an opposition so estranged from royal favour. Despite their ostensibly inimical attitude to him in the parliamentary votes, the Conservatives wanted Albert to come to see them as the true friends of the Crown. They desired him to see the grant reduction and denial of

precedence not as signs of their vindictiveness but of his being 'singularly unlucky in respect to the persons into whose hands it has fallen to
manage the affairs incidental to his elevation'.[81] Conservative newspapers expressed the hope that Albert's influence would mitigate the Queen's
prejudices, though *The Times* saw the selection of a husband even
younger than the Queen as regrettably diminishing the likelihood of
such influence being exerted.[82] The Tories were concerned that Albert
would be cocooned in a Whig household just as the Queen was, and, on
3 February, Inglis raised the question in the Commons of why important positions in the Prince's household had already been filled – by
Whigs – before Albert left for England.[83] The Duke of Buckingham
encapsulated the hopes of the Conservatives and of dispassionate observers when he wrote that the Queen's marriage should 'put an end to
an influence which had been exercised in a manner that was thought
had already affected the dignity of the Crown'.[84]

The course followed by Victoria in her two and a half years as a
virgin queen had to be amended: her partisanship had provoked a
constitutional crisis and accusations of 'back-stairs influence' and it had
become a commonplace that she was not queen of the nation but of a
faction – 'Queen of the Whigs'. Such partisanship and the arbitrary acts
of interference which almost necessarily went with it were untenable in
the political system that had been produced by the Reform Act – only
Peel's weakness in the Commons in 1839 had saved the monarchy from
the sort of head-on collision with parliament that it could not afford in
the modern age. Albert was looked to in 1840 as the man who would
mend Victoria's ways. In one superficial sense he was to end royal
partisanship but his ambitious plans for the Crown were to bring the
British monarchy into deeper political controversy than that of 1839.

1840–61: the impact of Albert

The view of Albert as the father of the contemporary constitutional
British monarchy, above party and above politics, has a long historical
pedigree. *The Times* obituary on the Prince Consort in December 1861
declared that 'by his influence her [the Queen's] steps have been directed in that path of constitutional conduct which has strengthened her
Throne'.[85] Albert's official biographer, Theodore Martin, wrote that it
was the Prince's resolution that, after the Bedchamber crisis, the Queen
'must not again be open to any imputation of being governed by political partisanship'.[86] Twentieth-century biographers have persisted in seeing him as a pioneer of British constitutionalism. Frank Eyck claimed
that Albert's 'most important achievement on the domestic scene' was

'his contribution to the theory and practice of constitutional monarchy. In spite of the Queen's opposition, he checked the essentially personal approach of the Hanoverian royalty as early as 1841. The Crown was to be kept free of a permanent attachment to one political party and was to act largely impersonally, according to certain rules.' After Albert's death, Eyck argued, 'The Queen's approach to politics returned to some extent to the personal one she had adopted early in her reign. In the long run the Prince Consort's conception of the role of the Sovereign prevailed and his son King Edward VII reverted to it ... In Britain he (Albert) had largely established his ideas on government'.[87] One of Albert's latest biographers, Robert Rhodes James has observed that 'it is now an accepted truism, that in the words of Cecil Woodham-Smith, the principle that "the Crown is disassociated from party, and, above party, is Prince Albert's contribution to British politics"'.[88]

However, as Rhodes James acknowledges, this orthodoxy 'requires some qualification'.[89] An examination of contemporary commentaries shows that it is at best a partial truth to say that Albert was the progenitor of the modern, non-partisan, limited monarchy. His was the decisive influence in disassociating the Crown from adherence to one party but this was only part of his conception of a powerful monarchy which, uniting all the nation behind it, could control the nation's destinies – a conception which far from providing the model for Edward VII and subsequent monarchs was to prove an embarrassment to the Crown during Albert's lifetime – especially in 1853–4 when it brought upon the monarchy the most fierce press attacks of Victoria's reign – and after his death – the further revelations, in Martin's biography, of his theory and practice of constitutional monarchy adding to the fears in the 1870s that there was a movement towards resurrecting old notions of the royal prerogative.

Albert had shown his concern about the overt partisanship of the British monarchy when, in 1840, he had unsuccessfully tried to dissuade Victoria from choosing an entirely Whig household for him. He also reminded Victoria, who had expressed her indignation at Tory attacks on Melbourne, that 'it need not trouble you as Queen, except for your friendship for the good lord Melbourne. Otherwise a constitutional sovereign may be indifferent to what is said against his ministry'.[90] Victoria's partisanship culminated in the ministry's making what *The Times* described as 'the broadest and most unconstitutional use of Her Majesty's name for the purposes of influencing the suffrages of her subjects'[91] in the 1841 election. The principal Whig newspaper the *Morning Chronicle* described the election as 'the Queen's appeal to the people' on behalf of her government and represented the Whig defeat as a defeat for the Queen.[92]

Albert was determined that, with the Tories now in an elected majority, the Queen's predilection for the Whigs would not, as it had done in
1839, interfere with the transference of power determined by a parliamentary vote. In his eulogy on Albert in 1862, Lord John Russell was to
cite a letter in which the Prince had told him that, in his opinion, a
constitutional sovereign did not 'exercise control or pronounce a decision on the choice of the First Minister of the Crown'.[93] To avoid a
repetition of 1839, Albert, through his private secretary, Anson, conducted a preliminary discussion with Peel, so that when the Conservative leader met the Queen to take office the question of changes in the
Queen's household had already been settled to both sides' satisfaction[94]
The Times noted 'that His Royal Highness Prince Albert, in conjunction
with Her Majesty, manifested an earnest desire to act in strict accordance with the spirit of the Constitution.'[95]

This was on one level the turning-point in the history of royal partisanship: though, as we shall see, the Crown did not entirely transcend
party strife in the next twenty years, Victoria was not henceforth, as she
had been in 1837–41, dubbed the 'Queen of a faction'. The Spectator
observed in 1843 that 'the Queen's name is not abused, as it was wont
to be, by being hacked on every occasion as a tool of party'.[96] The 1845
Windsor by-election was the first contest in the seat in which the
sovereign's name was not used as a party war-cry. Albert communicated
to Peel the Queen's wish that royal favour should no longer be conferred on one of the candidates where in 1841 The Times had written,
'Court officials endeavoured in the most tyrannical and unscrupulous
manner to intimidate and overawe the electors by the Castle influences'.[97]

The Crown was henceforth to be seen as a neutral umpire ratifying,
irrespective of personal opinion, the result of the parliamentary struggle
between the parties. When Albert in 1854 was, as we shall see below,
accused of unconstitutional conduct, his defenders were quick to point
out this new-found royal neutrality.[98] This was to be demonstrated at
the Princess Royal's wedding in 1858 when the mixing of party leaders
contrasted with the last royal wedding – the Queen's own – from which
the Conservatives were excluded.[99] Albert received much of the credit
for this. The Leeds Mercury writing of the royal visit to the town in
1858 praised the Prince Consort for the way in which he had 'wisely
held aloof from political partisanship'.[100] Albert's obituaries emphasized his role in disassociating the Crown from party.[101]

Yet Albert's contribution was a far more ambivalent one than historians have been prepared to acknowledge. His belief that the Crown
should not be identified exclusively with one party was but part of a
political outlook which led Disraeli to remark that 'If he had out-lived

some of our "old-stagers" he would have given us, while retaining all constitutional guarantees, the blessing of absolute government'.[102] This has not been taken seriously enough – Elizabeth Longford, for example, writes that 'there was nothing in Disraeli's gibe'[103] – but it was a commonly held view among the Prince's contemporaries. Lord Stanley felt that 'The Prince had undoubtedly a fixed determination to increase the personal power of the Crown',[104] and Viscount Esher surmised, 'Had he lived, his tenacity might have hardened into obstinacy: and the relations between him and a Government founded – like ours – on democratic institutions would have become very strained'.[105] The seriousness of the clash between, on the one hand, the Prince's ambitious and active conceptions of the monarchy's political role and of his political role as consort and, on the other hand, contemporary assumptions of what these roles entailed, has not been fully appreciated by historians. Even Robert Rhodes James, who recognizes that Albert's influence upon 'the development of the British Constitutional Monarchy is often misunderstood'[106] and that the Prince wanted 'the maximum political influence with the minimum of criticism',[107] ultimately fails to substitute a decisive new interpretation of the Prince's influence, and devotes only three pages to the crisis of royal unpopularity in 1853–4[108] which highlighted the extent to which Albert's ideas and practice were in collision with prevalent British opinion. Fulford, who describes Albert as urging 'action in a manner more reminiscent of a modern Prime Minister than of the Sovereign', dwells longer on the crisis of 1853–4 and at one point even acknowledges that, to some contemporaries, Albert's theory of constitutional monarchy may have 'seemed dangerous, provocative and continental'. However, in summing up Albert's political contribution, he dismisses as groundless and ahistorical the conjectures of twentieth-century writers – he had Lytton Strachey and Frank Hardie in mind – 'That the ability of the Prince was guiding the monarchy into absolutism or into a point where a clash with politicians was certain'.[109]

In 1858 the *Morning Chronicle* remarked that Albert 'for a time may have ... mistaken the complex machine of the British Constitution',[110] and it is indeed debatable as to whether he ever understood it, let alone, as biographers such as Eyck claim, fashioned its subsequent development. There were fears before his arrival of his Germanic education: the *Sunday Times* wished that the Queen would marry Prince George of Cambridge, 'by birth, habits and education, an Englishman, his mind continually imbued with the principles of our constitution', while Albert would 'come over to this country enveloped in a cloud of antiquated and obsolete opinions, cherishing in secret the doctrine of divine right and passive obedience, impatient of the checks imposed upon him and his Royal wife by the forms of our free commonwealth and disgusted by the limited powers which the constitution intrusts to our first magistrate'.[111] Albert's tutors in the art of kingship were his uncle, Leopold of Saxe-Coburg-Saalfeld, King of the Belgians, and Leopold's and then Albert's adviser, Baron Stockmar, who was intermittently present in the English court for the first twenty years of Victoria's reign. They taught Albert that the king should stand above faction so that he could legitimately guide the whole nation's destinies by controlling the policy of this government. Impartiality for the Coburgs was a means to more power, not, as most subsequent historians have assumed, an acknowledgement of parliamentary supremacy. Norman Gash commits this common error when he writes that Albert in mitigating Victoria's Whig prejudices 'accepted party rule as a political fact'.[112]

This hatred of faction or party as an obstacle to strong kingly government was a characteristic of the most atavistic English writings on the royal prerogative shared by Leopold, Stockmar and Albert. The 'Octogenarian' Tory denounced faction and asserted that the Queen, her prerogatives restored, should 'pilot the national vessel'.[113] In his early novels, Disraeli berated 'the selfish strife of factions'[114] and through one of his heroes looked to a 'free monarchy' under which 'the sectional anomalies of our constitution would disappear'.[115] Albert in an early memorandum to Anson wrote, 'Composed as Party is here of two extremes, both must be wrong'.[116] Stockmar's teaching, as embodied in a letter of 1854 subsequently published, with great controversy ensuing, in Martin's biography, was to hold in contempt the two parties and to look to the sovereign, 'patriotic ... free from party passion ... an independent judge', for leadership; he was the head of the whole nation, the Prime Minister merely of a faction temporarily in a majority.[117] Stockmar had drafted the Belgian constitution under which Leopold ruled through a puppet ministry – 'the country was clay, in Leopold's capable hands', to quote a biographer.[118] The preoccupation of historians with Albert's impartiality to the exclusion of the wider theory of royal authority of which it formed part is shown in Robert Blake's statement, intended to summarize Albert's beneficial effect on British constitutional development, that the Prince 'succeeded ... in converting the English monarchy from the Hanoverian to what might be called the Coburg model, if one uses Coburg in reference to the Belgian branch of the family'.[119]

The monarch in the Coburg model was to have an active, indeed decisive, political role. Leopold's advice to Victoria in January 1838 was to 'preserve these elements' of royal power and 'to contrive by every means to strengthen them again'.[120] Stockmar felt that 'Constitutional Monarchy has since 1830 been constantly in danger of becoming a pure Ministerial Government', especially as a result of the Reform Act and that 'no opportunity should be let slip of vindicating the legitimate position of the Crown'. The sovereign must reclaim what Stockmar saw as a constitutional right 'to be the permanent President of his Ministerial Council ... a permanent Premier, who takes rank above the temporary head of the Cabinet, and, in matters of discipline exercises supreme authority'. The sovereign would be the presiding genius of the administration, directing the tendency, of its policy while the 'substantial import' of measures was left to the ministers – though 'the sovereign may even take a part in the initiation and the maturing of the Government measures'.[121]

Albert's reply to Stockmar's letter was 'I heartily agree with every word you say'[122] and he himself had expressed the same philosophy of kingship in a memorandum of 1850: while he disclaimed any part for the sovereign in the choice of ministry – other than ratifying that of parliament – Albert contended that once the ministry was launched, 'the monarch had an immense moral responsibility upon his shoulders with regard to his government and the duty to watch over and control it'.[123] Frank Eyck writes that Albert's model of constitutional monarchy 'left a large sphere of influence to the Crown' but that it would be 'absurd' to criticize such influence as '"excessive" because it went further than democratic notions will allow in the twentieth century'.[124] The point is that Albert's view of royal authority went further than contemporary nineteenth-century notions would allow and this accounts for many of his difficulties and much of his unpopularity in Britain. Besides, Eyck's statement rather invalidates his own case that Albert is the father of the modern monarchy and shows that the Prince was setting his face against the evolution of the constitution rather than directing it. The prevalent opinion, held in diverse quarters, was that the days of serious royal authority were over. In 1842 *The Times* wrote that only 'in former days' did reformers need to concern themselves that 'the power of Royalty had increased, was increasing, and ought to be diminished, and set themselves to work in right earnest to curtail its sources of political influence'.[125] The opening number of the satirical paper the *London Pioneer* declared, 'England is not the land of kings, but the land of the people: and we send to Germany for kings, not, however, to rule over us, but to be ruled, and to sign our papers when we have drawn them out ourselves'.[126] One of the arguments of the republicans of the late 1840s and 1850s was that England already effectively had a republican form of government; 'our Monarchy is only a pretence', the sovereign 'only a supernumerary in the pageant'.[127]

Yet Albert's determined efforts to accumulate a comprehensive body of political knowledge and to pass it on to the Prince of Wales[128]

showed that he envisaged a better educated monarch playing an increased governmental role in the future; and the reactions provoked by
his own attempts to put his theories into practice showed how dangerous they were to the stability of the British monarchy. Albert failed to
see that the monarch's view of what was the national interest needs
must be as partial and personal as the next person's, and the spurious-
ness of the distinction that he drew between the 'partisan' championing
of men and the 'patriotic' championing of measures was demonstrated
in the way in which he drew the Crown into a sympathy with Peel, as
deep, if not as blatant, as it had had with Melbourne.

Albert shared Peel's political outlook and recognized a kindred spirit
when the Prime Minister claimed to base his actions on the national
interest, not on party prejudices. The Prince involved the Crown in
political controversy when in what could only be construed as a
gesture of support he appeared in the visitors' gallery of the House of
Commons on the night that Peel introduced the contentious bill for
the repeal of the Corn Laws, the product of a great middle-class
agitation but regarded by the landed interest of the Conservative party
as a heinous betrayal of their protectionist principles. Lord George
Bentinck, the Protectionist leader, said in his concluding speech in the
debates:

> We have heard a great deal in the course of these discussions about
> 'a limited monarchy' . . . to whisper a word in the ear of that
> illustrious and royal Personage . . . I cannot but think that he
> listened to ill advice when . . . he allowed himself to be seduced by
> the First Minister of the Crown to come down in this House to
> usher in, to give eclat, and as it were, by reflection from the Queen,
> to give the semblance of the personal sanction of Her Majesty.[129]

Albert had earned the lasting enmity of the Protectionists – intensified
in 1851 when he was the moving spirit behind the Great Exhibition, a
celebration of free trade.[130] Gladstone was convinced that Albert was a
Peelite and noted in 1846, '. . . the Prince is very strongly Conservative
in his politics and his influence with the Queen is over-ruling; through
him she has become so attached to Conservative ideas that she could
hardly endure the idea of the opposition Party as her ministers'.[131]

Gladstone's observation shows the political dominance of Albert over
the Queen. The Prince was in no doubt as to the importance of his role
as Victoria's consort. In 1850 in a letter to Wellington, he wrote that the
Queen's consort must:

> continually and anxiously watch every part of the public business
> . . . As natural head of her family . . . sole confidential adviser in
> politics and only assistant in her communications with the officers
> of the Government, he is, besides, the husband of the Queen, the

tutor of the royal children, the private secretary of the sovereign, and her permanent minister.[132]

Albert's perception of his role raised important constitutional questions for, as Gladstone wrote in his review of the first volume of Martin's biography, in which the letter was published, 'Minister to the Queen he could not be, because his conduct was not within the reach of and control of Parliament'.[133] Albert became steadily more important in the transaction of political business as Victoria was frequently removed by pregnancy. As well as serving as a Privy Councillor, he read and annotated the memoranda of cabinet ministers and was present at their interviews with the Queen.[134] Lord Stanley felt that 'had he lived . . . he might have made himself almost as powerful as the Prime Minister of the day'.[135]

What Albert failed to realize was that the British public took an entirely different view of his position. He was aghast at the outcry which the revelations of his political role produced in 1853–4; why, he asked Stockmar, should the public be surprised that 'an important personage has during all this time taken a part in governing them?'[136] The *Sunday Times*, *Daily News* and *Morning Herald* pointed to the 'general, although mistaken belief entertained by the public, that he carefully abstained from all meddling in political matters'[137] – and said that this was the prime reason for his being 'thought well of . . . up to the present time'.[138] The common view was that Albert channelled his energies into non-political activities and official duties, as a promoter of industry, patron of the arts and education, benefactor of the working class, scientific farmer and would-be hat-designer to the army,[139] while, as he could not be held constitutionally responsible for his actions, he abjured politics. The newspaper campaign waged against the Prince in December 1853–January 1854 alleged that he was undermining the British constitution and trying 'to establish a sort of Anglo-German despotism'.[140] The background to the furore was the coincidence of the onset of war with Russia with Palmerston's resignation from the cabinet and the disorder in the command of the army. Bellicose and suspicious, the radical and Tory press looked for an extraneous influence on which could be blamed what they saw as the timorous vacillation of the Whig-Peelite coalition in the face of Russian aggression against Turkey, the departure – albeit temporary – from the government of Palmerston, the 'minister of England', and the confusion in the army at so critical a time. Albert's foreign birth and high position made him the obvious scapegoat – and he was depicted as abusing his position to subvert British policy as part of a Coburg conspiracy in Russian interests.[141]

It was true that Albert disliked Palmerston both personally and politically and had been an active opponent of his policies as Foreign Secretary during the Russell administration of 1846–51, criticizing his policy documents in memoranda to Palmerston himself and to the Prime Minister. An internationalist, the Prince saw Palmerston's aggressive, chauvinistic style of diplomacy as a threat to European peace and his liberal posturings as an incitement to revolution on the Continent and the toppling of the relations of Albert and the British Royal Family from their thrones. Albert turned Victoria, who on her accession had been deferential to the experienced Foreign Secretary, into an ardent and zealously watchful critic of Palmerston and during the Russell ministry the royal couple fought a continuous battle with him over his failure to send Foreign Office dispatches to the Palace for the Queen's ratification.[142]

In 1851 Russell only just pre-empted the Queen in dismissing the Foreign Secretary over his unauthorized approval of Louis Napoleon's 'coup' in France.[143] There were rumours that Russell's hand had been forced by court pressure.[144] It was alleged that an agreement had been reached between the courts in Vienna and London that Palmerston should go, and that his dismissal was known of in Vienna before it was made public in England.[145] Only the Chartist newspaper, the *Northern Star* specifically cited Albert in the following warning:

> ... he (Palmerston) fell in consequence of a court intrigue against him, headed by one who up to this time has wisely kept himself aloof from such interference. It will be wise for him to continue that abstinence in future. The Court will maintain all the more pleasant relations both with the Parliament and the People if it refrains from mixing itself up with politics ... [146]

The international situation in 1853–4 was such that Palmerston's secession from the government led not this time to rumours but to an open and full-scale attack on Albert, led by the *Morning Advertiser*, long a supporter of Palmerston, which revived the speculation of 1851–2 and said that Palmerston's dismissal then and his enforced resignation now were the climaxes of a long-running attempt by Albert to undermine his position and to be rid of the one minister who stood up against his unconstitutional meddling in government.[147] The Tory newspapers, sensing a scandal which could undermine the coalition, joined in the attack – the *Morning Herald* published a letter from one styling himself 'M.P.', which detailed Albert's involvement in government.[148] Allegations were made that Albert completely altered cabinet decisions, sent contrary instructions to British diplomats abroad and corresponded secretly with foreign courts. One Tory newspaper, the *Standard* all but stated that if such allegations were true, the Prince was guilty of treason.[149] Albert was also accused of having deliberately weakened, through his interference, the British army so that it would be in no condition to fight a war.

The radical *Daily News* printed letters from one 'Miles' in which the resignations of several officers, including the Adjutant-General, General Browne, were explained by their outrage at such interference, and in which Lord Hardinge, the Commander-in-Chief was described as the Prince's compliant placeman.[150]

Many of the specific allegations about Albert's being a Russian agent and sending instructions contradictory to the government's to British diplomats, were gross calumnies, but the overall criticisms were substantive ones of Albert's views on kingly government and of his part in government. The *Daily News* warned that the Prince had been 'sedulously trained, at that period of his life when the mind is most accessible to lasting impressions, in the traditional maxims of those most inveterate of continental legitimists, the minor courts of Germany … it is an unanswerable reason for insisting that he should abstain from all interference with English politics'.[151] The *Morning Advertiser* wrote, that Germanic influences were 'rapidly undermining those free institutions which are the glory of Great Britain' and 'placing in imminent peril the very Throne itself'.[152] Albert's presence at the Queen's interviews with ministers and access to cabinet memoranda, made known for the first time, were regarded as wholly unconstitutional, as he was one 'on whom rests no responsibility … in the eye of the Constitution, a nonentity. He is a simple subject of the Crown.'[153] The *Morning Herald* identified Stockmar as a dangerous influence on Albert's conduct.[154]

The defence of Albert, conducted by ministerial newspapers during January and then in the parliamentary explanations in the new session at the end of the month, was of a confused nature, illustrating how indeterminate and difficult Albert's role as the Queen's consort was – showing that in effect he was a man trying to fill what was at that time a woman's role. The wilder accusations – of interference in the army and in instructions to British embassies – were denied out of hand in *The Times* and other pro-coalition publications[155] and disproved by statements from Generals and diplomats, cited in parliament.[156] On the question of Albert's governmental role there was, however, an embarrassing muddle. *The Times* acknowledged, 'No one presumes that in the confidence of married life the Queen and her husband may not converse upon public affairs' but stated that, apart from this, Albert's position 'had nothing to do with the duties of government'.[157] The explanations in parliament, far from denying that Albert was an important figure in the interplay of ministry and Crown, assigned a highly beneficial effect to his assistance to the Queen in her political tasks. Melbourne had deemed such a course to be wise, Peel had encouraged his attendance of the Queen's interviews with ministers and successive Prime Ministers had welcomed his advice – both front benches united in this definition of the Prince's duties, justifying it by the wisdom, impartiality and patriotism which had always marked his counsels.[158]

Political commentators observed that this showed that Albert occupied an unprecedented constitutional position, Prince George of Denmark, Queen Anne's consort, never having shown the interest or ability to play a part in government. The *Examiner* pointed to the inconsistency in the argument that Albert's erudition and intelligence entitled him to his apparently extensive involvement – 'the question of constitutional principle must be determined irrespectively of what we may describe as personal accidents'.[159] The basis of the case against Albert's having a political role had been, to quote the *Standard* of 14 January, that 'the constitution of England recognizes no irresponsible officer but the wearer of the crown';[160] and, therefore, wrote the *Spectator*, the only inference to be drawn from what had been said in parliament was that 'for the first time in the history of the country, the sovereignty is virtually shared by the consort of the sovereign, without the direct delegation conveyed to William the Third by parliament'.[161]

Radical newspapers were not satisfied by the parliamentary statements. The *Daily News* stressed that Albert was entirely irresponsible and that he must hope to give effect to his personal opinions when invited to comment on cabinet papers. It contended that there was enough to occupy Albert's talents usefully outside government business.[162] The *Morning Advertiser* was unrepentant about having started the press campaign against the Prince, which, it said, had exposed 'the creation and exercise of a great power in the State, wholly unrecognized by the Constitution. The Prince is . . . the real Premier, for what Minister . . . would have the moral courage to . . . set at defiance the wishes of the Prince and that, too, in the very presence of the Queen.'[163]

The Tory press, however, accepted the explanations: it had become worried by the way in which the ministry and its journals presented the anti-Albert agitation as a device of the Tory party.[164] The pro-ministerial press had attributed the calumnies to the longstanding antipathy of the Protectionists to the Prince[165] – and the opposition feared that a permanent rift might be created between them and the Queen. *John Bull*, a Tory paper which prided itself on loyalty to the Crown, blamed the ministers for allowing the radical press to originate the slanders against Albert to avert attention from their own errors and for then using Albert's 'name as an offensive weapon of party warfare' – which had 'a direct tendency to lower Royalty in the public eye'.[166] The *Standard* had towards the end of January begun to shift the attack from Albert onto the government, blaming the Prime Minister, Aberdeen, for allowing the Prince's interference and identifying Aberdeen himself as the agent of the Russian alliance.[167]

The crisis of unpopularity had shown that Albert's conception of royal authority and of his active role as consort contradicted general perceptions of the workings of Britain's limited monarchy – and as such was potentially dangerous to the monarchy. Republicans took revelations of Albert's activities as evidence that so-called constitutional monarchy was incompatible with the democratic tendency of the modern age.[168] Chartism had not been republican but the blatant examples of irresponsible personal power that had been brought to light caused the declining movement's organ, the *People's Paper* to remark that 'if there was no queen, there would be no prince ... The prince acts a prince's part, that is, as ever, one hostile to liberty, enlightenment and progress.'[169]

An entirely different view of royal authority and of Albert's activities was taken by the Foreign Affairs Committees of Russophobe Conservative MP David Urquhart. Urquhart, an expert on Near Eastern affairs, had developed a distrust of Russia, which he saw as augmenting its power in the Near East as a base for taking over the entire British Empire and dominating the world. Each nation's government had been impregnated with an agent of Russia's grand design and in Britain this was not Albert but Palmerston. Urquhart's other great preoccupation was the need for the reassertion of executive government in Britain, where the constitution had slid into legislative despotism. Palmerston had further precipitated this slide – and with the aim of subverting British policy in Russia's interests. The Crimean War made it essential to organize agitation for a vigorous prosecution of the war to destroy Russia's plans and for the restoration of the just prerogatives of the Crown, especially after Palmerston's appointment as Prime Minister in 1855. During the War, 145 of Urquhart's Foreign Affairs Committees were formed, mainly in the industrial towns of the North, with the same kind of artisanate membership as Chartism had, albeit on a much smaller and more ephemeral scale.[170]

The *Free Press*, published in Sheffield, was the organ of the Foreign Affairs Committees and expounded Urquhart's constitutional theories. Like other upholders of the royal prerogative, he saw the constitution as having been unbalanced by the shift of power to its legislative branch, which resulted in the dictatorship of the faction which enjoyed a temporary ascendancy in that branch. The cabinet exercised unchecked power, for as its composition was now determined by the majority in the House of Commons there was no parliamentary control over it. The right of the king to choose his ministers had to be reasserted and the Privy Council, now a shadow of its former self, restored as the active body where ministers and other expert councillors called up at specific times would meet under the presidency of the sovereign.[171]

Urquhart correctly identified Albert as one who wanted to restore power to the Crown – but unlike others who divined the Prince's political outlook Urquhart was in agreement with him. Urquhart saw the 1840s and 1850s in terms of a struggle between the Crown and Palmerston for control over foreign policy. The Queen, steeled in her resolution by the Prince, was, he argued, absolutely correct in insisting on her right to see Foreign Office dispatches before they were finally issued. The parliamentary explanations in February 1852 of Palmerston's dismissal in December 1851 had brought to light the Foreign Secretary's failure to send dispatches to the Queen. The Prime Minister, Russell had said that in failing to do so, in his unauthorized reception of the thanks of the pro-Hungarian delegation and, decisively, in his personal approval of Louis Napoleon's 'coup', Palmerston had usurped sovereign authority, 'passing by the Queen, and putting himself in the place of the Crown'. This statement of the Prime Minister's became a staple text of Urquhartism.[172]

Albert, Urquhart maintained, 'had detected that in the course pursued by the leading man in England, there was more than the reasons of State of a truly British minister'. Albert was no friend of Russia and could see Palmerston's treachery to British interests, and the necessity therefore of curbing his power and reasserting executive control.[173] Palmerston accordingly determined to negate Albert and did so by commissioning a pamphlet after his dismissal in 1851 which alluded to a conspiracy of despotic interests against the former Foreign Secretary. Palmerston held the threat of the pamphlet's supposedly dangerous contents over the Queen and Prince and as the price of suppressing it obtained a guarantee of a future recall to the government. Wildly exaggerated reports of the pamphlet's accusations had fuelled the anti-Albert agitation of 1853–4 occasioned by Palmerston's resignation,[174] and the upshot of that press campaign had been the chastening of the Prince from any further attempts to control Palmerston.[175] Urquhart went as far as to allege that Albert's premature death in 1861 from what had seemed to be a common cold was the final step in snuffing out any potential threat to Palmerston's running of the British government in Russia's interests. Russia, he wrote, had been known to murder its enemies. The Queen's grief would be used by *The Times* and other supporters of the Palmerston government as proof that she should abdicate, the heir apparent, whom *The Times* had begun to praise exorbitantly, was young and wholly under Palmerston's influence, and his accession would mark the conclusive reduction of the sovereign of England to a pliant tool of the ministry.[176]

Urquhart's views, particularly those as eccentric as the latter, were very much minority ones: the Foreign Affairs Committees flourished in numbers only briefly in 1855–6 as a product of popular frustration at the misconduct of the Crimean War – and were only to regain any momentum during the next major Eastern crisis in the later 1870s.[177] Commenting on an Urquhart speech in Newcastle in 1854, the *Northern Tribune* wrote that while his interpretation of the Eastern situation was an informed and popular one, his reverence for the royal prerogative was more appropriate to 'a Tory of the times of Anne', as he styled himself, than to the present age.[178] The more widespread reaction to failure in the Crimea was to blame remaining royal influence rather than to call for more. G.B. Henderson detailed Albert's extensive activities in war diplomacy, which 'sometimes exercised considerable influence'. The Prince, he argued, 'was thoroughly British in his outlook, and never allowed family interest or personal prejudice to colour his advice ... In short, under his care the Crown played the part reserved for it under a constitutional monarchy, and played it well.'[179] The public, however, was opposed to his involvement and convinced that he would act in the interest of foreign powers. The *Morning Advertiser* in October 1855 asked why Odessa had been spared by the British and French allies and concluded that Albert's 'pro- Russianism' was at the root of all such pusillanimity. Albert's conduct, the paper alleged, had 'put monarchical institutions on their trial'.[180] This was a paraphrase of Albert's speech at Trinity House earlier in the year in which he said that the war had placed free parliamentary government 'on its trial', as Russia's autocratic government was clearly at an advantage in waging a war: it did not have to suffer parliamentary opposition or press criticism and thus could proceed with much greater secrecy and fixity and unity of purpose. Some commentators, such as the *Spectator*, took the speech to be descriptive rather than prescriptive,[181] but those already hostile to Albert saw it as confirming their worst fears about his plans for the British monarchy. *Reynolds's Newspaper* described the speech as an 'anti-constitutional tirade' and 'a plain and unmistakable intimation that in this country the popular power is too ample and the royal prerogative too restricted'.[182]

Albert's political activities continued to be viewed with suspicion in the final years of his life. C.H. Stuart has described Albert's involvement in the complex ministerial politics of 1856–9 when the shifting parliamentary coalitions gave considerable scope to the Crown in trying to secure its favoured ministry. Stuart's study, like Henderson's of Albert's activities in Crimean War diplomacy, is an 'internal' one and at pains to argue that the Prince's motives were 'just and his purposes constitutional'.[183] The public, however, did not want him, an irresponsible figure, to play any part in their government. In 1859 the *Daily Telegraph*, the new voice of middle-class Liberalism was critical of the court when news leaked out that the Queen had initially sent for Granville instead of Palmerston. It expressed the hope that 'Knights of the Garter are not to be all-in-all in the Administration' and observed that at the Palace ... neither public nor Parliamentary opinion is very distinctly understood'.[184] T. Fontane, in England in 1857, had remarked on the feeling 'against "Germanism"' provoked by the rumours that Albert and Stockmar interfered in politics and that the Queen and Prince imposed conditions when appointing Prime Ministers.[185] The same year, a pamphlet entitled *Prince Albert. Why is he unpopular?* was reissued, having been first published in 1854. A great deal of his unpopularity stemmed, it said, from the belief that he interfered in government – a denial of unconstitutionalism had been made in 1854 but 'no regard [was] paid to it, and the former suspicions of the country remained unaltered'.[186] Popular jealousy with regard to Albert's political influence was such that ministers never acceded to the Queen's request that a bill conferring on him the title Prince Consort be introduced in parliament – and eventually, in 1857, the Queen decided to create him Prince Consort by letters patent.[187] When it was rumoured a year later that he would be made 'King Consort' there was great antipathy to the idea.[188] These rumours marred the wedding celebration of the Princess Royal. A Northampton radical, speaking against the proposed declaration of a public holiday, condemned the idea of such a title, recalling Albert's interference in 1854: he declared, 'I object to Germanism or any other ism which will take away the rights of working-men'.[189]

Conclusion

The view of Albert as the architect of the modern constitutional monarchy owes everything to his notions of royal impartiality and nothing to the broader conception of kingship of which these notions were but a part. One of his biographers, Daphne Bennett, writes that Albert's 'services to the monarchy' were 'to establish the monarchy on a more modern foundation by uniting Crown and nation and setting the throne above party' and to teach Victoria 'that in Britain it is not the monarch who governs but the Cabinet through Parliament'.[190] We have seen that Albert, schooled by Leopold and Stockmar, had as his ideal a powerful monarchy which would control the government. His inclinations were not to set the monarchy 'on a more modern foundation' but to hark back to earlier periods of royal authority. Robert Blake's article on 'The Prince Consort and Queen Victoria's Prime Ministers' is characteristic of the failings of historical interpretations of Albert. The Prince's constant 'nagging' of ministers is alluded to and his statement about the monarch's duty to 'control' the government quoted, with the observation that 'constitutional monarchy as seen by the Prince and the Queen was by no means the same as it became a century later'. But instead the focus is placed on impartial dealings with the leaders of political parties – 'his greatest contribution to the constitutional monarchy which Britain enjoys today'.[191]

The time has come for a complete reappraisal of Albert's contribution to the history of the modern monarchy, and a turning on its head of Blake's statement that 'If . . . the history of the British Crown has been one of the great success stories of the last hundred years, and if it remains one of the few institutions which have not in recent times come under serious as opposed to merely frivolous or spiteful criticism, the Prince Consort deserves a substantial share of the credit'.[192] The monarchy developed into a popular institution above politics in spite of and not because of Albert, who was responsible for much of the 'serious criticism' levelled at the Crown's political influence in this period and after his death. Far from being the architect of the modern monarchy, he had failed in his grand design of restructuring a powerful monarchy, while the personal political role he envisaged and tried to enact as consort had brought upon him suspicion and a welter of abuse, particularly in 1853–4. An assumption of much of the criticism of the Queen's abnegation of her ceremonial duties after Albert's death was that such duties were the only ones left to Britain's limited monarchy.[193] Albert's role as *paterfamilias* to the large Royal Family and as an indefatigable performer of public duties and patron of good causes set the tone for the future of the monarchy, as a domestic and philanthropic body,[194] far more than did his high-flown theories of royal authority. Politically, his legacy was ambivalent: he had helped to set the Crown above party but this had been merely a prerequisite of his constitutional scheme, and the full revelation of this scheme, in his biography in the 1870s, was to contribute to another major controversy over the Crown's political role. His death in 1861 eased the Crown's accommodation to the tendency towards democracy and the supremacy of parliament.

Notes

1. *Republican*, vol. 10 (April 1884), p. 4.
2. See Norman Gash on 'The End of the Hanoverian Monarchy', pp. 1–25 in *Reaction and Reconstruction in English Politics, 1832–1851* (London, 1965). The view of Albert as the architect of the modern constitutional monarchy is a common one among royal biographers – for example, Cecil Woodham-Smith, *Queen Victoria. Her Life and Times* (London, 1984 edn), pp. 199–200; Frank Eyck, *The Prince Consort. A Political*

Biography (Bath, 1975 edn), pp. 20–30, 40, 253–5; Hermoine Hobhouse, *Prince Albert: His Life and Work* (London, 1983), pp. 34–5. Of recent biographers, only Robert Rhodes James, *Albert, Prince Consort. A Biography* (London, 1983), p. 167, appreciates that 'Albert's dominant purpose was not to reduce but significantly to *increase* the real power and influence of the Monarch'. However, like Roger Fulford, who also acknowledges this in *The Prince Consort*, (London, 1949), pp. 57–8, 114, 133, 165–6, Rhodes James does not draw its full implications.

3. *Republican*, vol. 10 (April 1884), p. 4. Frank Hardie, *The Political Influence of Queen Victoria 1861–1901* (Oxford, 1935) argues that royal influence actually increased in the second half of the reign, as Victoria meddled more and more in politics. However, this interference was not generally perceived, partly because its effects were limited and never resulted in a head-on collision with parliament; and partly because Gladstone never made public his difficulties with the sovereign. Hardie in fact overestimates royal influence by conflating it with royal activity – the result of his absorption in the Queen's massive correspondence with her ministers. For a more accurate account of the extent of the Queen's effect on the workings of government see John P. MacKintosh, *The British Cabinet* (London, 1962), p. 111–28, 222–45, and John Cannon, *The Modern British Monarchy; a Study in Adaptation. The Stenton Lecture 1986* (Reading, 1987), pp. 12–13.

4. Gash, *Reaction and Reconstruction*, pp. 22–9.

5. Benjamin Disraeli, *Vindication of the English Constitution. In a Letter to a Noble and Learned Lord* (London, 1835), pp. 3–11, 167–99; idem, *Coningsby* (1st pub. 1844, Oxford, 1982 edn), pp. 31, 20–8, 232, 310–3, 323–4; *Sybil* (1st pub. 1845; London, 1980 edn), p. 38, 63–4.

6. Idem, *Vindication of the English Constitution*, p. 173.

7. Linda Colley, 'The Apotheosis of George III: Loyalty, Royalty and the British Nation 1760–1820', *Past and Present* no. 102 (1984), p. 102 points out that the King's career as figurehead of the nation could only begin after his political interference had ceased.

8. G.H.L. Le May, *The Victorian Constitution. Conventions, Usages and Contingencies* (London, 1979), p. 29.

9. Gash, *Reaction and Reconstruction*, p. 5.

10. Hardie, *The Political Influence of Queen Victoria*, p. 7.

11. See Gash, *Reaction and Reconstruction*, pp. 16, 19.

12. *Westminster Review*, vol. 27 (July 1837), p. 296.

13. *The Patriot Queen. To Her Most Gracious Majesty* Queen Victoria, The Humble Tribute of An Octogenarian. (London, 1838), pp. 5, 15–17, 20–5, 29, 50–4, 71–2, 78–81.

14. For example John Ashton, *Modern Street Ballads* (London, 1888), p. 271; *Sun*, 28 June 1838, p. 1.

15. *Westminster Review*, vol. 27 (July 1837), p. 246.

16. Disraeli, *Sybil*, pp. 40-1.

17. Brougham deplored the Queen's manifest favouritism in *Letter to the Queen on the State of the Monarchy. By a Friend of the People* (London, 1838), p. 13–22.

18. *The Times*, 15 June 1837, p. 15; 17 June 1837, p. 5; 20 June 1837, p. 4.

19. *Examiner*, 25 June 1837, p. 401.

20. *Quarterly Review*, vol. 59 (July 1837), p. 246.

21. *Westminster Review*, vol. 27 (July 1837), p. 246.
22. *The Times*, 17 October 1837, p. 2.
23. This interpretation was attacked in the Tory *Standard* 21 June, p. 2, cols 2–3.
24. *The Times*, 26 June 1838, p. 5; 29 June 1839, p. 7.
25. *The Patriot Queen*, pp. 78–9.
26. *The Times*, 21 May 1839, p. 4.
27. *Quarterly Review*, vol. 59 (July 1837), p. 246
28. In fact started by the Queen and her closest friend, Baroness Lehzen.
29. For the Lady Flora affair, see Woodham-Smith, *Queen Victoria*, pp. 164–80 and Elizabeth Longford, *Victoria R.I.* (London, 1983 edn.), pp. 117–31, 150–4. Lady Flora was suffering from a tumour on the liver, from which she died in July 1839. The Queen was hissed at Ascot and stones were thrown at the carriage that she sent to the funeral, one man in the crowd crying, 'What is the good of her gilded trumpery after she had killed her?'
30. *Morning Post*, 11 May 1839, p. 4.
31. *Morning Herald*, 11 May 1839, p. 2.
32. *Sunday Times*, 19 May 1839, p. 4.
33. *Morning Chronicle*, 13 May 1839, p. 2.
34. *Leeds Mercury*, 18 May 1839, p. 4.
35. *Standard*, 21 May 1839, p. 2; 23 May 1839, p. 2; 12 May 1839, p. 2.
36. Who declared in the Commons that 'no one could have expressed principles more strictly constitutional with respect to the formation of a new government ... than her majesty did on this occasion'. [A.C. Benson and Viscount Esher eds, *The Letters of Queen Victoria*, (1st ser. 3 vols, London, 1907), vol. 1, pp. 337–8; *Hansard*, vol. 48, col. 984.]
37. *Morning Herald*, 11 May 1839, p. 2; *Standard*, 13 May 1839, p. 2; *The Times*, 13 May 1839, p. 4.
38. Charles C.F. Greville, *The Greville Memoirs*, (ed. Henry Reeve, 8 vols, London 1888 edn, vol. 4, p. 215.
39. *The Times*, 13 May 1839, p. 5; *Morning Post*, 14 May 1839, p. 4, *Morning Herald*, 16 May 1839, p. 4; *Standard*, 13 May 1839, p. 2.
40. *The Times*, 18 May 1839, p. 4.
41. *Morning Herald*, 16 May 1839, p. 4; *The Times*, 13 May 1839, p. 4.
42. Quoted in the *Globe*, 17 May 1839, p. 2.
43. *Morning Chronicle*, 11 May 1839, p. 2.
44. *Morning Herald*, 13 May 1839, p. 2.
45. *The Times*, 11 May 1839, p. 4.
46. *Spectator*, 18 May 1839, pp. 453–4.
47. *Hansard*, vol. 48, cols 1164–86.
48. Victoria's letters show her to be quite distraught at the prospect of losing the ministry, and, at the first sign of conflict with Peel over the household, she wrote excitedly to Melbourne, 'Keep yourself in readiness, for you may soon be wanted'. [Benson and Esher eds, *The Letters of Queen Victoria*, (1st. ser.), vol. 1, pp. 204–5.]
49. *Letter to the Queen on the State of the Monarchy*, pp. 6, 20.
50. *Hansard*, vol. 48, cols 1164–86.
51. *A Letter to the Queen*. By A Councillor of the Crown (London, 1839), pp. 17–19, 21, 28–30.
52. *Spectator*, 24 June 1837, p. 577.

53. Ibid., 18 May 1839, p. 454.
54. *Globe*, 11 May 1839, p. 2.
55. *The Greville Memoirs*, vol. 4, p. 221.
56. *The Times*, 13 May 1839, p. 4.
57. *Berrow's Worcester Journal*, 16 May 1839, p. 3.
58. Quoted in the *Morning Chronicle*, 18 May 1839, p. 2.
59. *Northampton Mercury*, 18 May 1839, p. 3.
60. *Globe*, 20 May 1839, p. 2; 15 May 1839, p. 3.
61. Ibid., 18 May 1839, p. 2; *Examiner*, 26 May 1839, pp. 321–2.
62. *Northern Star*, 18 May 1839, p. 4.
63. Gash, *Reaction and Reconstruction*, p. 24.
64. *The Greville Memoirs*, vol. 4, pp. 216–18.
65. See below.
66. *Spectator*, 11 January 1840, p. 35.
67. *Standard*, 11 February 1840, p. 4.
68. *Morning Herald*, 25 November 1839, p. 2.
69. *Globe*, 26 November 1839, p. 2.
70. *The Times*, 25 November 1839, p. 4, dismissed such rumours and referred to orators such as Gregg as 'wine-warmed individuals' unrepresentative of the Conservative party.
71. *Leeds Mercury*, 15 February 1840, p. 3.
72. *Morning Herald*, 25 November 1839, p. 2.
73. *The Times*, 25 November 1839, p. 4; 27 November 1839, p. 2; 30 November 1839, p. 4.
74. *Hansard*, vol. 51, cols 11–42.
75. Ibid., vol. 51, cols 583–633.
76. *Morning Chronicle*, 12 February 1840, p. 6.
77. *The Times*, 27 January 1840, p. 4.
78. Ibid., 8 February 1840, p. 5.
79. *Morning Post*, 10 February 1840, p. 4; *The Times*, 11 February 1840, p. 4.
80. *Spectator*, 15 February 1840, p. 145.
81. *Morning Post*, 28 January 1840, p. 4.
82. *The Times*, 10 February 1840, p. 4.
83. *Hansard*, vol. 51, cols 1103–4. The letters exchanged between Victoria and Albert on this topic show the Prince to be anxious to have a mixed household of Whigs and Tories, while Victoria insisted, on Melbourne's instructions, that his establishment conform with hers. [Benson and Esher eds, *The Letters of Queen Victoria*, (1st ser.), vol. 1, pp. 252–6; K. Jagow ed., *Letters of the Prince Consort 1831–1861* (London, 1938), pp. 31–49.]
84. The Duke of Buckingham and Chandos, *Memoirs of the Courts and Cabinets of William IV and Victoria*, 2 vols (London, 1861), vol. 2, p. 402.
85. *The Times*, 14 December 1861, p. 6.
86. Theodore Martin, *The Life of His Royal Highness The Prince Consort*, 6 vols (London, 1875–87), vol. 1, p. 105.
87. Eyck, *The Prince Consort*, pp. 253–55.
88. Rhodes James, *Albert, Prince Consort*, p. 167.
89. Ibid., p. 167.
90. Jagow, ed., *Letters of the Prince Consort*, pp. 36–8.

91. *The Times*, 16 August 1841, p. 4.
92. *Morning Chronicle*, 28 August 1841, p. 4.
93. *Hansard*, vol. 165, col. 44.
94. Benson and Esher eds, *The Letters of Queen Victoria*, (1st ser.), vol. 1, pp. 337–46, 358–9, 379–90.
95. *The Times*, 31 August 1841, p. 4; 2 September 1841, p. 5.
96. *Spectator*, 29 April 1843, p. 385.
97. Norman Gash, *Politics in the Age of Peel* (2nd edn, London, 1961), p. 382; *The Times*, 1 July 1841, p. 5.
98. *Examiner*, 4 February 1854, p. 66, *Observations on the Character and Conduct of the Prince Consort* (London, 1854), p. 41
99. *Illustrated London News*, 23 January 1858, p. 73.
100. *Leeds Mercury*, 4 September 1858, p. 4.
101. *The Times*, 16 December 1861, p. 8, *Hansard*, vol. 165, col. 44.
102. W.E. Monypenny and G.E. Buckle, *The Life of Benjamin Disraeli, Earl of Beaconsfield*, 6 vols, (London, 1910–20), vol. 2, p. 117.
103. Longford, *Victoria R.I.*, p. 381.
104. John Vincent, ed., *Derby, Disraeli and the Conservative Party. Journals and Memoirs of Edward Henry, Lord Stanley 1849–1869* (Sussex, 1978), pp. 179–86.
105. M. Brett, ed. *Journals and Letters of Viscount Esher* (2 vols, 1934), vol. 2, p. 99.
106. Rhodes James, *Albert, Prince Consort*, pp. xii–xiii.
107. Ibid., p. 156.
108. Ibid., pp. 221–4.
109. Fulford, *The Prince Consort*, pp. 114, 165–6, 237–9. Frank Hardie makes a fleeting 'fanciful . . . speculation', based on Disraeli's comment, in the prelude to his study of the period after 1861 (Hardie, *The Political Influence of Queen Victoria*, pp. 18–19). Vernon Bogdanor, *The Monarchy and the Constitution* (Oxford, 1995), pp. 25–7 recognizes the dangers of Albert's views, but does not mention the furore his actions actually caused.
110. *Morning Chronicle*, 26 January 1858, p. 4.
111. *Sunday Times*, 24 November 1839, p. 4.
112. Gash, *Reaction and Reconstruction*, p. 28
113. *The Patriot Queen* pp. 80-1.
114. Disraeli, *Sybil*, p. 497.
115. Idem, *Coningsby*, p. 313.
116. Rhodes James, *Albert, Prince Consort*, pp. 104–5.
117. Martin, *The Life of The Prince Consort*, vol. 1, pp. 546–9.
118. Joanna Richardson, *My Dearest Uncle. A Life of Leopold, First King of the Belgians* (London, 1961), pp. 134–5.
119. Robert Blake, 'The Prince Consort and Queen Victoria's Prime Ministers' in John A.S. Phillips ed., *Prince Albert and the Victorian Age* (Cambridge, 1981), p. 31.
120. Benson and Esher eds, *The Letters of Queen Victoria*, (1st ser.), vol. 1, p. 134.
121. Martin, *The Life of the Prince Consort*, vol. 1, pp. 546–53.
122. Ibid., p. 558.
123. Brian Connell, *Regina v. Palmerston. The Correspondence Between Queen*

Victoria and Her Foreign and Prime Minister 1837–1865 (London, 1962), pp. 120–1.

124. Eyck, *The Prince Consort*, p. 253.
125. *The Times*, 17 March 1842, p. 4.
126. *London Pioneer*, vol. 1, no. 1 (30 April 1846), p. 1.
127. *English Republic*, vol. 1 (1851), pp. 355–8.
128. Jagow ed., *Letters of the Prince Consort*, pp. 72–3.
129. *Hansard*, vol. 84, col. 348.
130. Jagow ed., *Letters of the Prince Consort*, pp. 203–8; *John Bull*, no. 1586 (3 May 1851), p. 280, cols 1–2; *Morning Herald*, 1 May 1851, p. 4.
131. Rhodes James, *Albert, Prince Consort*, pp. 150-2. Victoria was in fact as distraught at losing Peel in 1846 as she had been on Melbourne's resignation in 1841. [Benson and Esher eds., *The Letters of Queen Victoria*, (1st ser.), vol. 1, pp. 75, 100–1.]
132. Jagow ed., *Letters of the Prince Consort*, pp. 156–8.
133. *Contemporary Review*, vol. 26 (June 1875), p. 9.
134. A reading of Albert's letters and of Martin's biography shows how active Albert was in keeping up a constant correspondence with ministers and drafting memoranda on political issues.
135. Vincent ed., *Derby, Disraeli and the Conservative Party*, pp. 179–81.
136. Jagow ed., *Letters of the Prince Consort*, pp. 203–8.
137. *Morning Herald*, 4 January 1854, p. 4.
138. *Sunday Times*, 8 January 1854, p. 4; cf. *Daily News*, 21 December 1853, p. 4.
139. For example, *Punch*, vol. 25 (1853), pp. 216–17.
140. *Reynolds's Newspaper*, 22 January 1854, p. 9.
141. For the strong anti-German element in the press campaign, see chapter 6.
142. Connell, *Regina v. Palmerston*, pp. 1–134 passim.
143. Ibid., p. 133–4.
144. For the background to the events of 1853–54 see Kingsley Martin, *The Triumph of Lord Palmerston* (London, 1963 edn) and Jasper Ridley, *Lord Palmerston* (London, 1970), pp. 395–7.
145. *Sunday Times*, 4 January 1852, p. 4.
146. *Northern Star*, 7 February 1852, p. 4.
147. *Morning Advertiser*, 19 December 1853, p. 4; 20 December 1853, p. 2; 4 January 1854, p. 4.
148. *Morning Herald*, 3 January 1854, p. 4.
149. *Standard*, 15 January 1854, p. 2 cols 1–2. Among the wilder reports in popular broadsheets was the news that Albert (some also stated the Queen) had been taken captive to the Tower. [Ashton, *Modern Street Ballads*, pp. 294–7.]
150. *Daily News*, 17 December 1853, p. 5; 21 December 1853, p. 4.
151. Ibid., 11 January 1854, p. 4.
152. *Morning Advertiser*, 20 December 1853, p. 2; 24 December 1853, p. 4.
153. Ibid., 22 December 1853, p. 4; 28 December 1853, p. 4.
154. *Morning Herald*, 14 January 1854, p. 4.
155. *The Times*, 18 January 1854, p. 8; *Globe*, 20 January 1854, p. 2; *Morning Chronicle* 16 January 1854, p. 4.
156. *Hansard*, vol. 130, cols 95–108, 182–91.

157. *The Times*, 18 January 1854, p. 8.
158. *Hansard*, vol. 130, cols 95–108, 182–91.
159. *Examiner*, 4 February 1854, p. 66.
160. *Standard*, 14 January 1854, p. 2.
161. *Spectator*, 4 February 1854, p. 124.
162. *Daily News*, 2 February 1854, p. 124.
163. *Morning Advertiser*, 2 February 1854, p. 4.
164. *Standard*, 1 February 1854, p. 7; *Morning Herald*, 2 February 1854, p. 4; *Hansard*, vol. 130, cols 95–108.
165. *Morning Chronicle*, 19 January 1854, p. 4.
166. *John Bull*, 21 January 1854, p. 40.
167. *Standard*, 18 January 1854, p. 2.
168. *English Republic*, vol. 3 (1854), p. 77; *Northern Tribune*, vol. 1, no. 3 (1854), pp. 42–3.
169. *People's Paper*, 21 January 1854, p. 5.
170. For Urquhart's early career, see Charles Webster, 'Urquhart, Ponsonby, and Palmerston', *English Historical Review*, vol. 62 (1947), pp. 327–51. For Urquhartism as a popular movement in the mid-1850s, see Richard Shannon, 'David Urquhart and the Foreign Affairs Committees' in Patricia Hollis ed., *Pressure from Without in early Victorian England* (London, 1974), pp. 239–61; Asa Briggs, 'David Urquhart and the West Riding Foreign Affairs Committee', *The Bradford Antiquary*, vol. 8 (1962), pp. 197–207; John Salt, 'Local Manifestations of the Urquhartite Movement', *International Review of Social History,* vol. 13 (1968), pp. 350–65; and Miles Taylor in Eugenio Biagini and Alastair Reid eds, *Currents of Radicalism: Popular Radicalism, Organized Labour and Party Politics in Britain, 1850–1914* (Cambridge, 1991).
171. *Free Press*, 3 November 1855, p. 1; 15 December 1855, p. 1; 9 February 1857, p. 202; 29 June 1859, pp. 61–3.
172. Ibid., 3 November 1855, p. 1; 24 November 1855, p. 1.
173. Ibid., 3 November 1855, p. 1.
174. Ibid., 24 November 1855, p. 1.
175. David Urquhart, *The Queen and the Premier. A Statement of their Struggles and its Results* (London, 1857), pp. 8–9.
176. *Free Press*, 1 January 1862, pp. 12–14.
177. Shannon, 'David Urquhart and the Foreign Affairs Committees', pp. 251–9.
178. *Northern Tribune*, vol. 1 (1854), no. 11, p. 389–92.
179. G.B. Henderson, 'The Influence of the Crown, 1854–1856', in idem, *Crimean War Diplomacy and Other Historical Essays* (Glasgow, 1947), pp. 68–97.
180. *Morning Advertiser*, 22 October 1855, p. 4.
181. *Spectator*, 16 June 1855, p. 616 cols 1–2.
182. *Reynolds's Newspaper*, 17 June 1855, pp. 8–9.
183. C.H. Stuart, 'The Prince Consort and Ministerial Politics 1856–9' in H.R. Trevor-Roper ed., *Essays in British History Presented to Sir Keith Feiling* (London, 1964), pp. 247–69.
184. *Daily Telegraph*, 13 June 1859, p. 4; 14 June 1859, p. 4.
185. T. Fontane, *Journeys to England in Victoria's Early Days, 1844–1859* (transl. Dorothy Harrison, London, 1939), p. 125.

186. *Prince Albert. Why is he Unpopular?* By F. Airplay, Esq. (2nd edn, London, 1857), pp. 58–9.
187. Connell, *Regina v. Palmerston*, pp. 238–50.
188. *Spectator*, 23 January 1858, p. 90.
189. *People's Paper*, 30 January 1858, p. 1.
190. Daphne Bennett, *King Without a Crown, Albert, Prince Consort of England 1819–1861* (London, 1977), pp. 377–8.
191. Blake, 'The Prince Consort and Queen Victoria's Prime Ministers', pp. 48–9.
192. Ibid., p. 49.
193. See below, chapter 5.
194. See below, chapter 7.

CHAPTER FIVE

Perceptions of Political Power and Partisanship, 1861–1901

We have seen that in the first twenty-five years of the Queen's reign contemporary opinion favoured a non-partisan monarchy which exercised little effective political power. Albert had directed Victoria away from the overt partisanship of her early years but his ambitious plans for the Crown's part in government and for his part as consort had embroiled the monarchy in political controversy, especially in 1853–4. His death must be seen as one of the factors operating gradually to remove the Crown from the realms of political contention.

There was, of course, a gulf between perception and reality: the Queen remained an ardent partisan – her hatred of Gladstone and infatuation with Disraeli were equally obsessive – and she continued to interfere unremittingly behind the scenes – but her virtual retirement from London in her widowhood made her seem very distant from the seat of power. Furthermore, the Reform Acts of 1867 and 1884 and the solidification of two cohesive political parties in place of the shifting coalitions of the earlier period made royal diversion of the course of parliamentary politics far more difficult – and far more hazardous; and the Queen, for all her party prejudices and belief in her right to participate in government, never induced a head-on collision with the now supreme popular branch of the constitution. Commentators were therefore inclined to praise the Queen's non-partisanship and constitutionalism. The dictums of Walter Bagehot on the monarchy in his essays on the English constitution written between 1865 and 1867 have subsequently acquired an authoritative status and Bagehot has been depicted as the prophet descending from the mountain with the tablets of modern constitutional kingship. In fact Bagehot was only one of many commentators remarking, albeit more apothegematically and in a more theoretical context, on the relegation of the monarchy to what he called a 'dignified' role. It was a commonplace that the Crown's political functions were now severely circumscribed and that its chief 'raison d'être' lay in its ceremonial ones.

However, the reality of the Queen's backstage activities sometimes intruded upon public perceptions – as, for example, in the Schleswig-Holstein crisis of 1864. Moreover, the survival in theory if not in common practice of the Crown's considerable prerogative power left room for controversy over this. Gladstone's use of the prerogative in 1871 to enact the Army Bill anticipated Disraeli's frequent recourse to it in his ministry of 1874–80. The printed (and subsequently reiterated) views of Disraeli on royal authority in his early novels gave rise to a serious debate on whether he was now attempting to resurrect government by royal prerogative – a debate intensified by the concurrent publication of the second and third volumes of Theodore Martin's biography of Albert detailing the Prince's minute involvement in politics and containing Stockmar's high-flown theories, endorsed by the Prince, of kingly rule. The debate revealed notions of an Urquhartite kind on the royal prerogative within the Conservative party.

The chapter first examines the years 1861–75 setting Bagehot's observations in the context of general assumptions about the monarch's role. The next section on 1876–9 draws attention to an entirely neglected episode in constitutional history and in Disraeli's relations with the Queen – the serious controversy provoked by the Royal Titles Act of 1876 and the subsequent use of the royal prerogative, which, taken together, were seen as a conscious attempt to exalt the power of the Crown and derogate parliamentary government, replacing it with a form of Caesarism as had been exemplified in France by Napoleon III. The employment of the middle volumes of Albert's biography as additional evidence that parliamentary government was under royal threat casts further light on how contemporaries distrusted the Prince's constitutional position. Next, we see how in the years 1880–7, with Disraeli departed from the scene, the impact of the biography of the Prince Consort receding and the triumph of democracy ensured by the third Reform Act, the Queen, for all her Tory bias and desperate intriguing to keep Gladstone and the Home Rulers out of office in 1885–6, at last attained a status above party and above politics. Finally the section on 1887–1901 shows how there was an increasing awareness of Victoria's partisanship but no widely-held fears that it could be used to subvert the course of parliamentary politics, though some Conservative claims about her political role did cause certain constitutional misgivings among Liberals and socialists.

1861–75: 'a beneficial substitution of influence for power'

In his review of the first volume of Theodore Martin's biography of Albert in 1875, Gladstone wrote:

> The weighty business of kingship has in modern times been undergoing a subtle and a silent, yet an almost entire transformation; and in this country at least the process has reached its maturity . . .

its substance may be perceived mainly in a beneficial substitution of influence for power.[1]

In the fifteen years following Albert's death, though the Queen continued assiduously to read cabinet memoranda and correspond with her ministers, her impact on the course of politics was perceived to be considerably lessened and her retirement to Osborne and Balmoral distanced her in the public mind from the ostensible workings of government. Throughout the 1860s commentators, among whom Bagehot was one, stressed the way in which the Crown had risen above party and abjured unconstitutional meddling in government, and one of the principal counters to the republican movement of the early 1870s was that full self-government already existed under Britain's limited monarchy. At the same time it must be noted that the precise definition of the Crown's political role was still an issue of debate. Not only the Urquhartites regretted that the Queen's retirement was detrimental to royal power. In this, in the criticism of possible royal interference with the handling of the Schleswig-Holstein crisis of 1864, in the use of the royal prerogative to enact the Army Bill in 1871 and in Disraeli's extolling of the Queen's political involvement in his 1871 speeches may be discerned the seeds of the controversy over the royal prerogative that was to break out in the late 1870s.

Erskine May's *Constitutional History of England*, published in 1861, depicted the triumph of parliamentary government and praised the Queen for her judicious, constitutional conduct. May wrote that William IV's failure to replace the Whig with a Tory ministry in 1834–5 was 'an instructive illustration of the effects of the Reform Act, in diminishing the ascendant influence of the Crown'. Victoria had erred once through false advice in the Bedchamber crisis, but 'Her Majesty was now sensible that the position she had once been advised to assert, was constitutionally untenable'. The only other constitutional controversy of her reign had been the circumstances surrounding the dismissal of Palmerston in 1851, when she was correct in asserting the right of the sovereign to be consulted and kept informed by ministers: 'From this time no question has arisen concerning the exercise of the prerogatives or influence of the Crown, which calls for notice. Both have been exercised wisely, justly, and in the true spirit of the constitution.'[2]

Royal celebrations of the early 1860s occasioned consensual reflections on the popularity won by the impartiality and constitutional conduct of the Queen. The *Saturday Review*, on the marriage of Princess Alice in 1862, wrote that 'the social supremacy of the Crown has only been confirmed and increased by the gradual transference of direct political power to Parliament and its nominees'.[3] The wedding of the Prince of Wales the following year augmented such observations. The

Daily Telegraph wrote, 'Shorn of a dangerous political power, the Throne in our days has assumed a new supremacy, and stands paramount over the moral state'.[4] The *Examiner* and *Sunday Times* both hailed Victoria as the first truly constitutional monarch, saying that, through her, the Crown had become a guarantee of, rather than a threat to, the liberty of which Englishmen were so proud.[5] *The Times* felt that the standing of the monarchy was inextricably linked with the great political reforms of the foregoing forty years: it was no longer at the head of the inequitable, corrupt old system but of a free and just polity.[6]

The Queen's widowed seclusion was seen to be further reducing the sovereign's political power. *The Times* argued that this was unbalancing the constitution.[7] The Queen's residence in Osborne or Balmoral made it difficult for ministers to consult her and to keep her informed of government business – and this was highlighted by the ministerial crisis of June 1866 when Russell had to travel to the Highlands to inform the Queen of his government's resignation.[8] The Queen's Private Secretary, Henry Ponsonby, observed, 'Ministers are getting rapidly reconciled to keeping her well away and in point of fact enjoy the outward appearance of having all the power in their own hands' – in 1873 the Secretary for War, Cardwell, infuriated the Queen by offering his personal congratulations to the troops instead of speaking on her behalf.[9] The Queen opened parliament in person on only three occasions in this period and the costly 'robes on the empty chair' was an important symbol of republican propaganda.[10] Frederic Harrison indeed argued that a republic was necessary for a re-assertion of executive authority: 'It was not given to forsee that the day would come when the monarchy would neither reign nor govern'.[11]

It was, however, recognized by some observers that the monarch's political role could still be an extensive one. Alpheus Todd, a conservative Canadian constitutionalist, produced his major work *On Parliamentary Government in England* in 1866 and stated in its preface, '. . . while I have elsewhere claimed for the popular element in our constitution its legitimate weight and influence, I have here sought to vindicate for the monarchical element its appropriate sphere . . . any political system which is based upon the monarchical principle must concede to the chief ruler something more than ceremonial functions'. While acknowledging the doctrine of royal impersonality – that the Crown can act only through ministers responsible to parliament – as the cornerstone of Britain's constitutional monarchy, Todd asserted that this doctrine

> only extends to direct acts of government. The sovereign retains full discretionary powers for deliberating and determining upon every recommendation which is tendered for the royal sanction by

ministers of the Crown and, as every important act of administration must be submitted for the approval of the Crown, the sovereign . . . is enabled to exercise an active and intelligent control over the government of the country.[12]

The Times too insisted that the Crown was not a mere ornament but an essential working part of the constitution. In an analysis more perceptive and realistic than most of the contemporary panegyrics to Victoria's constitutional practice and impartiality, it commented, '. . . nobody will deny to it [her reign] . . . a distinctive personal character, with Royal influences and a political tendency of its own, rendering Victoria, as much as Mary, Elizabeth or Anne, the object of partial regards, and, for all time to come, the subject of personal and even political criticism'.[13] *The Times* believed that 'the great mass of the nation' desired that the sovereign 'should even in political affairs use an individual judgement and discretion apart from the counsels of any set of politicians'.[14] It assumed that Victoria's successors would exercise an influence 'still most deeply felt in several departments of government'.

Above all in foreign affairs, *The Times* argued, the monarch's opinion would prevail 'over any that is not strongly proclaimed by the popular voice',[15] and in 1864 it was alleged that the Queen's pro-German sympathies had led her into unconstitutional interference to prevent the government from coming to the assistance of Denmark in the conflict with Prussia and Austria over the duchies of Schleswig-Holstein. The *London Review* wrote that the Queen had been moved 'by family feeling . . . to the exercise of forbidden powers', and was thus subjecting 'the principle of monarchical government' to 'the shock of confessed divergence between the monarch's and the nation's desires'.[16] Lord Ellenborough raised the matter in parliament, only to be assured by the Foreign Secretary, Russell, that 'there had been no one occasion on which . . . Her Majesty had not wholly followed their [the ministry's] counsels and adopted the Resolutions to which they had come'.[17]

Unsurprisingly the Queen was championed during the Schleswig-Holstein crisis by the Urquhartites who depicted her as heroically standing up for her constitutional rights.[18] Urquhart was however treading a lonely path. His divergence from popular opinion was illustrated by his condemnation of the reform agitation in September 1866: he urged the working class to avoid the corruption attendant on the franchise and present parliamentary government and to follow the example of their brethren in the Foreign Affairs Committees in the study of foreign affairs and the royal prerogative.[19] This singularity of Urquhartism was also demonstrated in the correspondence of 'a working man' – a member of a Foreign Affairs Committee – and the radical MP Dixon. Urged by his correspondent to press for the restoration of the Privy Council to its former powers, Dixon replied that progressive men such as himself looked for good government to 'the House of Commons – the elected representatives of the people' and not to the virtually obsolete Privy Council which was 'practically irresponsible to the people'.[20]

Even Urquhartites had to admit that they had seen the 'government of the Queen superseded by the government of the House of Commons'[21] and that 'the Crown has surrendered power and functions, and has avowedly become a Pageant'.[22] Todd acknowledged that since the 1832 Reform Act the Commons had been predominant, that most people saw the Crown as 'little more than an ornamental appendage to the state' and it would indeed be reduced to this if there were a further Reform Act (to which he was opposed).[23] *The Times*, in regretting Victoria's apparent withdrawal from government, warned, 'No reigning House can afford to confirm in its views those who suggest that the Throne is only an antiquarian relic and Royalty itself a ceremony'[24] but by the end of the 1860s it too was acknowledging that the future of the monarchy lay in its ceremonial and not in its political functions: 'Whatever may be said as to the political power of the Crown, there can be no doubt that even in these days the Sovereign has almost unlimited opportunities of . . . ennobling public occasions, and brightening the general aspect of things'.[25]

It is within this context that Bagehot's writings on the monarchy must be located. His articles in the *Fortnightly Review* between 1865 and 1867 were published as *The English Constitution* in 1867 and in a second edition in 1872. The work was quickly to gain an authoritative status – as is shown by Courtney's quoting from it as though it were constitutional law in the 1879 Commons debate on the royal prerogative.[26] This has led to an exaggeration of the originality of Bagehot's conception of the monarchy: Norman St.John-Stevas has written that Bagehot's 'most signal contribution to the lore of the Constitution was his formulation of the rights of a constitutional sovereign' – Bagehot was 'laying down the pattern of monarchy for the future'.[27] What Bagehot did was nothing more nor nothing less than to crystallize contemporary thinking on the monarchy. He observed a diminution in royal power, felt that this was desirable and that the monarchy's role henceforth would lie predominantly in its ceremonial duties. At the same time he saw the ambiguous areas of royal prerogative, in practice obsolete but in theory still extant. Bagehot was one of several journalists making this case – but his commentary was in the form of a work on the constitution and as such and through its succinct dictums it has come to stand as the integral constitutional text on the mid-Victorian monarchy.

Bagehot coined the terms 'dignified' and 'efficient' to describe the commonly observed division between the symbolic and effective parts of the constitution. This was a standard distinction of rational, Benthamite radicalism – the *Spectator* in 1840 likened the monarchy's part in the political system to that of the rites prescribed to be performed when drinking from a health-giving spring, merely incidental and symbolic and not producing the beneficial effect of cure or good government.[28] The pointless 'mummery' of the monarchy had long been a criticism made by radicals and republicans;[29] while the assumption of most loyal and republican critics of the Queen's retirement in the 1860s was that her visible ceremonial role was the only important one left to her. This was the background to Bagehot's assertion that the Crown was ceasing to be an 'efficient' and becoming a purely 'dignified' component, its roles as ceremonial and moral cynosure considerably enhanced as it became a symbol of unity and reverence above party and politics – the ostensible neutrality of the Crown, as we have seen, had been an object of praise since the early 1840s. Bagehot encapsulated prevalent opinion when he wrote, 'The nation is divided into parties, but the Crown is of no party ... We must not bring the Queen into the combat of politics or she will cease to be revered.' The ideal constitutional monarch was a 'thoroughly intelligent but perfectly disinterested spectator' who exercised only 'three rights – the right to be consulted, the right to encourage, the right to warn' – his 'greatest wisdom' lay in 'well-considered inaction'.

Bagehot's opinion of Victoria's constitutional practice reflected the contemporary view of her as non-partisan and discrete in her involvement in government – together with the contemporary awareness of the royal powers remaining in potential and of the influence that Albert had wielded. Having described the ideal monarch, Bagehot reflected that in the present reign 'the duties of a constitutional sovereign' had been 'well performed' for the first time in English history'.[30] He noted that 'under our present Constitution, a monarch like George III with high abilities would possess the greatest influence. It is known to every one conversant with the real course of the recent history of England, that Prince Albert did gain great power in precisely the same way'.[31] There remained to the Crown 'a hundred ... powers which waver between reality and desuetude'.[32] In his preface to the second edition he noted how the use of the prerogative to enact the Army Bill obstructed by the Lords had demonstrated the persistence of prerogative rights. Yet a frequent or comprehensive re-assertion of the prerogative was out of the question.[33]

Bagehot has been criticized for underestimating the role Victoria played[34] or by the same token praised for 'laying down' a better model for future monarchs.[35] His work has accordingly been seen as falsely descriptive or brilliantly prescriptive. How it was a mixture of description and prescription can be seen only by locating it within the contemporary perception of the monarchy as essentially and ideally neutral and increasingly limited. Ironically, Bagehot felt that the British people had an exaggerated notion of royal power and that an important role of the monarchy was to disguise the reality of the legislative power – 'The masses of Englishmen are not fit for an elective government. If they knew how near they were to it, they would be surprised and would almost tremble.' There is, however, little or no evidence that contemporaries thought in these terms.[36]

The republican movement of the early 1870s foundered above all on the constitutionalism of the British monarchy; on the widespread belief, expressed by *The Times* in 1871, that 'the Sovereign herself is so utterly powerless to do wrong, and so without political influence, except that of high personal character and Royal demeanour'.[37] The use of the prerogative in 1871 had been at Gladstone's request and despite the Queen's own opposition to the abolition of purchase of military rank included in the Bill – and had been invoked in order to overcome the House of Lords' obstruction of a bill passed by the Commons. Dilke, in his speech at Newcastle in November 1871 referred to a speech of Disraeli's which had stressed the Queen's continued involvement in government,[38] but newspapers were quick to refute his suggestion that Disraeli – who had stated that the Queen never signed anything of which she did not approve – equated the Queen's powers with those of the Emperor of Russia. The *Pall Mall Gazette* wrote, 'Great matters of home policy rarely come under the Queen's eye until they have been so thoroughly sifted in parliament as to leave no doubt that the nation has made up its mind about them.'[39] Much was made of John Bright's letter to the National Republican Conference at Birmingham in 1873 refusing its invitation to preside as he felt that all desirable reforms could be attained under Britain's limited monarchy. The *Saturday Review* remarked, 'The National Republican League is based on the declaration that in England all that a minority needs in order to get whatever it desires is the ability to convince their fellow citizens that what it desires is expedient. A country of which this can be truly said has already secured all that is really valuable in Republican government.'[40]

Thus, in the fourteen years following Albert's death, constitutional criticisms of the Crown were infrequent. In 1873 Peter Taylor, a republican and inveterate opponent of grants to the Queen's children, said in the Commons in opposing the grant to the Duke of Edinburgh, 'It is now acknowledged to the honour of the Queen, by both parties, that she is of no party and receives with equal readiness the right honourable Gentleman opposite and the right honourable Gentleman on this side'.[41] Gladstone, writing of the 'beneficial substitution of influence for power', observed that when, on a change of ministry, power was temporarily resumed by the sovereign, 'this resumption is usually brought about by forces distinct from the personal action of the sovereign'. Since the Bedchamber crisis, the ministry had changed twelve times, 'without the slightest jolt or friction in the play of the machinery. The thirty-six years, which have since elapsed, have been undisturbed even by a single shock in the relations between the Sovereign and her Government.'[42]

1876–9: Disraeli, 'imperialism' and the controversy over the royal prerogative

The 'special relationship' between Disraeli and the Queen during the former's ministry of 1874–80 has traditionally been depicted as a great turning-point in royal popularity. The Queen was transformed by her imaginative Prime Minister from the 'widow of Windsor' to the 'Faerie Queen'. He was the 'Grand Vizier' who made her Empress of India and filled her with a love of exotic pageantry, thus laying the foundations for the Crown's late century apotheosis as the symbol of empire and centre of national ceremonial.[43] What has been largely overlooked in such accounts is the storm of protest to which Disraeli's royal policies gave rise. The Royal Titles Bill, usually presented as the first step in the popularizing of the Crown as the figurehead of empire, was subjected to widespread attack. The term 'imperialism' was pejoratively ascribed to it even by the staunchest defenders of Britain's colonial power, for 'imperialism' in the 1870s conveyed the domestic sense of demagogic authoritarian rule, as practised by Napoleon III. Disraeli's frequent use of the royal prerogative was seen as a further manifestation of this. This whole episode has been ignored not only by historians of the monarchy but by constitutional historians and those concerned with Disraeli's career[44].

We shall see that the Prime Minister was accused of trying to 'imperialize' the English constitution by undermining parliament and exalting the status of the Crown. The Royal Titles Act and the excessive employment of the royal prerogative seemed to conform to the contempt for the 'Venetian' parliamentary constitution and the plan for a rejuvenated, populist monarchy found in the constitutional and fictional writings of the young Disraeli of the 1830s and 1840s. The coeval publication of Theodore Martin's biography of Albert, including Stockmar's theories and Albert's attempts to realize them, intensified the constitutional debate, provoking the allegation that under the mask of the supposed constitutionalism of the reign, two foreign influences, one German, one Jewish,[45] had been subverting English parliamentary government.

In 1876 both the manner in which the Royal Titles Act was passed and the Queen's new title of Empress of India were seen as an exaltation of the Crown at the expense of parliament and of a free, constitutionally governed people. In introducing the measure Disraeli did not specify what the change in the Queen's title would be – it would be proclaimed by the Crown once parliamentary assent had been obtained – and he denounced parliament's request to know the new title as an invasion of royal prerogative.[46] Disapproval of this course was so strong that he informed parliament that the new title was 'Empress of India', but though in the course of the debates he assured the House that it would not be used in England, he refused to incorporate this limitation in the Bill,[47] and it did not, as he had implied it would,[48] subsequently appear in the Proclamation[49] – it was merely to be left to the discretion of court, politicians, press and public to confine its usage to India. When Sir Henry James' motion in the Commons pointed out that Disraeli's assurances found no place in the Proclamation,[50] the *Spectator* supported him, accusing the Prime Minister of showing a contempt for parliamentary government. One of the most distressing elements of the debate on James' motion was the way in which ministers seemed 'to advance the theory that Parliament is factious in urging criticisms' in matters concerning the Crown.[51]

There was also a feeling that Disraeli had allowed the personal wishes of the Queen to dictate government policy. Lowe, in a speech at Retford, alleged that in Disraeli the Queen had at last found a Prime Minister malleable enough to accede to her request, made to his predecessors, that she be created an empress in order to be on an equal footing with the Emperors of Germany and Russia. Lowe had to withdraw his remarks in parliament,[52] but Samuelson, in the course of the debates, deplored Disraeli's constant references to how the 'pleasure and gratification of the Queen' would be obtained by the bill's passage.[53] The *Spectator* correctly detected the Queen's hand behind the measure[54] and the *Westminster Review* wrote of 'a belief . . . prevalent throughout the country that the bill had been introduced through Court influence and for Court purposes'.[55]

The title itself, wrote the same periodical, was 'wholly repugnant to the tastes, the temper, and the traditions of this country'.[56] Only the government majority which voted it through parliament seemed to have any enthusiasm for it. It was attacked inside and outside parliament for its autocratic overtones: emperors, historically and in contemporary Europe, were seen as tyrants; 'king' was the correct and traditional title for an English constitutional monarch. Gladstone summed up the opposition's dislike of the title when he said that it implied rule 'without the constraints of law and constitution';[57] and Cowen warned MPs, 'What the Ministers wished to do was to engraft upon their Constitutional forms the name and style of a military, autocratic, irresponsible and arbitrary power. They could not be too jealous of regal and despotic encroachments upon popular power and influence.'[58] There were Conservatives too who opposed the title as a dangerous innovation – Lord Shaftesbury, whom the *Sunday Times* described as looking 'at the question from a Conservative point of view',[59] begged an amendment to a title 'more in accordance . . . with the history of the Nation'.[60] A 'Septuagenarian Tory' who professed himself to prefer 'principle to party' wrote a pamphlet entitled, *Queen Alone, in every heart and on every tongue*, denouncing the Royal Titles Bill as revolutionary.[61]

Newspapers and journals reacted with the same hostility to the new title, reflecting, wrote the *Examiner*, 'the spontaneous feeling of the country': meetings were held in most principal towns and resolutions of protest passed with little opposition while as Cowen pointed out in the Commons, letters to newspapers were overwhelmingly against the Bill.[62] In the *Economist* Bagehot remarked on the 'exceeding attachment of the English people to old English traditions', which should have dissuaded Disraeli from an urge to 'meddle recklessly' with the monarchy – the title of empress could only diminish 'the liking of the masses for the throne . . . never heartier than it is now'.[63] Reverence for royalty, concurred the *Observer,* was 'reverence for antiquity'.[64] The *Spectator* felt that the only beneficiaries of such an exchange, would be 'the few Republicans in the country', and the republican *National Reformer* agreed.[65]

The *Spectator* saw the significance of the Royal Titles Act in relation to what it called 'English Imperialism'. The term 'imperialism' at this time referred not to Britian's foreign dominions but to a style of imperial government in which the masses were enlisted on the side of autocratic rule, as in France where the Second Empire had in the 1850s been successfully based on universal suffrage because of the support of the mass peasant electorate – an example which Bismarck had followed in embodying universal suffrage in the constitution of the German Empire. Disraeli, after the 1867 Reform Act, was seen as fitting into this new generation of radical conservative leaders, his policy being, argued the *Spectator*, to 'magnify the Crown and on the one hand and the wishes of the masses on the other and to make light of the constitutional limitations on either'.[66] This policy moreover was in accordance with his vision in *Coningsby* of a 'free monarchy' supported by public opinion – 'The House of Commons is the house of a few; the Sovereign is the sovereign of all. The proper leader of the people is the individual who sits upon the throne.'[67] The *Observer* wrote that, following the 1867 Reform Act, in the Royal Titles Act Disraeli had 'realized the

political principles foreshadowed in *Coningsby*. He has given us a Democratic suffrage under an Empire'.[68]

The 1876 Act could be viewed, wrote the *Spectator*, as 'a little
experiment on the popularity of the attempt to raise the titular magnificence of the Crown'. Like the *Bee-Hive*,[69] the *Spectator* observed that
the working class had been largely apathetic – the voices of protest at
the perversion of English traditions had been raised by middle-class
liberals and dissentient Tories. The journal pointed to the way in which
Disraeli in 1867 had 'persuaded his party to have confidence in the
Conservative tendencies of the Residuum, and proved by practical experiment that there is often less enlightenment in the masses than there
is in the higher strata of a civilized society'.[70] In *Sybil* in 1845 Disraeli
had described the Crown as the 'national chief' of 'the unenfranchised'
as the working classes then were. The 1832 Reform Act had been the
'mean and selfish revolution' of the middle class.[71] Though the *Spectator* believed that there was only a remote chance of an 'English Imperialism' undermining parliament and re-establishing the royal will as the
governing power appealing directly to mass support, it did not altogether discount such a possibility if there were 'an alliance between the
agricultural labourers, probably the most isolated, the least assimilated
of all the elements of our society, and an adventurer on the Throne'.[72]
Cowen too saw in the Royal Titles Bill a possible 'attempt to establish a
species of socialistic Empire'.[73] The *Daily News* warned of the dangers
of 'sham-Caesarism'[74] and the *Daily Telegraph* referred to the Act as
'another leap in the dark' – the phrase originally used to describe the
1867 Reform Act – which could prove to be the beginning of 'a sinister
revolution'.[75]

Controversy over Disraeli's conception of the constitution broke out
again in 1878 when his use of the royal prerogative to sign the Cyprus
Convention and to dispatch Indian troops to Malta coincided with
criticism of the second and third volumes of Theodore Martin's biography of Albert. A series of letters by one styling himself 'Verax'[76] to
the *Manchester Weekly News*, subsequently published as a pamphlet,
The Crown and the Cabinet, sparked off a series of review articles
debating the place of the Crown in the constitution, the career of Albert
and the policies of Disraeli. These set the events of the late 1870s in a
historical context – the Queen had become a historical figure, as her
earlier actions and those of Albert were set down in print for all to
evaluate. Martin's biography contained a wealth of detail on the royal
couple's minute involvement in politics, intended to glorify the Prince
by maximizing his contribution to British success and progress. But the
revelation of such comprehensive activity was greeted with disapproval
and provided ammunition for those suspicious of royal interference.

Similarly, Disraeli's novels of the 1840s were seen as the theoretical background to an attempt in office to reinstate government by royal prerogative.

'Verax' saw the third volume of Martin's biography as an unconstitutional political statement by the Queen, and the whole biography as showing Albert's theory and practice to have been alien to England's limited monarchy. The Queen, he alleged, planned the publication of the third volume, dealing with the Crimean War, as an attempt to convert public opinion back to its anti-Russian sentiments of that period in support of Disraeli's contemporary pro-Turkish policy in the current Eastern crisis – a policy which had become unpopular as a result of Gladstone's 'moral crusade' against the government's refusal to condemn the 'Bulgarian Atrocities', the massacre of Bulgarian peasants by Turkish troops.[77] The *Spectator* had observed that the Queen's unusual visit to Disraeli at his home at Hughenden in December 1877 was seen as an indication of royal countenance of the Prime Minister's policy at such a contentious time.[78]

The biography's description of Albert's constitutional opinions, learned from Stockmar, and of his extensive involvement in government should dispel, argued 'Verax', our illusion that 'our national policy' was 'decided not by hereditary brains, which may be wise or foolish, as accident determines, but by the select men of the nation'. The book 'seems to enshrine a courtly theory of the constitution, to exalt the prerogatives of the Crown, to debase the position of the Cabinet'. Palmerston was blatantly refused the support and confidence to which as a minister he was entitled and the Queen and Albert were entirely unconstitutional in demanding the superintendency of foreign affairs: 'The special functions claimed for the Crown in relation to foreign politics are a survival of a former age, when the monarch had a far larger share of direct power in most things than he has now'. Stockmar's 1854 letter to Albert on kingship was an appallingly frank indication of the damage that the German must have inflicted as an irresponsible adviser of the Crown for twenty years, and it probably still represented the Queen's constitutional outlook, which could explain why in the past six months 'our diplomacy has appeared to have a will of its own or to be inspired from unknown sources', and why she was now sending a direct and unprecedented 'Message from the Crown' in the shape of the third instalment of Albert's life.[79]

The *Westminster Review* agreed with 'Verax' that the biography showed 'that the chief characteristic of the Prince's mind was ... "meddlesomeness". He interfered with everybody and everything. The Cabinet was always being pelted with memoranda on every possible subject' – and these memoranda had the tone of 'orders'.[80] In 1873 the review had expressed alarm at the revelations in Stockmar's memoirs of the Baron's unconstitutional views and unconstitutional position as a 'secret and irresponsible minister'.[81] Now it was even more alarming to discover that Albert shared his mentor's disparaging opinion of parliamentary government as factious and inefficient, and his belief that the monarch should rule, initiating legislation through a compliant ministry. Albert's Trinity House speech of 1855 definitely, the *Westminster Review* asserted, expressed approval of despotic government. The biography showed Albert to be impatient of English constitutional constraints and to be continually striving to increase the Crown's influence over government. The constitutionalism of Victoria's reign had become a common-place but 'Now that we know the Sovereign, during the greater part of her reign, was in the hands of two secret advisers, each having high prerogative views, it must strike everyone as being equally remarkable and fortunate that throughout the reign there has been no collision between the Crown and the Houses'.[82] Gladstone, in his review of the second volume, wrote of Stockmar's theories, 'A congeries of propositions stranger in general result never, in our judgment, was amassed in order to explain to the unlearned the more mysterious lessons in the study of the British Monarchy'. They were 'based ... mainly upon misconception and confusion, such as we should not have expected from a man of the Baron's long British experience'.[83]

However, 'Verax's' pamphlet provoked an extraordinary riposte in the *Quarterly Review*, the literary organ of the Conservative Party, by W.J. Courthorpe. Entitled 'The Crown and the Constitution', it asserted the right of the Crown to control the nation's foreign policy and echoed the philosophy of Stockmar and of the young Disraeli in its call for a strong monarch to override the debilitating party warfare of parliament and place himself at the head of a united nation. Courthorpe argued that while the Stuarts upset the balance of the constitution in favour of the royal prerogative, the accretion of power by parliament had now disturbed the equilibrium in the opposite way and that the time had come for the Crown to regain its rightful powers.

This was especially the case with regard to foreign policy. Britain now operated on the principle of 'self-government', but according to Courthorpe, 'self-government is merely an application of the principle, that average common sense is capable of forming sound opinions on matters lying within its own experience' – and questions of foreign policy did not enter into this experience. Only the monarch, with unparalleled experience of international politics and an unequalled interest in the independence and standing of the nation could direct affairs. Britain would never hold its own against the autocratic powers of Europe if it spent its time debating courses of policy in parliament and fluctuating with public opinion. As Albert had done in 1855, Courthorpe explained Russia's success in the current crisis by the daring and speed with which, 'as the possessor of autocratic force, she had been able to direct her policy'.

Moreover, Britain had acquired a vast empire and parliament could not dispatch the welter of business before it as a result of its accroachment of royal power. For the first time in world history, he wrote, 'a free nation finds itself the master of a mighty empire'. Questions of empire were ones in which 'the whole unity of the nation is involved' and could not be 'settled by the distractions of party government'. His solution was drastic:

> When the Romans had acquired Empire, and found their old constitutional machinery was inadequate to the administration of their affairs, they deliberately chose to retain empire at the cost of liberty ... if they are the true children of their fathers, Englishmen will show that they know how to maintain both liberty and empire by placing full confidence in the Sovereign.

Like Urquhart, Disraeli and other Tory advocates of royal authority, Courthorpe saw the Crown as the salvation of the nation from faction, 'the centre to which all sound opinion ... should gravitate' and his message was essentially the atavistic 'The King and State are one' of the romantic Toryism of Bolingbroke, Sir Walter Scott and 'Young England': 'Her Majesty and all the members of the Royal Family have shown how clearly they understand that the interests of the Crown and the nation are identical'.

Courthorpe considered that even if 'parties disappeared, and Parliament, once more confining itself to its old office of control, left all initiative in the hands of the Executive', there would be no dangerous consequences. 'Ministers no doubt would be selected more at the discretion of the Sovereign' but this was proper, for, like Urquhart and Disraeli, he insisted that the ministry should not be parliament's but the sovereign's – in recent history ministers had become the 'creatures' of the people. The restoration of royal authority would not be despotic for, by tradition, 'the policy of Conservatism is municipal independence. It is to localize whatever is domestic, and to centralize whatever is imperial'. (In *Sybil*, Disraeli's ideal was 'a free monarchy . . . the apex of a vast pile of municipal and local government'.[84]) The prime imperial concern of the central royal authority was foreign policy. In the present crisis, Courthorpe concluded, the Queen, in the face of the vacillation of parliament, might have to exercise her prerogative of declaring war on Russia.[85]

The Liberal *Edinburgh Review* printed a reply to Courthorpe by W.N. Massey, who wrote that the former's article could be dismissed as the wild fancies of a nonentity were it not for its correspondence with the opinions of Albert revealed in his biography and of the Prime Minister revealed in his early novels and now apparently being put into practice by his government's use of the prerogative. The way in which the prerogative had been invoked to send the Indian troops to Malta with only the retrospective approval of parliament was a worrying precedent, as it undermined parliament's exclusive control over supply with its important implications for the levying of armed force by the sovereign. Furthermore, Derby, the Foreign Secretary, and Northcote, the Chancellor of the Exchequer, had 'recently spoken with contempt of public opinion on questions of foreign policy'. The government seemed intent on 'lowering the authority, and undermining the independence of parliament' – 'the business set before the house is of the quality which is dealt with by town councils and local boards', while great national issues were determined elsewhere, behind closed doors.

Massey cited Disraeli's novels as evidence that the Prime Minister was consciously implementing an unconstitutional theory of monarchical government. He quoted the passage from *Coningsby* referring to the monarch as the 'sovereign of all' and the Commons as the 'house of a few'.[86] Disraeli had been unstinting in his praise of Albert and there was a great affinity in their political beliefs. The Prince Consort was taught by Stockmar, who 'like all foreigners . . . was incapable of understanding the British constitution', and he had taken 'a more active part in public affairs than was conventional or becoming in one so highly placed'.[87]

A similar debate was staged in the *Nineteenth Century* journal between Henry Dunckley and T.E. Kebbel. Dunckley wrote that two foreign influences had diverted the course of English constitutionalism – the German Stockmar and the Jew Disraeli. He saw a consistency in Disraeli the novelist of the 1840s and Disraeli the Prime Minister of the 1870s. During his time as Prime Minister, 'the nation has begun to feel that it has not the same control as it once had over . . . its destinies'. The legislature was being down-graded and 'imperialism' on the French model established.

Dunckley recalled Disraeli's unconstitutional action during his brief ministry of 1868 when, refusing to resign when defeated over Gladstone's Irish Church Resolutions, he failed to tender to the Queen direct advice on whether to dissolve, 'thereby throwing upon the Queen a responsibility which he ought to have assumed, and enabling him to represent his remaining in office as an act of compliance with his personal wishes'. He had even told the Commons that, while he intended to govern until the Autumn, he could dissolve at any time with the Queen's dismissal if obstacles were thrown in his way. This embodied 'an advance upon the power to dissolve greater than had been made since the Revolution'. and since returning to power in 1874, wrote Dunckley, Disraeli had set about 'imperialising the Constitution'.

Dunckley feared a spectacular counter-revolution. The call-up of the Indian troops to Malta, which by-passed parliament's control of supply by using the Indian treasury, was ominous as now 'a telegram from London can give the Crown the command of resources enormously greater than those for which the Stuarts importuned Parliament in vain'. Disraeli's high-flown adulation of the Queen, initially laughed at was now imitated in a tone of 'Oriental adulation' – 'the effect upon the national character of a systematic servility of speech deserves to be taken into account'. Disraeli, as foreshadowed in his novels, would enlist the masses in a counter-revolution – he 'appeals over the head of Parliament to the passions of the multitude . . . to captivate the imagination of the people by startling exploits . . . and by such means to create a power outside of Parliament which shall dominate an existing Parliament while it lasts, and secure the return of successive Parliaments of the same sort'.[88]

Kebbel's rejoinder argued that Dunckley gave no real examples of the increase of 'personal government' at the cost of parliamentary government as there was no question of the Queen's interfering with the government and imposing her own policies against the advice of her ministers. As Dunckley himself admitted, the Crown still possessed considerable powers in theory and the call-up of the Indian troops and negotiation of the Cyprus Convention had been within the scope of these prerogative powers. Kebbel dismissed the notion of a Disraelian master-plan outlined in *Coninsby* and *Sybil* – these were novels, not political programmes, written in a purposively romantic style to excite the young. In so far as they represented a political theory, they were 'the tentative reveries of an original mind . . . meditating how best to restore the political equilibrium which the first Reform Bill had deranged'. If there were to be a revival of prerogative, it was more likely to come from popular 'dissatisfaction with the House of Commons', due to 'session after session wasted in factious wrangles', than from theories of a Stockmar or the actions of Disraeli.[89]

Dunckley took no comfort from Kebbel's article. It was Disraeli's use of the prerogative as a substitute for parliament, not the Queen's interference with government, which was at issue: 'Personal rule may flourish as luxuriantly through the interposition of a minister as when it is solely exercised, if indeed it can be exercised by the sovereign'. The Crown did indeed possess vast powers and there was no written constitution limiting the use of these powers, but it was the essence of English constitutional practice that these powers had, as Bagehot had written,[90] fallen almost entirely into desuetude. Disraeli lacked all discretion in his encouragement of the use of them. Kebbel's references to the disequilibrium of the constitution after 1832 – the chief lament of Stockmar – and to the 'factious wrangles' of the House of Commons illustrated the unconstitutional outlook of Disraeli's acolytes. To refute the argument that Disraeli's novels did not seriously represent his political philosophy one had only to point to his record in government: 'he is seeking by quiet and plausible steps to modify the Constitution in accordance with his autocratic opinions'.[91]

The controversy over the prerogative penetrated the House of Commons. In May 1878 in observations on the dispatch of the Indian contingent, Jacob Bright remarked that 'suspicions of a novel nature' as to 'personal government' were seizing the country, the grounds for such suspicions relating 'to the remarkable disclosures in the life of the Prince Consort, to the ideas on Constitutional questions advocated in the great Tory Review, to the character of the Prime Minister, and to the conduct of the government'. He pointed to the heavy sales of 'Verax's' pamphlet as evidence of public concern.[92] Two months later in the debate on the annuity to the Duke of Connaught on his forthcoming marriage, Plimsoll said that his constituents were opposed to the grant as a result of the late use of the prerogative. To vote for the annuity would imply support for claims for the prerogative 'compared with which those of Charles I were trivial'. Forster said that while public opinion over royal annuities was difficult to determine it was certain 'that there was no desire' to change the monarchy 'for Republicanism – or for what he believed to be a far greater danger – Imperialism'.[93]

In May 1879, Dillwyn, the Liberal MP for Swansea, moved that 'the mode and limits of the prerogative should be more strictly observed', as the government's policy had been to withdraw from the 'cognizance and control of the House matters relating within the scope of its powers and privileges'. He wished to make it clear that he had no 'intention whatsoever of reflecting upon the action of Her Majesty the Queen who thoroughly understood her duty as a Constitutional Sovereign, and who never interfered improperly in public affairs'. He cited the purchase of the Suez Canal shares, the dispatch of the Indian troops, the Cyprus Convention, the conduct of the Afghan War and the annexation of the Transvaal which led ultimately to the Zulu War, as cases in which parliament had been merely called upon to 'register the decrees of the Cabinet Council'. In the words of Leonard Courtney, who seconded Dillwyn's motion, Disraeli and his colleagues had 'protruded the name and authority of the Queen, so as to obtain undue power through the respect due to her name'. Courtney quoted Bagehot's dictum as to the limited 'three rights' of the sovereign – 'Not one of these rights suggested the power of initiation'. Gladstone, he recalled, had used the prerogative to ride rough-shod over parliament in 1871 to enact the Army Bill and Disraeli, whose principles were shown in his early writings such as *The Vindication of the English Constitution*,[94] was now making a systematic use of it.

Though Dillwyn disclaimed personal criticism of the Queen, he did allude to the rumours of political correspondence, independent of the government, between the Queen and the Viceroy of India during the Afghan War, and between the Queen and Sir Bartle Frere, the High Commissioner for South Africa, who had directly provoked the Zulu War. Jenkins, in supporting the motion, spoke of a widespread concern that 'the country was now falling on the system of secret influence' and pointed out that the Queen's telegram of sympathy to Lady Chelmsford on the recall of her husband after the disastrous defeat by the Zulus at Isandhlwana had effectively blocked any discussion of Chelmsford's competence in the House. The Chancellor of the Exchequer, in oppos-ing the motion, denied that there had been any abuse of the prerogative and said that the Queen's correspondence with Lady Frere had been of a private, apolitical nature and that her communication of encourage-ment to the Viceroy had been sent after the British troops had advanced in Afghanistan.

The speech of Sir Robert Montagu showed him not only to be in accord with W.J. Courthorpe but to have imbibed the writings of David Urquhart. He proposed an amendment to Dillwyn's motion to the effect that the sovereign should determine foreign policy. He argued that constitutional government consisted in good government and that good government was effected by those with knowledge and experience, and by the maintenance of 'secrecy in some affairs'. Referring to Courtenay's quoting of Bagehot, he denied the latter's status as a constitutional authority – Bagehot's essays were merely a gloss on the perversion of the constitution over the past two centuries. The worst aspect of this perversion was the accroachment of executive power by the cabinet, 'an illegal body'. The prerogatives of the Crown and the powers of the Privy Council had to be restored.[95] Lord Hartington refused to throw the weight of the opposition behind Dillwyn's motion, feeling that his colleagues had 'been led away by false and unnecessary alarm'. The opinions expressed by Montagu and in the *Quarterly Review* were held, he said, by only a few and were not government policy. The primacy of parliament was now such as to preclude a restoration of 'personal government'. Despite the protest of General Peel that the question was held to be of 'the utmost importance out-of-doors', the House moved on to other business and the matter was not returned to.[96]

The controversy over 'imperialism' and the royal prerogative shows that the Crown's political role was a contentious issue far later and

Disraeli's effect on royal popularity far more ambiguous than standard accounts allow. The Royal Titles Act was widely disapproved of: the title of Empress was feared as prefacing an accretion of more political power, and not seen as merely a colourful innovation which would serve the monarchy well in its ceremonial and symbolic functions. The debate on the prerogative revealed a diversity of views existing over a decade after Bagehot is supposed to have defined the remaining 'rights' of the Crown. With the defeat of Disraeli in 1880 and the return to power of Gladstone, the royal prerogative ceased to be an object of debate.[97] Attention had been focused mainly not on the Queen but on the Prime Minister; it was generally Disraeli's constitutional theories, not the Queen's, which were feared – in 1876 there had been a wholly mistaken belief in some quarters that the Queen was opposed to the Royal Titles Act.[98] The change of ministry and the absorption of the initial impact of Martin's biography caused a reversion to the overall trend of commentaries towards the apotheosis of the Crown's impartiality and political abstinence.

1880–7: above party and above politics

By the 1880s the Queen herself was as prejudiced and as inclined to meddle in politics as she had ever been. She violently disliked Gladstone and the Liberals and did what she could to thwart their policies, maintaining correspondences with those she considered moderate and safe members of the cabinet.[99] The gulf between the Queen as she really was and the constitutional paragon who appeared in contemporary writings was to be encapsulated in her complaint on the defeat of the Unionist government and return of Gladstone in 1892 that it was 'a defect in our much famed Constitution to have to part with an admirable Govt. like Ld. Salisbury's . . . merely on account of the number of votes'.[100] In 1880 she wrote that 'the way in which the present House of Commons is allowed to dictate and arrogate to itself the power of the executive, disregarding both the House of Lords and the Crown, ought to be firmly and strongly resisted'.[101]

The picture of the perfect constitutional monarch was not intruded upon by the reality of the Queen's ideas and conduct for two reasons. First, her interference produced little effect, and indeed one of her attempts to interfere was designed to avoid a clash between the popular and hereditary branches of the legislature. The Queen, worried about a public reaction against the House of Lords, which could extend to the other hereditary element in the constitution, the Crown, endeavoured to persuade the Conservative leaders to abandon their obstruction of the 1884 Reform Bill.[102] Secondly, Gladstone never made public the acute difficulties which he experienced with the sovereign. *The Radical Programme* of 1885 stated that 'if the Monarchy were proved to be the cause of real mischief, to minimize or endanger the freedom of popular government, no Radical, and probably no large class of Englishmen would exercise themselves to retain it'.[103]

Republicans were painfully aware of the distance between the Queen's practice and popular perceptions. Standring pointed to the Queen's readiness to open parliament for Conservative governments and reluctance to do so for the Liberals: 'Her Majesty ... is very fond of Tory administrations, and entertains a positive aversion to the policy and persons of the popular party'. He did not rule out the possibility of the Queen's refusing to invite an elected Liberal majority to form a ministry.[104] However, the Queen during her reign had exercised sufficient discretion to make republicanism seem a redundant cause and 'the whole tendency of politics in this country during the last sixty years' had been the decline of 'the power and influence of the royal and hereditary elements in the "Constitution"', while 'the democratic element has advanced in intelligence and organization'. He observed that 'Stockmar's advice, given forty years ago to the present Queen, to push forward the authority of the Crown upon every possible occasion, has clearly been regarded as inconsistent with security of tenure. The throne would topple over at the first collision with the people.'[105] As we have seen, Standring in 1886 changed the name of his newspaper to the *Radical* because republicanism had come to be regarded as 'an academic subject of comparatively little importance'[106] – *The Radical Programme* of the previous year had declared that 'so long as the functions of royalty are recognized as being ornamental and consultative ... Radicals have something better to do than to break butterflies on wheels.'[107]

Disraeli died in 1881, Urquhart in 1877, the Foreign Affairs Committees petered out after a last spasm of activity during the Eastern crisis of the 1870s,[108] and in the mid-1880s a consensus, illusive hitherto, was reached about the proper political function of the Crown and the Queen's fulfilment of it. The consensus was essentially Bagehot's picture of a neutral spectator exercising limited rights of being consulted, warning and encouraging. Victoria was enshrined as the model of such a sovereign in school textbooks[109] and in accounts of her life – 'She has always been a careful student of the political constitution of the country ... Being human, she must of course have had her personal predilections, but these have never interfered with perfect fairness.'[110] The *Daily Telegraph* remarked on the presence of all parties at the wedding of the Queen's youngest son Prince Leopold in 1882 – unlike in Germany, where the monarch ruled through one party, in England all parties were the Queen's and this gave to royal celebrations their 'healthy Constitutional character'.[111] The *Saturday Review*, looking back to the marriage of the Queen's eldest child in 1858, declared that 'in the twenty-four years that have elapsed ... the Queen has never once swerved from the path of constitutional duty'.[112]

1887–1901: Queen of the Tories

The final years of the reign brought both a revival of partisan political dispute around the monarchy and a renewal of concern about the Crown's political role. The first is explained by the gradual filtering out of reports of the Queen's antipathy to Gladstone and by the Conservatives' conscious association of monarchy with their own political programme – political continuity and the integrity of Empire, especially the Union with Ireland, the major political issue after Gladstone's commitment of the Liberal party to Home Rule in 1886. The coincidence of the great royal events of this period – the two Jubilees and the Queen's funeral – with Conservative ministries enhanced this relationship. An examination of partisan comment on royal events in this period makes it difficult to agree with Hugh Cunningham's contention that the Conservatives, because of the supra-party character of the Crown,[113] 'were curiously blind to the new focus of loyalty which was at that time [the late nineteenth century] being created: the monarchy'. (Whether this focus of loyalty was 'new' will be contested in chapter 7.) Furthermore, at a time when the Lords was under attack by the Liberals, the Conservatives in the 1890s began to emphasize the positive political influence of Victoria, as a way of asserting the beneficial effects of the hereditary branches of government. This provoked Liberal protest about unconstitutional ideas so that by the turn of the century the two parties were reflecting the old Whig/Tory divide over the role of the Crown. The paradoxical attitudes at the time of the Bedchamber crisis had been completely reversed and by the end of her reign Victoria was in some ways just as much 'Queen of the Tories' as she had been 'Queen of the Whigs' at its outset. Specific incidents contributed to the renewal of political controversy in this period: continued unease over the constitutional implications of the Queen's private fortune was highlighted by the 1889 debates over royal grants; and the Queen's intervention to prevent Labouchere's inclusion in the cabinet in 1892 aroused outrage in radical circles. Thus, while the biographies and newspaper tributes of these years were full of familiar statements about the removal of the monarchy from the political battle – and personal criticism of Victoria was rare – the full picture was a far more complex one and in fact even these apparently conventional statements sometimes had a subtle partisan message.

The Golden Jubilee took place in the immediate aftermath of the 1886 debates over Home Rule and the general election fought and won by the Conservatives over that issue. It was not an entirely consensual occasion as it was used by the ministerial press as an opportunity to celebrate the defeat of Gladstone's proposals. It is noticeable that treatment of the Jubilee in the main Liberal newspaper, the *Daily News* was far more restrained than the fuller, bombastic accounts in *The Times* and *Daily Telegraph*.[114] (The once radical *Telegraph* had formed part of the Unionist secession from Gladstone.) While newspapers of both parties commended Victoria's constitutional conduct, they used the Jubilee as an occasion for political debate over the rights and wrongs of Home Rule.

The Times and *Telegraph* in their Jubilee tributes to Victoria both praised the elevation of the monarchy above party in her reign[115] but proceeded to contradict this proposition or at least to put a novel interpretation on it in their own summations of the Jubilee. *The Times* hailed the frustration of Home Rule as 'the most momentous and far-reaching political triumph of the Victorian age'. Referring to the non-partisan nature of the Jubilee celebrations as seen in the Reform Club festivities of 15 June, the newspaper observed that a consensus had been reached because the aims of the reformers of 1837 had been fulfilled; those men would look with approval on the Conservative leaders of the present day, while under the influence of Gladstone, 'a political Mohammed', wild anarchical, socialistic, separatist radicalism had 'run riot in the outskirts of the Liberal party'.[116] Similarly, the *Daily Telegraph*, reflecting the co-operation of Liberal Unionists and Conservatives, presented Unionism as an apolitical national consensus and Home Rulers as a comparable threat to the nation as the French had been at the time of George III's Jubilee: 'Here are questions entirely non-political, facing Englishmen, Scotchmen, and Irishmen to think of the nation as a whole and not of any party sense'. The Queen's 'noblest claim is that she represents the unity of the realm ... above all party strife'. Hence her Jubilee should 'banish that accursed spirit of party which has been throughout our history, the cause of many disasters and the origin of many woes'. Effectively, Gladstonian Liberalism meant factionalism, and a monarchy above party and politics meant a Unionist monarchy. Association with the monarchy formed part of late nineteenth-century Conservatism's self-image, promoted since Disraeli's 1872 speeches, as the party of national consensus, defenders of the national institutions at home and of the national interest abroad – in Salisbury's words 'the administration of public affairs in the spirit of the constitution which held the nation together as a whole and levelled its united force at objects of national importance, instead of splitting it into a bundle of unfriendly and distrustful fragments',[117] as liberalism did. It is notable, as J.L. Lant has pointed out, that Salisbury asked the Queen to make a Jubilee visit to Birmingham in order to consolidate the Unionist sentiments of the city at a time when Chamberlain was considering rejoining Gladstone.[118]

Liberal and radical newspapers took a similarly partisan approach in their Jubilee issues. The *Daily News*, while full of praise for the Queen, argued that the perfect unanimity of the celebrations was marred by the discontent in Ireland, a regrettable feature which would have been avoided had Gladstone's Home Rule Bill been passed. The paper complained about the way in which Salisbury, in office purely because of Liberal disunity, had opportunistically secured 'honours and emoluments' for his colleagues in the Jubilee honours list.[119] Its retrospect on Victoria's reign referred to her marked preference for Disraeli over Gladstone, but wrote that she had accepted the 1880 general election result with 'that complete and ready acquiescence in the decision of the country which has always characterized her political actions'. It thus did not make any imputations of unconstitutional behaviour: 'The Queen, like all other human beings, has her likes and dislikes, her personal preferences for some statesmen over others, but she never allows these feelings to deflect from the straight line of constitutional practice'.[120]

An outspoken attack on the Toryism of the monarchy was found in the more radical *Reynolds's Newspaper*, whose republican critique of the Jubilee was discussed in chapter 3. It welcomed the honours list as soon the stage would be reached where every Conservative would be a knight, exposing the ridiculous nature of the monarchical system.[121] One verse printed in the paper said that the Queen's name was 'sacred to a Tory crowd'; another, a parody of 'God save the Queen' taken from an Australian paper, substituted 'Toryous' for 'glorious'.[122] *Reynolds's* observed that Gladstone was 'an object of deep aversion to the Queen and all her kith and kin'. At the same time it should be noted that this comment was made as part of an argument that the monarchy had no function – parliament was the real ruler and she had no power to prevent Gladstone from becoming Prime Minister when he had a majority.[123] Even a republican newspaper found it difficult in 1887 to make a case against the monarchy on the grounds of political interference.

Nonetheless, there was still an awareness of the potential power remaining with the Crown – W.T. Stead remarked ironically that some 'good' Radicals' had hoped that the Queen would veto the government's Irish Coercion Bill. Stead observed the dominant position of the

Emperor in the German constitution,[124] a theme he developed in an article on the Prince of Wales in 1891. He used the German example to argue that 'the old conception of the constitutional monarch, which made him, as Napoleon said, a fatted hog, is breaking down'. He contended that, with the exception of Home Rule, there were no real issues dividing the parties so it was easy for the Prince to take an active part in politics in a non-partisan way, for example on the housing question and the colonies.[125]

Few radicals, however, would have agreed with using the Imperial German constitution as in any way a guide for Britain. In 1891 *Reynolds's Newspaper* commented that a ruler like William II would provoke a revolution in Britain.[126] Radicals continued to keep a watchful eye on royal power and the existence of the Queen's private fortune outside parliamentary control was a source of constitutional concern. In 1873, 35 radical MPs had opposed the Third Crown Private Estates Act which altered the wording of the first such Act of 1800 in order to remove any obstacles to Victoria's bequeathing landed estates to her heir and to his disposing of them freely. Anderson said that no extension to the monarch's private property rights should be made while royal wills remained secret and he expressed concern at the constitutional implications of the current bill and the Second Crown Private Estates Act of 1862 which had removed the obstacle to the Queen's acquiring land in Scotland – so that she could inherit Balmoral from Albert.[127] Anderson had been supported in the radical press, *Lloyd's Weekly Newspaper*, for example, referring to a 'retrograde . . . reactionary constitutional course' which could lead to disaster.[128] Even *The Times*, while ultimately rejecting their seriousness, had acknowledged the possible constitutional fears arising from the monarch's building up independent wealth.[129] Attention was drawn to this again in 1889 when the extent of the Queen's savings on the Civil List became known as a result of the select committee on royal grants.[130] In the Commons debates Storey argued that the Crown should not have private wealth. He said that he agreed with the 'Whigs of the Revolution' – in future 'a rich king may corrupt public opinion by his riches, and thus buy the liberties of his country'.[131] The *Star* complained, 'We have a reigning House accumulating a vast fortune which may in good time be used against us'.[132] The paper wrote that Wilkes, Fox and Burke, those who had curbed the Crown in the past, were needed again.[133]

These expressions of disquiet were abstract and speculative but in the 1890s more came to light about Victoria's own involvement in politics and there were concrete radical criticisms of her role. The first revelation – contained in a biography of Archbishop Tait published in 1891 – did not cause criticism as it showed the Queen working with the popu-

lar will by interceding in 1869 to persuade the Lords to pass Irish
Church Disestablishment: though opposed on principle to the measure
she wished, as in 1884–5, to prevent a constitutional crisis.[134] However,
the *Pall Mall Gazette* observed, 'To many people, the revelation they
afford of the Queen's active participation in politics will come as a
surprise'.[135] Indeed the Labouchere incident the following year prompted
Reynolds's Newspaper to exclaim:

> We had thought that with the accession of the Queen, the days of
> personal government had vanished. The nation . . . had been bring-
> ing themselves to tolerate it [the Hanoverian dynasty] on the un-
> derstanding that the Sovereign was to be a mere lay figure, which
> should not dare to interfere with the processes of constitutional
> Government . . . In her old age, Victoria seems to be resorting to
> the methods which rendered her German Prince so deservedly un-
> popular.[136]

As we have seen, Labouchere was a regular and leading opponent of
royal grants, and his newspaper *Truth* was no respecter of the Royal
Family. The 1891 Christmas issue, in the wake of the Tranby Croft
affair, carried an illustration juxtaposing royalty in 1841 – a presentation of Victoria as the font of law and Christian virtue – with royalty in
1891 – the Prince of Wales in the midst of card-playing and horse-
racing.[137] The Queen refused to accept him as a member of Gladstone's
government unless he gave up his journalism. She also insisted that he
be outside the cabinet so that she would not have to receive him or his
wife (the Queen believed that they had lived together before marriage).[138] Labouchere refused to give up *Truth* and attacked the Queen
in it, dismissing Gladstone's characteristically loyal attempt to shield
her from criticism by saying that he himself had decided that Labouchere
was unsuitable as a minister of the Crown. Labouchere pointed to the
Queen's public expression of regret at the resignation of the Salisbury
ministry (in the Court Circular) and her publicized letter to Rosebery
urging him to become Foreign Secretary as corroborative evidence of
her interference. Referring to the pseudonymous letters published in
1878, Labouchere observed that 'Verax' had been right in his misgivings about Albert's and Victoria's conceptions of the Crown's political
role.[139] Labouchere was supported by *Reynolds's Newspaper*, which
condemned the Queen's ultimatum as an encroachment on the will of
the electorate and the freedom of the press.[140]

The Conservative response to the incident was to assert that if the
Queen had exerted any influence on Gladstone she was entitled to do so
– to quote the *Spectator*, 'It is a very reasonable and proper power
without which the Throne would become too much of a hollow form
and an empty name to entitle it to the respect of the people'.[141] A new

Tory emphasis on the active role of the monarch is detectable during the Diamond Jubilee celebrations and this did not go unnoticed by Liberals and radicals.

Salisbury in his Prime Ministerial Jubilee tribute in the House of Lords argued that the Queen's political role was now acknowledged more than at any time in the reign:

> When I was young it was fashionable to treat the sovereignty of the Queen as nominal, and the share which she took in the public business as unreal. I hear less of that language now [shouts of hear, hear] – and I speak to an Assembly where many could join with me in saying that no one could so describe the working of our institutions without an entire ignorance of the real method of their operation. The powers of the Sovereign are great; the responsibilities are enormous.

Kimberely, one of the leaders of the rump of the Liberal aristocracy which had not seceded from the party in 1886, agreed with Salisbury – 'the Sovereign of this country' had 'a constant, a wise, and a most important influence upon all the political events of the reign'[142] – but other sections of Liberalism took issue with the Prime Minister's speech. The *Nonconformist* wrote that it was 'weak and ill-judged' as he 'seemed disposed to exaggerate the personal influence of the Crown at the expense of its Ministers. To do this is certainly not to do any real good to the Crown itself.'[143] The *Spectator*, on the other hand, wrote that Victoria was rightfully 'one of the most influential members of the Cabinet' and that her being a woman had blinded the public at large to the extent of her political activities.[144]

Though the Diamond Jubilee did not take place at such a politically sensitive time as the Golden, the event cannot be seen as completely consensual as it occasioned partisan comments in the newspapers, with Home Rule still being brought into discussion of the Queen's reign. The *Daily News* remarked that the celebrations could not be complete while the grievances of Ireland remained[145] while the Unionist *Standard* in an allusion to Home Rule asserted that Englishmen shrank from 'any doctrine, principle, or method of government calculated to weaken or curtail' the Empire.[146] *St. James's Gazette* jibed that it was appropriate that Gladstone did not attend the celebrations as he 'could hardly be expected to sanctify by his presence the celebration of everything which he has so long striven to destroy'. This Jubilee, as we shall see in chapter 6, was very much an imperial affair and the newspaper presented it as a triumph for the Conservative policy of steadfast defence of Empire and of British interests abroad: '... to-day it [the nation] is doing more than honour the Queen. It is making a great manifestation of its revolt from the little, sordid, peddling spirit of Cobdenite and

Gladstonian Liberalism'.[147] Liberals criticized the proliferation of honours for their opponents in the Jubilee list as they had done in 1887,
and complained about the invitation only of Rosebery and Harcourt,
not the whole Liberal front bench, to St Paul's.[148]

The closer association of the Conservatives with the Crown was also
evident in the way that their celebration of the Jubilee had a greater
element of personal veneration of the Queen than the Liberals', which
was more of a commemoration of the advance of liberty during her
reign. The *Daily News* complained that Balfour's Jubilee Address in the
Commons had been too exclusively personal to the Queen whereas
Harcourt had struck the right balance by speaking of the advance of
democracy, in successive Reform Acts which the Queen had sanctioned,
as the foundation of national greatness in her reign.[149] It is interesting
to note that in York Conservative and Liberal councillors clashed over
how to mark the Jubilee: the Conservatives triumphed in their desire for
a statue of the Queen over the Liberals' wish for a public park.[150]

As in 1887, retrospects of the reign included references to the Queen's
contrasting attitudes to Gladstone and Disraeli. *The Times* wrote: '. . .
there is abundant proof that the policy of Mr Gladstone, from the
moment of Lord Palmerston's death, gave her much uneasiness', and
cited an equal royal approval of Disraeli's policies between 1874 and
1880.[151] The Liberal *Contemporary Review* speculated that the Queen's
dislike of the retired Liberal leader had been partly motivated by a
feeling that Gladstone had accroached regal status to himself through
his longevity as a public figure and the loyalty he aspired in his followers. It cited Gladstone's tour of Edinburgh in 1888, on which he followed the same route as the Queen had done in her progress in a similar
open carriage and during which Mrs Gladstone wrapped an ermine
tippet round his neck![152] (Elizabeth Longford writes that Victoria was
indeed 'profoundly jealous of Gladstone', calling his campaigns 'Royal
Progresses' and his press reports 'Court Circulars'.[153])

At the same time, however, these nuances did not detract too much
from the general feeling expressed in 1897 that Victoria had been a
model constitutional monarch and that the Crown had been removed
from political controversy during her reign. In one of the many books
produced to mark the anniversary, T.H.S. Escott wrote of the way in
which the monarchy had lost political and gained social authority.[154]
The Times contended that the Queen's personal political preferences
had 'never led her to swerve from the line of constitutional duty'. It
cited Bagehot and Maine as accurate commentators on the state of
constitutional monarchy in Britain and observed that while theoretical
prerogatives remained to the Crown, such as the rejection of Bills, the
imposition or refusal of a parliamentary dissolution and the exercise of

a personal preference in the choice of Prime and other ministers, 'These questions have ceased to have any serious importance in practical politics'.[155] Indeed, Kebbel, writing in the Conservative *National Review* reprised his familiar argument that the constitution had become dangerously unbalanced through the diminution of the Crown to the point where it 'has practically at the present day no will of its own'.[156] The *Contemporary Review*, having criticized the Albert/Stockmar doctrines which prevailed in the earlier part of the reign, observed:

> The Queen's reign has never been so beneficial as since she has stood alone. England is a country of such unbroken tradition that a very active or busy sovereign is liable to do more harm than good ... Since 1861 the Queen has *governed* less than she did before.[157]

The *Spectator* wrote that the monarchy now 'works with a democracy more easily than it ever worked with an oligarchy'.[158] One of *Reynolds's Newspaper*'s republican arguments was that the monarch now possessed only the 'shadow and show of authority'.[159]

In 1901 obituaries and reflections on the monarchy praised Victoria as 'steeped in the spirit of the constitution'[160] and referred to Britain as a 'crowned Republic'[161] but there was definite dispute between Conservatives on the one hand and Liberals and socialists on the other over the precise scope of the Crown's role. Salisbury in the Lords said that Victoria 'always maintained and practised a rigorous supervision over public affairs' and Balfour in the Commons cited the mass of government papers which had built up during her short illness as evidence of her diligent role in public affairs and argued that with the expansion of Empire and development of the self-governing colonies linked together by the monarchy, 'the importance of the Crown in our Constitution is not a diminishing but an increasing factor'.[162] The *Daily Telegraph* took up Balfour's reference to the papers to say that 'the vital part played by the Queen in the actual working of the Constitution will be revealed to the imagination of her subjects who had never grasped it during all the years of her long reign'.[163]

The *Daily News* expressed concern at Balfour's words and their echo in the Conservative press. It wrote that he had 'spoken lightly of the increasing power of the Crown' and it feared that 'the Government may contemplate giving some striking proof of the light value which they attach to those conditions by virtue of which the Royal power in this realm has its existence[164] – presumably a change in the arrangements over royal finance.[165] The socialist *Clarion* on 26 January 1901 commended the Queen's 'exemplary attitude of non-interference in government, so scrupulously maintained' but a week later, having absorbed the Conservative assertions of Victoria's contribution, it wrote:

they startle us with a new-sprung claim that the late Queen did actually counsel and control our country's diplomacy and many features of our home government ... we socialists must make it clear that in joining in the general expressions of regard and praise for the late Queen, we did so whilst sharing also in the general belief that the Queen had deserved especially well of her country by 'doing nothing in particular, and doing it very well'. We all admired her, not for any great deeds that were attributed to her, but because of her supposed loyalty to the people in constantly abstaining from interference with that which was solely the people's business.[166]

Paradoxically, another article in the *Clarion* expressed the hope that Edward VII would use his position to further the advanced views which he apparently held on social issues,[167] and this is an example of the way in which the loyal left, just as the right, projected its own political views where possible onto the monarchy in apparent contradiction of its doctrine of royal non-intervention. (Even republicans were not immune from this – Keir Hardie claimed that the Queen was opposed to the Boer War[168] and *Reynolds's Newspaper* praised Albert's intercession in favour of peace when the Trent affair threatened war with the USA in 1861, and looked to the new King to intervene on the progressive side.[169])

In the case of loyal Liberals the purpose of such a projection of their ideals onto the monarchy can be seen as a way of diluting the association of the monarchy with Conservatism, which, as we have seen, was so strong in this period. The Liberals were out of office for all but three years between 1886 and 1905 and the Conservatives made much political capital out of the coalescence of the heyday of imperialism and the frequent royal ceremonial of these years. The Liberal response was to equate the monarchy as much as possible with the progressive, tolerant and pacific aspects of the Victorian age. In 1897 the *Contemporary Review* wrote that Victoria had used her influence as a 'standard of international morality to her ministers'.[170] In 1901 when Balfour asserted that 'we intimately associate the person of Queen Victoria with the great succession of events which filled her reign, with the growth, moral and material of the Empire over which she ruled', Campbell Bannerman responded by speaking of the Queen's 'personal and sincere devotion to the cause of peace and freedom and uprightness[171] – a pertinent association of the Queen with these Liberal principles in the middle of the Boer War to which the Liberals were opposed. The *Daily News*, while acknowledging 'her essentially Conservative mind', argued that the Queen 'was Liberal in the sense of tolerance'[172] and the *Nonconformist* at the time of the Diamond Jubilee quoted a sermon praising 'God who has given us a Queen under whom we have enjoyed freedom to worship'.[173]

Perhaps the most interesting way in which progressives used the Queen's political involvement to their advantage was over the cause of female emancipation and enfranchisement. In 1887 W.T. Stead took an unusual line in his editorial on the Golden Jubilee in the *Pall Mall Gazette* when he hailed it as 'A Woman's Jubilee'. He predicted that historians would write of the Victorian era as 'the era of the Emancipation of Women'. Victoria had played her part in this as she had 'accustomed the nation to the spectacle of a woman whose discharge of the highest political functions never impaired her womanliness ... never interfered with the ideal of the wife and the mother, or destroyed the homeliness of the home'.[174] Thus Stead used the example of Victoria to confront one of the essential arguments of anti-suffragists. The *Englishwoman's Review* in its Golden Jubilee issue wrote:

> The workers in the suffrage cause, while they have never yet received any direct encouragement from Her Majesty [this was scarcely surprising as we now know the Queen to have been a violent opponent of it], unite in telling us how ... any allusion to the steady political work which a woman was doing on the throne touched a fibre of sympathy in all those with whom they were pleading for a small share of political influence ... with all this devotion to public business she has fulfilled with exemplary fidelity and care her duties as wife, mother, and friend ... she has illustrated once for all the absurdity of the statement that political duties are incompatible with the tenderer sympathies of a woman's life ...[175]

In 1895 Milicent Fawcett, the leader of the National Union of Women's Suffrage Societies, wrote a biography of the Queen in a series of lives of eminent women and in it made the same case: 'politics and political responsibilities of the weightiest kind have not unsexed her'.[176] (Disraeli speaking in parliament in 1848 had said, '... in a country governed by a woman ... I do not see, where she has so much to do with the State and Church, on what reasons, if you come to right, she has not a right to vote'.[177]) Emily Crawford writing in the *Contemporary Review* in 1897 argued that the 'Queen's accession brought forward very slowly the question of Women's rights'[178] and *Reynolds's Newspaper*'s obituary of the Queen reflected:

> Her life has had one great use. It has taught us the power we are wilfully allowing to go to waste in the womanhood of the nation. If Victoria has been all her flatterers say, then there are many thousands of possible Victorias in the kingdom. No longer can it be argued ... that women are unfitted for public duties. The feature of the twentieth century probably will be the utilization of this rich reserve of force. If it be so, that will be the greatest result of the reign of Queen Victoria.[179]

Conclusion

There was an increasing tendency towards a view of the monarchy as above politics in the 1860s – and Bagehot's picture of the constitutional monarch was the expression of this. But the controversy of the late 1870s, hitherto ignored by historians, showed that the Crown's prerogatives could still be the centre of debate. In retrospect, Disraeli as Prime Minister has been regarded as one of the architects of the monolithically popular late-Victorian monarchy, but a study of contemporary attitudes sheds a new light on his relations with the monarchy. It is by looking at contemporary perceptions – a perspective not adopted by constitutional histories – that we see how controversy over its political role was an integral not an incidental feature of the Victorian monarchy. The incorporation into the debate of the 1870s of material from the 1840s and 1850s, by then published in historical accounts, reinforces the argument that, throughout the period under my examination, the Crown's political role could be a highly contentious one.

The disapproval of Albert strongly expressed in the reception of his biography further undermines the common historical judgement that he was the father of the modern constitutional monarchy. Indeed, his departure from the scene in 1861 was, one should infer from retrospective comments of the 1860s and 1870s, a prerequisite to the Crown's gradual assumption of an apolitical status in the period 1861–87. *Reynolds's Newspaper* wrote in 1862: 'The late Prince Albert, it is well-known, was by no means enamoured of the "British constitution", and would not have had the least objection to a considerable enlargement of the sphere of the sovereign's power'.[180] The prospect of the heir apparent following his example in the practice of kingship was not a pleasing one to contemporaries – a revealing passage appeared in the *Daily Telegraph* at the time of the Royal Titles Bill: 'if this Bill passes the present generation may hear Empress oftener than Queen, and the next may live under an Emperor Albert I instead of a King Edward VII'.[181]

The influence which Albert and his adviser, Stockmar, had wielded was seen by the *Westminster Review* in its article on Stockmar's memoirs, as a pernicious corollary of a female reign and as proof that 'our system of parliamentary government does not so completely, as we had hitherto thought, prevent the existence and influence of Court favourites and secret and irresponsible ministers'. The solution to this problem lay not in the abolition of the monarchy but in the completion of the 'omnipotence of the House of Commons'.[182]

Even in the final years of the reign there was some political controversy as Victoria's Conservatism and dislike of Gladstone became better known. However, as this was not seen to be interfering with the course of politics – the Conservatives did win general elections in 1886, 1895 and 1900 – and as the Liberal leaders did not make an issue of it, the monarchy was able from the 1880s on to appear in its now paramount ceremonial and domestic roles as the figurehead of the whole nation.

Notes

1. *Contemporary Review*, vol. 26 (June 1875), p. 10.
2. T. Erskine May, *The Constitutional History of England Since the Accession of George the Third 1760–1860* 2 vols (London, 1861), vol. 1, pp. 126–7, 131, 135.
3. *Saturday Review*, 5 July 1862, p. 1.
4. *Daily Telegraph*, 10 March 1863, p. 4.
5. *Examiner*, 7 March 1863, p. 145; *Sunday Times*, 8 March 1863, p. 4.
6. *The Times*, 20 February 1863, p. 9. This view was echoed in the *Leeds Mercury's* statement that the throne had 'ceased to be oppressive'. (11 March 1863, p. 2.)
7. *The Times*, 15 December 1864, p. 8.
8. *Punch*, 30 June 1866, p. 272.
9. Elizabeth Longford, *Victoria R.I.* (London, 1983 edn), p. 493.
10. See above, chapter 3.
11. *Fortnightly Review*, vol. 11 (June 1872), pp. 637–8.
12. Alpheus Todd, *On Parliamentary Government in England* 2 vols (London, 1867), vol. 1. pp. x–xi, 201.
13. *The Times*, 15 April 1868, p. 8.
14. Ibid., 15 December 1864, p. 8.
15. Ibid., 6 November 1862, p. 6.
16. *Remarks on Certain Anonymous Articles Designed to Render Queen Victoria unpopular: With an Exposure of their Authorship* (Gloucester, 1864), pp. 11–14. (The pamphleteer believed that John Bright was the writer in the *London Review*.)
17. *Hansard*, vol. 175, cols 606–16. That the Queen exerted considerable influence and triumphed – with the support of the rest of the cabinet – over Palmerston and Russell, the Prime Minister and Foreign Secretary, is shown in W.E. Moss, 'Queen Victoria and her Ministers in the Schleswig-Holstein Crisis 1863–64', *English Historical Review*, vol. 78 (1963), pp. 263–83; and K.A.P. Sandiford, 'The British Cabinet and the Schleswig-Holstein Crisis, 1863–1864', *History*, vol. 58 (1973), pp. 360–83.
18. *Free Press*, 6 January 1864, p. 10; 3 February 1864, p. 22; 6 April 1864, p. 37; 6 July 1864, pp. 61–2.
19. *Diplomatic Review* (continuation of *Free Press*), 5 September 1866, pp. 113–14.
20. Ibid., 20 April 1872, pp. 83–92.
21. Ibid., April 1873, pp. 94–5.
22. Ibid., 5 August 1868, p. 116.
23. Todd, *On Parliamentary Government*, vol. 1. pp. x–xi, 15–117.
24. *The Times*, 15 December 1864, p. 8.
25. Ibid., 21 October 1869, p. 6.

26. See below.
27. *The Collected Works of Walter Bagehot Vol. 5* ed. Norman St John-Stevas (London, 1974), pp. 81, 89.
28. *Spectator*, 28 November 1840, p. 1140.
29. See chapters 2 and 3.
30. *The Collected Works of Walter Bagehot, Vol. 5* pp. 226–58.
31. Ibid., pp. 254–5.
32. Ibid., p. 243.
33. Ibid., p. 182.
34. Frank Hardie, *The Political Influence of Queen Victoria, 1861–1901* (Oxford, 1935), pp. 23–7.
35. St John-Stevas, introduction to *The Collected Works of Walter Bagehot, Vol. 5*, pp. 81, 83, 89.
36. *The Collected Works of Walter Bagehot, Vol. 5*, pp. 240–1.
37. *The Times*, 21 March 1871, p. 8.
38. Charles Dilke, *On the Cost of the Crown* (London, 1871), pp. 19–20.
39. *Pall Mall Gazette*, 9 November 1871, p. 1; *Examiner*, 11 November 1871, pp. 1109–10; *Daily News*, 9 November 1871, p. 5.
40. *Saturday Review*, 17 May 1873, p. 641.
41. *Hansard*, vol. 217, cols 1337–48.
42. *Contemporary Review*, vol. 26 (June 1875), pp. 10–12.
43. For example, Kingsley Martin, *The Crown and the Establishment* (London, 1962), p. 21; David Cannadine, 'The Context, Performance and Meaning of Ritual: the British Monarchy and the "Invention of Tradition" c 1820–1977' in Eric Hobsbawm and Terence Ranger eds, *The Invention of Tradition* (Cambridge, 1983), p. 124.
44. G.H.L. Le May, *The Victorian Constitution. Conventions, Usages and Contingencies* (London, 1979), pp. 94–6, briefly discusses the parliamentary debate of 1879 on the prerogative but not the broader controversy from which it arose; Hardie, *The Political Influence of Queen Victoria*, p. 216, quotes, without comment, a reference in the Queen's correspondence to parliamentary criticism of her in 1879; while there is no mention whatever in Robert Blake, *Disraeli* (Suffolk, 1978 edn). P.R. Ghosh, 'Disraelian Conservatism: a financial approach', *English Historical Review*, vol. 99 (1984), p. 292, alludes briefly to the attack on personal government made in the Liberal election campaign of 1880.
45. *Nineteenth Century*, vol. 4 (November 1878), pp. 785–92.
46. *Hansard*, vol. 227, cols 407–10.
47. Ibid., vol. 228, cols 1094–5.
48. Ibid., vol. 228, cols 1097–8.
49. Ibid., vol. 228, Appendix.
50. Ibid., vol. 229, col. 51.
51. *Spectator*, 13 May 1876, p. 613, col. 2.
52. *Hansard*, vol. 228, cols 202–4; vol. 229, cols 52–3.
53. Ibid., vol. 227, cols 1727–30.
54. *Spectator*, 25 March 1876, p. 392, col. 2.
55. *Westminster Review*, vol. 106 (October 1876), pp. 313–15.
56. Ibid.
57. *Hansard*, vol. 227, cols 1733–46.
58. Ibid., vol. 228, cols 503–4.
59. *Sunday Times*, 9 April 1876, p. 4.

60. *Hansard*, vol. 228, col. 1039.

61. *Queen Alone, in every heart and on every tongue*. By a Septuagenarian Tory (London, 1876).

62. *Examiner*, 18 March 1876, p. 310; 8 April 1876, p. 393; *Hansard*, vol. 228, col. 501.

63. *The Collected Works of Walter Bagehot, Vol. 5*, pp. 447–9.

64. *Observer*, 19 March 1876, p. 4. *Punch* depicted the prevalent mood in an engraving showing Disraeli as the villain in Aladdin trying to persuade the Queen (Aladdin's mother) to exchange the truly magical lamp (the kingly crown of England) for a false one (the imperial crown). [*Punch*, vol. 70 (15 April 1876), p. 147.]

65. *National Reformer*, 30 April 1876, pp. 273–4; *Spectator*, 18 March 1876, p. 360.

66. *Spectator*, 8 April 1876, pp. 457–8.

67. Benjamin Disraeli, *Coningsby* (1st pub. 1844, Oxford, 1982 edn.), pp. 312–13.

68. *Observer*, 14 May 1876, p. 5.

69. *Bee-Hive*, 1 April 1876, pp. 9–10; 6 May 1876, pp. 10–11.

70. *Spectator*, 8 April 1876, pp. 457–8.

71. Benjamin Disraeli, *Sybil. Or the Two Nations* (1st pub. 1845; London, 1980 edn), pp. 343, 497.

72. *Spectator*, 8 April 1876, pp. 457–8.

73. *Hansard*, vol. 228, col. 509.

74. *Daily News*, 18 February 1876, p. 4.

75. *Daily Telegraph*, 17 March 1876, p. 4.

76. In fact Henry Dunckley – see Agatha Ramm, ed., *The Political Correspondence of Mr Gladstone and Lord Granville 1876–1886, vol. 1 1876–1882* (Oxford, 1962), p. 85.

77. *The Crown and the Cabinet. Five Letters on the Biography of the Prince Consort* by 'Verax' (Manchester and London, 1878), pp. 3–12.

78. *Spectator*, 22 December 1877, pp. 1, 605.

79. *The Crown and the Cabinet*, pp. 6–44 passim.

80. *Westminster Review*, vol. 109 (April 1878), p. 438.

81. Ibid., vol. 93 (April 1873), pp. 472–503.

82. Ibid., vol. 109 (April 1878), pp. 430–64.

83. *Church Quarterly Review*, vol. 3 (January 1877), pp. 473–4.

84. Disraeli, *Sybil*, p. 313.

85. *Quarterly Review*, vol. 145 (April 1878), pp. 277–328.

86. Disraeli, *Coningsby*, pp. 31, 266.

87. *Edinburgh Review*, vol. 148 (July 1878), pp. 262–94.

88. *Nineteenth Century*, vol. 4 (November 1878), pp. 785–808. Gladstone approved of Dunckley's arguments and suspected that Stockmar's schooling had made the Queen susceptible to Disraeli's views of the constitution – see Ramm, ed., *Political Correspondence*, p. 85. Gladstone resolved to re-publish his 'Kin beyond the Sea' and his reviews of Martin's biographies, which appeared together as *Gleanings of Past Years 1843–78 vol. 1. The Throne and the Prince Consort; the Cabinet and the Constitution* (London, 1879). In 'Kin beyond the Sea', originally published in the *North American Review*, vol. 127, no. 264 (Sept.–Oct. 1878), pp. 179–212, Gladstone gave an account of the English constitutional monarchy which owed much to Erskine May and Bagehot.

89.   *Nineteenth Century*, vol. 4 (December 1878) pp. 1139–50

90.   *The Collected Works of Walter Bagehot, Vol. 5*, p. 243.

91.   *Nineteenth Century*, vol. 5 (February 1879), pp. 344–61.

92.   *Hansard*, vol. 240, col. 790.

93.   Ibid., vol. 242, cols 779–80, 791–4.

94.   See above, chapter 4.

95.   The Urquhartites hailed Montagu's speech as a 'storehouse' of constitutional truths. [*Diplomatic Review* (Supplement), no. 59, p. 8; *Diplomatic Fly-sheets*, vol. 2 (1879), nos 83–96 passim.]

96.   *Hansard*, vol. 246, cols 242–325.

97.   It played a part in the election campaign, as P.R. Ghosh has noticed ('Disraelian Conservatism', p. 292), alongside Liberal attacks on the ministry's high-spending and militarism. See Bernard Holland, *The Life of Spencer Compton, Eighth Duke of Devonshire*, 2 vols (London, 1911), vol. 1, p. 207 for a speech of Hartington's on personal government.

98.   For example, *Pall Mall Gazette*, 4 May 1876, p. 1; *Daily Telegraph*, 5 May 1876, p. 4.

99.   G.E. Buckle ed., *The Letters of Queen Victoria*, (2nd ser. 3 vols, London 1926–8), vol 3, passim.

100. Elizabeth Longford, *Victoria R.I.* p. 650.

101. Buckle ed., *The Letters of Queen Victoria*, (2nd ser.), vol. 3, pp. 135–6.

102. C.C. Weston, 'The Royal Mediation in 1884', *English Historical Review*, vol. 82 (1967), pp. 296–322, attributes the crisis' resolution to the Queen. Andrew Jones, *The Politics of Reform, 1884* (Cambridge, 1972), pp. 241–2 points out that 'however neatly the intervention of the Queen coincided with peace' this was a 'coincidence' – 'Politicians kept far ahead of the Queen to render superfluous and obsolescent her every move'. The episode in fact shows that the Queen could at least appear to have had her way only when she worked with and not against the grain of parliamentary politics.

103. Chamberlain, *The Radical Programme*, pp. 38–40. Publication of *More Leaves from the Journal of a Life in the Highlands* in 1884 (see below, chapter 7) further contributed to the view that the Queen, her concerns apparently entirely domestic, played no real political role – see H.C.G. Matthew, *The Gladstone Diaries vol. 10* (Oxford, 1990), p. clxv

104. *Republican*, vol. 9, no. 11 (February 1886), pp. 84–5.

105. Ibid., vol. 10, no. 1 (April 1884), p. 4.

106. Ibid., vol. 12, no. 6 (August 1886), p. 36.

107. Joseph Chamberlain, *The Radical Programme* (London, 1885), pp. 38–40.

108. Shannon, 'David Urquhart and the Foreign Affairs Committees', in Patricia Hollis, ed., *Pressure from Without in Early Victorian England*, (London 1974), p. 259.

109. Valerie E. Chancellor, *History for their Masters. Opinion in the English History Textbook: 1800–1914.* (Bath, 1970), p. 44.

110. *The Queen and the Royal Family. Anecdotes and Narratives, based on Contemporary Records* (London, 1882), pp. 180–1.

111. *Daily Telegraph*, 27 April 1882, p. 6.

112. *Saturday Review*, 29 April 1882, pp. 515–16.

113. Hugh Cunningham, 'The Conservative party and patriotism' in Robert

Colls and Philip Dodd eds, *Englishness: politics and culture 1880–1920* (Kent, 1987 edn), pp. 300–2.

114. Contrast the space devoted to and language used about the event in the newspapers on 21 June 1887, Jubilee day.

115. *The Times*, 20 June 1887, p. 9; *Daily Telegraph*, 21 June 1887, pp. 4–5.

116. *The Times*, 21 June 1887, pp. 8–10; 16 June 1887, p. 9.

117. Robert Taylor, *Lord Salisbury* (London, 1975), pp. 79–80..

118. Lant, *Insubstantial Pageant*, pp. 158–9.

119. *Daily News*, 20 June 1887, p. 4.

120. Ibid., 22 June 1887, p. 4.

121. *Reynolds's Newspaper*, 12 June 1887, p. 2.

122. Ibid., 19 June 1887, p. 1.

123. Ibid., 26 June 1887, p. 1.

124. *Pall Mall Gazette*, 22 June 1887.

125. *Review of Reviews*, July 1891, pp. 30–2.

126. *Reynolds's Newspaper*, 17 January 1891, p. 4.

127. *Hansard*, vol. 217, cols 693–716, 1006. It was during these debates on the Second Crown Private Estates Act that the principle was acknowledged, for the first time, by the Solicitor-General, George Jessel that the private wealth of the sovereign could in future be taken into account when calculating the Civil List (*Hansard*, vol. 217, col. 709.) Hall, *Royal Fortune: Tax, Money and the Monarchy*, p. xix draws attention to this whereas Kuhn, 'Queen Victoria's Civil List', p. 662 sees it as a precedent established by the 1889 settlement.

128. *Lloyd's Weekly Newspaper*, 27 July 1873, p. 6. See also *National Reformer*, 3 August 1873, p. 72; *Reynolds's Newspaper*, 27 July 1873, p. 1.

129. *The Times*, 23 July 1873, p. 9.

130. See above, chapter 3.

131. *Hansard*, vol. 338, col. 1304.

132. *Star*, 2 July 1889, p. 1.

133. Ibid., 27 July 1889, p. 1.

134. Thomas Randall Davidson, William Benham, *Life of Archibald Campbell Tait, Archbishop of Canterbury*, vol. 2 (London, 1891), pp. 8–9, 23–4, 36, 40–1.

135. *Pall Mall Gazette*, 3 June 1891.

136. *Reynolds's Newspaper*, 28 August 1892.

137. *Truth*, Christmas number, 25 December 1891.

138. Longford, *Victoria R.I.*, pp. 651–2.

139. *Truth*, 25 August 1892, pp. 385–6, 441–2.

140. *Reynolds's Newspaper*, 4 September 1892, p. 1.

141. *Spectator*, 3 September 1892, p. 308; see also *The Times*, 1 September 1892, p. 7.

142. *Hansard*, 4th ser., vol. 50, cols 417–21.

143. *Nonconformist*, 24 June 1897, p. 497.

144. *Spectator*, 19 June 1897, pp. 856–7.

145. *Daily News*, 22 June 1897, p. 4.

146. *Standard*, 21 June 1897, p. 6.

147. *St James's Gazette*, 14 June 1897, p. 3; 15 June 1897, p. 3.

148. See the *Nonconformist*, 24 June 1897, p. 497 and the *Daily News*, 23 June 1897, p. 8.

149. *Daily News*, 22 June 1897, p. 4; *Hansard*, 4th ser., vol. 50, cols 439–46.

150. Sarah Duffield, 'Queen Victoria: the sad fate of a statue', *York Historian* 8 (1988), p. 60.
151. *The Times*, 22 June 1897, p. 9.
152. *Contemporary Review*, vol. 72 (1897), p. 50.
153. Longford, *Victoria R.I.*, p. 663. There has been speculation that a similar relationship existed recently between the present Queen and Mrs Thatcher.
154. T.H.S. Escott, *Social Transformations of the Victorian Age* (London, 1897), p. 274.
155. *The Times*, 22 June 1897, p. 9; 21 June 1897, p. 13.
156. *National Review*, vol. 29 (June 1897), pp. 542–8.
157. *Contemporary Review*, vol. 72 (1897), pp. 51–4.
158. *Spectator*, 26 June 1897, p. 904.
159. *Reynolds's Newspaper*, 20 June 1897, p. 1.
160. *The Times*, 23 January 1901, p. 7
161. *Spectator*, 26 January 1901, pp. 129–30; also *Daily Telegraph*, 24 January 1901, p. 8.
162. *Hansard*, 4th ser., vol. 89, cols 7–9, 19–23.
163. *Daily Telegraph*, 26 January 1901, p. 8.
164. *Daily News*, 4 February 1901, p. 6.
165. In fact, while the Civil List was increased, though less than Edward wanted, the government resisted the new King's desire to be relieved of income tax – see Kuhn, 'Victoria's Civil List', pp. 663–5.
166. *Clarion*, 2 February 1901, p. 33.
167. Ibid., p. 34.
168. *Labour Leader*, 26 January 1901, p. 28.
169. *Reynolds's Newspaper*, 27 January 1901, pp. 1, 5.
170. *Contemporary Review*, vol. 77 (1897), pp. 53–4.
171. *Hansard*, 4th ser., vol. 89, cols 19–26.
172. *Daily News*, 31 January 1901.
173. *Nonconformist*, 24 June 1897, p. 503.
174. *Pall Mall Gazette*, 20 June 1887.
175. *Englishwoman's Review*, 15 June 1887, pp. 242–3.
176. Milicent Fawcett, *Life of Her Majesty Queen Victoria* (London, 1895), p. 224.
177. Quoted in Constance Rover, *Women's Suffrage and Party Politics in Britain 1866–1914* (London, 1967), p. 33.
178. *Contemporary Review*, vol. 719 (1897), p. 763.
179. *Reynolds's Newspaper*, 27 January 1901, p. 1 cols 1–2.
180. *Reynolds's Newspaper*, 6 July 1862, p. 1.
181. *Daily Telegraph*, 17 March 1876, p. 4.
182. *Westminster Review*, vol. 43 (April 1873), pp. 502–3.

CHAPTER SIX

The Monarchy, Patriotism and Nationalism

The Jubilee celebrations of 1887 and 1897 and the mourning of 1901 were seen by contemporaries as expressions of the way in which the monarchy embodied the British nation and British Empire. Historians concerned with patriotism, nationalism and imperialism and those who have written on the monarchy all concur that the Crown became a symbol of nation and empire in the last quarter of the nineteenth century as Britain's standing and role in the world became a major preoccupation.[1] Hugh Cunningham has written, 'It was the monarchy which provided the new focus for patriotism in the late nineteenth and early twentieth century'.[2] This may be contrasted with earlier periods in the reign, when the Crown and Royal Family – in particular, Albert – were stigmatized as German; above all, in 1853–4, when a popular patriotic outcry blamed foreign influence at court for the vacillation of British policy in the Near East and the resignation of Palmerston, 'the Minister of England'.

This chapter poses two connected questions – to what extent did contemporary perceptions of the relationship between the Victorian monarchy and patriotism undergo a transformation of the kind outlined above; and what light do such perceptions shed on the 'language of patriotism', a topic which had attracted much recent attention among modern British historians? Hugh Cunningham has argued that from the 1840s on the 'language of patriotism' began to be conquered by the state, having previously been the language of popular rights and of radical protest against the state, until, 'by the late 1870s the shift of patriotism to the political right had been established'. Palmerstonian Liberalism represented a turning-point in this process, as Palmerston was the first government minister to tap the chauvinism of one strand of patriotic radicalism as a source of popular support. By the late 1870s, however, patriotism had ceased to have this liberal content and Palmerston's mantle had been inherited, not by Gladstone's Liberal Party, but by Disraeli and the Conservatives.[3]

Evidence from writings on the monarchy can be produced to support Cunningham's thesis. On the coronation of Victoria, an octogenarian Tory, hailing her, in the manner of Bolingbroke, as 'The Patriot Queen' lamented that patriotism was currently taken to signify 'a decided partiality for the popular part of the constitution';[4] while in 1879, the *Sunday Times* declared 'The patriotism of the English people is concentrated upon the Crown',[5] and a writer in the *Republican* in 1886 denounced patriotism as narrow, selfish and aggressive and primarily the creed of monarchs.[6] However, both ends of the time-scale also furnish contradictory evidence. The work of Linda Colley on the late eighteenth-century monarchy, calls for a reappraisal of the chronology of the 'language of patriotism'. During the war with France, George III, as a counter to the republican sentiments which the French Revolution had inspired and as a necessary symbol of the nation in time of conflict, was presented as the personification of England, in the guise of John Bull and St George. Radical, libertarian patriotism was 'forced . . . on the defensive' – 'increasingly, the nation would be celebrated in a very different way'. The King replaced Wilkes as the archetypal 'Patriot': on Jubilee Day in 1809 an Oxford clergyman preached, 'How are we best to manifest our patriotism? Surely, my friends, one principal mode of proving its reality is to pray for our King. The safety of the King is the safety of the state.'[7] The same assertion was made at the outset of Victoria's reign.

Conversely, even at the end of my period the time had not been reached when it was mutually exclusive to be critical of the Crown and at the same time claim to be patriotic – indeed, the MPs who voted against the grant to Princess Louise on her wedding in 1871 were described by the *Saturday Review* as 'misguided patriots';[8] while the *Republican*, in 1886 printed a 'Patriotic Song', extolling the Commonwealth.[9] The Royal Family continued to be reviled as German by radicals and republicans. While Cunningham has cited 'the liberalization of the English state' as a factor facilitating its appropriation of the 'language of patriotism',[10] we have already seen that 'the Old Corruption', the oppressive state, continued to be part of the radical discourse.[11]

All this suggests that there was no conclusive appropriation of the 'language of patriotism'. Throughout this period, the right and the left, the supporters and the critics of the monarchy claimed to be patriotic. To love one's country might mean to one loyalty to the throne and to another defence of popular freedoms and of the interests of the common weal. Less ambiguous were notions of Englishness and nationalism, and, despite the protestations of the loyal earlier in the reign and the continued criticisms of radicals towards the end, the monarchy was indisputably more English after the death of Albert in 1861. It was thus able to become the focus of a new assertive nationalism and imperialism emerging in the last quarter of the nineteenth century as Britain's international and industrial pre-eminence was threatened by the newly consolidated German Empire and the United States of America and by the attempts of all the European powers to catch up with Britain's lead in colonial possessions. Hugh Cunningham has written of 'the aggressive and conservative nationalism which became common in western Europe in the 1870s'[12] and John M. MacKenzie observes:

> If the wedding of European nationalism to the New Imperialism was a response to what seemed to be the outrageous and unmerited scale of British power, so in Britain the national convergence took a distinctly imperial form in the defence of real and imagined colonial interests.

The result was a 'British imperial cult', in which the 'Queen was swiftly transformed from petulant monarch to imperial matriarch'.[13]

The identity of the monarchy with national greatness and national cohesion does become increasingly noticeable from the 1870s on, as does a new emphasis on the Crown as the symbol of imperial unity, though it must be noted that the introduction of the title Empress was very unpopular in 1876. The libertarian patriotism of the 'free-born Englishman' resonated in disapproval of the foisting of a foreign, 'despotic' title onto the English, 'constitutional' one of king – the *Sunday Times* wrote that 'all patriotic Englishmen should protest' at this.[14] However, 'imperialism', used pejoratively in 1876 to describe Disraeli's apparently despotic plans for the English constitution, was to come to mean in Rosebery's definition 'a greater pride in empire, which is a larger patriotism',[15] and the monarchy was to be a figurehead in this creed.

The first section of the chapter considers the period 1837–61 – the patriotism of radical and republican critics of the monarchy, including the chauvinistic radicals and the way in which their attacks on Albert blended with those of Tory xenophobes in 1853–4; and, on the other hand, the monarchical patriotism of the loyal. The second section looks at 1861–87 – both the persistence of a patriotism critical of the monarchy and the connection of the Crown with the new nationalism and imperialism.

1837–61: different patriotisms; chauvinistic dislike of Albert

William Linton in 1852 wrote in the *English Republic* of true and false patriotism. True patriotism was that of a Cromwell or a Mazzini; in contrast to the debased kind arising from the confusion of patriotism with loyalty to a false, monarchical sovereign. A patriotic poem by 'Spartacus' was appended to the article:

'Let us serve our Country!
   Whether times be good
Or disaster overwhelm her
   Like a winter flood . . . [16]

Such sentiments would also be professed by patriotic supporters of the
monarchy who saw their loyalty and patriotism as synonymous. The
Morning Herald on the birth of the Prince of Wales in 1841 connected
'British greatness' with the 'golden chain of sovereignty' in which the
new Prince formed the latest link;[17] and the mayor of Northampton
addressing a public meeting on the marriage of the Princess Royal in
1858 declared that there could not be 'a British heart here present that
would not have responded to the sentiment expressed in that single
word, loyal'.[18] This section on 1837–61 will consider these different
kinds of patriotism in relation to the monarchy and show how Albert's
presence militated against those who sought to identify the Crown with
Britishness.

The language of patriotism was a natural mode of expression for
radicals in the eighteenth century. Patriotism entailed the common good,
the upholding of popular rights against the narrow class which wielded
political power.[19] George III may have been portrayed as the patriotic
father of his people during the French war but radicals were in no
doubt that it was true patriotism that had been suppressed – the *Secret
History of the Court of England*, published in 1832, denounced 'the
persecutions . . . against patriotism' that had taken place during the
war, when it 'became sedition to hint at Parliamentary Reform'.[20] Patriotism and democracy went hand in hand as they involved the whole
nation in government by the people for the people, and to quote Hugh
Cunningham, 'In Chartism the vocabulary of radical patriotism reached
a new peak, similar to that of the 1790s'.[21]

This radical patriotism, directed against the oppressive state, had an
added anti-monarchical tinge because of the foreignness of the ruling
house of Brunswick. Tom Paine's picture of 'the Norman yoke' under
which Britons slaved linked the rumours in the 1790s that the King
would call on foreign troops to suppress the reformers with the Norman invasion and with the Stuarts' attempts to find foreign military
support.[22] The republicanism inspired in certain Chartists by the 1848
revolutions claimed to be truly English and patriotic in contrast to the
foreign dynasty into whose hands the country had fallen. Linton, in the
opening number of the *English Republic* recalled 'the brief day of our
Commonwealth as the grandest day of English history'.[23] The pages of
the *English Republic* were full of eulogies to the heroes of the Commonwealth so that, wrote Linton, 'our Republicanism, though enriched by
many a lesson, may be of English growth, characteristic of the genius of

our people'.[24] Republicanism, as Mazzini taught, was the corollary of patriotism as only in a republic did everyone enjoy full citizenship and undertake the duties concomitant with such rights – all the people, 'not of one class only' could unite in 'our notion of republicanism, of patriotism, of duty'.[25]

Those loyal to the throne conceived of patriotism entirely differently. George III had declared, 'Born and educated in this country, I glory in the name of Briton' and much was made of the Duchess of Kent's speech to the Corporation of London on the occasion of Victoria's coming of age on 24 May 1837 in which she stated that she had not allowed the perilous seas to thwart her determination in 1819 to travel from her native Leiningen to give birth to Victoria in Britain.[26] The Queen herself and the institution of the monarchy were identified with national pride and national greatness. The *Courier* argued that 'the Patriot' would see in the coronation of 1838 a 'sublimely impressive spectacle',[27] and those radicals who criticized it as a barbaric rite were, wrote *Berrow's Worcester Journal*, 'neither Englishmen by habit, heart, nor education'.[28] The *Morning Chronicle* wrote on coronation day, 'The annals of the British Empire, will, perhaps, never be able to boast a day more memorable than the present'.[29] The promotion of the monarchy as a symbol of national unity and consensus above class divisions, was not, as some historians such as Freda Harcourt have argued, an innovation of the 1870s in response to the enlargement of the urban electorate in 1867.[30] That the monarchy was a beneficent, unifying institution atop an equitable political system was a commonplace of the liberal middle class after the Reform Act of 1832, countering the Chartist argument that the unenfranchised were oppressed by the class legislation of a narrow ruling order. The refrain of the middle-class press on the births of the royal children in the 1840s and 1850s was that the whole nation united in joy.[31] Similarly, after the Queen's abandonment in the early 1840s of overt political partisanship, the monarchy was seen as transcending party divisions, and royal celebrations, such as the Princess Royal's wedding, occasions for a truce between parties as they paid homage to a higher national loyalty.[32] 'Papal Aggression' in 1850 was denounced as a threat to the common allegiance to the Queen of Englishmen of all denominations.[33]

The most ardent protesters of the Crown's patriotic leadership were the Tories. *John Bull* began in 1820 at the instigation of, among others, Walter Scott, to support George IV in the Queen Caroline affair[34] and was a weekly newspaper bluntly purveying the 'protestantism, protectionism and no popery' philosophy of Tory backwoodsmen. Its patriotism was of the variety identified by Hugh Cunningham as that which 'evoked the world of roast beef, plum pudding and good beer'.[35] National life centred on and gained its distinctiveness from the monarchy. Of the coronation of Victoria it wrote:

> We think, Englishmen as we are, we may with confidence . . . ask . . . in which capital in the universe could have there been such an unbounded display of devotion to Monarchy, such a spontaneous declaration of attachment to the ancient institutions of a country?[36]

The birth of the heir apparent in 1841 was a special cause for national celebration as 'with the very title "the Prince of Wales", some of the best and proudest of our national feelings are associated'.[37]

The most high-flown Tory associations of the Crown with the nation were in the writings of those who followed Bolingbroke's *The Idea of a Patriot King* in seeing the sovereign as ridding the land of faction and ruling with the united weight of national sentiment behind him. Into this category came the octogenarian author of *The Patriot Queen*, the young Disraeli in his early novels and the Russophobe MP David Urquhart. In *The Patriot Queen* it was argued that patriotism would be best demonstrated by the Queen's reassertion of her prerogatives and by the expulsion of a Whig government composed 'of Catholics and Dissenters, of Atheists, Heretics, and Republicans', who were undermining the monarchical and Protestant constitution of England.[38] Disraeli, whose novels were the manifestos of Young England's romantic Toryism, a fusion of Walter Scott and Bolingbroke, also felt that the ancient, English constitution had been supplanted by a 'Venetian' one, in which the monarch was reduced to the status of Doge by the oligarchy which dominated parliament, now all-powerful, though it was successive monarchs who had made English history so glorious.[39] The only remedy was the rebirth of royal power based on the support of the whole nation – 'Before such a royal authority, supported by such a national opinion, the sectional anomalies of our country would disappear'.[40] Urquhart too was a firm believer in the royal prerogative.[41] The Crown, he wrote, was 'the only branch of the legislature which is still English'[42] and, during the Crimean War, his Foreign Affairs Committees, formed mainly in the north of England, insisted that conduct of national policy was safe only in the Queen's hands.[43]

However, Urquhart's views were very much those of a minority, for it was the Near Eastern crisis of the mid-1850s which occasioned the greatest crisis of royal unpopularity in Victoria's reign – arising from charges of unEnglishness in sentiment and actions directed at Prince Albert. The Prince's German nationality had been a source of criticism from his arrival in England. The patriotism of some radicals was bound up with a chauvinistic pride in the constitutionalism of England, contrasted with the despotism of Continental states, and their support for the monarchy was conditional upon its recognition of the limited nature of its power and the essential liberalism of the English constitution. Much of the antipathy to Albert as a German was attributable to fears that he would subvert this liberalism. The *Sunday Times*, at this time an irreverent radical paper, wished that the Queen had chosen, 'Prince George of Cambridge ... by birth, habits and education, an Englishman, his mind continually imbued with the principles of our constitution'.

The other principal cause of anti-German sentiment was the feeling that the nation was once more being robbed by the annuity paid to Albert out of taxes on the British people. The ruling House had come from Germany and subsequent and costly royal spouses had been brought from Germany, so, wrote the *Sunday Times*, there were serious objections to 'importing a new foreign specimen of royalty, with foreign tastes, foreign habits, foreign preferences, and connections who must necessarily be displeasing to the people of this realm, naturally and justly prejudiced against these nests of adventures the petty courts of Germany'. In these courts 'princes are hatched by scores to be drafted off to any country who will be at the expense of maintaining them'.[44] Albert's house, of Saxe-Coburg, was particularly notorious in this respect, and his uncle Leopold, King of the Belgians, was already in receipt of a British pension as a result of his marriage to Charlotte, Princess of Wales, who had died in child-birth in 1817. *The Royal Wedding Jester*, a ribald anthology of satire, contained an obscene parody of the wedding procession, including:

> The Sausage of State
>   Born by Lord Melbourne.
> This singular emblem of German ingenuity is worthy of especial notice as it has been the very root and aggrandizement of the House of Coburg ... The sausage of state brought over by Prince Albert ... (is) both longer and stronger than Leopold's and, therefore, not so likely to result in a miscarriage.

It was ironically remarked that Albert would have no difficulty in keeping the wedding oath to endow Victoria with all his worldly goods, as he had none. A more bitter note was struck in a poem included in the anthology contrasting the Whigs' provisions for the British pauper with the German one, Albert.[45] The Chartists' newspaper, the *Northern Star* drew the same comparison, describing Albert as 'an idle foreigner'.[46]

The sexual scandals associated with the Georges left another anti-Germanic prejudice engrained. Even the *Spectator*, the rational mouthpiece of Benthamism, wrote of the unwisdom of the £30,000 annuity granted to Albert 'a Prince unaccustomed to money, and in the very heyday of his blood' when 'the looseness of the marriage-tie and of sexual morality in German estimation, is notorious and remarked by every traveller'.[47] The *Sunday Times* declared, 'It may be said, with great truth, that we have already had quite enough of German Princes and Princesses' and their 'coarse manners' and 'lax morality'.[48]

Not only chauvinistic radicals disapproved of the choice of a German Prince as the Queen's husband. The Tory *Standard* regretted that the Royal Marriages Act of George III's reign 'as hitherto acted upon, ensures the exclusion of British blood from all approach to the Throne, and condemns the country to be governed for ever by sovereigns at least half foreign by descent ... it is only by the Royal Family making itself thoroughly English in spirit and habit that the monarchy can be made secure in the times in which we live'.[49]

In the prevalent view of Albert as an alien we find none of the 'racial Anglo-Saxonism' and belief in 'English-German kinship' which, according to Reginald Horsman, was emerging strongly in the first half of the nineteenth century.[50] This may have been the era of the Gothic revival and intellectuals such as Carlyle, Arnold and John M. Kemble may have been emphasizing the Saxon heritage and Teutonic origins of the English people[51] but Albert was not seen as a brother Saxon but ridiculed as German and as a Coburg. Intellectual trends in racial philosophy had not percolated down to the compilers of *The Royal Wedding Jester*, whose collection was full of jibes against Germans and against Saxe-Coburg-Gotha.[52] Albert's utterances were printed so as to render a thick German accent in this and other satirical publications.[53] In 1842 *The Times* remarked that Albert, '*foreigner as he is*', was attaining the respect of the English public.[54]

But Albert's position as the Queen's consort put him in a particularly exposed and delicate position. In advocating an English husband, the *Sunday Times* had pointed out that the influence of a male consort on a queen regnant was bound to be greater than that of a queen consort on a king.[55] Albert was indeed to exercise considerable influence over Victoria and it was unfortunate that one of the chief results of his influence was to put the court in conflict with Palmerston, the man popularly known as the 'minister of England' because of the assertive style of his foreign policy.[56]

Palmerston's apparent championing of liberal and nationalist movements on the Continent horrified Albert and the Queen, who feared that it would encourage revolution and war and the toppling of their relatives from their thrones, but won him the support of the patriotic radicalism led in the Commons by Roebuck and voiced in the press by the *Morning Advertiser*, *Daily News* and *Sunday Times*, a radicalism which wanted the dissemination of British liberal constitutionalism through the despotic states of Europe. Though its bellicosity alienated the Manchester school of radicals led by Bright, whose patriotism was of a pacific, non-chauvinistic kind, Palmerston's approach appealed to the patriotic radicalism expressed in working-class publications such as *Reynolds's Newspaper* and the republican papers of G. Julian Harney. Palmerston could also rely on the support of xenophobic Tories.[57] This whole weight of patriotic feeling was to be directed against the Crown in 1853–4 when Palmerston's resignation from the Cabinet at a time of great tension in the Near East provoked accusations of treacherous interference in government by Albert. Having examined the constitutional criticisms of Albert in a previous chapter,[58] here I shall look more specifically at the patriotic, anti-German thrust of the press campaign waged against him.

The parliamentary explanations of Palmerston's dismissal in December 1851 had brought to light the divergence between him and the court, and at that time there had been rumours that his removal from government had resulted from collusion between the British and Austrian courts.[59] Only the Chartist *Northern Star* referred directly to Albert and warned that the Court should refrain from 'mixing itself up with the politics or the personal policy of foreign powers'.[60] In December 1853 the *Morning Advertiser* was certain that 'Lord Palmerston is, as he was in December 1851, again the victim of a German conspiracy against him ..'. 'Coburg influence is at work . . . and Lord Palmerston is too faithful, patriotic and national in feeling not to incur its hate.'[61] Over the following weeks, it was alleged that Albert, with the Prime Minister, Aberdeen, as his tool, was twisting British policy in the interests of the Austro-German-Russian alliance of which the Coburgs, including King Leopold, were a part, and that this explained the vacillation of Britain in the face of Russian aggression against Turkey.[62] All Albert's 'prepossessions and predilections are in favour of Germanism' and under his influence and that of his entourage 'Germanism has notoriously everything its own way. The Court and Cabinet have alike ceased to be English.'[63] The paper adopted as its motto, 'England for the English', which should be the rallying cry of all those who desired the expulsion of the German, 'which is synonymous with Russian . . . influences at Court, which are not only rapidly undermining those free institutions which are the glory of Great Britain, but which are placing in imminent peril the very Throne itself'.[64] This was characteristic of radical patriotism – 'Germanism' threatened the free constitution of England as 'All that is German in government is ignorant, tyrannous and dark'.[65]

The public response in letters to the *Morning Advertiser* showed how deep the anti-German sentiment ran and how damaging associations with 'Germanism' were to the Royal Family. One correspondent, whose notions of the Saxons did not include the Germans, wrote, 'The people of England, I doubt not, have yet enough of the old Saxon blood in them not to allow their constitution to be trifled with by any foreigner'.[66] Another, styling himself, 'Anti-German John Bull', congratulated the *Morning Advertiser*: 'You have raised your voice against the dominance of German influence in the British Court. Your conduct is spirited, and to be admired by all straightforward Englishmen.'[67]

Only the newspapers supporting the Aberdeen ministry did not join in the anti-Albert/anti-German campaign spearheaded by the *Morning Advertiser*. The other main radical daily of the middle classes, the *Daily News*, stated, 'It is indispensable that at such a time the national councils should not only be united, resolute, but thoroughly and exclusively English'.[68] *Reynolds's Newspaper*, the radical paper of artisans, wrote of 'the conquest of England by the Coburgs'. The Queen, however 'pure and patriotic' her sympathies, was 'in the hands of a gang of needy German relatives ... The Court is composed of those who are aliens in blood, in language, and in sympathy; we need not, then, wonder that British honour and interests shall be deemed secondary and subordinate to Coburg, Belgium, and Russian considerations.'[69] *Reynolds's* had always objected to the subsidy of Albert and other Germans by the British taxpayer: 'John Bull has been fleeced and pillaged, scoured and plundered, bamboozled and robbed, by happy hordes of petty German Princes'. The time had surely now come for them to be deported. In the most virulent language, *Reynolds's* declared that 'the German heart, when in the breast of a Royal or Princely personage is inherently base', and that Baron Stockmar, long-time adviser of Leopold and Albert, should be sent back with other 'slimy Germans emanating from their murky holes abroad', just as the Queen's erstwhile German companion, Baroness Lehzen, had been 'packed off to her native pigsty'.[70] Republicans saw the affair as confirmation of the alien character of the English monarchy: Linton asked in the *English Republic*, 'Have England's honour or England's interest ever been consulted in any European question since – as a natural consequence of our glorious Dutch Revolution – we were first cursed with a German family?'[71]

The Protectionist Tory press also turned on Albert, who had been seen as an enemy ever since his public support for Peel's repeal of the Corn Laws.[72] (The Protectionist voice had been a dissentient one at the Great Exhibition in 1851, a celebration of free trade and internationalism organized by Albert – the *Morning Herald* expressed displeasure at the number of 'foreigners' drawn into London by the Exhibition.)[73] In 1854 the *Standard* stated:

> George the Third was beloved as a good man, a good King, but above all, as a thoroughly good Englishman. 'Born and educated in

this country I glory in the name of Briton' ... Why is it that the Consort of our beloved Queen is never spoken or thought of as an Englishman?[74]

The *Morning Herald* revived the 1839 rumours that Albert was a Catholic (provoked by the omission of the phrase 'Protestant Prince' from the declaration of engagement to the Queen[75]) and said that this would divert English policy in the favour of Belgium and Austria and undermine the Protestantism so integral to the national character. Moreover, Albert's interest in educational reform, including reform of the curriculum at Cambridge University, where he was Chancellor, was part of his plan to bring all the country's institutions 'nearer to a German model'.[76]

The penetration of the newspaper campaign into the popular mind was shown by the rumours that Albert – some stated Victoria as well – had been taken to the Tower for high treason, and by the anti-German sentiments in popular ballads.[77] Greville noted in his journal on 15 January: 'At present nobody talks of anything else, and those who come up from distant parts of the country say that the subject is the universal topic of discussion in country towns and on railways'. He 'could not remember anything like the virulence and profligacy of the press' and regretted that 'it is not to be denied or concealed that these abominable libels have been greedily swallowed all over the country and a strong impression produced' – the sales of the *Morning Advertiser*, he noted, had increased enormously since it began its attacks on the Prince.[78] The *Advertiser* was the paper of the licensed victuallers' trade[79] and, available in public houses, its readership was in any case larger than its normal circulation of 6,600 suggested.[80]

Pamphlets were written in Albert's defence in an attempt to mitigate the crisis of royal unpopularity. One protested that as husband of the Queen of England and father of her children 'the first and strongest intuitions of the Prince's heart are all English rather than German'.[81] Another asserted: 'Never has there been, in the last two centuries, less of "German influence" at the British Court, than at present. It has been very honourably said of the Prince, that it has been his study to become an Englishman.'[82] When parliament reassembled, statements were made refuting the allegations of the Prince's treason to British interests.[83] However, the anti-Germanic distrust of Albert persisted and setbacks in the Crimean War were blamed on his unpatriotic interference. The *Morning Advertiser* in an article entitled 'Why has Odessa been spared?' claimed the answer lay in 'the pro-Russianism which exists in the Court ... Germanism and Russianism are convertible terms' – and Albert was, it was clearly implied, the source of such an influence.[84]

Albert exacerbated matters when, at the height of the war, he made a speech which seemed to express envy at the despotic government of

Russia which was able to prosecute the war with complete secrecy and freedom from criticism – the circumstances of war had, he said, placed the parliamentary institutions of England 'on their trial'. This provoked the indignation of radical patriotism which saw Albert as proposing to 'Germanize' British institutions.[85] *Reynolds's Newspaper* once more drew the picture of the German Prince feeding from the body of John Bull: 'Why cannot this fat foreigner gorge himself with the national plunder in peace, without both insulting and libelling the people of this country?'[86] The *Sunday Times*, in an article on 'Royalty and National-ity', viewed the concurrent absence of the Queen and Albert from Ascot – the premier event of the 'sport which above all others, is characteristic of the English nation' – as further evidence of the Prince's refusal 'to accommodate himself to the national humour', a signal failing in one 'nourished by all the tid-bits that the national purse can afford'. Albert's snub to horse-racing, a sport not practised in his native Germany, was an example of his desire to 're-model him (John Bull) according to some foreign school'. This was also manifested in his proposals to make the academic curriculum of the universities more rigorous at the expense of sport:

> The absence of manly exercise is one of the defects of the German universities, and, in spite of the erudition of his professors, the German student is, in all that regards bodily training, a far inferior animal to the Oxonian or the Cantab. Our national systems of instruction call loudly for reform, but no true patriot could wish to see the boating, the cricketing, the riding of Oxford and Cambridge banished from the precincts of learning.[87]

There was no single major stirring of patriotic sentiment against Albert after the Crimean War but an anti-German feeling continued to be directed against him during his remaining years and posthumously. A pamphlet entitled *Prince Albert. Why is he unpopular?*, first published during the uproar of 1853–4, was reissued in 1857, when it remained the case that 'in this world of contradiction, there is one fact that not even a Jellinger Symonds can be found to countravert, and that is the unpopularity of His Royal Highness Prince Albert'. Albert served as 'a *butt* against whom to launch our shafts of temper and ridicule when-ever we feel inclined', and 'one of the great cries against the Prince has its origin in his German relations'.[88] Theodor Fontane in England in 1857 remarked on the feeling 'against "Germanism"' and the rumours that Albert and Stockmar interfered in politics and that the Queen had imposed upon Palmerston as the condition of his appointment as Prime Minister that he under no circumstances press for a declaration of war on Prussia.[89] In 1858 celebration of the Princess Royal's wedding was marred by speculation that Albert was to be created 'King Consort'.

Alluding to this, a Northampton radical recalled Albert's alleged meddling with the government and declared, 'I object to Germanism or any other ism which will take away the rights of workingmen'.[90] The *Spectator* dismissed the speculations as groundless as Albert was 'not likely ... to add even a feather's weight to any jealousy of the German element in our Court; for the lightest of the feathers may be "the last"'.[91] While obituaries to Albert in the middle-class press in 1861 were, out of deference to the Queen, eulogistic, even in those newspapers which had attacked him during his life,[92] *Reynolds's* retrospective references to him were as a 'German'.[93] F.W. Soutter observed that the unpopularity of Albert's nationality was one of the causes of the republican movement's emergence in the early 1870s.[94]

Albert was indeed as a ball and chain for the monarchy to drag after it as far as its identity with patriotism and the national character was concerned; without him the Royal Family would undeniably be more English. The Queen was already regarded as the epitome of English domestic virtues – to quote the *Morning Post*, 'the highest type of English lady, English wife and English mother'.[95] The *Daily Telegraph*, like the Post, commenting on the Princess Royal's wedding, wrote:

> We will not remember, on this morning, that a German lineage mingles in the succession to the British throne, for whatever heralds may demonstrate, history, patriotism, reciprocal chivalry has made Victoria English, and the blood of England will mount to-day, to the cheeks of the royal bride ... [96]

Yet such sanguine views of the Royal Family's Englishness were not universally held. The *Spectator* wrote that there was a European 'royal class' – perpetuated by inter-marriages such as that of the Princess Royal to the heir to the Prussian throne – which transcended the national identity of all the countries over which its members ruled. Thus, while 'our own Queen is English in her opinions, attachments, and policy' she was above all a member of the royal class with its transnational concerns and when a minister of the Crown 'is "explaining" in Parliament it is impossible to tell how much of his motives, purposes and plans, belong to this country, or are foreign'.[97] In an article entitled 'The Royal German Legion', *Lloyd's Weekly Newspaper* observed that in the wedding procession 'there is hardly an English person' – it was 'a list of carefully disposed foreigners – connections of the royal family of England'. It warned that the court did not fully escape 'the great reproach which the English nation had to make against the early Georges ... their Germanism'.[98] The removal of Albert could not and, as we shall see, did not in itself put an end to all charges of foreignness against the Royal Family, though it was to remove the major obstacle to its identification with Englishness.

Furthermore, while the *Daily Telegraph* and the *Morning Post* were employing a 'language of patriotism' focused on the monarchy, the radical 'language of patriotism' was still being voiced in other quarters. At the beginning of this section I quoted the mayor of Northampton who was trusting in 1858 to the sentiments that the word 'loyal' would evoke in every 'British heart'. However, the mayor's appeal to the loyalty of his townsfolk failed as his proposal for a public holiday on the wedding of the Princess Royal was defeated because those assembled saw patriotism as lying elsewhere – in responsibility to the common people who had already lost enough money through the wedding in the costly ceremonial arrangements and the Princess Royal's annuity.[99] These two patriotisms continued to coexist, but in changing circumstances in the ensuing period.

1861–87: from patriotic criticism to the 'new nationalism'

In this period republicans and radical critics of the monarchy and Royal Family continued to consider themselves patriotic and specifically to use patriotic language as a weapon against the Crown: thus, it cannot be said that the 'language of patriotism' was conclusively appropriated by the state and by the right. However, this period was distinguished from the foregoing one in that patriotism began to be denounced by the emerging socialistic elements of the left as it came into more frequent and bellicose usage by the right. Socialism, which believed in internationalism and the brotherhood of the workers of different nations, disapproved of the patriotism which consisted in aggressive nationalism and imperialism – phenomena which were becoming more and more prevalent in the increasingly competitive international climate of the second half of the nineteenth century.

The *Spectator* wrote in Albert's obituary in 1861 of 'that newest form of idolatry, the worship of the reflection of one's own face', which had been manifested in 'that outburst of vanity' about Britain's supremacy at the Great Exhibition of 1851, designed by Albert as a celebration of international progress and peaceful goodwill.[100] It had been hailed as such in many quarters[101] but had also provoked boasts about 'the confidence of England in itself'[102] and about 'the most powerful Monarch in the earth'.[103] National assertiveness was to increase as doubts about the maintenance of Britain's world leadership set in, after the deficiencies exposed by the Crimean War[104] and with the establishment of a united Germany and the catching-up of the rest of Europe and the United States with Britain's industrial and colonial lead. The new nationalism and imperialism which historians have described[105] was to find a potent symbol in the Crown, better able to serve as such after Albert's death. However, the Prince Consort's removal was not enough to silence radicals' patriotic attacks on the Crown and it is these which will be considered before looking at the Crown's place in the new national and imperial cult.

In the 1860s, 1870s and 1880s the Royal Family was still seen as German by patriotic radicals, the situation being exacerbated by the marriages of several of the Queen's children to German princes and princesses. Attacks were made on the Crown's alleged pro-German interference with British foreign policy and on the bleeding of the British taxpayer to maintain foreigners in idle splendour. The radical language of patriotism lived on in the republican movement of the early 1870s which regarded itself as truly patriotic.

In the 1860s patriotic criticism centred on the royal marriages and on the Queen's involvement in the Schleswig-Holstein crisis of 1864. *Reynolds's Newspaper* was foremost in its denunciation of all things royal and German. Of the marriage of Princess Alice to the Prince of Hesse-Darmstadt in 1862 and the accompanying pensions and sine-cures to the newly-weds, it wrote: 'We submit to these bleedings for the sake of starveling Germans ... a portion of this golden blood ... should be allowed to re-enter into the well-drained veins of the plundered industry of our own country'.[106] The *Sunday Times* continued to berate German affiliations. Prince Christian of Schleswig-Holstein who married Princess Helena in 1866 was immediately styled 'His Royal Highness' and granted a major-generalship in the British army in addition to his wife's handsome dowry – the paper observed, 'These German princes may well find it desirable to get hold of an English princess in the bonds of "holy matrimony"'.[107]

The Queen's German ancestry, her attachment to the memory of Albert and the marriage ties of her children were held to cloud her judgement of international affairs and to lead her to interfere with British policies in the interests of the German powers – especially dangerous in the 1860s and early 1870s when Prussian aggrandizement was creating a unified Germany. In 1864 it was rumoured that the Queen had prevented her ministers from coming to the aid of Denmark to prevent Prussian and Austrian annexation of the duchies of Schleswig-Holstein.[108] The matter was raised in parliament by Lord Ellenborough who stated that 'in all public questions relating to Germany, Her Majesty's Ministers have as much difficulty in carrying out a purely English policy as was experienced ... in the reigns of the two first sovereigns of the House of Hanover'.[109] The question of the Queen's pro-Germanism again reached parliament in 1870 when she was seen to be favouring Prussia in the war with France.[110] We have seen how the French republic formed after Napoleon III's defeat at Sedan in September 1870 inspired the sympathy of British radicals, and the belief that the Queen was an ally of Prussia in its war against the republic was a further stimulus to the emergence of a British republican movement.

The republican movement of the early 1870s set great store by its patriotism and by the lack of patriotism of the 'kings and queens ... bred from special foreign stocks'[111] imported to rule a people whose true character was one of independence and self-government. The *Daily Telegraph* asserted at the time of the Thanksgiving for the Prince of Wales' recovery in 1872 that 'Nobody thinks of her (the Queen) as a Guelph – as a descendent of that Elector of Hanover'[112] but one only had to read the columns of Charles Bradlaugh's *National Reformer*, the organ of the Republican Clubs, to be disabused of this illusion. Bradlaugh wrote of the present Royal Family, 'I loathe these small German breastbestarred wanderers ... In their own land they vegetate and wither scarcely noticed; here we pay them highly to marry and perpetuate a pauper prince race.' This was the conclusion to his 'Impeachment of the House of Brunswick' in which all the Hanoverian monarchs from George I to Victoria were indicted for, among other things, Germanic treachery to the country over which they ruled.[113] The memoirs of Stockmar, published in 1873, showed 'how the small German family whom we pay to be our chief magistrates, regard their own petty interests rather than those of the nation'.[114] Prince Albert had 'dictated a German continental policy to Lord John Russell'[115] and the Queen, as in 1864, had continued to do so after her consort's death.[116]

The loyal press accused the republicans of lacking 'patriotism'[117] – the *Sunday Times*, becoming conservative by this time, wrote that Dilke's criticisms of the Queen at Newcastle in November 1871 would have no effect on the 'patriotic discrimination of the great British public'.[118] Republicans regarded such statements as perversions of patriotism. C. Charles Cattell, president of the first Republican Club, formed at Birmingham, wrote that republicans were 'patriots' in that they were 'enlightened' and acted upon the 'first principles of political justice'.[119] Some radical societies of this period were known as Patriotic Societies[120] and some of these societies became Republican Clubs or maintained close links with them.[121] The House of Commons which voted overwhelmingly in 1870 for the annuity to Princess Louise on her marriage was ironically described as 'patriotic'.[122] The real patriots were the delegates convening at Birmingham for the national conference of Republican Clubs in 1873: 'To assert human freedom, has been the mission of England ... England, vibrating with enlightened patriotism, will not prostrate herself before a man, an institution, or a name'.[123]

The same identification of patriotism and republicanism was made by George Standring, who, after the collapse of the organized movement in the mid-1870s, maintained a republican propaganda for another ten years.[124] Republicanism, wrote Standring, entailed 'the people legislating for themselves, elevating themselves ... in patriotism'.[125] The *Republican* also contained virulent attacks on the 'German paupers' in receipt of pensions and sinecures: 'Whether under a Monarchy, or under a Republic, England should at least be governed by Englishmen'.[126]

As we have seen,[127] republicanism was fading into insignificance from the mid-1870s, but attacks on the foreignness of the Royal Family remained part of the popular radicalism of *Reynolds's Newspaper*. In 1873 it wrote, 'All the royal family are Germans. There is not a drop of English blood in their veins.'[128] The royal marriages of the 1880s were derided in the same way as those of the 1860s and 1870s. Prince Leopold's was regarded as a device to pension 'the daughter of a beggarly little German prince', as the chronically ill Leopold had not long to live. His wedding was merely the pretext for 'a flight of locusts' to descend 'on our shores' – as ever, from Germany.[129] The wedding of Victoria's youngest child Beatrice in 1885 brought the last in a long line of German additions to her family, Prince Henry of Battenberg, whose new 'mother-in-law will provide him lucrative appointments at the expense of John Bull, just as she has done Christian, Gleichen, Leiningen, and other princely sweepings of German workhouses'.[130]

At the same time, however, we find patriotism being spoken of pejoratively by certain radicals and republicans. This is explained by the emergence of the internationalist creed of socialism and by the cultivation of an aggressive patriotism by the right. In the *Republican*, the newspaper running from 1870 to 1872 as the organ of the socialistic Land and Labour League, there was an ambivalent attitude to patriotism. On the one hand republicanism was described as patriotic[131] and the monarchy denounced as 'German-plated',[132] but there were also attacks on patriotism. One correspondent saw patriotism as part of the state's apparatus for dominating the people – 'The whole tendency of things in England is to crush and grind down the poor ... Death and glory, Queen and country, drink and tobacco, will get them into the required condition of devoted loyalty and patriotism'.[133] Patriotism here was seen as what current Marxians would call 'false-consciousness', deflecting from true class loyalty. The paper stated that patriotism served to 'keep mankind isolated', by 'dividing and *localising* the human family into geographical clans or groups called nations'. This was again presented as a deliberate device of the ruling classes to deceive the workers into false loyalties: '... the political traffickers have deluded their victims under the plea of patriotism, sinking them pell-mell into the most disastrous wars for the support, glorification, and perpetuation of Kings, Emperors, Aristocracies, and Oligarchies'.[134] The positive radical picture of patriotism as service to the whole community was here replaced by a negative one of patriotism as subjection to the ruling class's partial definition of the national interest.

This divergence is seen in Standring's *Republican* in the 1880s. On the one hand it was located in the tradition of libertarian patriotism but it also set itself in the new socialist trend of thought.[135] 'Modern jingoism' was attacked[136] and in an article, 'Internationalism versus Patriotism', patriotism was presented as synonymous with such jingoism. 'Patriotism has little regard for the interests of other communities, and is almost essentially in continual antagonism to them.' It was characterized by a national vanity which prompted imperialist expansion, and was the creed of the ruling class: 'those who are mostly interested in patriotism are the monarchs to whom it brings larger revenues and the aristocratic satellites who share the spoil'.[137]

It was the assertive new nationalism and imperialism of the final quarter of the nineteenth century which enforced a strong bond between the monarchy and a chauvinistic, authoritarian patriotism. Loyalty and service to the throne was an important theme in the writings of those propounding a competitive nationalism in response to the foreign challenge to British supremacy. Even a writer declaring himself to be of liberal, pacific views argued in 1875 that Britain must look to her hereditary rulers to forge a united, national spirit if she were to retain her industrial and commercial lead. The success of Prussia was attributed to her clearly defined structure of social command.[138]

Hugh Cunningham has fixed on the jingoism orchestrated by the Conservatives during the Eastern crisis of 1877–8 as the moment at which patriotism became a right-wing ideology.[139] It was in the 1870s that Disraeli identified the Conservatives as the patriotic party; defenders of the nation's ancient institutions and, in the ministry of 1874–80, exponents of an aggressive foreign policy promoting Britain's world role – admittedly more by accident in Afghanistan and the Transvaal, but definitely by design in the brinkmanship towards Russia in the crisis of 1877–8. The mantle of Palmerston had descended on Disraeli and this time the Crown, with Albert departed and Victoria an ardent supporter of her Prime Minister, was linked with these forward policies rather than seen as opposed to them. Whereas in the Eastern crisis of the mid-1850s Albert and the court were accused of pro-Russianism, explaining British pusillanimity, in 1877–8 the Crown was firmly associated with the Russophobe pro-war party. The Queen's unusual visit to Disraeli's home at Hughenden was believed to indicate her approval of his basing his Eastern policy squarely on British interests in the face of Gladstone's moralistic condemnation of upholding the despotic Turkish government. The expression of anti-Russian sentiments in the authorized biography of the Prince Consort was taken to be a direct message from the throne; the publication in late 1877 of the volume dealing with the Crimean War being timed, Liberals alleged, to influence public opinion unconstitutionally.[140] Conservatives openly linked the Queen with their policies – in the party's literary organ, the *Quarterly Review*, W.J. Courthorpe wrote that the Queen would be justified in using her prerogative to declare war on Russia.

Courthorpe's overall argument was that a coherent national policy directed by the Crown was needed if Britain were to hold her own against the autocratic powers of Europe. If time were wasted in factious parliamentary debate and in following the fluctuations of public opinion, Britain would be decimated in the modern world of 'Realpolitik', where force was the decisive factor in international politics. The answer to the problems of international competition was an iron dawn of authoritarian patriotism in which the Crown provided 'the head which thinks and the arm which strikes'.[141]

This smacked of Urquhartism and of the romantic Toryism of Disraeli's early novels, and, as we have seen, there were serious fears that Disraeli, in his magnification of the royal title and his use of the prerogative to commit Britain to dangerous undertakings in foreign policy, was acting according to a grand theory, foreshadowed in *Sybil* and *Coningsby*, of royal supremacy, in which the Crown as head of a united nation superseded the factions of parliament.[142] The Crown had played an important part in Disraeli's rhetoric in opposition in the early 1870s presenting the Conservatives as the national party, the defender of the institutions fundamental to national character and greatness, in contrast to Gladstonian Liberalism, depicted as an alien, cosmopolitan creed which fostered republicanism. Gladstone, however, was as ardent a monarchist as Disraeli. Anxious to check republicanism, he organized the Thanksgiving of 1872 to rebuff the republican movement through a solemn celebration of the nation's consensus in its allegiance to the monarchy as an integral part of the national life.[143]

Royal ceremonials from the Thanksgiving onwards occasioned paeans to the Englishness of the monarchy combined with defiant, self-conscious comparisons of the English nation with her foreign rivals. *The Times* described the Thanksgiving as a 'great National Solemnity', one of those 'national acts' which serve 'to awaken national sympathy'. This was important as at this time there must be no 'weakening of the national spirit, of patriotic zeal ... An occasion such as this gives the public the opportunity of proving ... that it is as capable as ever of national enthusiasm, and that if another time of trial should come the manly virtues of our forefathers would again be conspicuous.' In an era of individualism, loyalty to the Crown provided the necessary 'national spirit' – the Queen was 'a living symbol of this great union, as well as a link between the glorious past and brightening future of this Empire'.[144] The *Sunday Times* wrote that 'all patriotic Englishmen' would be satisfied by the Thanksgiving: 'Had it been a failure it would have exposed our national weakness, but since it was a success foreigners will remember that England is strong because she is united'.[145] The *Illustrated London News* saw the ceremonial as 'a nation's renewed homage to the glorious principles that have maintained that nation in the foremost place of the world, and which will so maintain it while England is true to herself and her noble traditions'.[146] According to the *Daily Telegraph* the Thanksgiving gave 'a new sense of national strength, and a new spirit of patriotism and pride'. It served as proof that 'the history of the Mother of Empires is not nearly finished, nor her proud glories half unfolded, if she had carried to modern times these ancient and sterling qualities of unity, loyalty, piety and ideal nationality which was yesterday so splendidly exemplified'.[147]

The marriages of the Queen's children became occasions for the expression of such sentiments by the loyal and nationalistic. The *Saturday Review* observed that the entry of the Duke of Edinburgh with his Russian bride in March 1874 was a more imposing ceremonial than Britain had been accustomed to and conjectured that the return of the Conservatives to power might explain this and the greater military element in the procession: 'Instead of a paltry guard, there was an inspiring body of troops on the ground, and the troops were picked regiments of whom any nation might be proud'.[148] Royal ceremonials were important, wrote the *Daily Telegraph*, in displaying to the world Britain's 'great wealth and unsurpassed rank among nations'.[149] The *Observer* wrote that staging a fine ceremony was a matter of 'national self-respect'.[150] We have seen the fierce, xenophobic attacks made by the popular radical press on the choice of German spouses, but the middle-class press now wrote of the racial and historic links between the Saxon peoples of England and Germany – the *Daily News* on Arthur's wedding to Louise, Princess of Prussia, declared, 'We and the people of the (German) Empire are akin, after all, and beneath superficial differences, the two national characters are not very unlike'.[151] The *Saturday Review*, when Leopold married Helena, Princess of Waldeck-Pyrmont, reflected that given the close connections between the English and the Germans, 'the prepossession of Englishmen against all that comes from Germany is, to say the least remarkable'.[152]

An important element in the new nationalism was an increased pre-occupation with the British empire. The earlier Victorian period had not been 'anti-imperialist'[153] and statements of pride in the empire can be found in the 1840s and 1850s.[154] But there was not that self-con-sciousness about imperial unity, glorification of empire and naked asso-ciation of it with national power which became familiar from the 1870s.[155] Earlier references to Victoria as head of the empire had usu-ally dwelt on the way in which her sovereignty was a safeguard of the liberties of her subject peoples – as for example in 1858 when the formal assumption by the Crown of the powers of the East India Company was hailed as bringing hope for fairer government to the Indian people, in the wake of the Mutiny.[156] It is from the 1870s that the Crown's role as the symbol of imperial unity and strength becomes more pronounced. While the title of Empress of India in 1876 was an unpopular one because of its despotic overtones, the opponents of 'imperialism' as a system of government could be devotees of Britain's imperial power. The *Daily Telegraph* viewed the Royal Titles Act as a 'sinister revolution'[157] but styled itself at this time an 'imperial' newspa-per.[158] In 1873 it decried the republicans at Birmingham for ignoring that as Englishmen they were 'born aristocrats', part of their inheritance being 'the pride and honour of all these English possessions which belt the earth with the colour of England's heraldic rose, and daily hear "the Queen's morning drum beat round the world"'.[159] One reason for its opposition to the Royal Titles Bill was that imperial unity would not be best served by giving a distinct title to the Queen's sovereignty of one part of the empire.[160] *The Times*, which was opposed to the new title, had been enthusiastic about the Prince of Wales' concurrent visit to India as it would strengthen the ties of empire.[161] Mundella in the Commons defended the heavy expenditure on the Prince's tour, saying 'The monarchy ought to represent the greatness and wealth of the empire'.[162] The first of the Delhi Durbars, organized by the Viceroy, Lytton, in 1876 to commemorate the Queen's new title, ushered in an era in which royal and imperial ceremonial were to be indissolubly linked.[163]

At home royal ceremonials were coming to be seen as celebrations of empire. The *Daily Telegraph* wrote upon the reception of the Duke of Edinburgh and his bride in 1874, 'Those brave officers who have won so great a victory for Civilization in the heart of Africa marched for Her Majesty; and for "Her Majesty's cause" there are hundreds of thou-sands more ready to "go anywhere and do anything"'.[164] In the paper's account of Prince Leopold's wedding in 1882 the Queen was described as the ruler 'of the greatest and mightiest empire ever submitted to a woman's sway'.[165] *The Times* regretted that the colonial leaders would not be in England for the Jubilee in 1887, as they were visiting in the Summer of 1886 – the Jubilee should be an imperial event.[166] The Imperial Institute was opened in 1886 as part of the colonial leaders' visit and the Foreign Secretary, Rosebery, a Liberal imperialist, wanted the Queen to be in state dress – he wrote to Ponsonby, the Queen's Private Secretary, 'The symbol that unites this vast Empire is a Crown not a bonnet'.[167]

1887–1901: the Imperial Crown

The final phase of the reign marked the culmination of the identification of the monarchy with nationalism and imperialism and of the attainment of a near monopoly on the currency of patriotism by the right. Both Conservatives and Liberals identified the monarchy as the institution which bound the nation and the empire together but the former group, as we saw in chapter 5, went further in using royal events as a celebration of the assertive foreign policy and imperialism with which they were associated. Meanwhile the radicals of *Reynolds's Newspaper* still sometimes used the language of patriotism in its old democratic idiom but were generally concerned with attacking what they saw as a pernicious new 'jingo' imperialism – as were the new socialist newspapers, where we can find a negative view of patriotism as synonymous with such jingoism and imperialism. It is noticeable that attacks on the Royal Family as German persisted in *Reynolds's Newspaper* but also noticeable that the *Labour Leader,* with its internationalist, socialist outlook did not share with the older radicalism this form of patriotic pride in English freedom set against Continental despotism.

The monarchy and its ceremonials were depicted as the focal point of patriotism in the mainstream press. For *The Times* the Golden Jubilee was a 'festival of patriotism'. It termed a cheering East Ender 'a sturdy patriot'.[168] The *Daily Telegraph* described the 'unrestrained patriotism' which the Jubilee summoned up.[169] At a time of increasing concern in Britain about growing international rivalry, colonial, military and economic,[170] royal events were opportunities to celebrate and demonstrate the strength of the nation. *The Times* wrote in 1887 of armament in Europe, the resurgence of France, the 'struggle for existence' and 'commercial contest for the control of markets'[171] and observed that, while Britain's army was comparatively small, foreign princes attending the Golden Jubilee would have been impressed by its evidence that 'if a time of trial were to come upon the English race, English men, we are sure, would be ready, for adequate reasons, to incur sacrifices which would place them on a level in point of armed force with their neighbours'.[172]

For *Lloyd's Weekly Newspaper* the congratulations from around the world to Victoria were a tribute to 'the greatness of the Anglo-Saxon race'.[173] In 1897 *The Times* wrote that the Diamond Jubilee was a time of 'heightened national consciousness' through pride in the Queen.[174]

Obituaries of the Queen, especially from the Conservative side, emphasized patriotism as a personal characteristic and as a force bound up with the monarchy. Salisbury spoke of her 'passionate patriotism'[175] and *The Times* used the same phrase about Disraeli to explain the Queen's warm approval of him.[176] The *Daily Telegraph* wrote that the Queen was part of 'our sense of England' and asked, 'Who can think of the nation and the race without her?' as she was 'the golden link of the race'. *The Times* reflected that people needed to follow the Queen's example to prolong national glory at a time when foreign states had caught up and improved on Britain's industrial lead while the spirit of innovation had died out at home. The *Telegraph* exhorted people to raise the monument left in their hearts by the Queen's funeral 'ever higher by vigilant and steadfast patriotism and a spirit of national duty that will never slumber or flinch'.[177]

The strongest patriotic theme in this period was the role of the Crown as the binding force in an expanding Empire. These years saw the scramble for Africa, the reconquest of the Sudan and the Boer War, and British colonial interests were involved in confrontations with France and the United States and a worsening of relations with Germany. The two Jubilees, especially the second, were celebrations of imperial strength and the Queen's funeral, taking place in the middle of the Boer War, was a strongly military ceremony and the occasion of much assertiveness about the importance of empire (and also criticism from opponents of the war).

The development of the empire was one of the features of the reign emphasized in 1887. *The Times*, reviewing one of the many commemorative books produced, wrote, 'If it were sought to sum up the effect of the book in a single phrase, that phrase would be the expansion of England'.[178] The newspaper usually prefaced references to the empire with the word 'vast'[179] and reflected that the 'ancient polity of England is, in its totality, no mean part of the civilization of the world'.[180] An effect of the Jubilee would be to impress on the visiting foreign princes 'the extent in territory, in resources, and in population of the British Empire, with its rich and varied domains in every clime'.[181] The *Standard* wrote of the 'great Pan-Britannic procession'.[182] The uniting force of the Queen's popularity throughout the empire was alluded to – *The Times* stated that no toast was drunk with greater enthusiasm or more frequently 'throughout the vast British Empire than that of "the Queen: God bless her"'.[183] Liberal newspapers also hailed the 'great Empire on which the sun never sets' and the celebration throughout it of the Queen's Jubilee.[184] The Conservative *National Review* pointed out that as the self-governing white colonies had their own legislatures they 'find the symbol of Imperial unity not in the British Parliament . . . but in the person of the British Sovereign'.[185]

Such was the importance of the monarchy to the empire and of the empire to the monarchy that the *Spectator* suggested in 1893 that, while enthusiasm for the monarchy might not be on the increase in Britain – part of a 'decline . . . in the ancient English patriotism' – it certainly was in the empire and this would in the long run ensure the future of the British monarchy against any possible upsurge of republicanism in the 'English proletariat' – 'The Empire would not adhere to a Republic . . . and as the Empire nourishes England, the people are by no means willing to give it up'.[186]

The journal pursued this theme at the time of the Diamond Jubilee, arguing that the major reason for the enhanced standing of the monarchy was the growth of 'Imperial spirit'. The words 'Imperial' and 'Empire' were increasingly being used in place of 'loyal' and 'kingdom'. The throne now stood at the 'centre not of a kingdom, but of a world-wide Empire, of a congeries of nations, races, sections of mankind . . . the link which binds us to so many is the golden circlet which marks sovereignty'. The British people were proud to have a monarch who ruled a quarter of humanity: 'The pride of Sovereignty has in fact entered into the people', as shown by their 'almost ludicrous' appreciation of the colonial Prime Ministers and colonial troops in the procession. The monarchy was now made secure by the British people's love of empire – if it disappeared the monarchy 'might, as they clearly see, carry with it the bond which makes of New Zealanders and Englishmen one people'.

The Spectator wrote of the Diamond Jubilee, 'Imperialism was the note of the entire festivity'.[187] While the colonial Prime Ministers had attended the Golden Jubilee – and the first Colonial Conference had been held in London as a result – they were the central guests in the second Jubilee due to the Queen's desire not to invite the crowned heads of Europe, who had been present at the first. Chamberlain, Colonial Secretary and the most ardent 'new Imperialist' in the government saw the possibility of the colonial Prime Ministers filling the gap and of the participation of colonial troops in the procession as a striking demonstration of imperial unity and strength.[188] The *Daily Telegraph* saw the Jubilee as an endorsement of Chamberlain's idea of imperial federation, as 'Imperial unity was yesterday incarnate'.[189] *The Times* wrote of the procession, 'Seldom has the immensity and the unity of the Empire been brought before the imagination more powerfully more powerfully'.[190] The key newspaper of the populist 'new journalism', the Conservative, imperialist *Daily Mail* on the day after Jubilee day, trumpeted:

> Until we saw it passing through the streets of our city we never quite realized what the Empire meant . . . It makes life worth living . . . to feel oneself part of this enormous, this wondrous machine, the greatest organization the world ever saw.[191]

When the Queen died, Balfour, in his obituary speech in the Commons, singled out as the most notable feature of her reign, 'the growth, moral and material of the Empire over which she ruled'.[192] The *Daily Telegraph* wrote that Victoria's life had been bound up with the 'heritage and destiny of Empire'. Of the imposing military ceremonial of the funeral, it observed, 'the procession . . . was the epitome of Empire'.[193] *The Times*' retrospect on her reign remarked on the way in which 'the Imperialist sentiment had lately become a powerful factor in the national life' and on how Chamberlain had used this to turn the Diamond Jubilee into 'not a family festival, not a democratic festival, but a festival of the British Empire'. The newspaper's own coverage of the funeral stressed the 'great Imperial realities of which naval and military honours to the dead Queen are but symbols'. It wrote of the carriage of her body across the Solent that it was fitting for Victoria 'to pass to her rest . . . amid the booming guns by which her Empire has been maintained and extended'.[194]

Royal ceremonial of these years also occasioned cautious and critical comment on imperialism from the left. The Liberal *Pall Mall Gazette* warned against unthinking celebration in 1887: 'Does our Empire stand everywhere for peace, for liberty, for justice, and for right?'[195] In 1901 some opponents of the Boer War in a divided Liberal party expressed distaste over the government's association of the monarchy with the aggressive imperialism of recent years. Emily Crawford in The *Contemporary Review* deplored the 'Jingo Imperialism' into which Britain had lapsed in response to its 'relative inferiority' now in strength to other nations. The Diamond Jubilee had been an unwise 'glorification of material power'.[196] The *Daily News* regretted that the main funeral procession was 'too exclusively military' and that 'inordinate greed for wealth', as exemplified by the desire for the gold of the Transvaal, had become so strong in Britain.[197]

The most outspoken criticism of the imperialism of royal ceremonial came in *Reynolds's Newspaper* and in the socialist press. *Reynolds's* still sometimes used the old radical language of patriotism – for example it described the opponents of the 1889 royal grants as 'its [the Commons'] more patriotic representatives'[198] and, in an article calling on Edward VII to be a 'Patriot King', it condemned the burning of a Boer village and commented, 'It is not unpatriotic to be just'.[199] The newspaper lamented the 'baneful new Imperialism' which had characterized the latter part of Victoria's reign[200] and at the time of the Diamond Jubilee ironically suggested an alternative procession including the ghosts of the Maori race, 'any remnant of the aboriginal Australians who survived the murder and rapine of the most Christian monarch Victoria'; any Kaffirs, Zulus and other African tribes surviving the '"civilizing" and "Christianizing" process for which England has earned notoriety'; 'a representative contingent of loyal and contented East Indians' and 'a deputation of Egyptians mad with joy at the English rule'.[201]

The new, socialist left was fiercely critical of aggressive imperialism and we can find in its press the use of 'patriotism' as a pejorative term identical with such imperialism and the preserve of glorifiers of the monarchy. The *Clarion*, complaining about the extravagantly eulogistic obituaries of the Queen from supporters of the Boer War, argued that 'the outburst is not unnatural when we remember the Jingo fever of the last 2 years, and the patriotic bluster of the same men'.[202] Keir Hardie analysed the Diamond Jubilee in socialist terms – 'the statesmen are there because Empire means trade, and trade means profit, and profit means power over the common people'.[203] A staunch opponent of the Boer War, he objected in parliament to what he saw as the excessively militaristic style of the Queen's funeral, where, he said, the 'dead body of England's Queen was used as a recruiting sergeant to help the military designs now being carried into effect'.[204]

The Royal Family's 'Germanness' was irrelevant from Keir Hardie's perspective but still a target of attack for *Reynolds's Newspaper*. In 1887 the Queen was described as a German determined to import an endless line of relations to bleed the British taxpayer dry, and the Royal Family addressed as 'ignorant blockheads who are unable to spell your own mother tongue correctly':

> The very dogs in England's Court
> They bark and howl in German.[205]

In 1897 the Diamond Jubilee was described as 'more a German triumph than an English celebration'.[206] That supporters of the monarchy were aware of such potentially damaging views can be seen in the efforts in the loyal press to emphasize the Englishness of the Royal Family. In 1893 when Princess May of Teck assumed the role of future Queen by marrying the Duke of York, much was made of the Prince of Wales's statement that he was 'proud to think' that his son was marrying 'one born in this country, living in this country, and having the feelings of an

Englishwoman'.[207] (*Reynolds's Newspaper* scoffed that she was 'the most German Princess they could find to keep up the thoroughly foreign character of the ruling family'.[208]) Edward VII was hailed on his accession as possessing the 'truest and sincerest patriotism' and his Danish Queen as 'a true Englishwoman'. We can thus see the concern about the unpopularity of any perceived foreignness that would lead soon to the change in the dynasty's name to an English one in the First World War.

Conclusion

Throughout this period the relationship between the monarchy and patriotism remained a complex one. In 1873 republicans considered themselves patriotic as they assembled for their national convention at Birmingham, while loyal newspapers such as the *Daily Telegraph* condemned their political faith as a vain attempt to 'turn Englishmen into Frenchmen'.[209] Patriotism defied a simple definition – a satirical pamphlet on the debate over the Royal Titles Bill wrote that 'patriotism' was the name given when 'hundreds and thousands of people grumbled together' to form a political party opposed by another party of 'patriotic' grumblers.[210] It was always difficult to locate patriotism on the political spectrum. Hugh Cunningham has pinpointed the jingoism of 1877–8 as marking the decisive shift of patriotism from right to left. Radical and republican writings on the Crown do reveal a certain aversion to patriotism as a ruling class ideology in the 1870s and 1880s but on the whole republicans and radical critics of the monarchy continued to call themselves patriots.

What we do find from the 1870s on is the incorporation of the monarchy in an assertive nationalism and imperialism. The Crown had of course been identified with the national character and with national glory earlier in the reign – and in the time of Victoria's Hanoverian predecessors, most notably George III – but it becomes a more prominent and consistent feature of writings on the monarchy in the second half of the period here under examination. This is partly due to the more self-conscious national and imperial sentiments of these decades and partly to the death of Albert, which made it easier for the Crown to be a symbol of Englishness. Attacks on the 'Germanism' of the Royal Family persisted but were far less general and less serious than those levelled in Albert's day. The ruling house in Britain had always faced the dilemma of a dual identity – its members belonged to the transnational royal caste, interrelated and intermarrying, but were also heads of the British nation and British Empire. In the later Victorian period the

Royal Family became decisively national and imperial: the Diamond Jubilee was a far more imperial event than the Golden, when the Queen's foreign relations, the crowned heads of Europe, were the chief guests. The nationalization of the ruling dynasty was to be completed during the War with its change in name to Windsor. Consideration of the monarchy's relation to patriotism and nationalism shows that in some ways a transformation did occur – the Crown in 1853–4 portrayed as the enemy of English interests abroad was by 1887 on the threshold of an era where it was seen to embody these interests – but that this transformation was not of a straightforward linear character. Throughout this period different people projected very different images onto the monarchy, onto 'patriotism' and onto 'the nation'.

This chapter has concentrated on the different perspectives on patriotism from the left and right and on the 'Englishness' or otherwise of the monarchy in the reign of Victoria. Linda Colley's seminal book on patriotism in the preceding period has addressed two other vital issues – the way in which the British national identity created in the eighteenth century was a Protestant one forged on the anvil of conflict against Catholic France; and the extent to which the constituent parts of the United Kingdom were assimilated into this British identity. These are not areas which I can claim to have examined in any depth but my reading of the Catholic and Jewish press at the time of important royal events shows that on the British mainland non-Protestant subjects proclaimed their deep loyalty to the Crown and that they celebrated Victoria's reign as an epoch in which they had gained equality and membership of the nation. Before looking at these, it is instructive to quote *The Times*' contrast in 1901 between patriotism in the ages of Victoria and of her predecessor – it wrote that 'William IV was English after the manner of a sailor, who could not separate religion from patriotism, nor patriotism from fighting'.[211]

The leading Catholic newspaper, the *Tablet* showed perhaps the most reverence of any journal towards the monarchy because of its belief in the divinely sanctioned nature of royal authority. At the time of the Prince of Wales' wedding in 1863 it wrote that its loyalty was 'a principle of religion, and our fidelity an obligation of conscience'. Describing the enthusiasm of the crowds, it questioned the Liberals' insistence that such displays of loyalty in Continental states were the result of coercion and attacked the contradiction between loyalty to the monarchy in Britain and the government's recent policy in Italy, where it had acquiesced in the deposition of legitimate rulers by Garibaldi and Piedmont.[212] In 1887 it again emphasized that 'Catholic loyalty is loyalty with a difference' and implied criticism of those newspapers which stressed Victoria's personal virtues, considerable though they were –

loyalty should not be based on 'personal liking'; the 'Sovereign, even in a constitutional country like this, is the representative of God'.[213]

The *Tablet* celebrated the advances enjoyed by Catholic subjects during the reign. In 1887 it hailed the presence of a Papal envoy in Britain for the first time in 200 years in honour of the Golden Jubilee as 'a symbol of the happy change which has come over the conditions of Catholicism in the reign of Queen Victoria'. The Queen herself was credited with never having shown herself inimical to Catholicism and, since she doubtless had some political influence, with not having used it to hinder their progress.[214] Given the rabid anti-Catholic sentiments of ultra Tories at the outset of the reign and the desire of some of them to see the like-minded heir presumptive, the Duke of Cumberland, on the throne, it is not surprising that the *Tablet* had expressed great satisfaction at the birth of the Prince of Wales in 1841. It wrote, 'A beloved Queen has added one more safeguard to the stability of the throne'.[215]

The *Jewish Chronicle* in 1863 expressed the rejoicing of 'loyal Jewish subjects' at the Prince of Wales's wedding, 'in common with all Englishmen ... for is not England our dear country, Queen Victoria our beloved Sovereign, and the Prince of Wales also our hope and pride ... ?'[216] In 1887 it reflected on the 'wondrous improvement which has taken place in our position during the Queen's happy reign ... No longer an alien the English Jew is now an integral part of the nation, as closely identified with its interests as any other Englishman.'[217] In its obituary Victoria was praised for her own example of 'enlightened toleration' as shown in her especial regard for Disraeli; while the new King's friendships with prominent members of British Jewry was remarked on.[218]

A study of Irish, Scottish and Welsh discussion of the monarchy is beyond the scope of this book though I have come across contributions from MPs for these parts of the United Kingdom in parliamentary debates on the monarchy and have read pioneering essays by other historians on an issue which should attract further research. As we have seen, Irish nationalist MPs objected to arrangements for the Golden Jubilee, arguing that Ireland had no cause to celebrate the events of the reign. In 1897 Dillon and Redmond made the same case about the Diamond Jubilee and O'Kelly went furthest, saying that the Irish were 'disloyal because they were not free, and that they were proud of their disloyalty'. They were countered by Colonel Sanderson, the MP for Protestant Armagh, who spoke of Irish loyalty,[219] and an essay by D.G. Boyce stresses that the Crown became the rallying point for Ulster Protestants faced by the Nationalist and Liberal Home Rule policy.[220]

Victoria's fondness for Scotland was reciprocated by its inhabitants according to several Scottish MPs contributing to the 1889 debates on the royal finances. Brown, MP for Hawick, speaking strongly *against* the grant, asserted that 'nowhere is [the Queen's] greatness and goodness more recognized than in Scotland'. Some Scottish representatives were more restrained. Campbell, MP for Kirkcaldy, said that he 'could not go into any gushing strain with reference to the institution of the Monarchy'. Philipps, MP for mid-Lanarkshire, while not commenting on the loyalty of his constituents said that not half a dozen of them would support the grant.[221] Christopher A. Whatley does not find any evidence of opposition to the Victorian monarchy in his essay on riot on the celebration of the sovereign's birthday in Scotland, but, as he stresses, his piece is a speculative, exploratory one and is more concerned with the 'meaning' of riot than with attitudes to the monarchy.[222] Antony Taylor, in a survey of dissentient voices in 1887, notes disdain for the Jubilee in a Scottish radical weekly advocating Home Rule.[223]

John Davies' essay on Victoria and Victorian Wales points out that the Queen spent only seven nights in Wales compared with a total of seven years in Scotland. However, he finds that Nonconformist Wales was largely approving of a monarch whose reign brought advances in religious liberty and equality. At the same time, he contends that there was considerable grass-roots republicanism in Wales but mainly through a dislike of royal grants (as seen in Mabon's intervention in the Commons debates of 1889 – see chapter 5) and concern over the moral character of the Prince of Wales, rather than through any nationalist feelings – there was, he writes, 'little that was specifically Welsh about Welsh anti-royalism'.[224] Since the late nineteenth century was a time of renewed national consciousness in Wales, with Welsh MPs and extra-parliamentary radicals in some measure following Irish examples, it would be instructive to see this argument tested further. It is interesting to reflect that the three areas of conflict identified by *Reynolds's Newspaper* as proof of discord at the time of the Golden Jubilee were coercion in Ireland, the tithe war in Wales and the crofters' war in Scotland – *Reynolds's* viewed them not as nationalist fights but as clashes between an oppressive state and the common people[225] (though elsewhere in its pages it cited the love of freedom felt by the Irish and Scots in contrast to the submissive English[226]) but they could also be seen as evidence of an unassimilated Celtic fringe.

Notes

1. Kingsley Martin, *The Crown and the Establishment* (London, 1962), pp. 21, 53–4; David Cannadine, 'The Context, Performance and Meaning of Ritual: the British Monarchy and the "Invention of Tradition",

c 1820–1977' in Eric Hobsbawn and Terence Ranger eds, *The Invention of Tradition* (Cambridge, 1983), p. 124; Tom Nairn, 'The glamour of backwardness', *The Times Higher Education Supplement*, no. 636 (11 January 1985), p. 13; idem, *The Enchanted Glass. Britain and its Monarchy* (London, 1988), p. 285; John M. MacKenzie ed., *Imperialism and Popular Culture* (Manchester, 1986), p. 3; idem, *Propaganda and Empire. The Manipulation of British Public Opinion, 1880–1960* (Manchester, 1984), pp. 3–4; Hugh Cunningham, 'The Language of Patriotism', *History Workshop*, issue 12 (Autumn 1981), pp. 23–4; idem, 'The Conservative Party and Patriotism' in Robert Colls and Philip Dodd eds, *Englishness. Politics and Culture 1880–1920* (London, 1986), p. 301; Miles Taylor, *The Decline of British Radicalism 1847–1860* (Oxford, 1995).

2. Cunningham, 'The Conservative Party and Patriotism', p. 301.
3. Idem, 'The Language of Patriotism', pp. 8–33.
4. *The Patriot Queen. To Her Most Gracious Majesty, Queen Victoria* The Humble Tribute of an Octogenarian. (London, 1838), p. 72.
5. *Sunday Times*, 16 March 1879, p. 4.
6. *Republican*, vol. 12 (June 1886), pp. 19–20.
7. Linda Colley, 'The Apotheosis of George III: Loyalty, Royalty and the British Nation 1760–1820', *Past and Present*, no. 102 (1984), pp. 94–129.
8. *Saturday Review*, 25 March 1871, p. 363.
9. *Republican*, vol. 11, no. 10 (January 1886), p. 75.
10. Cunningham, 'The Language of Patriotism', p. 19.
11. See above, chapter 3.
12. Cunningham, 'Jingoism and the Working Classes 1877–78', *Society for the Study of Labour History*, Bulletin no. 19 (Autumn 1969), p. 8.
13. MacKenzie, *Imperialism and Popular Culture*, p. 3.
14. *Sunday Times*, 19 March 1876, p. 4.
15. C.C. Eldridge, *England Mission. The Imperial Idea in the Age of Gladstone and Disraeli.* (London, 1983), p. 242.
16. *English Republic*, vol. 2 (1852), pp. 185–8.
17. *Morning Herald*, 10 November 1841, p. 2.
18. *People's Paper*, 30 January 1858, p. 1.
19. See, for example, Linda Colley, 'Whose Nation? Class and National Consciousness in Britain. 1750–1830', *Past and Present*, no. 113, (1986), pp. 97–117.
20. Cunningham, 'The Language of Patritoism', p. 17.
21. Ibid., p. 17.
22. Christopher Hill, *Puritanism and Revolution. Studies in Interpretation of the English Revolution of the 17th Century.* (London, 1958), pp. 101–2.
23. *English Republic*, vol. 1 (December 1850), pp. 3–4.
24. Ibid., vol. 1 (1851), p. 251.
25. Ibid., vol. 3 (1854), pp. 1–2; and see above, chapter 2.
26. For example the *Observer*, 14 November 1841, p. 4 cols 2–3. In fact, the Duke of Kent was persuaded to send his wife to England for the birth by acquaintances, including Joseph Hume, who saw the significance of such a move – see Cecil Woodham-Smith, *Queen Victoria. Her Life and Times 1819–1861* (London, 1983 edn), pp. 24–5.

27. *Courier*, 28 June 1838, p. 3.
28. *Berrow's Worcester Journal*, 5 July 1838, p. 3.
29. *Morning Chronicle*, 28 June 1838, p. 2.
30. Freda Harcourt, 'Gladstone, Monarchism and the "New Imperialism", 1868–74', *Journal of Imperial and Commonwealth History*, vol. 14, no. 1 (October 1985), pp. 20–51.
31. See below, chapter 7.
32. See above, chapter 4.
33. See, for example, *The Times*, 19 October 1850, p. 4.
34. H.R. Fox Bourne, *English Newspapers. Chapters in the History of Journalism*, 2 vols (London, 1887), vol. 2, pp. 5–6.
35. Cunningham, 'The Language of Patriotism', p. 21.
36. *John Bull*, 1 July 1838, p. 304.
37. Ibid.,13 November 1841, p. 546.
38. *The Patriot Queen*, pp. 68, 71–2, 78–9.
39. Benjamin Disraeli, *Sybil. Or the Two Nations* (1st pub, 1845, London, 1980 edn), pp. 38, 40–1, 63–4.
40. Idem., *Coningsby* (1st pub. 1844; Oxford, 1982 edn.), pp. 312–13.
41. See above, chapter 4.
42. *Free Press*, 10 May 1856, p. 2.
43. See above, chapter 4.
44. *Sunday Times*, 24 November 1839, p. 4.
45. *The Royal Wedding Jester or Nuptial Interlude. A Collection of the Wedding Facetiae Displayed on this Joyful Event*. The whole collected and arranged by Rigdum Funnidos (London, 1840), pp. 73–4, 14–15, 12–13.
46. *Northern Star*, 25 January 1840, p. 4.
47. *Spectator*, 11 January 1840) pp. 34–5.
48. *Sunday Times*, 24 November 1839, p. 4.
49. *Standard*, 25 January 1840, p. 4. *The Times*, 22 April 1843, p. 4 described the Royal Marriages Act as 'an insult to the commonalty, to the peerage, to the Majesty of this realm. It has perpetuated a consobrinal continuity of intermarriages which can only ensure moral and physical evils'.
50. Reginald Horsman, 'Origins of Racial Anglo-Saxonism in Great Britain before 1850', *Journal of the History of Ideas*, vol. 37, no. 3 (July–September 1976), pp. 387–411).
51. Ibid., pp. 399–403.
52. Described as such a tin-pot kingdom that it could not be found on the map, even with magnifying glasses, until recourse was taken to the 'famous oxy-hydrogen microscope at the Gallery of Practical Science'. [*The Royal Wedding Jester*, pp. 23, 57, 97.]
53. Ibid., passim.
54. *The Times*, 31 May 1842, p. 4 (my emphasis).
55. *Sunday Times*, 24 November 1839, p. 4.
56. See Brian Connell, *Regina v. Palmerston. The Correspondence between Queen Victoria and Her Foreign and Prime Minister 1837–1865*. (London, 1962), pp. 1–150.
57. Though the greatest Russophobe of them all, David Urquhart, regarded him, and not Albert, as the foreign agent subverting British foreign policy. (See above, chapter 4.)

58. Chapter 4.
59. See above, chapter 4.
60. *Northern Star*, 7 February 1852, p. 4.
61. *Morning Advertiser*, 19 December, 1853, p. 4; 20 December 1853, p. 2.
62. Ibid., late December 1853 passim; 5 January 1854, p. 4.
63. Ibid., 22 December 1853, p. 4.
64. Ibid., 24 December 1853, p. 4.
65. Ibid., 20 December 1853, p. 2.
66. Ibid., 13 January 1854, p. 5.
67. Ibid., 12 January 1854, p. 4.
68. *Daily News*, 11 January 1854, p. 2.
69. *Reynolds's Newspaper*, 1 January 1854, p. 7.
70. *Reynolds's Newspaper*, 15 January 1854, p. 1; 22 January 1854, p. 9.
71. *English Republic*, vol. 3 (1854), p. 77.
72. See above, chapter 4.
73. *Morning Herald*, 1 May 1851, p. 4.
74. *Standard*, 13 January 1854, p. 2.
75. See above, chapter 4.
76. *Morning Herald*, 4 January 1854, p. 4.
77. John Ashton, *Modern Street Ballads* (London, 1888), p. 294; Albert wrote incredulously to Stockmar that a crowd had assembled to see him and the Queen led captive to the Tower [K. Jagow ed., *Letters of the Prince Consort 1836–1861*, (London, 1938), pp. 203–8.]
78. *The Greville Memoirs* (ed. Henry Reeve, 8 vols, London, 1888 edn), vol. 7, pp. 127–30.
79. Bourne, *English Newspapers*, vol. 2, p. 159
80. Ibid., *Lloyd's Weekly Newspaper*, which did not join in the attacks on the Prince, told its more respectable old artisanate and shopkeeping readership that the *Morning Advertiser* was a 'pot-house' print. (5 February 1854, p. 6).
81. *Who's to blame, the Prince, the Press, or the Ministry? A letter to Lord Aberdeen*. By Plain Speech (London, 1854), p. 8.
82. *Prince Albert's Defence* (London, 1854), p. 29.
83. See above, chapter 4.
84. *Morning Advertiser*, 22 October 1855, p. 4.
85. See above, chapter 4.
86. *Reynolds's Newspaper*, 17 June 1855, pp. 8–9.
87. *Sunday Times*, 10 June 1855, p. 4. Philip Ziegler, *King William IV*, (London, 1971) p. 288 describes Ascot as 'one of those hallowed feasts at which the tribal chief ritually immerses himself in the convocation of his subjects'. In the twentieth century the Royal Family has not been accused of antipathy to horse-racing or non-attendance of Ascot.
88. *Prince Albert. Why is he unpopular?* By F. Airplay, Esq. (2nd edn, London, 1857), pp. 6, 21, 40. Roger Fulford, *The Prince Consort* (London, 1949), p. 99 remarkably states that there is 'no evidence' that Albert's unpopularity had anything to do with his being a foreigner.
89. T. Fontane, *Journeys to England in Victoria's Early Days, 1844–1859*. (transl. Dorothy Harrison, London, 1939), p. 125.
90. *People's Paper*, 30 January 1858, p. 1.
91. *Spectator*, 23 January 1858, p. 90 col. 1.
92. See below, chapter 7.

93. For example, 6 July 1862, p. 1; 25 December 1864, p. 1.
94. F.W. Soutter, *Fights for Freedom. The Story of My Life.* (London, 1925), pp. 117–18.
95. *Morning Post*, 26 January 1858, p. 4 and see below, chapter 7.
96. *Daily Telegraph*, 25 January 1858, p. 3.
97. *Spectator*, 30 January 1858, p. 121.
98. *Lloyd's Weekly Newspaper*, 24 January 1858, p. 6.
99. *People's Paper*, 30 January 1858, p. 1.
100. *Spectator*, 21 December 1861, p. 1387.
101. For example, *Illustrated London News*, 3 May 1851, p. 359; *Sunday Times*, 4 May 1851, p. 5; *The Times*, 21 April 1851, p. 4.
102. *Morning Chronicle*, 1 May 1851, p. 4.
103. *Observer*, 11 May 1851, p. 2.
104. For example, *The Times*, 24 November 1855, p. 6.
105. Cunningham, 'Jingoism and the Working Classes 1877–78', p. 8; MacKenzie, *Imperialism and Popular Culture*, p. 3.
106. *Reynolds's Newspaper*, 6 July 1862, p. 1.
107. *Sunday Times*, 8 July 1866, p. 2 col. 1.
108. *Remarks on Certain Anonymous Articles designed to render Queen Victoria unpopular: with an Exposure of their Authorship* (Gloucester, 1864), pp. 9, 13, 24–6. The Urquhartites were convinced that this was part of Palmerston's plot to force the Queen to abdicate in favour of the Prince of Wales, whom they saw as a pliant tool of the Prime Minister (see above, chapters 4 and 5 also *Free Press*, vol. 12 (1864), passim.)
109. *Hansard*, vol. 175, cols 606–10.
110. Ibid., vol. 204, cols 866–8.
111. *National Reformer*, vol. 15, no. 15 (10 April 1870), p. 25.
112. *Daily Telegraph*, 27 February 1872, p. 4.
113. *National Reformer*, 1 September 1872, pp. 130–1; 23 July 1871, pp. 49–50.
114. Ibid., 13 April 1873, p. 234 and see above, chapter 5.
115. Ibid., 3 August 1873, p. 66 col. 1.
116. Ibid., 1 September 1872, pp. 130–1.
117. *Daily Telegraph*, 11 November 1871, p. 4.
118. *Sunday Times*, 12 November 1871, p. 2.
119. *National Reformer*, 13 March 1873, pp. 194–5.
120. Cunningham, 'The Language of Patriotism', p. 18.
121. *National Reformer*, 17 December 1871, pp. 398–9; 25 August 1872, pp. 124–5.
122. Ibid., 18 December 1870, p. 391.
123. Ibid., 13 April 1873, p. 228.
124. See above, chapter 3.
125. *Republican*, vol. 4,(January 1879), p. 75.
126. Ibid., vol. 5, no. 3 (June 1879), p. 118.
127. See above, chapter 3.
128. *Reynolds's Newspaper*, 4 May 1873, p. 4.
129. *Reynolds's Newspaper*, 30 April 1882, p. 4; 30 March 1884, p. 4.
130. Ibid., 26 July 1885, p. 4.
131. *Republican*, no. 12 (1 June 1871), pp. 4–5; no. 24 (1 December 1871), p. 2.

132. Ibid., no. 6 (February 1871), p. 7; no. 10 (1 May 1871) p. 7; no. 25 (1 January 1872), pp. 6–7.
133. Ibid., no. 7 (March 1871), p. 8.
134. Ibid., no. 4 (December 1870), p. 5.
135. See above, chapter 3.
136. *Republican*, vol. 10 (April 1884), p. 3.
137. Ibid., vol. 12(June 1886), pp. 119–20
138. *Fraser's Magazine*, vol. 92 (October 1875), pp. 411–36.
139. Cunningham, 'The Language of Patriotism', pp. 22–3.
140. See above, chapter 5.
141. *Quarterly Review*, vol. 145 (April 1878), pp. 277–328.
142. See above, chapter 5.
143. See Harcourt, 'Gladstone, Monarchism and the New Imperialism', pp. 20–51; William M. Kuhn, 'Ceremony and Politics: The British Monarchy 1871–1872', *Journal of British Studies*, vol. 26, no. 2 (April 1987), pp. 133–62.
144. *The Times*, 23 February 1871, p. 9; 24 February 1871, p. 9; 26 February 1871, p. 9.
145. *Sunday Times*, 3 March 1872, p. 4.
146. *Illustrated London News*, 2 March 1872, p. 203.
147. *Daily Telegraph*, 28 February 1872, p. 6.
148. *Saturday Review*, vol. 37, no. 959 (14 March 1874), pp. 328–9.
149. *Daily Telegraph*, 27 April 1882, p. 6.
150. *Observer*, 30 April 1882, p. 5.
151. *Daily News*, 13 March 1879, p. 5.
152. *Saturday Review*, 29 April 1882, pp. 515–6.
153. John Gallagher and Ronald Robinson, 'The Imperialism of Free Trade', *Economic History Review*, vol. 6, no. 1 (1953), pp. 1–15.
154. Ronald Hyam and Ged Martin, *Reappraisals in British Imperial History* (London, 1975), pp. 91–106.
155. Ibid., p. 117; Eldridge, *England's Mission*, p. 231; MacKenzie, *Imperialism and Popular Culture*, p. 3.
156. *Punch*, vol. 35 (1858), p. 106, col. 1.
157. *Daily Telegraph*, 12 May 1876, p. 4.
158. Stephen Koss, *The Rise and Fall of the Political Press in Britain. Vol One: The Nineteenth Century* (London, 1981), p. 203.
159. *Daily Telegraph*, 13 May 1873, p. 5.
160. Ibid., 18 February 1876, p. 4.
161. *The Times*, 25 March 1875, p. 9.
162. *Hansard*, vol. 225, col. 1512.
163. Buckle ed., *Letters of Queen Victoria*, 2nd ser., vol. 2, pp. 460–3.
164. *Daily Telegraph*, 12 March 1874, p. 5.
165. Ibid., 27 April 1882, p. 6.
166. *The Times*, 24 March 1886, p. 9.
167. Arthur Ponsonby, *Henry Ponsonby. Queen Victoria's Private Secretary. His Life from his Letters.* (London, 1942), p. 79.
168. *The Times*, 22 June 1887, p. 5
169. *Daily Telegraph*, 20 June 1887, p. 4.
170. An article in *Vanity Fair* in the week of the Jubilee asked 'Stands England where she did?' and concluded that Britain was now '*un quantite negligeable*' in international affairs. (Cited in Caroline Chapman and

Paul Raben eds, *Debrett's Queen Victoria's Jubilees, 1887 and 1897* (London, 1977).)

171. *The Times*, 20 June 1887, p. 9.
172. *The Times*, 24 June 1887, p. 9.
173. *Lloyd's Weekly Newspaper*, 26 June 1887, p. 1.
174. *The Times*, 22 June 1897, p. 9.
175. *Hansard*, vol. 89, col. 9.
176. *The Times*, 23 January 1901, p. 7.
177. *Daily Telegraph*, 23 January 1901, p. 8; 4 February 1901, p. 8; *The Times*, 23 January 1901, p. 11.
178. *The Times*, 15 June 1887, p. 6.
179. Ibid., 20 June 1887, p. 9; 21 June 1887, p. 5.
180. Ibid., 10 June 1887, p. 9.
181. Ibid., 24 June 1887, p. 9.
182. *Standard*, 21 June 1887, p. 5.
183. *The Times*, 21 June 1887, p. 5.
184. *Lloyd's Weekly Newspaper*, 19 June 1887, p. 6; 26 June 1887, p. 1; *Daily News*, 22 June 1887, p. 6.
185. *National Review*, vol. 9 (July 1887), p. 589.
186. *Spectator*, 6 May 1893, p. 592.
187. Ibid., 26 June 1897, p. 904.
188. Lant, *Insubstantial Pageant*, pp. 217–20.
189. *Daily Telegraph*, 21 June 1897, p. 8.
190. *The Times*, 23 June 1897, p. 14.
191. *Daily Mail*, 23 June 1897, p. 4.
192. *Hansard*, 4th ser., vol. 89, cols 19–23.
193. *Daily Telegraph*, 23 January 1901, p. 8; 4 February 1901, p. 8.
194. *The Times*, 23 January 1901, p. 8; 1 February 1901, p. 9.
195. *Pall Mall Gazette*, 21 June 1887.
196. *Contemporary Review*, vol. 79 (February 1901), pp. 153, 157.
197. *Daily News*, 4 February 1901, p. 6.
198. *Reynolds's Newspaper*, 14 July 1889, p. 1.
199. Ibid., 5 February 1901, p. 1.
200. Ibid., 27 January 1901, p. 5.
201. Ibid., 20 June 1897, p. 1.
202. *Clarion*, 2 February 1901, p. 33.
203. *Labour Leader*, 19 June 1897, p. 203.
204. *Hansard*, 4th ser., vol. 91, cols 1204–6.
205. *Reynolds's Newspaper*, 19 June 1887, p. 1.
206. Ibid., 27 June 1897, p. 1.
207. *Lloyds's Weekly Newspaper*, 9 July 1893, p. 8; see also *Pall Mall Gazette*, 6 July 1893, p. 1.
208. *Reynolds's Newspaper*, 7 May 1893, p. 4.
209. *Daily Telegraph*, 13 May 1873, p. 5.
210. *The Pin in the Queen's Shawl. Sketched in Indian Ink on "Imperial Crown". From a Conservative Stand-Point.* (London, 1876), pp. 6–7.
211. *The Times*, 23 January 1901, p. 3.
212. *Tablet*, 14 March 1863, p. 168.
213. Ibid., 18 June 1887, p. 961.
214. *Tablet*, 18 June 1887, p. 961; 25 June 1887, pp. 1001–4.
215. Ibid., 13 November 1841, p. 729.

216. *Jewish Chronicle*, 6 February 1863, p. 4.
217. Ibid., 17 June 1887, pp. 10–11.
218. Ibid., 25 January 1901, pp. 8–9, 16–17.
219. *Hansard*, 4th ser., vol. 50, cols 446–55.
220. D.G. Boyce, 'The Marginal Britons' in Robert Colls and Philip Dodd eds, *Englishness: Politics and Culture* (Kent, 1987 edn), pp. 233–4.
221. *Hansard*, vol. 338, cols 1335, 1486, 1657–8; vol. 339, cols 341–2.
222. Christopher A. Whatley, 'Royal Day, People's Day: The Monarch's Birthday in Scotland, c. 1660–1860' in Roger Mason and Norman McDougall eds, *People and Power in Scotland, Essays in Honour of Christopher Smout* (Edinburgh, 1992), pp. 170–88.
223. Taylor, '*Reynolds's Newspaper,* Opposition to the monarchy', p. 336.
224. John Davies, 'Victoria and Victorian Wales' in Geraint H. Jenkins and J. Beverley Smith eds, *Politics and Society in Wales 1840–1922; Essays in Honour of I.G. Jones*, pp. 7–28.
225. *Reynolds's Newspaper*, 26 June 1887, p. 4.
226. Ibid., p. 1.

CHAPTER SEVEN

Reverence and Sentimentality Towards the Monarchy and Royal Family

The glorification of the monarchy in the last years of Queen Victoria's reign, encompassing the two Jubilees, has been remarked upon by historians, who have viewed it as a new phenomenon in the history of the modern monarchy. Kingsley Martin wrote that 'not until the later part of the century . . . could the politically conscious democracy allow itself to indulge its national capacity for devotion to an idealized personality . . . Until the last quarter of the century Queen Victoria seemed likely to be the last British monarch.' A new period of royal popularity began only 'with the growth of imperialism in the last quarter of the century'.[1] Those interested in the 'new nationalism' and 'new imperialism' of the late nineteenth century, such as Tom Nairn, Freda Harcourt, and John M. MacKenzie have made similar allusions to the monarchy: MacKenzie writes, 'Reverence for the monarchy developed only from the late 1870s, and when it did it was closely bound up with the monarch's imperial role'.[2] Nairn sees such reverence as a response not only to the enemies without – 'powerful foreign empires' – but within – 'new urban masses': 'One aspect of the ruling order's mobilization against them was to be an equally intense and permanent exaltation of the Crown'.[3] Harcourt argues that 'monarchism' was a 'new national ideology' forged by politicians of both main parties in the early 1870s as a means of 'bridging class ideology'.[4] P.S. Baker, in a discussion of the two Jubilees, contends that only in the last decades of the nineteenth century did the monarchy come to 'represent values of "community", "unity" and "motherhood"' due to its 'mobilization' by the ruling class as a 'means by which it hoped to re-establish its domination', threatened by class conflict.[5]

In his concluding chapter Baker makes an acknowledgement of the limits of his analysis: 'It is necessary to gain a wider perspective on the novelty of the presentation of the monarchy in the late nineteenth century'.[6] Subsequently, Linda Colley has demonstrated the veneration of the monarchy during the Napoleonic Wars when George III was presented as the father of his people, the Crown as the symbol of national unity.[7] Tom Nairn has recognized the importance of this work:

'a template had been cast and tested which, when circumstances demanded, could easily be revived'. However, this template was revived not, as Nairn writes, 'from the 1870s onwards' but in 1837 when the accession of a young, virgin Queen promised a new lease of life for the monarchy after her aged and uninspiring predecessors, George IV and William IV. Of course, Nairn is correct in writing that in the nineteenth century 'Monarchy was to traverse moments of even deeper unpopularity than it had known in the eighteenth century'[8] – and the rest of this book shows how contentious the Crown remained in all its aspects to the end of this period – but this chapter demonstrates the existence of reverence for the monarchy and for Victoria and of sentimental writings on the Royal Family from the outset of the reign, and analyses the content of such veneration.

Veneration for the monarchy did not begin suddenly in the late 1870s but had always been voiced in the middle-class press and in special publications on the Royal Family. Such veneration existed alongside the critical, questioning attitude to the monarchy which has been discussed in previous chapters. There is no justification for Martin's assertion that it was widely held, up to 1875, that Victoria would be the last British sovereign – we have seen that active republicans were always in a distinct minority, however much general controversy specific events involving the Crown provoked. Though a reputable intellectual journal such as the *Spectator* professed a theoretical republicanism founded on its Benthamism,[9] the rest of the mainstream London and provincial newspapers, irrespective of their political affiliations, maintained a deference to the institution of monarchy and, for most of the time, to the person of the sovereign. Their middle-class readership had been incorporated into the political establishment in 1832 and saw the monarchy not, as did the Chartists, as the symbol of an oppressive, exclusive ruling order but as the symbol of the political and economic status quo to which they belonged and which they wished to maintain.

To argue that the monarchy became an object of adulation only to counter class tensions in the last quarter of the century is to suggest that not only veneration of the monarchy but class conflict was an experience unique to these years. This would strike a student of Chartism as remarkable – and we shall see that supporters of the established political and social order were keen to emphasize the monarchy's beneficent, unifying role as a means of smoothing the social conflicts of earlier decades. In the previous chapter we have seen that the 'new nationalism' was indeed important in consolidating a much-trumpeted position for the monarchy as the figurehead of nation and empire. However, we also saw that the position had always been claimed for the monarchy by the enthusiastically loyal, but that it was better equipped to fill the role of national symbol after the death of the German Prince Consort. It was the attenuation of criticism of the Crown by the 1880s, as organized republicanism disappeared and as the Crown became less prone to accusations of seclusion, partisanship, political interference and foreignness, which produced a more consonant setting for the praises of the monarchy, Queen and Royal Family which had always been sung. The welter of celebratory literature occasioned by the two Jubilees was to be a natural commemoration of these events in a long tradition of panegyrics to the Victorian monarchy, not a novel departure in the presentation of the Crown.

This chapter examines this veneration of the institution of monarchy and of the persons of the Queen and Royal Family. The common theme of the loyal was that an historical reverence for the Crown had been intensified and turned into a personal affection for Victoria through her devotion to duty and care for the welfare of her people; she was the paragon of womanhood and English domestic virtues, and the loving mother of the whole nation. Moreover, there was a common identification with the whole Royal Family as a family going through the same cycle of birth, marriage and bereavement known to all. A sentimental and trivial interest in all the doings of the Royal Family was evinced in what radicals dismissed as 'gush' literature in the press and special books, this literature offering escape to a fairy-tale world of princes and princesses but at the same time encouraging the reader to see the members of this world as a typical middle-class family whom one could know intimately. Just as there were, as we have seen, diverse forms of criticism of the monarchy and of Victoria, so, throughout the reign, there were different species of praise – from quasi-religious reverence for the Crown and the person of the Queen to domestic affection for the Royal Family as familiar human figures.

The first section of the chapter, on the period 1837–61, looks at the excitement on Victoria's accession and at the consolidation of the monarchy's reputation after the marriage to Albert, with the unfolding of the family saga and the presentation of the royal couple as the exemplars of duty, domesticity and devotion to the people. The second section, on 1861–87, shows that the Queen's widowed seclusion, as well as prompting the criticism discussed in chapters 3 and 8, itself became the object of sentimental idealization. The marriages of her children continued the family cycle, while the ageing Queen became a venerable matriarch and embodiment of the national progress and successes achieved during her long reign. Both she and the Crown were extolled as symbols of historical continuity in an epoch of unparalleled change. The final section on 1887–1901 shows the culmination of these themes but also that praise for the monarchy was dependent on at least ostensible fulfilment of these idealized domestic roles by members of the Royal Family.

1837–61: from virgin Queen to mother of the nation

1837–40

By 1837 the Crown's repute had fallen since the 'apotheosis' of royal popularity under George III described by Linda Colley. More detailed work on George IV and William IV would no doubt reveal a strand of veneration for these monarchs, and both certainly had their admirers.[10] But the tone of their obituaries showed that both had been found wanting as inspiring examples of kingship. George IV, debauched and latterly reclusive, had become a grotesque figure of detestation. *The Times* pronounced the savage epitaph, 'There never was an individual less regretted by his fellow creatures than this deceased king. What eye has wept for him? What heart has heaved one throb of unmercenary sorrow?'[11] William IV had presented a more respectable front than his brother, his marital infidelities having been committed in the distant past, but he too was an elderly monarch at his accession and laboured under a coarse and stolid stupidity. Though in 1837 parliamentary condolences were obsequious in tone[12] and obituaries drew attention to his industry, patriotism, honesty and generosity, they also referred to 'his feeble mind',[13] his 'very confined understanding and very defective education', his rudeness and vulgarity.[14]

The new sovereign, a young woman of eighteen, was a fitter object of reverential devotion. While a radical such as Brougham saw the accession of a virtual girl as exposing the insecurity of hereditary monarchy,[15] the acceding monarch's circumstances also inspired chivalric sentiments and visions of a bright new era for the Crown and nation under a young, virgin Queen. Mark Girouard in his work on the concept of chivalry in nineteenth-century England has described the importance of the new sovereign as a figure of romance: often depicted in medieval contexts.[16] *The Times*, somewhat guarded in its praise because of the identification of the new regime with the Whigs,[17] observed that 'the accession of a youthful sovereign to the throne is wont to fill the hearts of nations with eager faith and sanguine assurance of prosperity'.[18] The ministerial press was particularly fulsome and in the month following the King's death, wrote Greville, 'Everything that could be said in praise of the Queen, of her manners, conduct, conversation and character, has been exhausted'.[19]

The coronation was seen as the symbolic inauguration of the new epoch. In the sermon preached at the ceremony, Bishop Blomfield hailed the 'freshness and fullness of youthful hope and promise' which would revive 'the ancient but not forgotten glories of a female reign'.[20] The middle-class press viewed the coronation as a reaffirmation of the nation's attachment to the institution of monarchy, an attachment intensified by devotion to the person of the young Queen.[21] Tory papers rejoiced in the 'spontaneous'[22] national loyalty and respect for tradition manifested in the celebrations – England was at heart deferential to its old hereditary institutions.[23] Liberal papers wrote of the unparalleled 'union of freedom with subordination' which had obtained in England thanks to political reform and which produced a rational loyalty to the Crown and to Victoria.[24] The *Manchester Guardian* expressed the common attitude of both the Liberal and Tory press to the coronation in describing it as a 'great national solemnity'.[25]

After the initial enthusiasm accompanying her accession to the throne, the reputation of the young Queen was somewhat tarnished and her court brought into disrepute by the Lady Flora Hastings affair, and it was not until her wedding that the Crown could begin in earnest to cement the reputation for industrious duty and domestic probity that was to become the hallmark of Victoria's reign. The marriage to Albert in 1840 was the beginning of the domestic iconography of the British monarchy in the nineteenth century – the first of the successive family events which were the object of so much sentimental attention.

All details of the wedding were minutely covered in the London and provincial middle-class press. The Chartist newspaper, the *Northern Star* was contemptuous of this treatment of what it regarded as trivia: 'Every trifling and minute circumstance is made subject matter of an outrageous puff. The pageant-monsters chronicle how lords and ladies strutted like dunghill cocks in breeding time and their accomplices and dupes cry "La, how grand!"' This could only be an attempt to divert attention from the serious class issues which were agitating the country.[26] Indeed, one of the *Star's* middle-class opponents, the *Manchester Guardian* wrote that no political comments would appear in its pages on the occasion of the wedding: '. . . an occurrence of much greater and more permanent interest'.[27] Another, the *Leeds Mercury*, in its editorial, presented the wedding as a symbol of national consensus and the Queen and her consort as at once figures of romance and paragons of domestic virtue, and a couple with whom its middle-class readership could identify. The picture was of a harmonious nation united in loyalty to a throne which represented an equitable status quo. The union of Victoria and Albert was such as adorned fairy-tales and captured the imagination:

> No event so calculated to excite unmixed gladness and warmth of
> heart has taken place in England for centuries. Never before has

England seen a Queen in the first bloom of youth and beauty, uniting herself to the man of her heart . . .

At the same time, 'the conduct of the happy pair towards each other was such as might have characterized the most loving couple in the middle class of society'.[28]

The wedding was marked by a plethora of special publications commemorating the event in maudlin prose and verse.[29] An architect, G.R. French, produced tables of the couple's ancestry, concluding them with the remark that the Queen was an 'illustrious lady for whose welfare the pulse of a great nation throbs with the affectionate and heartfelt interest of personal solicitude and loyalty'.[30] Accounts of the Queen's life were published, in response, it was said, to a desire in the country 'to obtain the fullest and most authentic information respecting the education and early life of so interesting a personage'.[31] Similar books on Albert were brought out, praising the Prince's character and his family's history – partly to counter the hostile, chauvinistic reaction to his arrival described in chapter 6.[32] The wedding had launched the Victorian monarchy on its domestic career.

1840–61

In the 1840s and 1850s the praises sounded at the coronation and wedding augmented as the Queen and Albert were deemed by loyal writers to have, through their industry, devotion to the nation and its people, and their example of domestic probity, enhanced public reverence for the monarchy and to have deepened this reverence into an affectionate identification with them and the large family which grew up around them. An examination of enthusiastic writings in the press and special publications shows the emergence in this period of themes normally associated only with the last years of Victoria's reign and subsequent history of the Royal Family – veneration for the Crown as a symbol of historical continuity and present prosperity, and as an agent of social harmony; idealization of the Queen and her family; and a preoccupation with the common, family experiences of the royal caste.

Kingsley Martin argued that until late in the reign the set of the national mind was, on rational and democratic principles, anti-monarchical and unprepared to indulge in idealized personalities,[33] but the constant refrain of the middle-class press was that expounded by a liberal newspaper, the *Morning Chronicle* on the birth of the Prince of Wales – that 'loyalty which is paid as a debt to a sovereign as being the fountain of law, in whose person the majesty of the law is honoured' was united with 'the warm regard and admiration won by her Majesty from all classes of her subjects since her accession to the Throne'.[34] We have seen that there was considerable criticism of the monarchy on rational and economic grounds by middle-class radicals and that the republican movement of the 1870s was led by middle-class politicians who wanted a meritocratic overhaul of inefficient aristocratic institutions. But republicanism was always the creed of a minority and the great body of the middle class after 1832 wished merely to preserve the status quo of which they, with the monarchy and aristocracy, now formed a part.

Moreover, as the most exalted and venerable part of the status quo, the monarchy was to be courted as it could confer the ultimate acknowledgement of middle-class worth and of the place of contemporary industrial and commercial progress in the nation's long and distinguished history. *The Times* wrote of Albert's opening of the Royal Exchange in 1842:

> These great occasions are not far from being an integral portion of our constitution. To the middle classes, who may now almost be considered the ruling class of England, it has become nearly a right ... that the great men of the country ... should pay them the compliment – we might say the homage – of appearing periodically ... to give a tone to their thoughts ... [35]

This was true of the receptions accorded to royal visitors by the industrial magnates who were the burghers of northern cities. *The Times* wrote that while Manchester, a utilitarian city without tradition, a creation of the modern age, would have seemed an unlikely place to entertain royalty, civic pride in associating its industrial greatness with Britain's history came to the fore: 'The corporation, after a faint struggle, arrays itself in robes of scarlet and black, according to its degrees, to be fit for the Royal presence'. In the Queen they 'see ... a link between themselves and antiquity ... They have learnt that this nation is not simply what it is made from day to day ... but the growth of ages, knit together by an ancient constitution.'[36] When the Queen visited Leeds in 1858 to open the Town Hall the corporation wore ceremonial robes for the first time in its history.[37] The *Leeds Mercury* voiced the civic pride of the Leeds bourgeoisie: 'When the Queen opens our Town Hall, she will be giving her express sanction to Municipal self-government' – and depicted the industrial world pursuing its profits with the blessing of royal antiquity and in a just and settled political and social order topped by the Queen:

> She inherits the pretensions of Norman and Saxon, of Plantagenet, Tudor, Stuart, and Brunswick, ... Under her shield, life is sacred, property is secure, the husbandman sows and reaps, the capitalist invests his money safely, and the labourer goes forth to his work and to his labour till the evening.

She would encourage the people of Leeds 'in their industrial undertakings, to combine enterprise and perseverance with sobriety and unswerving uprightness – in their local interests, to cherish the spirit of improvement, without forgetting the duty of economy'.[38]

According to *The Times* the principal reason, above 'historical associations, family greatness', for the 'heartfelt attachment to the Crown' in places such as Leeds, with their radical politics and large working-class populations, was the Queen's 'identity with the interests and aspirations of the community'.[39] At a time when Chartists attacked the political settlement of 1832 as exclusive and the ruling order, of which the monarchy was the figurehead, as oppressive, the Crown was presented in the middle-class press as a beneficent friend of the whole community, allaying class conflicts and thus proving the fitness of existing constitutional and social arrangements. The Queen's 'munificent offer' to submit herself to the new income tax in 1842 was, wrote *The Times*, 'of inestimable advantage in refuting those who are ever anxious to prove our political and social constitution to be a mere juggling machinery for enabling the rich and great to plunder the poor and feeble'.[40] The *Spectator*, though republican on principle, saw the value of the Royal Family in this respect – of the Duke of Sussex, a staunch reformer and by far the most popular of the royal dukes, it wrote 'Such men are the oil poured over the tempest-tossed surface of society to make the waters abate'.[41]

On the birth of the heir apparent the *Observer* made extravagant claims for the way in which the Royal Family bound the nation together regardless of differences in wealth – rejoicing was universal, for 'among the manufacturing towns suffering most from distress there was for the moment an abandoning of all consideration of personal sufferings. A beam of sunshine had pierced the darkness of their sorrows and loud was the lightsome tumult of their joy.'[42] *The Times* lapsed into equally fanciful prose to make the same case on the wedding of the Princess Royal: it wrote of the London crowd of working people:

> They shouted for the Queen and the youthful pair, and gave them rough blessings as they passed, all in a manner which might befit a simple people of the Middle Ages who had never heard of democratic principles, or the tyranny of capital, or the inalienable right of man.[43]

From a radical perspective, *Lloyd's Weekly Newspaper* concurred that the incontinent enthusiasm of the crowd had been a setback to hopes for a popular movement for franchise reform – it showed the low political consciousness of the people, whose 'self-abasement' manifested 'that side of the English character, which has unhappily survived the emancipation of the serfs'.[44]

However, while it disapproved of extreme demonstrations of idolatry for the monarchy and criticized the cost of the appendages of the court, *Lloyd's*, with its mass old artisanate and lower middle-class readership, was by no means republican and itself wrote of the beneficial effects of the Queen's rule: upon the birth of Princess Alice in 1843, it prayed that the Queen 'may be spared many more years to witness the blossoming of these buds, with which the fair garden of royalty seems destined under her auspices to be adorned'.[45] In 1854 it regretted the concern that the calumnies on Prince Albert must be causing to the Queen, for while George IV in his seclusion cared nothing for the odium in which he was held, the Queen, ever in the eyes of her subjects, had been eager to cultivate their love and had deservedly received it.[46]

The Queen's identity with the interests and aspirations of the community was openly displayed in the visits which she and Albert paid to different parts of the country and in the many public engagements and philanthropic activities undertaken by the couple.[47] In the early 1840s a series of royal progresses was made in Scotland and England. These were commended by *The Times* as 'they cement the union between the Crown and the people by a reciprocity of confidence', when previously it had been supposed 'that the English Sovereign was necessarily doomed to a perpetual seclusion at Windsor or Pimlico'.[48] Many souvenir pamphlets with engravings on the Queen's progresses were produced, one describing them as 'the most remarkable regal tours which have occurred for many centuries ... proof that she was most warmly interested in the welfare of her people'.[49]

Britain's avoidance of revolution in 1848 was attributed to the peaceful reforms of preceding decades and to the attachment to the Crown built up by the unremitting efforts of Victoria and Albert to associate themselves with the people's welfare. Albert's assumption of the presidency of the Society for Improving the Condition of the Labouring Classes in early 1848 was well calculated 'at a time when it is much easier for Royal personages to lose popularity than to win confidence'.[50] On the royal opening of the British Coal Exchange in 1849, *The Times* referred to the royal couple's 'constant solicitude and occasional presence in the industrial regions of this metropolis'.[51] The Great Exhibition was hailed as not only a celebration of industrial progress but of the stability of the British monarchy – a 'second and more glorious inauguration of their sovereign',[52] earned by 'an universal and well-won popularity'.[53] *Punch* heaped ridicule on the English republicans known to be in collusion with revolutionary refugees from the Continent and contrasted the upheavals abroad with the tranquillity at home – Victoria was happy in:

The loyal line of a great people, knowing
That building up is better than o'erthrowing
That freedom lies in taming of self-will.[54]

Republicans were scornful of efflorescent accounts of the people's loyalty to a caring monarchy. However, the lining of the London streets
from five o' clock in the morning to see the Queen pass on her way to
open the Great Exhibition caused G. Julian Harney to reflect, 'No
doubt the spirit of flunkeyism yet inspires a large number of the people'.[55]
What Harney dismissed as 'the spirit of flunkeyism' has been seen as a
desire for respectability by the historians who have been concerned to
show that the political radicalism of Chartists and republicans was but
one tradition of the working class and that an alternative belief in self-
improvement within the existing political and social framework was
positively held by working people and not foisted onto them by the
middle class. T.W. Laqueur in *Religion and Respectability. Sunday Schools
and Working Class Culture 1780–1850* argues that in the Sunday schools,
whose proliferation was brought about by the working-class hunger for
education, the values taught by working people to the children of their
class reflected the 'widespread working-class adherence to the main
outlines of the political order'. Among these was an exuberant loyalty
to the throne, marked by outings to royal palaces and celebrations of
royal events.[56]

G.W.M. Reynolds wished that working people would stay away from
such events – though he felt that the middle class was more 'childish
and puerile' in its propensity to gape at royalty, it was the susceptibility
of the working class which grieved him.[57] Yet he was not above exploit-
ing it as a businessman – another of his popular publications, *Reynolds's
Miscellany*, contained illustrations of the Royal Family and articles
praising, for instance, the five-year-old Prince of Wales' 'intelligence,
giving promise of high mental qualifications'.[58]

Such sycophantic praise of the Royal Family struck republicans as a
national malaise. William Linton pointed out that while Victoria was
'just an ordinary young woman, with no great gifts either of nature or
acquirement, not even remarkable for her appearance', she was a 'divin-
ity for public worship' merely because she was royal and managed to
'behave decently'. The latter ability made her 'undoubtedly our best
Monarch for centuries' but this could not justify the exorbitant language used by her 'idolaters'.[59] *Punch* was loyal to the throne but
viewed the excesses of reverential newspapers with a satirical eye. In
1844 it printed an imaginary royal proclamation to the effect that:

> foolish language, touching Ourself, our Royal Consort, and Be-
> loved Babies ... be discontinued, and that from henceforth all
> Vain, Silly, and Sycophantic Verbiage shall cease ... Be it known,

> That the Queen of England is not the Grand Lama; And further be
> it remembered that Englishmen should not emulate the vain idol-
> atry of speech familiar in the mouths of Eastern bondmen.[60]

The Queen was revered in the middle-class press as the ideal sovereign
and the ideal woman. The qualities which she and the Royal Family
were held up to exemplify were those prized as the foundations of
Victorian society – hard work, thrift, probity and the sanctity of the
home and family. As sovereign and consort, Victoria and Albert were
the models of devotion to duty, of industry and minute use of time;
values which needed to be inculcated in a successful commercial society.[61] A book on the Queen for the instruction of the young dictated
'Her Majesty and Prince Albert set a very good example of industry.
They rise rather early, and both of them spend the day in active and
useful pursuits.'[62] Albert became renowned for the breadth of his activities – he appeared indefatigable in working for social, industrial, educational, cultural and military improvement.[63] However, we have seen
the way in which the Prince was ridiculed and strenuously attacked as a
foreigner, and even in the praise of his industry there was, as Norman
Gash has noted, a tone of amused condescension – for example, in
Punch's 'Industrious Boy' and 'H.R.H. at it again'.[64]

By contrast Victoria was idealized as a woman in sentimental writings from her accession through to her death, encompassing the successive stages of marriage, motherhood and bereavement. She was the
cynosure of the domestic virtues which a woman and particularly an
Englishwoman was supposed to embody. 'The court', wrote the London Pioneer, 'is principally of use to the century as a moral agent': while
George IV had set a profligate example, the reign of a female sovereign
was 'more favourable to the development of the domestic virtues'.[65]
The marriage of Victoria and Albert quickly became a by-word for
probity. The Times described the royal couple as the ideal parents – the
Queen 'more pure and womanly than Queen Elizabeth', Albert noted
for his 'exemplary life . . . strong affections finding their sufficient gratification within his exalted home'.[66] On the wedding of Princess Royal,
the Morning Post declared, '. . . in our Queen we see the highest type of
English lady, English wife, and English mother'.[67]

Indeed, wrote the Morning Chronicle of the same event, 'We have
become so accustomed to regard Queen Victoria as a pattern and
example of the "household virtues", to venerate the Sovereign for her
discharge of domestic duties' that 'it coincides with all our preconceived
ideas to look upon the marriage of her eldest daughter – also the "eldest
daughter of England" – as a domestic rather than a State event'.[68] With
the emphasis on the role of the Queen as an exemplar of domestic
virtue, it became common to depict the Royal Family less as royal and

more as a family – certainly one to be venerated as the ideal but also a family with whose experiences every household in the land could identify. Victoria, it was argued, became 'mother of the nation' in a very special way – not only in a traditional sense as beneficent monarch but as the mother in a family which people likened to their own. The Victorian cult of the home and the family was nowhere more marked than in its application to the highest family in the land.

Bagehot was to write in the 1860s, 'A family on the throne is an interesting idea also. It brings down the pride of sovereignty to the level of petty life . . . a royal family sweetens politics by a seasonal addition of pretty events'.[69] With the Queen so young at her accession her reign was to include the full saga of a family coming into being and growing up. In 1858 *The Times* wrote, 'It is long – we will not venture to say how long – since there was a Royal family in England that was the object of so much domestic interest as that of Queen Victoria' – it was 'of the number and of the age that everywhere awakens sympathy'.[70] Linda Colley has pointed out that Brougham wrote of the death of Princess Charlotte in 1817, 'it really was as if every household throughout Great Britain had lost a favourite child',[71] but the royal generation preceding Victoria – the sons of George III – had come to the throne in their old age and there could not be the accumulation of family events that was to characterize her reign: before the birth of the Princess Royal in 1840 it had been 63 years since the birth of a child to a reigning British monarch; between 1840 and 1857 there were nine such births. The *Spectator* observed in 1844, 'As the race of George the Third's family is gradually disappearing . . . , a new generation is growing up to occupy the vacant stage'. The outgoing generation had tended to excess and disrepute, the new was entering into 'a more rational condition of royal society – less peculiar, less pampered, less open to vicious indulgences, less restrained in all that is the refined but genuine enjoyment of human existence'[72] – in other words, a home life more identifiable with that of their subjects. The *Spectator* wrote at the time of the Prince of Wales' birth that the English were 'remarkable for their appreciation of home comforts . . . There is a neighbourly disposition among the English on such occasions which does not detract from their reverence.'[73] Royal births were held to touch every family in the realm in fellow-feeling. For the *Observer*, 'It was a pleasure to behold, even in the public streets, how, as friend met friend there was a mutual congratulation, as if each had to thank Providence for some signal blessing poured down on him and his children'.[74]

The domestic rather than the regal aspect of the Royal Family was emphasized as it grew up. Simon Schama has commented on the 'domestication of majesty' in Royal Family portraiture. He contrasts

Landseer's *Windsor Castle in Modern Times* of 1841–5 with Nocret's *Allegorical Portrait of the Family of Louis XIV* of 1670: 'They stand at opposite ends of a process that transformed the image of a ruling dynasty from a clan of deities to a domestic parlour group'. The process began with the family of George III and became complete with the mass production in the 1840s and 1850s of calotypes and daguerreotypes of nursery album pictures of the Queen's children.[75]

In the same way, writers described the Royal Family as unaffected and homely in its displays of affection. It was considered important that Albert's and Victoria's had been a love-match, more than just a calculating one of state,[76] and we have noted the description of their behaviour at their wedding as 'such as might have characterized the most loving couple in the middle class of society'.[77] Accounts of the progresses in Scotland in the early 1840s celebrated their informality – unlike George IV, who had put the 'external and dazzling trappings of Royalty' between him and his people on such progresses, the Queen appeared 'as the attached and virtuous wife – as the fond and happy mother – as the kind and considerate mistress'.[78] *Punch*, in its imaginary royal proclamation, ridiculed the awed reports of royal informality in Scotland: 'That our beloved Child, the Princess Royal, shall be permitted to walk "hand in hand" with her Royal Father, without exciting such marked demonstrations of wonderment at the familiarity, as has been made known to Me by the public press'.[79] Such familiarity was still sending the press into ecstasies at the opening of the Great Exhibition in 1851 – the *Morning Chronicle* wrote of the 'honest domestic delight which hailed the Queen, and her husband, as they joined the procession, holding by the hand, the Royal mother a Prince of Wales, and her Consort the Princess Royal'.[80]

Punch also bemoaned the attention paid in the press to trivia concerning the Royal Family. It imagined the Queen's wish: 'It shall be permitted to our Royal Self to wear a white shawl, or a black shawl, without any idle talk being passed upon the same'.[81] A column headed 'Royal Nursery Circular' satirized the minute interest taken by the press in the Royal Family's doings.[82] The *Spectator* was similarly amused by the amount of detailed coverage devoted to the particular of royal events. On the eve of the birth of the Princess Royal it observed, 'The Court historiographers, who did such ample justice to the Royal Bridecake, are already hard at work on the Royal Cradle'.[83] The *Illustrated London News*, which began publication in 1842 was to contain much pictorial presentation of the Royal Family: it wrote of the birth of Prince Alfred in 1844, 'Our readers will naturally desire to become acquainted with every circumstance connected with this happy event'[84] and this was the attitude of all the London newspapers; the *Observer* wrote that such was the attachment of the people to the Queen that the birth needs must deflect attention from the concurrent events in Tahiti which were so important to Britain.[85]

The greatest royal event of this period – the wedding of the Princess Royal in 1858 – was marked by comprehensive newspaper coverage sentimentally emphasizing the family aspect of the occasion; the first severance of family ties with the marriage of the first child and her departure to a foreign land. The *Globe* reported the words of a 'sturdy labourer' in the crowd as expressing the common national sentiment: 'it's John Bull a-marrying of his eldest daughter'.[86] For the *Daily Telegraph*, the excitement of the wedding lay in its combination of the romantic pageantry of state with the commonly known experiences of the family:

> Within a narrow space were confined numerous princes, English and foreign, the proudest ranks of the aristocracy, the highest dignitaries of the Church, and all the banners of heraldry were spread in the Palace corridors, and yet, upon the glittering dais . . . the ritual was performed, amidst all those demonstrations of familiar felicity and love who confer a charm upon every season of domestic rejoicing . . . those human and fireside graces that vivify the domestic manners of a palace . . .[87]

It was in fact 'a great drama of domestic happiness'. The actors in this drama were the Royal Family – they 'live in the sight of the nation; their movements are chronicled; their characters are known; millions of persons regard them with more than a public interest'.[88] There was also pathos in the drama as 'the Royal circle is for the first time about to be broken' and 'these millions . . . will follow with wistful eyes the departure of her whom they have known, as it seems, from infancy'.[89]

A cataclysmic fracture occurred in 1861 with the death of Albert, described in 1858 as 'the distinguished head' of 'that august family circle'.[90] Earlier in the year the Queen had lost her mother, the Duchess of Kent, and newspapers wrote of the commonly-felt sympathy with her bereavement. *The Times* reflected:

> . . . there is no family on which they (Englishmen) so much love to think on as . . . the Royal Family . . . They watch its growth, they note its characteristics, they cherish its well-known features, they inquire into its inner life, they speculate on its future destinies, with an interest only less than they feel for their own households.[91]

Every family would feel Albert's loss as 'a personal wound'.[92] *Lloyd's Weekly Newspaper* told its massive readership, 'there is not a fireside that in the midst of Christmas revelry will not be, now and then, overshadowed by the remembrance of Queen Victoria's bereavement'[93] for, wrote the *Morning Chronicle*, 'a bereavement such as this melts away the distinction of class'.[94] The *British Workman*, a temperance publication with the broader aim of making working men pious, industrious and deferential to their superiors, printed 'Lines by a Working Man on the Death of Prince Albert', which were said to have been 'sung with overpowering effect ... at a large assembly of working men in Surrey Chapel' to the tune of 'God Save the Queen!':

> Lord, heal her bleeding heart
> Assuage its grievous smart
>   Thy heavenly peace impart
> God save thy Queen.[95]

The obituaries to Albert showed how greatly the monarchy and Royal Family had risen in repute in the 1840s and 1850s. Their eulogistic tone contrasted with the respectively damning and guarded pronouncements on the careers of George IV and William IV. Even in newspapers which had criticized him during his life, the import was:

> His life was gentle, and the elements
> So mixed in him, that Nature might stand up,
> And say to all the world, 'This was a man!'

The Royal Family had come to enshrine the virtues which the middle-class press felt should be exemplified to the rest of society. Albert was praised for his unstinting endeavours in performing a wide variety of public duties and for his spotless probity as the head of the family. The *British Workman* exhorted its readers, 'Cherish his memory. Emulate by being the sober, industrious, skilful, and economical, pious men he desired to see you.'[96] Moreover, Victoria and Albert had, to quote the *Spectator*, 're-established that personal relationship between Englishmen and their Sovereign which ceased with the death of the last of the Stuarts'. The English people had 'for a hundred years ... lavished sarcastic invective on its monarchs' but now 'the lowest compiler of broadsheets does not offer a verbal discourtesy to the Queen'.[97]

Thus Kingsley Martin erred in asserting that 'not until the later part of the century' did the Victorians reconcile their belief in self-government with their 'capacity for devotion to an idealized personality'. By 1861 the monarchy was already venerated in the middle-class press as the beneficent head of a perfect constitutional system and the historic link of modern industrial and commercial achievement with the nation's past; while the Royal Family were the exemplars of the virtues which underpinned the society's achievement. The domestic saga of the Royal Family was chronicled with its dual appeal to flunkeyism – on the one hand, rank and its gorgeous trappings, on the other, the belief that the reader could identify intimately with the figures in the pageant as they passed the common landmarks of family life.

1861–87: the widow and her children

In chapter 3 I traced the emergence of a republican movement in England from the 1860s to the early 1870s and its decline in the 1870s and
1880s. Here the period is viewed from the obverse perspective. The first
section, on 1861 to 1871, considers the continued veneration of the
Queen and Royal Family in a decade usually noted by royal historians
only for the increase in criticism of the monarchy because of the Queen's
virtual retirement. The second section, on 1872 to 1887, shows that the
panegyrics to the Crown in this period were not as some historians have
argued a novel phenomenon but a continuation of the themes familiar
from the early years of the reign – praise of the Crown seemed more
resounding because of the weakening of republican criticism.

1861–71

John Cannon has written that the death of Albert 'interrupted . . . the
evolution of a domestic monarchy'.[98] The widowed seclusion into which
the Queen retreated certainly prompted accusations that expenditure
was wasted on the monarchy and this accounted for the increased
support given to republican views.[99] However, the domestic iconography of the Royal Family was not halted. The Queen's widowhood
was not only an object of criticism but of exaltation for the sanctity of
her grief, the intensity of her suffering. Meanwhile, the royal children
whose births had been celebrated in the 1840s were now getting
married and their weddings were feted in the same way. This section
examines the sympathy for the Queen stimulated by her bereavement,
the sentiments occasioned by the royal weddings, and the criticism of
the press's sycophantic and trivial preoccupation with the Royal Family
made in the radical and republican publications and in the more
detached intellectual journals.

The journalists who had in the 1840s and 1850s celebrated the
'auspicious events' in the life of the Royal Family as concomitant with
events in the reader's own household, now mourned the Prince Consort
and sympathized with the widowed Queen in the same cathartic manner. *The Times* wrote in April 1862, 'We believe that a deeper and more
sincere sentiment never pervaded this nation than the regret for the
Prince we have lost . . . A friend has been taken from us in whose
character discretion can find no fault.'[100] As Elisabeth Darby and Nicola
Smith have observed, 'the popular acclaim which had eluded the Prince
Consort in life was heaped upon his memory'.[101] It was easier to revere
the dead Albert than the living one – we have seen how his foreignness
and his ambitions for the Crown's and his own political role had

brought distrust and unpopularity upon him during his life. While Darby and Smith have described the erection of statues and buildings commemorating him throughout the land as the 'cult of the Prince Consort', this is more properly termed, as Norman Gash has pointed out, 'the iconography of the Prince Consort' for there was none of the devotion to the person of the Prince that goes to make a cult.[102] As Darby and Smith acknowledge, Victorians quickly tired of the regular erections of Albert's statues and the phenomenon disappeared as his memory faded[103] – and its initial impetus, write the two historians, came from the contemporary 'fashion for extravagant mourning' and from 'genuine compassion for the widowed Queen'.[104]

This compassion was the overriding sentiment in articles on the Queen in the early 1860s. Far from distancing her from her people, her widowhood was held by some to have brought her nearer to their hearts. The *Daily Telegraph* wrote, 'The bond of loyal love between the Queen and her people has been so riveted by sympathy for her great sorrow that we may think of her to-day with reverent affection and rightful solicitude'.[105] The sombre mood of Princess Alice's wedding in 1862 was respected by newspapers, which focused their attention on the Queen's grief. The *Morning Post* lamented, 'The ceremony of yesterday re-opens the wound in the heart of the nation'.[106] Since her bereavement, praise for the Queen was more excessive than ever. The *Morning Herald* declared, 'Mortal as she is, to her subjects her Majesty has no faults'.[107] The *Examiner* considered the Queen personally responsible for the social harmony in which the Prince of Wales' wedding was celebrated in 1863: 'It is the Queen who has cleared England of Chartism.[108]

When *The Times* criticized the Queen in 1864 for prolonging her absence from the public duties of state,[109] it was attacked by some of the other newspapers. The *Observer* described the Queen's loss as 'irreparable' and stated that the time of her return to public life 'must evidently be left to herself' – she was scrupulous in fulfilling the vital constitutional duties which did not entail public appearance.[110] The *Sunday Times* referred to what was effectively a message from the Queen, printed in the Court Circular in *The Times*. This spoke of the 'utter and ever-abiding desolation which has taken the place of her former happiness'; and, wrote the *Sunday Times*, 'the magnitude of the calamity which has been thus frankly revealed to the nation' should silence demands for her return.[111]

The publication of the regally directed, *Early Years of . . . the Prince Consort* in 1867[112] and of the Queen's own *Leaves from the Journal of Our Life in the Highlands* in 1868 constituted another direct statement from the Queen of the happiness of her married life and the calamity of her loss, and perpetuated the cult of retrospection and mourning. In her review of *The Early Years of . . . the Prince Consort* in *Blackwood's Edinburgh Magazine*, Margaret Olliphant mawkishly described the book as 'the story of a blue-eyed boy born over the seas and plains in a little German principality' and the marriage of Victoria and Albert as 'so perfect a union'.[113] *Leaves from . . . Our Life in the Highlands*[114] sold 20,000 copies immediately and ran quickly into several editions. It was, Elizabeth Longford has written, another landmark in the 'Queen's love affair with the middle classes' and the Queen 'believed the *Leaves* would in future look after her popularity, rendering a drastic alteration in her way of life unnecessary'.[115] In 1871, at the time of Princess Louise's wedding, the *Illustrated London News*, citing the way in which the Queen 'threw open to us the whole story of her life in the simple and genial record composed by herself', asserted that 'of late years, the Queen, though actually in comparative retirement, has in good truth, been more with us and in our hearts than ever'.[116]

Furthermore, while the Queen was in rarely-broken seclusion, the marriages of her children kept the domestic history of the Royal Family fluid and public, complementing the unchanging pathos of her widowed retirement. Bagehot wrote, 'A princely marriage is the brilliant edition of a universal fact, and, as such, it rivets mankind'[117] and the *Saturday Review* described the double-edged appeal of royal weddings – fabulous and mundane – when it pronounced upon that of Princess Alice:

> The domestic joys and sorrows of the Royal Family are watched with a stronger interest, because they produce on a conspicuous stage the familiar events of ordinary life. A Princess is probably the ideal of every girl, and a marriage between the descendants of two great Royal Houses pleases the youthful imagination like the climax of a novel.[118]

The wedding, wrote the *Morning Herald*, was another reminder of 'how admirably our Queen represents the deep national sentiment which governs us, perhaps more than all others, and which finds its expression in the one simple word – Home'.[119]

The *Daily Telegraph* summed up the press' descriptions of Princess Louise's wedding in 1871 when it announced, 'There is a wedding in the family to-day'.[120] This would be literally true in many families, said the *Daily News*, as such was the common identity with the Royal Family that couples would have chosen the same day for their weddings – and they would ever compare landmarks in their married lives with those in Princess Louise's. The paper pointed to the way in which people followed the fashions of members of the Royal Family seen in photographs. Photography, it argued, had been important in making the Royal Family seem 'so much like any other family'.[121]

The florid and minute descriptions of royal events and the attention paid to trivial matters concerning the Royal Family were criticized in the more intellectual journals and in the organs of popular radicalism and republicanism. Under the ironic title, 'Important Rectification', the *Examiner* in 1864 quoted *The Times*' correction of the details previously given of a cap worn by the Queen, and rebuked the 'utter futility' of 'such trash'.[122] The *Spectator* found the newspapers in the week of Louise's wedding 'filled with the most rubbishy prose epithalamiums it was ever our ill-fortune to peruse'. It singled out *The Times*' metaphor of 'a ray of sunshine' which 'gladdened every habitation in this island, and forced its way even where uninvited' and the *Daily Telegraph's* obsession with flowers – the bridegroom, Lord Lorne had such good fortune that 'felicitations would fall upon him like flowers upon a garden', and the nation's wish was that 'the pleasantest roses of life may grow with the old heraldic roses about their home'.[123] *The Times* had written that 'privacy is the charm of English life', but what privacy, asked the *Saturday Review* had its accounts and those of its contemporaries left to the Royal Family?[124]

The middle-class press was taken to task by *Reynolds's Newspaper*, the radical paper of the artisan. At the time of the Prince of Wales' wedding, it wrote, 'The intemperate sycophancy which depicts the Prince as the hope and the saviour of England, and the Princess as the fairest and most virtuous of her sex, would be intolerably loathsome, were it not so intensely ludicrous'. Underpinning such sycophantic praise was the commercial exploitation of the wedding: 'the "princely pair" have been employed to advertise the nostrums of quack doctors, puff the work of slop tailors, short-measuring and adulterating grocers ... The Prince is praised, in order to bring grist to the mill.' It was naive to believe that the images of the couple were emblazoned on products merely 'to manifest the unselfish loyalty of upright English tradesmen'.[125] The Princess of Wales it feared would become an object of trivial adulation – an 'inanimate doll, for fashion to ape and extravagance to deck' or an idol of the values held dear by the middle class: 'a domestic paragon ... who would condemn thirty millions to perpetual mourning, and haggle over a yard of bombazine'.

Most grievous was that the people had been duped into participating in the middle-class and aristocratic celebration of spurious royal virtue – 'greater crowds' assembled to 'deify princely puberty' than had lined the route of the funeral of Wellington who had given a lifetime of service to his country.[126] The newspaper saw the intense public interest in the Mordaunt divorce case of 1870 – in which the Prince of Wales was cited – as further proof of the sorry and undiscriminating fascination of people with the Royal Family. G.W.M. Reynolds himself exploited this fascination in his non-political publications, laying himself open to charges of hypocrisy from *Figaro*, which pointed out that while *Reynolds's Newspaper* constantly vilified the Royal Family and in particular the Prince of Wales – described as a 'rat' and his dead infant a 'louse' – *Bow Bells*, printed in the same office, had issued a 'Prince of Wales's number' containing laudatory biographies and illustrations of him and his family.[127]

Republicans were filled with revulsion by the divine aura surrounding royal personages and the insatiable curiosity in them. It had become customary for large numbers of leisured English families to spend their holidays wherever the Prince and Princess of Wales were sojourning – described by *The Times* as 'royalty hunting'[128] – and William Macall in the *Republican* reported that there had been a 'fierce contest' between 'a number of English gentlewomen' for the stones of cherries which the Princess had eaten. Such was the sycophancy of the English, Macall despaired, that 'ought not the electric telegraph to inform every town and village what royal personages are doing at each moment of the day and of the night?'[129] The 1860s had seen an increase, in radical quarters, of republican sentiments but no diminution in the loyal's capacity for veneration of the Royal Family.

1872–87

It was this capacity for veneration of the monarchy which was self-consciously mobilized against republicanism by Gladstone in 1872 in the Thanksgiving for the recovery of the Prince of Wales.[130] Freda Harcourt has argued that this marked the beginning of 'monarchism' as a 'new national ideology': both Gladstone and Disraeli arrived at this strategy in response to the creation of a large urban electorate in 1867; a consensual image of the nation was needed if the politics of class were to be avoided. Disraeli's speeches in 1871–2 exalting the monarchy and linking it with British imperial greatness showed the Tory leader's intent to make his the 'national party'; while Gladstone staged the Thanksgiving as an attempt to make loyalty to the Crown a unanimous national creed – he wrote, 'What we should look to . . . was not merely meeting [republicanism] by a more powerful display of opposite opinion, but to getting rid of it altogether, for it could never be satisfactory that there should exist even a fraction of the nation republican in its views'.[131] Other historians of the 'new nationalism'[132] and 'new imperialism', such as Tom Nairn and John M. MacKenzie, have also presented veneration of the monarchy in the 1870s and 1880s as a new phenomenon, associated with assertive nationhood and the imposition of a notion of national unity in which class conflict would be sublimated.[133]

It is true that the monarchy acquired greater prominence as a symbol of the nation and empire because of the greater self-consciousness of British nationalism and imperialism in this period.[134] However, this chapter has shown that the reverential literature of the 1870s and 1880s on the monarchy needs to be located not only in its contemporary context but in a long tradition of exaltation of the Crown and of Queen Victoria as the universally popular emblem of the whole nation, binding classes together in a common loyalty. The 'conservative working man', to whose existence Disraeli after all trusted in bringing in the 1867 Reform Act, was a familiar figure of newspaper editorials describing popular jubilation at royal events. Gladstone viewed the republicanism which emerged in the early 1870s as the aberration of 'a fraction' caused by the Queen's abstention from public duties: far from framing 'a new national ideology' he was seeking a complete return to what he saw as the customary and proper loyalty of the English people. When Disraeli championed the Crown in the early 1870s he was appealing to moderate opinion, putting the Conservatives forward as the defenders of tradition against the dangers of Gladstonian Liberalism, of which republicanism, he argued, was a symptom.

In analysing laudatory writings on the monarchy, Queen and Royal Family in this period, we shall find the familiar themes of preceding decades, their emphasis slightly changed with the passage of time – for example, as the reign lengthened, the Queen's lifetime became a yardstick of progress. It is in the mid-1870s that contemporaries began to refer to themselves as Victorians.[135] What made the period seem a novel one in its depiction of the monarchy was the gradual weakening of dissentient voices – it became more appropriate to extol the Crown as a symbol of unity and of the nation, as its political interference and partisanship and its foreign associations seemed to have decreased and provoked fewer attacks. The core of remaining active republicans in the late 1870s and 1880s despaired as their criticisms of the Crown were overwhelmed by the 'gush' which they deplored.

The press, as Gladstone had hoped, took full advantage of the Thanksgiving to rebuff the republicans by pointing to the cheering crowds as proof that the nation was one in its loyalty and that the monarchy was seen as a glorious living link with the nation's history.[136] Republicans were convinced of the press's importance in manufacturing spurious enthusiasm for the event. Frederic Harrison wrote that it was the role of 'the press to beat gongs and bawl one deaf'. The effect was to create 'a state religion; with the monarchy as its Melchisedek, its prophet, priest and king'.[137] *The Times* described the Thanksgiving as a 'great National Solemnity'. Loyalty had burst forth: 'the sentiment which attaches the nation to a particular family as the representative of its historical tradition ... in spite of many differences, in spite of a large diffusion and separation of interests, and in spite of much inequality in the distribution of national blessings'.[138] The *Sunday Times* was hyperbolic: the Thanksgiving was '... the greatest demonstration of popular feeling ever witnessed in any age or in any country'.[139] The intensity of loyalty wrote the *Daily Telegraph* was a tribute to the personal qualities of the Queen – the '"Mother of the People" in every sense', she had led a 'faultless life' and exhibited 'unprecedented virtues'.[140] Whereas of old there had been a 'superstitious' loyalty to monarchs personally undeserving, Englishmen now freely gave their love to the Queen, 'because she had been a good wife, a good mother and a kind neighbour.[141]

This veneration of the institution of monarchy and of its incumbent continued through the 1870s and 1880s together with full and sentimental description of the further unfolding of the 'great drama of domestic life' in the Royal Family – the marriages of the rest of the Queen's children and the premature deaths of two of them. *The Times*, on the occasion of the Duke of Edinburgh's entry into London with his Russian bride, Princess Alexandra, in 1874, reflected that 'loyalty and the homage which in one form or other is paid to all sorts and degrees of royalty is a very indestructible element'. Despite the utilitarians' teaching that men should be judged according to their merit and contribution to the general well-being of the community 'the ordinary British mind is not so constituted. It still puts Crowns and coronets, even when they encircle the brows of reflected or delegated royalty, far before the goodness or even the goodness that comes of itself.'[142] The newspaper with the largest circulation, *Lloyd's Weekly*, while it criticized attempts to equate popular loyalty with political quiescence,[143] was contemptuous of republican agitation again so fully rebutted by the reception of the Princess: 'The loyalty of the English people is always hearty on these occasions, and the display of it yesterday was enough to prove that we are still a long way off from the Republican Utopia, that is to be the portion of England when certain Soho debators and bye-street politicians are to be believed'.[144] The republican organ, the *National Reformer* bleakly drew the same conclusion: 'the excitement of the large crowds assembled in the snow and cold demonstrated the monarchical and aristocratic instincts of the people'.[145]

The loyal press's explanation for the popularity of the Crown was that reverence for tradition had been sustained by the reforms and improvements that had taken place under the monarchical constitution and had been augmented into devotion to the person of the monarch by the Queen's supreme example of regal and domestic virtue. Opponents of Disraeli's Royal Titles Bill in 1876 were averse to imperial additions to the old title of king of England with its venerable associations: the

Observer warned, '. . . the feeling of loyalty has its roots in history . . . the survival of the monarchical idea depends upon reverence for antiquity'.[146] The monarchy, wrote *The Times* in 1882, was a 'golden thread running through our chequered history, and giving it a unity and a meaning'[147] – to quote the *Daily Telegraph*, it provided 'mediaeval ornament to our progress'.[148] Moreover, the monarchy had presided over this progress, over the alleviation of discontent with the old unreformed system: *The Times* wrote that the Prince of Wales' visit to Sheffield in 1875 showed that the Crown acted as a symbol of national unity where it once 'half a century ago', might have seemed an instrument of the classes against the masses:

> It is the unanimity which particularly distinguishes the welcome in the present day. No one rails against the Sovereign or her House, and this shows how great an advance we have made, partly by the removal of political grievances, partly by the development of wealth and industry.[149]

The Queen was given personal credit for much of this transformation. She had always 'striven to identify herself with . . . all classes of her subjects'[150] and had attained 'unexampled popularity'.[151] As her reign lengthened, biographies of the Queen appeared, praising her constitutional and domestic probity, in homage to which, wrote one biographer, her people 'have risen up and called her blessed'.[152] School history textbooks held up the Queen's domestic qualities as exemplary,[153] as did the *Girls' Own Paper* in its first number in 1880.[154]

The Queen's children, now taking a prominent part themselves, were also praised for their devotion to duty. While the Prince of Wales appeared in radical and republican prints as a successor in debauch and riot to George, the Prince Regent, in the loyal press he was the industrious inheritor of his father's mantle, tirelessly discharging innumerable public functions, and doing so with great geniality and eclat.[155] His tour of India in 1875–6 was seen as a special personal triumph and received heavy coverage in the press.[156] Against charges that the Princes were parasitical wasters, it was argued that they earned their annuities through their worthy public appearances.[157] When Princes Alfred and Leopold visited Manchester for such a purpose in 1881, the *Manchester Guardian* asserted that the people of the city saw in the Princes, 'no drones, but worker bees of the most admirable sort'.[158]

Above all, wrote the *Daily News* in 1882, 'It is as the first family in the land that the Royal Family are chiefly thought of. It is in their cultivation of domestic ties that they have one of their firmest holds on the public esteem.'[159] The marriages of the Queen's younger children in this period all elicited newspaper comments on the importance of domestic feelings in the loyalty of the British people. The *Illustrated*

London News, upon the marriage of Prince Alfred in 1874, wrote that 'we all identify ourselves in some degree with the family of Queen Victoria' – their 'joys and sorrows ... become part of our personal experience, enlarge by engaging our sympathies, and raise us into a higher and broader sphere of daily life and experience'.[160] The *Daily News* stressed the importance of photography 'in dispelling the mystic halo which was once supposed to surround Royal persons'. Seeing the Royal Family in 'little domestic groups', wearing ordinary clothes encouraged an intimate association with them, as 'no one who hears the common social talk about those members of the Royal family who are most liked will think of denying'.[161] *The Times* cited the influence of the press as education was diffused and communications improved: 'Millions who in other times would scarcely have heard of George IV or William IV, and who would have been only awakened to any sympathy with Royalty by such a calamity as the death of Princess Charlotte ... now know and take an interest in every detail of a Royal Marriage'.[162] The *Daily Telegraph* saw royal weddings as pre-eminently English: there was no precise foreign equivalent for the English word 'home' and it was 'the idea of "home" and "family" ... which her Majesty represents concretely and paramountly to English minds'.[163] Royal bereavements were treated in the same way. *The Times* wrote that the death of Prince Leopold in 1884 produced 'throughout ... the land a universal shock of surprise and grief'.[164]

Several of the serious weekly and monthly journals disapproved of the familiar and sentimental terms in which the Royal Family was discussed. The *Sunday Times* found the 'hysterical professions of popular happiness and jubilation' at Prince Arthur's wedding 'manifestly preposterous' when couched 'in terms of endearment such as only should be reserved for the closest intimacies of kindred and friendship'.[165] The *Westminster Review* felt similarly about the Queen's own publication, *More Leaves from the Journal of a Life in the Highlands. From 1862 to 1882,* which came out in 1884 as a tribute to her deceased servant John Brown, just as the first *Leaves* had been a memorial to Albert. While *The Times* was enchanted that the Queen had 'taken her subjects into full-confidence as to the great domestic sorrows of her past' and 'told in artless language the story of her life',[166] the *Westminster Review* asked, '... was it worthwhile to publish such a book?', containing as it did 'such trivialities' as endless descriptions of the Queen's taking tea and betraying 'a want of dignity in a royal or indeed in any author' in the detailed and lengthy description of how Brown's legs were cut by the edges of his wet kilt.[167] Moreover, the extravagant lament for Brown – 'His loss to me is irreparable' – was likely to be 'misunderstood, misrepresented, and ridiculed', provoking as it did the reflection that 'The memory of her servant's loss seems to have overclouded even her memory of her lost consort'. The reviewer concluded with the wish: 'which arises from our unfeigned respect for its Royal and gracious author – that it had never been published'.[168]

Overblown praise for royal personages and minute and mawkish articles on royal weddings offended the discriminating observer. In 1874 the *Examiner* complained about the 'nauseating flattery' heaped upon Prince Alfred and his bride, 'two young people whose sole claim to distinction is that they have lived within the shadow of the throne'.[169] In 1879 at the time of Prince Arthur's wedding, the *Pall Mall Gazette* found 'what is vulgarly but expressively called "gush"' in the newspapers 'not only foreign to the character of the English people but ... impertinently obtrusive'.[170] Yet it was such "gush" which held sway in the press. A correspondent to George Standring's *Republican* wrote to congratulate the periodical on its survival as 'a brave little outpost ... in sight of a huge and overwhelming enemy' – 'the sickly "loyalty" of the age ... a fashion frequently followed with preposterous zeal and effusiveness'.[171]

The Queen's reign was itself becoming an historical period, a yardstick of the nation's progress. Her visit to Europe in 1879 prompted the observation that her 'reign spans a wide chasm in the history of modern Europe', an epoch of revolutions abroad and peaceful change at home.[172] When it was announced that the Jubilee celebrations would take place after the completion of fifty years on the throne, *The Times* concentrated on the historical significance of the event – it would be not just a 'personal' commemoration but a 'national' one, signifying that 'No great State has passed a half-century of national existence so abounding in vitality of every kind'. Victoria was indissolubly bound up with the political, economic, social and scientific advances of her reign – 'Her praise is that it is difficult to think of her reign of fifty years apart from the British nation, and impossible to think of that without her.[173] *Punch*'s almanacs for 1886 and 1887 both anticipated the Jubilee with double-page engravings of the Queen against a backcloth depicting all the varied national achievements of her reign.[174]

1887–1901: apotheosis

The themes discussed above reached their climax in the press coverage of the two Jubilees and the Queen's death and in the proliferation of biographies of the Queen in these landmark years.[175] That the monarchy was lavishly praised at the end of the reign is not a matter of historical dispute and it is necessary to take only a sample of a cross section of mainstream London newspapers to illustrate the kind of approval which was heaped on the Queen in these final years. One feature of note which does emerge is that it was less the institution than the sovereign herself who was lauded extravagantly, the import of such commentaries being that the stability of the throne did to a certain extent depend on the perceived qualities of its occupant.

Erstwhile critic of the monarchy, Henry Labouchere remarked at the time of the Golden Jubilee that 'love of Royalty' was 'firmly established in the middle-class English breast'[176] and the middle-class press certainly reflected that love in its coverage of the events. Editorials professed a respect for the institution of monarchy but above all emphasized the way in which the personal qualities of the Queen had been responsible for cementing its popularity.

The Times asserted that 'Britons, in spite of their confirmed habit of grumbling, look upon their ancient institutions with steadfast affection and reverence'. At the same time it acknowledged that 'their attachment to the monarchy has blended with respect for the character of the Queen'.[177] The newspaper felt that 'personal affection' for the Queen was 'the largest element' in 'this unprecedented movement of popular feeling'.[178] The *Illustrated London News* reported in the crowds lining the streets comments which showed an 'honest friendship to the Royal family – not profoundly reverent or ardently enthusiastic, but manifestly the outcome of sound popular opinion'.[179] Similarly the *Spectator* observed in the popular attitude 'a change indescribable, but unmistakable; an increase of kindliness and affection, but a decrease of awe. It was a friend of all who was welcomed, rather than a great Sovereign.'[180]

The high moral tone of the monarchy under Victoria was seen as the principal cause of her popularity. The *Daily News* referred to her reign as 'a new era', with old Royal debts paid off and no new ones incurred, and cited the 'purity of the Court, the exemplary conduct of the Queen and her Consort who were regarded as a pattern father and mother of a pattern family'.[181] *The Times* struck the same note, arguing that 'nothing in the rich and various history of the past 50 years is more worthy of record than the purification and refinement of social life and manners to which the influence of the Court has most powerfully contributed'. This explained the 'vast . . . change' for the better in 'the tone in which royalty and royal persons are spoken of' compared with the early nineteenth century. The paper approvingly quoted John Bright's speech of 1858 in which he had stated his hope that the monarchy would be perpetual if 'the throne of England be filled with so much dignity and so much purity as we have known it in our time'.[182]

Thus the tone was of massive approval of the monarchy but none the less there was a realization that such approval was conditional upon the monarch. W.T. Stead writing in the *Pall Mall Gazette* explained the monarchy's popularity by the fact that it was the only institution currently doing its job satisfactorily – the Commons being feeble, the Lords overweening – and, as mentioned in chapter 3, he pondered, looking on the Prince of Wales, how long the monarchy would last after the Queen.[183] *Lloyd's Weekly Newspaper* clearly saw the importance of issues of personal popularity when it wrote that the Jubilee was a greater event than the Thanksgiving of 1872 not only because the Prince of Wales was merely heir to the throne but also because he 'was not, perhaps, quite so popular then as he is now'.[184]

Victoria's longevity was another factor enhancing the standing of the Crown as the Jubilee presented an opportunity to associate the progress of the past 50 years with her reign. *The Times* remarked that her reign spanned the entire or greater part of the lives of the current generation and that her name was identified with all the achievements which had taken place during her reign in all aspects of human endeavour.[185] *Lloyd's Weekly Newspaper* with its democratic outlook stated, 'In honouring the Queen we honour the progress of the people during the term of her reign'.[186]

While Labouchere spoke of the *middle class*' love of the monarchy and *Lloyd's* wrote that the Jubilee could not obscure class inequalities and conflicts,[187] the middle-class press emphasized the consensual nature of the occasion, referring to the 'common rejoicing of all classes of Her Majesty's subjects'.[188] The *Standard* proclaimed, 'We are one people'.[189] *The Times* explained the 'warmth of attachment' to the Queen felt by 'all sorts and conditions of her people' by her own 'large fund of perfect loving sympathy and . . . inexhaustible spring of pure affection for them.[190]

Familiarity of the people with the Queen was another theme arising from this for, not only, wrote *The Times* had the Queen 'associated herself with all the joys and sorrows and all the happiness of her people' but she had allowed her subjects to be 'the sharers in her own personal joys and sorrows' and this had created the unique 'personal character of the relations which the Queen's long reign has established between the nation and its Sovereign'. The Queen's embracing of her children was seen as 'the one touch of nature which made the whole assembly kin'.[191]

The years between the Jubilees were largely significant for events involving the Prince of Wales' family. We have noted in chapter 3 the criticism aroused by grants to his children, by his involvement in baccarat and by the 'gush' surrounding the death of Albert Victor and marriage of George. Here we will consider more favourable presentations of these episodes.

The marriage of the Prince's daughter, Louise to the Earl of Fife in 1889 was hailed in familiar terms by *The Times* as a love-match: 'A marriage of affection, however exalted the station of the bride, goes straight to the English heart'.[192] Even *The Times* was moved to censure the Prince in 1891 over his apparent addiction to baccarat, warning that 'in these democratic days' such a 'personal default' was a 'shock' to the monarchical principle. At the same time it acknowledged the mitigating 'monotony of a Royal existence' and the 'assiduity, the tact, and the unfailing good humour with which the Prince performs these duties'.[193] W.T. Stead took a similar line in a balanced profile of the Prince in the *Review of Reviews*. He argued that the Prince above all needed to be given more responsibility and that he did, for all his faults, possess 'all the elements of a democratic Prince', as evinced by his interest in working-class housing. He would surely now effect a Henry V-style transformation.[194] The furore surrounding the baccarat scandal and the references to potential republicanism in even the loyal press illustrate again that the stability of the monarchy was contingent on individuals in the Royal Family. Stead boasted that before publication of his profile of the Prince, Gladstone was worried that 'I was setting a match to a mine that would blow the Constitution heavens-high' and that the Prince of Wales clutched an unopened copy of the article in terror and needed Lady Warwick to read it for him.[195]

The betrothals in quick succession of May of Teck first to Prince Albert Victor and then after his death to his younger brother George, Duke of York, were both greeted in the same newspapers as love-matches, *Lloyd's Weekly Newspaper* commenting, '. . . there is an air of romance associated with a young woman captivating two brothers'.[196] The *Daily News* went as far as to say that Royal betrothals were 'not of State convenience' but 'just as the poorest peasants might have formed a love match'.[197] The death of Albert Victor prompted a fulsome obituary in *The Times* quite at variance with the reality of a dissolute, uneducatable Prince:[198]

> whether as a sailor, as undergraduate, or as soldier, he behaved with unassuming modesty, with grave propriety, and with steady application . . . (He) led the uneventful life of the serious student . . . with the simplicity, modesty, and zeal of an English gentleman . . . (demonstrating) his fitness to occupy at some distant date the position of a constitutional ruler . . . [199]

The *Spectator*, which took a more detached view of events, observed that Albert Victor had not according to reports been 'a strong man' and said that there was only 'subdued approval' for the marriage of May to the brother of her deceased betrothed. Nevertheless it commented that while a republic would be the higher ideal if human nature were fit for it, the British monarchy played an important role as 'the apparent pivot and centre of our race, the silent but everywhere visible standard-bearer of the flag which represents the unity of our people, their history, and their pride' – a figurehead role which Albert Victor could have filled. The Prince of Wales had become a far more popular figure since 1872 and 'the feeling for the throne . . . is deep and genuine'. People viewed the Royal household as 'the central household of them all'. The marriage of the future heir, the Duke of York, was popular in that it would probably secure a popular dynasty and gave every likelihood that the future king would be happily married. A happily married king was a cornerstone of the monarchy's continued success since 'a disreputable Court in England would soon be a Court shaking in every breeze'.[200] The *Daily News* on the occasion of the wedding celebrated the 'dignity and historic grandeur of a great line of sovereigns' but stressed that 'we are no believers in the principle of unconditional loyalty' – loyalty had to be 'reciprocal' from rulers to the people.[201]

The *Spectator* pursued its theme concerning the potential dangers of a male sovereign in its commentary on the Diamond Jubilee. The throne was safer with a woman since people were 'unwilling to pry too much into the secret history of her reign' – to examine whether royal political influence had been exercised. Victoria, the journal asserted, had 'rehabilitated the monarchy' since 'the German dynasty had never been genuinely popular'.[202] The *Daily Telegraph* described Victoria as 'the best-loved monarch that ever ascended a Throne'.[203]

The press once more emphasized the intimacy of the Royal Family's connection with the people. The *Pall Mall Gazette* wrote of 'the romance of Royalty in the reality of its individual nearness to the poorest and humblest'.[204] Emily Crawford in the *Contemporary Review* contended that the advent of the Penny Post, with the Queen's portrait becoming visible to all, had been important in building up her familiarity. She noted that Louis Napoleon, as President, had instituted the same system as a way of consolidating his popularity in France.[205]

The Queen's high moral conduct and her sympathy with her subjects were, as ever, central themes, and her influence on matters such as 'improving the lot of animals' and lessening dangers to sailors and workmen were commended.[206] Praise of the Queen was quite without bounds as *The Times*' over-blown analysis of the Queen's simple Jubilee message to her subjects shows: 'From my heart I thank my beloved people. May God bless them.' The newspaper wrote, 'All, the simplest as well as the most cultured, feel the spell of language which is of rare eloquence in its absolute freedom from affectation'.[207]

Adding to the Jubilee enthusiasm was the new-style, populist paper the *Daily Mail*, which had a rampantly pro-monarchical stance and which reported events in a knock-about, colloquial style with many neologisms around the word 'Jubilee': 'The jubilonged-for day is upon us at last . . . jubiline the streets . . . jubilluminate them'.[208]

In a more reflective mood, W.S. Lily in the *Nineteenth Century* argued that the message of the Jubilee was that, contrary to much contemporary thought, imagination and emotion were 'still far more masterful than logic with the vast majority of men'. The emotion of loyalty was still clearly alive in Britain: 'In Englishmen there is innate a veneration for the men and women in whom the institutions of the country seem – so to speak – embodied in visible form'. He painted a Whiggish picture of the 'growth of English freedom' under the aegis of an increasingly constitutional monarchy whose 'uprightness and honour' ensured a 'national unity' and 'national stability'.[209]

When the Queen died in 1901, the unequivocal tone of obituaries in the mainstream press was that the whole nation united in mourning the dreadful loss of a Queen who had been an exemplary monarch and woman, whose parting marked the end of an era and whose reign stood as a benchmark of extraordinary national progress.

The Queen's strength of character, sense of duty and unmatched accumulation of experience were common sources of praise. The *Daily News* singled out her 'strength of character, and length of days' as the reasons for her unprecedented popularity.[210] The *Spectator* wrote that while subtlety and imagination were not among her attributes she had a 'plain, simple character, fortified by large experience and wide knowledge'.[211] Even a quite critical obituary which appeared in the *Quarterly Review* some months after the Queen's death agreed that Victoria though 'a rather ordinary mortal' had 'fine instincts, considerable mental capacity, and a certain vital persistence'. (The article also cited her obstinacy, philistinism, political prejudices and unconstitutional interference resulting from a belief in divine right and 'chimerical conviction of her own indispensability'.[212])

The Queen's domestic virtues were to the fore in all accounts. The *Daily Mail* referred to a 'perfect court and model home',[213] *The Times* to 'the ennobling example of her private life' as 'an excellent daughter, wife, and mother'.[214] *Lloyd's Weekly Newspaper* explained that as she had experienced as a mother 'all the primal and essential ties that bind men on this earth' so all classes could feel sympathy for the Royal Family and feel as Rosebery had said that the loss of the Queen was the loss of a friend[215]. The *Daily Mail* wrote that because of the Queen's care for her subjects she had left 'tender memories. It seemed as if of all the millions there was not one of her subjects who had not some cherished personal reminiscence of the Queen.'[216] This made her, to quote the *Spectator*, a 'well-loved mother' to all her people since her 'devotion to and love for' them 'knew no limits'.[217] Her death, wrote the *Daily Telegraph*, meant that a 'desolate void lies cold upon the heart of the nation'.[218]

Such a situation, reflected *The Times*, showed what a transformation the Queen had effected in the standing of the monarchy. Inverting its stinging obituary on George IV, the newspaper exclaimed, 'What eye has not wept for her? What heart has not heaved with many a throb of unbought and quite irresistible sorrow?'[219]

It was acknowledged that the national success which her reign had encompassed had added to the Queen's lustre. The *Spectator* reflected, 'Something of the glamour which is produced by continuing and amazing success undoubtedly entered into the heartfelt worship which was ultimately paid to the Queen.[220] *The Times* wrote that 'Victorian' was an appropriate epithet for a period in which Britain had enjoyed continuous progress and extraordinary stability.[221]

It was the loss of this stability represented by the Queen which was now feared by the *Spectator*. It wrote with *fin de siècle* foreboding that the 'Victorian age, the longest, the greatest, and the noblest in our annals' was closing 'in storm' as Britain was engaged in a war unpopular with the rest of Europe. The Queen's death made people feel 'a distinct and an unexpected diminution in their faith in the stability of things'.[222] However, the journal repeated the much-used analogy of a reformed Prince Hal to describe the new King and praised his patriotism, courage, political knowledge, tact, judgment of men, charm and abilities of chairmanship, and called his consort 'a true Englishwoman'.[223] These sentiments were echoed in the rest of the press, the *Pall Mall Gazette* declaring that there was 'no more popular figure in the world to-day than His Majesty King Edward VII'[224] and the *Daily News* pronouncing his wife 'the idol of the people'.[225] Alexandra was likened to the late Queen in the way in which she had not allowed personal bereavement to overcome her sense of public duty.[226] *Punch* depicted its eponymous character telling Edward, 'Your Coronation awaits your Majesty's pleasure, but you are already crowned in the hearts of your people'[227] – the seamless transition to a new phase of veneration of the monarchy had been made.

Conclusion

The picture presented in the middle-class London press late in the reign was one of unanimous loyalty to the Crown and of deep devotion to the persons of the Queen and Royal Family. Yet such panegyrics were not, as has been argued, a new phenomenon, created to forge a 'new national ideology' in which class conflict would be sublimated. Certainly there was greater authority about statements of popular approval of the Crown as active republicanism dwindled – the Crown apparently rising above politics and purged of much of its foreignness could be less ambiguously cast as an emblem of national unity. However, the same newspapers had been venerating the monarchy, the Queen and her family from the outset of the reign – the Crown, identifying itself with the people's interests, bound classes together in a reformed and equitable political system, while the home life of the Queen, Albert and their children provided a cynosure of probity and of family life lacking in the royalty of England since the earlier years of George III's reign. An indication of the continuity of reverential writing on the monarchy is the historical perspective of the loyal press late in the reign: the monarchy's standing throughout the reign was the constant feature in a much-changed world. Comparing the period of her first daughter's wedding in 1858 with that of her last son's in 1882, the *Saturday Review* reflected, 'The range of history ... is considerable, and much has been altered in the interval. But of all things that which has altered least is the position of the Royal Family in the country.'[228]

The attitude of the middle-class press towards the monarchy reflected the deference of a class which, though it prided itself on self-made success, needed the approbation of those born to their riches and status – the hunger for royal visits was comparable with the common desire of industrialists to buy their way into the landed aristocracy. The deification of the Royal Family for their possession of the favourite bourgeois virtues of thrift, industry, sobriety, domestic probity and, as Frank Prochaska has pointed out, philanthropy,[229] was another aspect of flunkeyism. We have observed how much of the veneration of the monarchy consisted in veneration of the family. The cycle of family events in the royal household held a romantic, fairy-tale appeal but was also related to that of a typical English family – and the Royal Family often appeared in paintings and photographs as a bourgeois domestic group. The gratifying self-image of the middle-class family's behaviour and values was very much projected onto Victoria's family, for, in its strained relations between parents and children, its rigid etiquette and arranged marriages, its reality was far from the informal, affectionate ideal presented in the press and in fact closer to the bizarre, self-enclosed world inhabited by Victoria's Hanoverian predecessors.[230] That contemporaries were prepared to suspend disbelief for this Royal Family is explained by its far greater respectability – the Prince of Wales notwithstanding – when compared with its predecessors and to the less controversial role of the monarchy in politics; as well as to the desire of the middle class to see its values affirmed in the highest family in the land.

The importance of the Victorian period as a turning-point in the history of the British monarchy can now be better appreciated. In previous chapters we have seen how rigorous discussion of the monarch's utility, cost, political power and patriotism persisted from earlier periods. Here we have seen that alongside such debate there was the veneration of the Royal Family and preoccupation with the trivial details of their lives, which was to become for most of the twentieth century virtually the only discussion of the monarchy heard as a greater consensus was reached on those areas of earlier contention. This position sheltered form controversy did, however, depend on a fulfilment, at least ostensibly, of the virtuous, harmonious family life which the press had ascribed to the Royal Family – not to mention a general willingness by the press not to delve into and publicize any deviations from this ideal.

Notes

1. Kingsley Martin, *The Crown and the Establishment* (London, 1962), pp. 20–1.
2. John M. MacKenzie, *Propaganda and Empire. The Manipulation of British Public Opinion, 1880–1960.* (Manchester, 1984), pp. 3–4.
3. Tom Nairn, 'The glamour of backwardness, *The Times Higher Education Supplement*, no. 636 (11 January 1985), p. 13; idem, *The Enchanted Glass. Britain and its Monarchy* (London, 1988), pp. 282, 349.
4. Freda Harcourt, 'Gladstone, Monarchism and the "New Imperialism" 1868–74', *Journal of Imperial and Commonwealth History*, vol. 14, no. 1 (October 1985), pp. 20–51.
5. P. S. Baker, 'The Social and Ideological Role of the Monarchy in late Victorian Britain' (unpub. MA, Lancaster, 1978), pp. 2, 16, 62.
6. Ibid., p. 65.
7. Linda Colley, 'The Apotheosis of George III: Loyalty, Royalty and the British Nation 1760–1820', *Past and Present*, no. 102 (1984), pp. 94–129.
8. Nairn, 'The glamour of backwardness', p. 13.
9. See above, chapters 2 and 3.
10. See Christopher Hibbert, *George IV* (London, 1976 edn), pp. 599–604, 622–6, 782, 787; Philip Ziegler, *King William IV* (London, 1971), pp. 151–5, 292–4.
11. Hibbert, *George IV*, p. 783.
12. *Hansard*, vol. 28, cols 1547–63.
13. *Westminster Review*, vol. 27 (1837), p. 243.
14. *Examiner*, 25 June 1837, p. 401.
15. See above, chapter 2.
16. Mark Girouard, *The Return to Camelot. Chivalry and the English Gentleman.* (New York and London, 1981), pp. 112–25.
17. See above, chapter 4.
18. *The Times*, 21 June 1837, p. 4.

19. Charles C.F. Greville *The Greville Memoirs*, (ed. Henry Reeve, 8 vols. London, 1888 edn), vol. 4, pp. 14–15.
20. C.J. Blomfield, Lord Bishop of London, *A Sermon Preached at the Coronation of her Most Excellent Majesty Queen Victoria* (London, 1838), pp. 15–18.
21. For example, *Observer*, 1 July 1838, p. 2; *Leeds Mercury*, 30 June 1838, p. 4.
22. *Standard*, 29 June 1838, p. 2; *Berrow's Worcester Journal*, 5 July 1838, p. 3.
23. For example, *John Bull*, 1 July 1838, p. 304.
24. For example, *Leeds Mercury*, 30 June 1838, p. 4; *Globe*, 28 June 1838, p. 3.
25. *Manchester Guardian*, 30 June 1838, p. 3.
26. *Northern Star*, 15 February 1840, p. 4.
27. *Manchester Guardian*, 12 February 1840, p. 2.
28. *Leeds Mercury*, 15 February 1840, p. 3.
29. *Victoria and her People; or the Covenant*. A poem by a Member of one of the Inns of Court. (London, 1841), p. 15; The Rev. R. Kennedy, *Britain's Genius: A Mask. Composed on the Occasion of the Marriage of Victoria* (London, 1840), p. 15.
30. G.R.French, *The Ancestry of Her Majesty, Queen Victoria, and of His Royal Highness, Prince Albert*. (London, 1841), pp. 348–9.
31. *Anecdotes, Personal Traits and Characteristic Sketches of Victoria the First*. By 'A Lady' (London, 1840); see also A. Strickland, *Queen Victoria. From Her Birth to Her Bridal* 2 vols (London, 1840).
32. For example, *Prince Albert, His Country and Kindred*. (London, 1840); *The Marriage of the Queen to Prince Albert Considered in A Letter to the People of Great Britain* (London, 1840).
33. See above.
34. *Morning Chronicle*, 10 November 1841, p. 2.
35. *The Times*, 18 January 1842, p. 4.
36. Ibid., 13 October 1851, p. 4.
37. Ibid., 9 September 1858, p. 6.
38. *Leeds Mercury*, 7 September 1858, p. 2. See also, Asa Briggs, *Victorian Cities* (London, 1980 edn), pp. 170–7.
39. *The Times*, 9 September 1858, p. 6.
40. Ibid, 17 March 1842, p. 4.
41. *Spectator*, 29 April 1843, p. 395.
42. *Observer*, 14 November 1841, p. 4.
43. *The Times*, 26 January 1858, p. 6.
44. *Lloyd's Weekly Newspaper*, 31 January 1858, p. 6.
45. Ibid., 30 April 1843, p. 4.
46. Ibid., 5 February 1854, p. 6.
47. For details of these activites, see Prochaska, *Royal Bounty*, pp. 67–99.
48. *The Times*, 8 December 1843, p. 4.
49. *The Progresses of Her Majesty Queen Victoria and His Royal Highness Prince Albert in France, Belgium and England* (London, 1844), p. 144; also, *The Progress of Her Majesty Queen Victoria and His Royal Highness Prince Albert to Burghley House, Northampton* (Northampton, 1844); *Queen Victoria in Scotland* (London, 1842); Sir Thomas Dick

Lauder, *Memorial of the Royal Progress in Scotland* (Edinburgh, 1843); John Grant, *Her Majesty's Visit to Scotland* (Woolwich, 1842).

50. *The Times*, 19 March 1848, p. 4.
51. Ibid., 31 October 1849, p. 4.
52. Ibid., 2 May 1851, p. 4.
53. *Illustrated London News*, 10 May 1851, p. 392.
54. *Punch*, vol. 20 (1851), pp. 183–95.
55. *Friend of the People*, 10 May 1851, p. 189.
56. T.W. Laqueur, *Religion and Respectability. Sunday Schools and Working Class Culture 1780–1850* (New Haven, 1976), pp. 202–3, 239–40.
57. *Reynolds's Political Instructor*, 24 November 1849, p. 17.
58. For example, *Reynolds's Miscellany*, 5 December 1846, pp. 73–4.
59. *English Republic*, vol. 1 (1851), p. 355.
60. *Punch*, vol. 7 (1844), p. 138.
61. For example, *The Times*, 23 November 1840, p. 4; 11 November 1841, p. 4.
62. *Talk to Young Folk on the Voyages and Visits of the Queen and Prince Albert to France and Belgium*, by Grandfather Philip (London, 1844), p. 23.
63. See, for example, *The Times*, 24 November 1855, p. 6.
64. Norman Gash, 'A gifted public man', *Times Higher Education Supplement*, no. 577 (25 November 1983), p. 20.
65. *London Pioneer*, 20 August 1846, p. 270.
66. *The Times*, 10 November 1841, p. 4.
67. *Morning Post*, 26 January 1858, p. 4.
68. *Morning Chronicle*, 25 January 1858, p. 4.
69. *The Collected Works of Walter Bagehot, Vol. 5*, (ed. Norman St John-Stevas, London, 1974), p. 229.
70. *The Times*, 20 January 1858, p. 8.
71. Colley, 'The Apotheosis of George III', p. 125.
72. *Spectator*, 10 August 1844, p. 746.
73. Ibid., 13 November 1841, p. 1081.
74. *Observer*, 14 November 1841, p. 4.
75. Simon Schama, 'The Domestication of Majesty: Royal Family Portraiture, 1500–1850', *Journal of Interdisciplinary History*, vol. 17 no 1 (Summer 1986), pp. 155–83.
76. See, for example, *Spectator*, 29 April 1843, p. 385.
77. See above.
78. *Queen Victoria in Scotland*, pp. iii–iv; Lauder, *Memorial of the Royal Progresses in Scotland*, pp. 3–6.
79. *Punch*, vol. 7 (1844), p. 138.
80. *Morning Chronicle*, 2 May 1851, p. 6.
81. *Punch*, vol. 7 (1844), p. 138.
82. Ibid., vol. 4 (1843), p. 90.
83. *Spectator*, 21 November 1840, p. 1116. Newspapers carried details of the cradle and of all other provisions for the new babe; for example, *Observer*, 21 November 1840, pp. 2–3.
84. *Illustrated London News*, 10 August 1844, p. 86.
85. *Observer*, 11 August 1844, p. 2.
86. *Globe*, 26 January 1858, p. 2.
87. *Daily Telegraph*, 26 January 1858, p. 3.

88. *Observer*, 31 January 1858, p. 5.
89. *Daily Telegraph*, 25 January 1858, p. 3.
90. *Morning Chronicle*, 26 January 1858, p. 4.
91. *The Times*, 23 December 1861, p. 6.
92. *Manchester Guardian*, 16 December 1861, p. 2.
93. *Lloyd's Weekly Newspaper*, 22 December 1861, p. 1.
94. *Morning Chronicle*, 16 December 1861, p. 4.
95. *British Workman*, 1 February 1862, p. 342.
96. Ibid., no. 8 (1 February 1862), p. 342.
97. *Spectator*, 21 December 1861, p. 1387.
98. John Cannon, 'The Survival of the British Monarchy', *Royal Historical Society Transactions*, 5th Series, no. 36 (1986), pp. 150–1.
99. See above, chapter 3.
100. *The Times*, 23 April 1862, p. 8.
101. Elisabeth Darby and Nicola Smith, *The Cult of the Prince Consort* (London, 1983), p. 1.
102. Gash, 'A gifted public man', p. 20.
103. See below, chapter 8.
104. Darby and Smith, *The Cult of the Prince Consort*, pp. 1, 58–9, 88–9, 101, 104–5.
105. *Daily Telegraph*, 1 July 1862, p. 4.
106. *Morning Post*, 2 July 1862, p. 4.
107. *Morning Herald*, 2 July 1862, p. 4.
108. *Examiner*, 7 March 1863, p. 145.
109. See below, chapter 9.
110. *Observer*, 18 December 1864, p. 4.
111. *Sunday Times*, 10 April 1864, p. 4.
112. The Hon. C. Grey, *The Early Years of His Royal Highness the Prince Consort* (London, 1867).
113. *Blackwood's Edinburgh Magazine*, vol. 102 (September 1867), pp. 375–84.
114. Queen Victoria, *Leaves from the Journal of Our Life in the Highlands From 1848 to 1861*. (ed. Arthur Helps, 1st pub. 1868, Folio Society, London 1973, with an introduction by Elizabeth Longford).
115. Longford, *Victoria R.I.*, pp. 470–1.
116. *Illustrated London News*, 25 March 1871, p. 282.
117. *The Collected Works of Walter Bagehot, Vol. 5*, p. 229.
118. *Saturday Review*, 5 July 1862 p. 1.
119. *Morning Herald*, 2 July 1862, p. 4.
120. *Daily Telegraph*, 21 March 1871, p. 4.
121. *Daily News*, 22 March 1871, p. 4; 21 March 1871, p. 4.
122. *Examiner*, 16 April 1864, p. 244.
123. *Spectator*, 25 March 1871, pp. 337, 346–7.
124. *Saturday Review*, 25 March 1871, pp. 362–3.
125. For illustrations of the use of the Royal Family in advertising see Robert Opie, *Rule Britannia. Trading on the British Image* (London, 1985), pp. 8–9, 43–9. Thomas Richards describes the apothesis of the Queen in advertising in 1887 in 'The Image of Victoria in the Year of the Jubilee', *Victorian Studies*, vol. 31 no. 1 (Autumn 1987), pp 7–32.
126. *Reynolds's Newspaper*, 15 March 1863, p. 1.

127. *Newspaper Warfare! The Great Pen and Ink Battle Between the 'Figaro' and 'Reynolds's Newspaper'* (London, 1872), pp. 1, 16.
128. See *The Times*, 4 August 1869, p. 9.
129. *Republican*, no. 16 (1 August 1871), pp. 1–2.
130. See above, chapter 3.
131. Another ardent monarchist, Tennyson was as delighted as Gladstone by the defeat of republicanism. In 'The Last Tournament' written in 1871, the Red Knight, the epitome of evil challenging Arthur's court, was an amalgam of a Communard and a British republican, and the 1872 edition of *Idylls of the King* contained a preface denouncing the republicans and extolling Victoria and the memory of Albert. (Gwyn A. Williams, *Excalibur. The Search for Arthur's Britain* (London, 1994), pp. 197–200 and see pp. 192–7 for the veneration for the Victoran monarchy underlying *Idylls of the King* as a whole.)
132. Harcourt, 'Gladstone, Monarchism and the "New Imperialism"', pp. 20–51.
133. Nairn, 'The glamour of backwardness', p. 13; idem, *The Enchanted Glass*, p. 282; MacKenzie, *Propaganda and Empire*, pp. 3–4.
134. See above, chapter 6.
135. See *The Oxford English Dictionary*, vol. 12.
136. For the way *Punch* and other illustrated papers 'wrote up' the Thanksgiving, see Frankie Morris, 'The Illustrated Press and the Republican Crisis of 1871–2', *Victorian Periodicals Review* 25 (1992), pp. 114–26.
137. *Fortnightly Review*, vol. 11 (June 1872), p. 635.
138. *The Times*, 23–6 February 1872, passim.
139. *Sunday Times*, 3 March 1872, p. 4.
140. *Daily Telegraph*, 27 February 1872, p. 4.
141. *Daily News*, 28 February 1872, p. 7.
142. *The Times*, 12 March 1874, p. 9.
143. For example at the time of the Thanksgiving – *Lloyd's Weekly Newspaper*, 3 March 1872.
144. Ibid., 8 March 1874, p. 6
145. *National Reformer*, vol. 23, no. 12 (22 March 1874), pp. 178–9.
146. *Observer*, 20 February 1876, p. 4; 19 March 1876, p. 4.
147. *The Times*, 28 April 1882, p. 9.
148. *Daily Telegraph*, 12 March 1874, p. 5.
149. *The Times*, 12 March 1875, p. 7.
150. Ibid., 14 May 1887, p. 13.
151. *Daily Telegraph*, 27 April 1882, p. 6.
152. *The Life of her Most Gracious Mmajesty the Queen*, By Sarah Tytler, 2 vols (London 1885), vol. 2, p. 234; see also, *The First Lady in the Land* (London, 1884); *A Diary of Royal Movements and of Personal Events and Incidents in the Life and Reign of her Most Gracious Majesty, Queen Victoria* (London, 1883), *The Queen and the Royal Family. Anecdotes and Narratives, Based on Contemporary Records* (London, 1882).
153. Valerie E. Chancellor, *History for their Masters. Opinion in the English History Textbook: 1800–1914* (Bath, 1970), pp. 42–3.
154. Jane MacKay and Pat Thane, 'The Englishwoman' in Robert Colls and Philip Dodd eds, *Englishness. Politics and Culture 1880–1920* (London, 1986), p. 18. Brian Harrison alludes to the importance of the domestic

example of the Royal Family in the propaganda of the Girls Friendly Society, founded in 1880, in 'For Church, Queen and Family: the Girls Friendly Society 1874–1920', *Past and Present*, no. 61 (1973), pp. 127–8, 131–2.

155. *The Times*, 15 August 1882, p. 9. For details of the charitable activities of the Prince and the Queen's other children, see Prochaska, *Royal Bounty*, pp. 109–30.

156. For example, *Illustrated London News*, 1876, passim; *Punch*, vol. 69, Almanac for 1876; vol. 70 (1876), p. 191.

157. *The Times*, 8 September 1880, p. 9.

158. *Manchester Guardian*, 13 December 1881, p. 5.

159. *Daily News*, 28 April 1882, pp. 4–5.

160. *Illustrated London News*, 14 March 1874, p. 238.

161. *Daily News*, 12 March 1874, p. 4.

162. *The Times*, 13 March 1874, pp. 8–9.

163. *Daily Telegraph*, 27 April 1882, p. 6.

164. *The Times*, 29 March 1884, p. 11; cf. the death of Princess Alice, ibid., 16 December 1878, p. 8.

165. *Sunday Times*, 16 March 1879, p. 4.

166. *The Times*, 29 March 1884, p. 11.

167. The reviewer suggested that 'if "poor Brown" had not worn the dress of a Highland cattle stealer of bygone days and had been content to wear the ordinary femoral habiliments of the nineteenth century he would have escaped this accident'. A satire *John Brown's Legs or Leaves from a Journal in the Lowlands* was dedicated 'To the Memory of those extraordinary Legs, poor bruised and scratched darlings'. (Longford, *Victoria R.I.*, pp. 577–8.)

168. *Westminster Review*, vol. 65 (April 1884), pp. 420–9.

169. *Examiner*, 14 March 1874, p. 250.

170. *Pall Mall Gazette*, 13 March 1879, p. 1

171. *Republican*, vol. 5 (July 1879), p. 125.

172. *The Times*, 3 April 1879, p. 9.

173. Ibid., 20 November 1885, p. 7.

174. *Punch*, vol. 89, Punch's Almanac for 1886; vol. 91, Almanac for 1887.

175. G.B. Smith, *Life of Her Majesty Queen Victoria* (London, 1887); W.B. Tulloch, *The Story of the Life of Queen Victoria for Boys and Girls* (London, 1887); J.C. Jeafferson, *Victoria, Queen and Empress*, 2 vols (London, 1893); Alfred E. Knight, *Victoria; Her Life and Reign* (London, 1896); Richard Davey, *Victoria, Queen and Empress* (Westminster, 1897); R.R. Holmes, *Queen Victoria* (London, 1897); G.B. Smith, *Life of Her Majesty Queen Victoria* (London, 1897); Sarah Tytler, *The life and times of Queen Victoria with which is incorporated 'The domestic life of the Queen'*, 2 vols (London, 1901).

176. Lant, *Insubstantial Pageant*, p. 49.

177. *The Times*, 20 June 1887, p. 9.

178. Ibid., 16 June, p. 9.

179. *Illustrated London News*, 25 June 1887, p. 706.

180. *Spectator*, 25 June 1887, pp. 857–8.

181. *Daily News*, 22 June 1887, p. 3.

182. *The Times*, 20 June 1887, p. 9, 21 June 1887, p. 5.

183. *Pall Mall Gazette*, 22 June 1887.

184. *Lloyd's Weekly Newspaper*, 19 June 1887, p. 6.
185. *The Times*, 16 June 1887, p. 9 .
186. *Lloyd's Weekly Newspaper*, 19 June 1887, p. 6.
187. Ibid., 26 June 1887, p. 1.
188. *The Times*, 10 June 1887, p. 9 .
189. *Standard*, 21 June 1887, p. 5.
190. *The Times*, 21 June 1887, p. 5.
191. Ibid., 22 June 1887.
192. *The Times*, 27 July 1889, p. 11.
193. Ibid., 10 June 1891, p. 9.
194. *Review of Reviews*, July 1891, pp. 23–34.
195. Frederic Whyte, *The Life of W.T. Stead*, 2 vols (London, 1925), vol. 2, pp. 103–4.
196. *Lloyd's Weekly Newspaper*, 9 July 1893, p. 8. See also *The Times*, 7 December 1891, p. 9; *Daily News,* 4 May 1893, p. 4.
197. *Daily News*, 15 January 1892, pp. 4–5.
198. See Philip Magnus, *King Edward the Seventh*, pp. 202, 215, 275.
199. *The Times*, 15 January 1892, p. 9.
200. *Spectator*, 16 January 1892, p. 76; 6 May 1893, p. 592.
201. *Daily News*, 6 July 1893, p. 4.
202. *Spectator*, 19 June 1897, pp. 856–7; 26 June 1897, p. 904.
203. *Daily Telegraph*, 23 June 1897, pp. 8–9.
204. *Pall Mall Gazette*, 22 June 1897, p. 1.
205. *Contemporary Review*, vol. 71 (June 1897), p. 762.
206. *The Times*, 22 June 1897, p. 9; *Daily Telegraph*, 21 June 1897, p. 8.
207. *The Times*, 23 June 1897, p. 14.
208. *Daily Mail*, 22 June 1897, p. 4.
209. *Nineteenth Century*, vol. 41 (June 1897), pp. 853–64.
210. *Daily News*, 23 January 1901, p. 6.
211. *Spectator*, 26 January 1901, pp. 133–4.
212. *Quarterly Review*, vol. 193 (April 1901), pp. 301–38.
213. *Daily Mail*, 23 January 1901, p. 4.
214. *The Times*, 23 January 1901, p. 3.
215. *Lloyd's Weekly Newspaper*, 3 February 1901, p. 12.
216. *Daily Mail*, 22 January 1901, p. 5.
217. *Spectator*, 26 January 1901, p. 125.
218. *Daily Telegraph*, 23 January 1901, p. 8.
219. *The Times*, 2 February 1901, p. 9.
220. *Spectator*, 26 January 1901, p. 129.
221. *The Times*, 23 January 1901, pp. 8–11.
222. *Spectator*, 26 January 1901, pp. 128–9.
223. Ibid., pp. 129–30.
224. *Pall Mall Gazette*, 24 January 1901.
225. *Daily News*, 24 January 1901, p. 4.
226. *Daily Telegraph*, 23 January 1901, p. 8.
227. *Punch*, 6 February 1901, p. 115.
228. *Saturday Review*, 29 April 1882, p. 515.
229. Prochaska, *Royal Bounty*, p. 85.
230. See David Cannadine, 'The Last Hanoverian Sovereign? The Victorian Monarchy in Historical Perspective 1688–1988' in A.L. Beier, David Cannadine and James M. Rosenheim eds, *The First Modern Society:*

Essays in English History in Honour of Lawrence Stone (Cambridge, 1989).

CHAPTER EIGHT

Attitudes to Royal Ceremonial

Of all the themes treated in this book, royal ceremonial has received the most prior attention from historians. In *Insubstantial Pageant. Ceremony and Confusion at Queen Victoria's Court*, J.L. Lant examined the staging of the two Jubilees and provided an introductory chapter on the reign's previous royal events. Lant was concerned primarily with the behind-the-scenes arrangements for the ceremonies[1] – as is William M. Kuhn in his article on the aims of the organizers of the Thanksgiving of 1872[2] – but David Cannadine in 'The Context, Performance and Meaning of Ritual: the British Monarchy and the "Invention of Tradition" c. 1820–1977' provides an historical equivalent of what the anthropologist Clifford Geertz calls 'thick description' – the locating of public attitudes to ceremonies within their social and, in this case, historical context. This produced an account of the evolution of royal ceremonial which paralleled the standard interpretation, pioneered by Kingsley Martin, of the transformation in the repute of the Crown in Victoria's reign. Just as Martin asserted that until the last quarter of the nineteenth century Victorians were too rational and preoccupied with political progress to indulge their 'capacity for devotion to an idealized personality',[3] so David Cannadine argues that the utilitarian early- and mid-Victorian epochs held pageantry in low esteem. Moreover, the partisan political involvement of the Crown, the criticism of its cost and the periodic slurs on its patriotism all militated against its ceremonial glorification as the symbol of the nation. This explained the shoddiness and drabness of early ceremonial arrangements – remarked upon by Lant. In the last decades of the reign, however, the monarchy, rising above party and politics and republican and radical criticism, became, in an era of imperialism and intense international competition, an unequivocal emblem of the nation, to be fêted as such in ceremonies for which, it was found, there was an increasing public taste; the age of reason had given way to 'the rebirth of the irrational in politics', and, world-wide, democracies 'invented' ceremonial 'traditions' with mass appeal.[4]

The foregoing chapters of this book are the basis for a 'thicker description' of the ceremonial of Victoria's reign, as they provide a deeper and more complex analysis of contemporary attitudes to the monarchy than has hitherto existed. This can now be allied to a more detailed examination of writings on ceremonial to modify the conclusions on this period found in Professor Cannadine's chronologically broader and, of necessity, more schematic and exploratory essay. Just as we have seen the need to amend Martin's linear model of the progression of royal popularity, in the light of the veneration of the institution of monarchy and the person of the Queen early in the reign and the persistence of criticism later on, so we shall find a concomitant enthusiasm for pageantry in the first half of this period, which is obscured by a blanket categorization of the era as utilitarian:[5] it was not always mutually exclusive to favour economy in government and the mounting of spectacle worthy of the name. (We shall also find continued attacks on the irrationality of ceremonial later in the reign.) It was the Queen and court who were reluctant to respond to the appeal which existed *throughout* this period for pageantry to be more splendid and more public. This is explained by the Queen's obsessive dislike of the physical and mental rigours of state ceremonies[6] – never fully overcome despite her gratification at the success of the Golden Jubilee[7] – and her belief that the monarchy's ceremonial duties were trivial in comparison with its political ones[8] and that 'ostentatious pomp' was 'utterly incompatible' with and 'unsuitable to the present day'.[9]

In this latter opinion of the Queen, expressed in 1872 in protest at Gladstone's plans for the Thanksgiving celebrations, we find evidence in support of the view that a disparaging 'economic' and rationalist view of ceremonial obtained until the final quarter of the century. This I shall dispute, but I have written of 'modifying' rather than over-turning previous work on ceremonial, for one effect of my more detailed examination will be to reinforce some of Professor Cannadine's contentions. My argument has been that this period was a turning-point throughout which two strands of discussion of the monarchy, one critical, one reverential, coexisted, with the former overwhelming the latter by 1887, and we see this pattern repeated in the debate on ceremonial. As staunch radical and republican critics of the monarchy stood fast by their beliefs to the very last but acknowledged by the 1880s that there was an unbreachable sentiment in favour of the Crown, so while the opponents of royal ceremonial continued to criticize it on rational and economic grounds they latterly admitted that the spirit of the age was with those who had always proclaimed the emotional need for pomp and circumstance.

It is also the case that, as attacks on the political role of the Crown and on its 'Germanism' became less frequent and less serious – its Olympian distance from politics and its Englishness more widely believed in – its role as national ceremonial figurehead became a more natural one. The initial partisanship of the Queen and court meant that the coronation and wedding were the occasion of party bickering in the ministerial and opposition press – later ceremonies were marked by observations on the temporary party truce sealed for such events. Above all, the contemporary belief in the continuous reduction of the political power of the Crown, described in chapters 4 and 5, had as its corollary a belief that the role of the monarchy henceforth lay in the discharge of its ceremonial duties – the writings of Bagehot encapsulated this trend of thought. So, ceremonial became more important to the monarchy, and it also acquired a new significance to the nation in the latter part of the period when the monarchy, as we have seen, became the focus of a new assertive nationalism and imperialism, spawned by the threat to Britain's world leadership. While upon the coronation of Victoria there was a complacent contempt for the Continental powers whose talent lay in grandiose pageantry – Britain's strength was real, not illusory – by the 1870s and 1880s a display of national greatness at royal ceremonials was viewed as essential for foreign eyes. The effect of this greater national and imperial self-consciousness can be seen in a seman- tic analogy taken from two events on either side of the Queen's reign. *The Times* regretted in 1837 that William IV's fairly simple obsequies had been marred by an undue amount of ceremonial and by the milit- arism of 'booming guns',[10] but in 1901 the same newspaper exulted in the elaborate and martial ritual of Victoria's funeral and declared it most apposite that the Queen should 'pass to her rest ... amid the booming guns by which her Empire had been maintained and ex- tended'.[11]

The chapter approaches its theme through the time-scale convention- ally applied to the movement of opinion on royal ceremonial – the first section looks at 1837–61 when, it has been contended, pageantry was little valued; the second at the 1860s, viewed as a turning-point as the complete collapse of royal pageantry during the Queen's widowed se- clusion provoked calls for more and better ceremonial; the third exam- ines the 1870s and 1880s, seen as the beginning of a new era of popular and spectacular royal ritual; and the final section deals with the climax of ceremonial in the Jubilees and the Queen's funeral.

1837–61: royal ceremonial in the age of utility

At the time of Victoria's accession, elaborate royal ceremonial was out of fashion in England. An impressive ritual had centred on George III during the Napoleonic wars – culminating in the Jubilee celebrations of 1809[12] – and George IV's belief in the magnificence of majesty was demonstrated in the medieval pomp of his coronation.[13] However, George had latterly been forced into a reclusive existence by his ill-health and

unpopularity, and his successor William, who had no taste for ceremony and who saw lack of simple domesticity as one of the causes of
his elder brother's unpopularity, meticulously shunned ostentation. The
informality of his manner upon his accession in 1830 caused Wellington
to observe, 'This is not a new reign, it is a new dynasty'[14] – and the
effect on the outward appearance of the British monarchy was similar
to the contemporary replacement of the Bourbons with the house of
Orleans in France; Hobhouse remarked that William and Adelaide were
'like wealthy bourgeois . . . in contrast with our late Asiatic monarch'.[15]

Victoria inherited this attitude and perpetuated it. The major royal
events of this period – the coronation, the Queen's wedding, the Princess Royal's wedding and Albert's funeral were pared down in scale and
the weddings and funeral were private rather than public occasions.
The Royal Family but rarely appeared in the robes of state and, as we
have seen, contemporaries were much given to remarking on royal
informality and on how the Queen's resembled a typical middle-class
family.[16] In commentaries on royal ceremonial in this period we do find
a disparaging view, based on economic and rational principles – but
mainly amongst those who were critical of the institution of monarchy
itself or at least of its costliness. Generally, there was an enthusiasm for
such ceremonial as took place and a feeling that the spectacular aspects
of monarchy should not be neglected but could exist alongside the
cultivation of an appealing domesticity.

While the coronation of Victoria was on a grander and more expensive scale than that of William IV it was still a much curtailed version of
the traditional ceremony. The Whig government decided to omit the
banquet and the procession of the estates of the realm and, in all its
arrangements, observed the Duke of Buckingham, seemed 'to stand in
awe of the strictest economical principle', when 'it was hoped that the
affair would be conducted in a manner characteristic' of so wealthy a
nation.[17] The planned ceremony drew forth protests from diverse quarters. The radical, satirical newspaper, *Figaro in London*, though no
friend of expensive courts, was desirous of a fine show for the people of
the capital and decried the government's penny-pinching.[18] London
tradesmen petitioned parliament for a postponement of the coronation
'that it might then be conducted on a scale of grandeur befitting the
occasion'.[19] The Tory weekly, *John Bull* lamented the absence of such
spectacle as was seen at the coronation of its idol, George IV, and
criticized the chaos of the unrehearsed ceremony, whose disasters have
been well described by other historians:[20] 'nothing', it declared 'could
be much worse – ill-arranged, ill-managed, and ill-regulated'.[21]

However, the ministerial press contended that the arrangements were
more in keeping with the spirit of the age than what the *Globe* called

'the gorgeous and in many respects silly pageantry which marked the coronation of George IV.'[22] The radical *Sunday Times*, ever a critic of the cost of the Crown, dismissed 'the senseless cry of injury to trades-men by the curtailment of the useless pageantry, to be provided at public expense'.[23] Lord Fitzwilliam also employed the rational language of utility when the tradesmen's petition reached the House of Lords: he described the ceremony as 'little better than an idle and ridiculous pageant . . . fit only for barbarous or semi-barbarous ages' and 'half-educated people'.[24] The Benthamite *Spectator*, on principle republican, agreed with him: 'any atom of rational purpose is so smothered in a garnish of antiquated follies'.[25] The Chartists also regarded the corona-tion as 'idle show' and 'a palpable waste of the national resources'. For them expenditure on ceremonial was another example of the ruling order despoiling the people for its own gratification.[26]

We may also detect in the derogation of the coronation a species of national self-confidence: pageantry was dismissed as an unnecessary and meaningless display of vanity which sought to mask deficiencies in true national strength. The *Sunday Times* observed that the foreign ministers at the coronation easily surpassed the British nobility in their splendour, and that the enthronement of the Emperor of Austria would be a far more grandiose affair: 'In embroidery and lace they (foreign nations) go far beyond us in richness, style and effect. But it is not in vain parade, or gorgeous trappings that our national superiority exists; it is based on far better excellence.'[27] There seemed to be an inverse correlation between national greatness and the inclination to stage im-posing ceremonial. Buckingham commented that now, at the height of its wealth and power, 'the British Empire was condemned to stand in the eyes of foreigners as too poor to crown her Monarch, which, when much poorer, the nation had willingly afforded'.[28]

Nonetheless, there was, in juxtaposition to the attitude which be-littled pageantry, an enthusiasm for such spectacle as the coronation provided and affirmation of the continued importance of such ceremo-nial in the modern age. The Tory and Church of England newspaper, the *Record*, criticized the utilitarian view of the coronations: 'he who would govern by an abstract appeal to reason, has yet to learn the very rudiments of the science of human nature'.[29] The liberal *Courier* agreed that imagination was as important as the mind in human behaviour. The philosopher might scoff at pageants as fit for children and peoples in their infancy, but perhaps children were wiser than their elders in this respect: 'In short we must learn the art of being happy at a corona-tion'.[30] The *Leeds Mercury*, a voice of provincial liberalism, described the coronation as 'one of the most splendid and interesting ceremonials which the world can furnish'.[31]

Thus, though the late nineteenth century is usually seen as the period of 'the rebirth of the irrational', there was a widespread belief at the outset of the reign that politics should not consist merely in the rational and effectual, and that the ceremonies of royalty were not out-moded forms. Moreover while J.L. Lant has written that ceremonies of this period were 'courtly pageants', in which the bulk of the nation neither expected nor wanted to participate,[32] this was not true of the coronation. The general opinion of contemporaries was that while the courtly pageantry itself had been circumscribed, 'the gratification of the people', to quote the *Morning Chronicle*, 'has been an object of peculiar and unusual solicitude'. Defending the government's omission of the coronation banquet, it wrote, 'That exclusive system which sacrificed a quarter million of the public money for the sake of feasting the already well-fed has been abandoned for the purpose of extending its enjoyment to its utmost verge'.[33] There was a fair in Hyde Park, fireworks in Green Park and in the evening all the theatres were thrown open to the public. Greville observed, 'The great merit of the coronation is, that so much has been done for the people: to amuse and interest *them* seems to have been the principal object'. Far from being uninterested in the event, the people of London had decorated the shops and houses on the route of the procession, and it was estimated that a million people lined the route. There were numerous spontaneous illuminations as the night set in.[34] Given the meanness of the government and court, wrote the *Standard*, 'The grandeur of the spectacle is due solely to the people'.[35]

The Queen's wedding in 1840 provided another example of contemporary enthusiasm for pageantry not fully reciprocated in the courtly arrangements and execution of the event. The wedding took place in the Chapel Royal, St James's rather than in the more public setting of Westminster Abbey or St Paul's Cathedral. The whole proceeding was unrehearsed: Albert's escort took a wrong turning on the way to the Chapel, disappointing the large crowd assembled to see him at St James's Park,[36] and during the ceremony the Prince, at times plainly at a loss, was prompted by the stage-whispered advice of Dowager Queen Adelaide.[37] Several of the male guests neglected to don special court dress[38] and Greville complained of the 'very poor and shabby style' in which the royal couple left Windsor.[39]

That the Queen was inclined to view the wedding as a private rather than a state event was shown in her rebuttal of Melbourne's suggestion that more members of the opposition be invited to the ceremony: she replied that this is 'my marriage' and that she would 'only have those who are sympathetic with me'[40] – Wellington and Liverpool were the only Tories present, reflecting the Queen's detestation of the opposition, intensified by the Bedchamber crisis. When Tory newspapers objected

that the exclusivity of the Queen's guest-list had 'denigrated this national solemnity into a mere pageant', they meant that the ceremony
had been stripped of its deeper meaning – it should express the unity of
the nation in allegiance to the Crown.[41] As it was, leading articles in
ministerial and opposition papers were preoccupied with party attacks.[42]
Until the Crown was elevated above party politics royal ceremonies
could not be the unequivocal celebration of national unity.

However, while leading articles were concerned with the contentious
political overtones of the wedding, articles in the same newspapers –
both Whig and Tory – on the ceremonial *per se* evinced unqualified
interest and excitement. Full details of the procession, service, wedding
breakfast and departure were carried in all the main papers and some
gave complete lists of all the decorations and illuminations in the city.
The *Standard* was impressed by the 'magnificence and splendour' of 'so
novel' an event – the first marriage of a Queen regnant in England for
over a century;[43] and the *Morning Chronicle*'s delight in the romantic
and exotic elements of a royal wedding defies a description of this
period as solidly rationalist: 'To be able to describe the gorgeous splendour of the train by which her Majesty was preceded and succeeded,
would be to possess the powers of the far-famed story-teller of the
Arabian nights'.[44]

The early ceremonials of Victoria's reign thus reveal a contemporary
interest in well-mounted pageantry, and in the 1840s and 1850s criticism of ceremonial as irrational and extravagant was not universal but
confined to those who criticized the monarchy itself as an irrational and
costly institution. Moreover, these critics of ceremonial were in agreement with its supporters that pageantry was an important function of
monarchy and that it held great popular appeal. It was also commonly
held that the arts of pageantry were ill-sufficiently cultivated in Britain.

William Linton in the *English Republic* in 1851 argued that with the
decline of its political power ceremony remained the only purpose of
the English monarchy and that the expenditure of money on such folly
would not be tolerated in an age of utility.[45] However, 'Ceremony',
Disraeli had written in *Coningsby* in 1844, was 'not an idle form' –
through it the people could 'constantly and visibly . . . comprehend that
Property is their protector and their friend'.[46] In the previous chapter I
argued that the majority of the middle class did not wish to supplant
the monarchy as an archaic, irrational, hereditary institution blocking
the complete triumph of meritocratic principles, but, after their incorporation into the ruling order in 1832 and triumph over the Corn Laws
in 1846, promoted the monarchy as the beneficent head of a just status
quo. Ceremonial, as Disraeli argued, could play an important part in
the presentation of an equitable, unified society, celebration of the

Crown's rituals transcending class divisions and helping to allay the tensions which could threaten the political settlement. The *Morning Chronicle* wrote of the Great Exhibition, a monument to industry, 'Royal pageantry is never so suitably employed as in adorning the festive occasions which unite all classes of the community in a common interest'.[47]

The middle-class press was as enthralled with the pomp of royalty as it was with the minute details of its domestic life. The *Illustrated London News* printed full-page engravings of the Queen's opening of the Exhibition and revelled in 'all the splendour of Court ... all the pomp and pageantry of a royal procession'.[48] I wrote in the last chapter of the middle class's desire for royal approbation, and the ceremonial trappings of royalty were the supreme ornament to commercial achievement. The *Daily News* described the Queen's inauguration of the Exhibition, a monument to industry and trade, as the blending of 'the prestige of regal state' and 'modern intellectual power'.[49] All the Royal Commissioners responsible for the Exhibition – other than Richard Cobden – wore court costume for the occasion.[50] Similarly, we have seen how for the Queen's visit to Leeds in 1858 councillors for the first time wore the traditional robes of a medieval corporation.[51]

Republican critics of royal ceremonial described it as anachronistic and irrational like the institution of monarchy itself, but had to acknowledge that, despite the 'march of the mind', show still held an emotional appeal for the people. In the opening number of the *Democratic Review* in 1849, G. Julian Harney declared that Englishmen had 'some respect for our youthful and virtuous Queen, but the "barbaric pomp" with which she is surrounded alike arouses their laughter, contempt and scorn'.[52] However, the same year, commenting on the cheering crowds at Albert's opening of the Coal Exchange, G.W.M. Reynolds admitted:

> ... that these traditional specimens of barbaric mummery would not be persisted in at all, were it not for the species of enthusiasm that appears to welcome their appearance.[53]

Yet royal pageantry was not that frequent, splendid or well-performed. The *Red Republican* wrote of the 'annual farce' of the state closing of parliament, 'They do things much *better* at the Italian Opera, and much *cheaper* at Astley's Amphitheatre'.[54] In the same paper a satirical drawing of Britain's coat of arms depicted a bonnet instead of a Crown surmounting the whole.[55] As we have seen in the previous chapter, it was the quasi-bourgeois domesticity of the Royal Family which struck observers in this period. Though Gladstone was in 1878 to write that Albert was 'one of the few, the very few characters on the active stage of modern life in whom the idea of duty seems to be actually personified, and to walk abroad in the costumes of state',[56] the frequent royal progresses of the 1840s and 1850s were characterized by their inform- ality, in contrast with the pomp of George IV.[57] *Punch* noted that the inhabitants of Jersey did not recognize the royal couple dressed in ordinary clothes and reserved their loudest cheers for a liveried servant whose two large epaulettes made them think that he was the Prince[58]. Albert devoted little time to ceremonial organization[59] – he was preoc- cupied with what he saw as the true, business-like role of the Crown; extensive involvement in government and in industrial, social, educa- tional and artistic improvement.[60] He disliked the glittering, hedonistic high society life which had traditionally orbited around the court[61] and this accounted for the lengthy absences of the royal couple from Lon- don, favouring instead the more secluded, rural royal residences.

Though the middle-class press delighted in the domesticity of the Royal Family and liked to see a reflection of the behaviour and virtues of its own class reflected in the ruling house, it also wanted the magnifi- cence of monarchy to be displayed for public gratification, the import- ance of its ceremonial role to be recognized and the quality of pageantry to be improved. *The Times* in 1857 wrote, 'We are confessedly the worst hands at a spectacle in the world. For State ceremonies, we have lost the simplicity of nature without acquiring the ingenuity of art.'[62]

Enthusiasm for royal ceremonial and dissatisfaction with the current provision of it was expressed upon the first wedding of one of the Queen's children – the Princess Royal's in 1858. The *Spectator* re- mained true to its philosophic radicalism in arguing that 'to modern eyes this parade of millinery and carpentry, burlesques and overlays the majesty of the event'. However, the rest of the press was filled with and enraptured by the prospect of grand ceremonial.[63] In fact, newspapers complained that the event had not been spectacular or public enough. Apart from the wedding service in the Chapel Royal, St James's – glittering in itself but witnessed by few – there was little ceremonial, the procession being merely along the shortest line from Buckingham Pal- ace to the Chapel and affording opportunity for the crowds to get no more than a fleeting glimpse, at best, of the finery of the participants and guests. The *Illustrated London News* asserted 'If the popular voice was followed, the ceremonial would have been next only to a corona- tion in splendour and extent'. The shortcomings were symptomatic of a general national deficiency – 'In this country we have few, if any, public pageants; and the materials of their composition are sparse and ineffect- ive'.[64] The *Daily Telegraph* ventured that in France there would have been illuminations, a distribution of largesse, a grand military display and a fuller public marriage procession. The service would have taken place in a cathedral so that 'the nation would have entered into the revelry of the Court'.[65]

Not only the service, but the festival performances at Her Majesty's Theatre were the preserve of the court and foreign aristocrats,[66] so that, wrote *The Times*, there was 'no opportunity for even the middle classes to pay a tribute of loyalty to the Sovereign's family'.[67] The *Daily Telegraph* regretted the 'bareness of the day's exhibition' and the 'growing system of reserving the exclusive enjoyment of State ceremonials and spectacles for particular classes'. While on the coronation and Queen's wedding, theatres had been thrown open to the public, this time 'some of the gratuitous places of popular resort were actually closed'. The Royal Family, wrote the paper, the daily organ of middle-class liberalism, was expensively maintained by the nation, so 'it is not too much to ask, when opportunities occur for grand and imposing demonstrations, that the people should be allowed to participate'.[68] The same sentiments were expressed in *Lloyd's Weekly Newspaper*, the high-circulation radical newspaper of the old artisanate and lower middle class: 'since there are tens of thousands of people who do care for a show, since tinsel is loved and is largely paid for . . . from John Bull's purse . . . it would be a slight courtesy . . . to refresh the said John Bull with a sight of satin and diamonds'.[69]

Writings on the wedding of the Princess Royal confirm the existence of an interest in and taste for ceremonial in Britain normally associated only with later decades of the century. The occasion was also unmarred by party squabbles, unlike the Queen's wedding: the apparent elevation of the monarchy from party politics was manifested in the mingling of government and opposition politicians among the guests and by the mixture of children of Tory and Whig families among the bridesmaids.[70] This consensus and the common perception of the reduced governmental role of the Crown were to make its national ceremonial functions seem all the more appropriate and important henceforth. However, there was a discrepancy between public demand and the willingness of the Queen to provide courtly pageantry – to be exacerbated after Albert's death as without the support of her husband she refused to perform the public duties which she had always found stressful.

Albert himself had not favoured elaborate ceremony: his funeral was a private affair at Windsor, performed with the minimum of state and pomp, as he had expressly requested. Whereas the simplicity and privacy of previous ceremonies had been criticized, the press respected the Queen's grief and Albert's wishes and agreed that it was better to bury the Prince 'out of sight with a grief as sincere as unostentatious'.[71] Royal funerals had become less grandiose and elaborate over the previous two centuries[72] and, commenting on Albert's obsequies, the *Daily*

Telegraph wrote that the funeral of William IV had been a fitting contrast to 'the garish splendour formerly lavished on Royal funerals'. In 1861 the memory remained of George IV's grotesque funeral with paid mourners, whose tears were the only ones shed, following a hearse that was stoned. At all events, the consensus in favour of a private funeral did not denote an aversion to royal pageantry: indeed, the *Daily Telegraph* wrote approvingly that, though simple and private, Albert's funeral was 'from its commencement to its termination, a most sumptuous and magnificent ceremony'.[73]

Thus, there was considerable interest in royal ceremonial in a period hitherto characterized as unfavourable to pageantry. Those who attacked the ceremonial of the monarchy as irrational and costly were, on the whole, those who viewed the monarchy itself as irrational and costly. A more common criticism was that the performance of royal ritual was inadequate – and it was the complete absence of such ritual, after the Queen's period of mourning should have ended, which was to provoke disappointment and some measure of criticism in the 1860s.

1861–71: the call for more and better ceremonial

The 1860s have been seen as a turning-point in which the retirement of the Queen prompted novel calls, especially in the writings of Walter Bagehot,[74] for a more magnificent and public monarchy.[75] In fact there had always been such calls and they were intensified, not created, by a decade in which the Queen opened parliament only three times and in which the royal weddings – of Princess Alice, the Prince of Wales, Princess Helena and Princess Louise – were drab, private events, pervaded by continued mourning for the Prince Consort. The lack of pageantry, together with the contemporary perception of the reduced political role of the Crown, did focus attention more on ceremonial, now seen to be the chief function – almost the justification – of monarchy. This resulted in writings on ceremonial of a more considered, generalized nature – but not only from Bagehot. When examining attitudes to royal political power we saw that he was but one of several commentators observing a change in the monarchy's role from what he called the 'efficient' to the 'dignified' functions of the constitution'.[76] There was a general belief in the importance to the monarchy of its ceremonial duties and a fear that the Queen's neglect of them was endangering the Crown itself: we have examined the 1860s from the perspective of radical critics of the monarchy and seen the way in which the republican movement grew out of attacks on the Queen's hoarding of public money;[77] here we shall see the loyal criticism provoked by the same perception – and the contrary demand to which it gave rise; not the abolition of the monarchy, but a more consistent and spectacular public profile for the monarchy to ensure its popularity. Like radical criticism, this demand grew in volume during the 1860s as the Queen showed no sign of abandoning her mourning but more requests for annuities to her children were made to parliament.

The wedding of Princess Alice in July 1862 prompted the first mild criticism of the inactivity of the court since Albert's death. *The Times* described the wedding as 'a day snatched from mourning, with not a colour and scare a shade of brighter hue to mark the exception to the uniform gloom'.[78] It was hoped that 'After a brief period of retirement and quiet . . . the Throne has repaired its losses and that England is not without men and women born in the highest state and prepared to take their turn of duty with all the rest'. The theme of the duty of the Queen and court to undertake their public engagements became the constant refrain of the press.[79]

However, the wedding of the Prince of Wales the following year was scarcely different. It again took place away from London – at Windsor – and there were no other provisions for ceremonial or festivities, apart from the entry of the bride, Princess Alexandra, into London. This was a nondescript event: *The Times* said that there was little 'to gratify curiosity and a love of display'.[80] The wedding itself took place in the funereal atmosphere of Windsor, where Albert had died. The Queen, dressed in black, made her way to the chapel in private, through a specially-constructed covered way, and did not attend the wedding breakfast. So intently was the court geared towards mourning that arrangements for the wedding were chaotic: carriages proceeded from Windsor Castle in utter disorder and at the railway station there was a frantic scramble for seats in which one guest was robbed by members of the uncontrolled crowd.[81]

The absence of any state provision for celebration of the wedding of the future king gave rise to commentaries on the general ineptitude of the British nation in ceremonial planning. The *Illustrated London News* observed that in any other nation such an event would have moved the government to mount grand public displays but that in Britain even the declaration of a national holiday had been 'rather forced upon the Government by the strength of public feeling than spontaneously undertaken on their official responsibility'. The general paucity of public celebrations in Britain, the paper speculated, was attributable to the inclement weather, a national reserve of character, the hierarchical social structure and the restrained form of the Protestant religion.[82]

Robert Cecil, writing in the *Saturday Review* agreed: 'If there be a weak place in English institutions it is our lamentable deficiency of public shows'.[83] He had been remarking upon this since 1861 when he wrote of the farcical nature of the opening of parliament: an aptitude for ceremonial, he surmised, was 'generally confined to the people of a Southern climate and of non-Teutonic parentage'.[84] The opening of parliament lost such lustre as it had possessed after the widowed Queen declined to perform it in person[85] and the nation was left only with the 'burlesque upon John Bull' constituted by Lord Mayor's Day – 'archaic ceremonial', badly executed and holding little appeal, was tenaciously clung to when the need was for imaginative innovation.[86] He was most disappointed with the arrangements for the Prince of Wales' wedding: relegated to the obscure village of Windsor it would have been 'a real pleasure to the whole population of London' for the excitement of the crowds at the passage of just six carriages with mourning livery from one railway station to another showed that 'In spite of the march of the intellect ... people, both high and low are still passionately fond of shows'.[87]

The monarchy, Cecil argued, should be the cynosure of such show: the chief duty of the English monarch, he wrote in March 1864, when it was rumoured that the Queen would never return to London, was to be the 'centre alike of the pomp of the state and of the gaieties of the well-to-do world'. The monarchy had become superfluous enough to the workings of government to allow a sovereign to neglect administrative duties; but for that very reason ceremonial ones could not be by-passed – if the monarchy were to survive loyalty needed a 'visible object'; 'Seclusion is one of the few luxuries in which Royal personages may not indulge. The power which is derived from affection or from loyalty needs a life of almost uninterrupted publicity to sustain it'.[88]

The Times pursued the same line of argument, repeatedly enjoining the Queen to resume her public duties and taking every rare appearance of the Queen hopefully as a sign that she was about to. When in October 1863 she ventured to Aberdeen to unveil a statue to Albert it wrote, 'Two years, it must be said are a long period to be consumed in unavailing regrets. .... It is too often the result of such an occupation to become possessed, with an exaggerated estimate of one's misfortunes.'[89] In March 1864 posters appeared outside Buckingham Palace announcing 'These commanding premises to be let or sold, in consequence of the late occupant's declining business' and on 1 April The Times announced, 'Her Majesty's loyal subjects will be very pleased to hear that their Sovereign is about to break her protracted seclusion'. This may, as Elizabeth Longford suggests, have been 'a leg-pull' but it was the preface to a very serious article on the reasons why the prediction should be fulfilled – those who lived in seclusion:

will find themselves fading in the eye of man, losing hold on the general interest ... Everybody must show himself in his appointed place ... He must walk his walk, and fill his post, and that actually and visibly, otherwise the view dissolves and another picture takes his place.[90]

However, the Queen had a disclaimer published in the paper's Court Circular, stressing that she was unable to undertake public ceremonial without such harm to her health that she would be incapacitated for the fulfilment of what she saw as her far more important governmental duties.[91] The third anniversary of the Prince Consort's death – normally considered the utmost limit of mourning – occasioned blunt advice from The Times to abandon 'the indulgence of an unavailing grief'. The Prince's memory would be best respected not by obsessive mourning or the unveiling of countless statues but by the regular resumption of public duty: 'he submitted to fatiguing ceremonials of State, even when they were meaningless'.[92]

It is within this context that the writings of Walter Bagehot must be located. In the essays published in the Fortnightly Review in 1865–6 and subsequently collected as The English Constitution, Bagehot defined the political role of the monarchy as limited to the three rights to be consulted, to encourage and to warn,[93] and described the Queen as the 'head of our society', of the 'pageant of life'[94] – the ruling house 'sweetens politics by a seasonal addition of nice and pretty events'.[95] Yet, he acknowledged that since Albert's death 'the court has always been in a state of suspended animation'[96] – the Queen was 'a retired widow' walking on the slopes at Windsor.[97] However, Bagehot was not preoccupied with the Crown's ceremonial in these essays – the 'dignified' functions of the Crown on which he dwelled more fully were its religious sanction to government,[98] its moral leadership[99] and the way in which it disguised the true operations of the constitution.[100] Indeed, Bagehot did not here align himself with those who 'have of late objected to the English royalty that it is not splendid enough', that it cut a drab figure alongside the magnificence of the French Emperor. The French sovereign, Bagehot countered, was the state, the actual ruler, and the Queen's could not be compared with his rituals of power. Moreover, 'We have voluntary show enough in London' from ostentatious aristocrats, and 'we do not wish it encouraged and intensified, but quieted and mitigated'.[101]

It was in subsequent articles in the Economist that Bagehot made his famous formulations about the prime importance of ceremony to the monarchy – by 1874 he was convinced that 'the usefulness of the monarchy in almost all countries ... is bound up with ceremonial display', and was encouraging lavish outlay to provide suitably imposing royal show in Britain.[102] The evolution of Bagehot's thought in the late 1860s and early 1870s shows that he was following contemporary opinion on ceremonial, rather than creating it. There were false dawns in 1866 and 1867 when the Queen opened parliament in person twice[103] and in July 1867 when she attended the naval review for the Sultan of Turkey and Viceroy of Egypt. These were the first foreign visitors for some time to have been entertained with a certain state and ceremony – there had been much criticism of the initial decision to put the Viceroy in a hotel, as recent dignitaries had been – and there was widespread excitement and approval for the London festivities, in which the Prince of Wales played a prominent part.[104]

Bagehot, writing at the conclusion of the popular visits, and with an eye on the Reform Bill, wrote, 'The more democratic we get, the more we shall get to like state and show, which ever pleased the vulgar'. Napoleon III's reception of the Sultan at the International Exhibition had outstripped Britain's, and Bagehot approved of Disraeli's bill for a special palace for the entertainment of foreign princes, to remedy the nation's shortcomings. Contradicting the view he had expressed in *The English Constitution*, he wrote, 'In such matters, the English must be guided by the French. We can hardly allow ourselves to be altogether outdone in tasteful and cordial hospitality without sinking in the scale of nations'. Here we find the new defensive preoccupation with Britain's standing in the world: 'the present position of the English state in the eyes of foreign nations, and as upholding English dignity, is a new subject; that the public mind must be educated to consider it'. We noted that at the time of the coronation when British self-confidence was at its height little attention was paid to outward shows of magnificence. Now, however, Bagehot wrote that as in society where 'you are esteemed not by what you are, but by what you seem', so with nations.[105]

Bagehot's thoughts on ceremonial were influenced by the democratization of British politics and the changing position of Britain in the world – but above all by the unpopularity of Victoria's seclusion which seemed to be putting the very existence of the monarchy in doubt. There was no regular resumption of royal duties in the late 1860s and criticism of the Crown intensified, from those of republican inclination and those ardently loyal. When the Queen once more declined to close parliament in August 1869, *The Times* sensed in the simplicity, 'even to baldness' of the resulting ceremony a foreboding similar to that of the chamberlain who ushered in the buckleless Ministre Roland to Louis XVI at Versailles.[106] The Prime Minister, Gladstone, convinced of the need for royal ceremonial, vainly tried to persuade the Queen to break her retirement.[107] On one of the few occasions on which he was successful – the Queen's visit to the city in November 1869 to open Blackfriars

Bridge and the Holborn Viaduct – *The Times* wrote of the value of such appearances in strengthening the status quo, as the crowd would go home 'much better disposed towards the governing power in the State and less inclined to quarrel with it, simply because they had seen its Royal representative'. Moreover, pageantry had an enduring appeal: 'It is hard even for the philosophers to conceive a state of things in which human nature will be so changed as not to find delight in the sight of glittering jewels and gay robes'.[108] Indeed, the newspaper argued, the modern, industrial world was especially in need of such ornament and it was the chief role of the monarchy to provide it:

> Whatever may be said as to the political power of the Crown, there can be no doubt that even in these days the sovereign has almost unlimited opportunities of giving a pure pleasure ... ennobling public occasions, and brightening the general aspect of things in a world which certainly wants it. Progress wants cheering and utility should have grace.[109]

However, the wedding of Princess Louise in 1871, though performed with more state than the entirely private one of Princess Helena in 1866, was, in the *Sunday Times'* estimation, 'not a state ceremony at all'.[110] Again a royal wedding was staged at Windsor and, observed the *Spectator*, 'London ... was rather sulky and did not illuminate, having an idea that Royal ceremonials ought to be transacted in the capital, and not in provincial villages'. With an amused superiority, the *Spectator* also noted the fascination with the ceremonial aspects of the marriage shown in the rest of the press.[111] The *Illustrated London News* was full of engravings of the couple, the Chapel, the service, the bridesmaids and even the wedding gifts.[112] The *Daily News* expressed disappointment at the lack of public ceremonial. The Royal Family had come to be loved as an ordinary domestic group but it was to be regretted if this was at the expense of the romantic, splendid element of monarchy: 'it may be imagined by many that a charming young Princess might, perhaps, have wished to see more imposing ceremony at her wedding – a ceremony more in accordance with the precedent which invariably rules such occasions in the highly-coloured nursery tale'.[113]

The absence of royal ceremonial, set against the repeated requests made for grants, additional to the Civil List, to the Queen's children had produced a serious crisis of royal unpopularity by mid-1871.[114] Bagehot in July 1871 penned his most critical article on the Queen's neglect of her ceremonial duties. He wrote that she 'has done almost as much injury to the popularity of the monarchy by her long retirement from public life as the most unworthy of her predecessors did by his profligacy and frivolity ... it is the essence of the showy parts of the Constitution to acquire importance and popularity by being shown'. He

warned that 'people who (are) constituent elements of pageant are
likely to be valued very much in degree to the value they set upon
themselves' – and the Queen appeared to set very little.[115] When Dilke
used the information of the pseudonymous pamphlet *What does she do
with it?* in his attack on the cost of the Crown at Newcastle in November 1871, the more considered journals of the loyal press, while deplor-
ing his criticism of the Queen, agreed that the best way to rebut it was a
reassertion of the Crown's ceremonial role, neglect of which had led to
support for Dilke's views.[116]

Thus, in the decade 1861–71 there was a great deal written about the
ceremonial of monarchy. Examination of the period 1837–61 has shown
that the taste for pageantry expressed in the 1860s in attacks on the
Queen's abandonment of it was not a new-found one. Rather it was the
importance of pageantry to the Crown which was fully appreciated for
the first time in this decade because of the Queen's refusal to perform it.
As the Queen's retirement from the centre of political power strengthened the commentators' view that the governmental role of the Crown
had declined, the question was raised of what purpose the monarchy
then served if not to embody the nation in state ceremonials. We see this
realization dawning in the writings of Bagehot between 1865, when he
did not place great emphasis on spectacular pageantry, and 1871 when
he was forecasting the disappearance of the monarchy if it did not
provide such pageantry. The popularity of show had always been commented on form the outset of the reign, but it was Bagehot at the time
of the Reform Bill of 1867 who formulated a logical link between
democracy and regular, grandiose ceremonial. Also discernible in his
and others' writings was a new belief that imposing state pageantry was
necessary as a display of national strength – and this belief was to
impart a new meaning to the royal ceremonial of the 1870s and 1880s
as the international climate became an increasingly competitive one.

1872–87: 'the rebirth of the irrational'

As historians have observed,[117] it was in the 1870s and 1880s that royal
ceremonial became more public and imposing – and did so in a calculated manner. The rise of a republican movement had shown the dangers of neglecting ceremonial and as Britain became more self-consciously
nationalist and imperialist the pageantry of the Crown became a vehicle
for displays of national and imperial unity and strength. For the first
time in the reign efforts were made to create ceremonial occasions – the
thanksgiving for the recovery of the Prince of Wales as a rebuttal of
republicanism in 1872 and the reception of the Duke of Edinburgh and

his Russian bride in 1874, after the wedding had taken place in the Princess's homeland. However, the contrast between the 'utilitarian' 1840s and 1850s and a 'rebirth of the irrational' in the 1870s and 1880s should not be overdrawn. The continued place of the imagination in public life and the popularity of show had been dwelled on from the outset of the reign. It was in the latter decades that rationalist critics of ceremonial – who were usually also republicans – acknowledged the survival and triumph of the irrational, just as they did that of the monarchy itself. Conversely, the Queen's and court's response to the demand for pageantry continued in the 1870s and 1880s to lag behind public opinion: the weddings of her children still took place at out-of-the-way Windsor, the Queen remained largely in seclusion and governments had to fight determinedly with her desire to keep state to a minimum on her appearances.

Previously in the reign royal ceremonial had only occurred when necessitated by the coronation or a wedding in the Royal Family. In the 1870s, however, there were two Prime Ministers, Gladstone and Disraeli, who had strong beliefs in, respectively, the importance of the Crown's ceremonial duty and the magical appeal of pageantry to the imagination of the people. In 1872 Gladstone resolved to turn the recovery of the Prince of Wales to account against the republicans by bringing the Queen out of seclusion to preside over a special celebration; a religious thanksgiving complemented by state pageantry.[118] Gladstone's efforts to plan the thanksgiving on as large a scale as possible were constricted by the court, which regarded pageantry as its prerogative,[119] and by the Queen who wanted a simple service without any ceremonial trappings, and little public participation. St Paul's Cathedral, the most suitable venue for a large service, was decided upon but there was outcry in *The Times* and other newspapers when it was announced that only 7–8,000 people would be admitted. Protests enabled Gladstone, with the Prince of Wales' intercession, to raise the number to 13,000 and also to make the route of the procession to the Cathedral longer and more conducive to large crowds.[120]

The resulting compromise between the Prime Minister's ambition and the Queen's caution produced in the press the usual acclaim for royal ceremonial – intensified by the relief it had resurfaced after so long an absence – and the customary observation that Britain did not match other nations in its staging. *The Times* hoped that the thanksgiving would mark an end of 'the tendency of modern habits ... to curtail or abandon pageantry'; it looked for a return to the pomp of George III. The thanksgiving for the restoration of his health in 1789 had included a procession 'which was national and not merely courtly'.[121] The *Pall Mall Gazette* noted how much excitement had been generated by the plans for the celebration: 'We are not a ceremonial people; . . . But little by little the ceremony of today worked upon the imagination of the people till a little alarm mixed with our gratification.'[122] The *Daily News* saw in the celebrations support for Renan's contention that the Celtic spirit was gaining ascendancy over the Teutonic in the English national character.[123] Yet the pageantry presented to the people was far inferior to what might be seen on the Continent – as the *Saturday Review* observed, 'Nine carriages do not make much of a show'.[124] The significance of the ceremony lay, wrote this journal, the *Daily News* and *Daily Telegraph,* in the spontaneous and unanimous demonstration of loyalty by the people, which could not be equalled anywhere. We may still detect a rather dismissive attitude to 'mere pageantry':[125] 'If we do not shine in the arts of State ceremony, it is because we do not esteem them'.[126]

Nonetheless, commentaries on the thanksgiving show how certain tendencies were investing royal ceremonial with a greater national significance. One was the effort of the government to make the thanksgiving truly national by allocating seats in the Cathedral to representatives of working-class organizations and the free churches – previously the services at the centre of royal ceremonials had been the preserve of the ruling elite.[127] Another was the orderly behaviour of the crowds, widely remarked upon as contrasting with the London 'mobs' of old. An aspect of this behaviour was the good-natured, apolitical reception of leading figures of both parties, whereas royal events early in the reign had been occasions for the crowd to clap and hiss different politicians according as they pleased or displeased them.[128] The thanksgiving had demonstrated national unity, irrespective of class, religious and party differences and *The Times*, in calling it a 'great national Solemnity', called for more such 'national acts' of ceremonial to preserve and foster the national spirit – as we noted when discussing the relationship of the monarchy to the 'new nationalism', the thanksgiving was the first royal event marked by the forebodings as to Britain's future standing in the world, and references to the need for royal pageants to engender 'national enthusiasm'.[129]

The opportunity to stage another such 'national act' was taken in 1874 when the Duke of Edinburgh returned with his Russian bride. The *Daily Telegraph* once more wrote, as it had of the thanksgiving, that the ceremony would not, as it would for example in Russia, be a splendid, state-regulated one but remarkable as a spontaneous popular demonstration.[130] In fact, a greater ordering of the ceremony and attention to detail were apparent. The *Spectator* noted that open carriages were used and that the procession passed at a much slower rate than normal, to afford the crowd the greatest possible opportunity of seeing the

Queen and her new daughter-in-law.[131] This and the unusually imposing body of troops assembled had something to do with the return of
the Conservatives to power, the *Saturday Review* speculated. The
journal wrote, 'There is nothing in the simple and honest enjoyment of
a good show to be ashamed of . . . It is an old and natural instinct.' The
British people were pleased to witness 'something of the state which in
the popular idea ought to surround the sovereign of a great country. It
is obvious that if these things are to be done at all, they ought to be
done handsomely and graciously, and this was the peculiar merit of
Thursday's proceedings.' Dilke and those who complained of the cost of
the Crown should take note – there was no 'desire on the part of
Englishmen to effect a paltry saving by stripping the fringe and gliding
from the throne'. Any popular discontent 'had its origin in a feeling that
the sovereign had become too much of an abstraction and that what
was needed was more and not less of monarchy'. The *Sunday Times*
agreed that 'Royal pageants are nowhere more popular than in England[132] and the *Daily Telegraph* approved of the festive decorations,
whose quality, it felt, should dispel the myth that England was inept in
this respect.[133]

Republicans continued to criticize royal ceremonials but could see
that the tide was against them. *Reynolds's Newspaper* denounced the
procession of 1874 as testimony to the dictum that monarchy is 'more
adapted to a barbarous than a civilized state', governing men by their
senses not their understanding,[134] and the *National Reformer* described
the proceeding as a 'Royal Farce' – the Royal Family were described as
members of a seasoned theatrical troop, the effect of whose performances upon the public mind was 'pernicious and degrading'. Yet the
paper admitted that the 'Royal performance' of its sort 'was a praise-
worthy presentment' and that it held popular appeal. It was admitted
that republicanism must not rest its case solely on reason – it too
needed to appeal to the imagination of the people, which the popularity
of ceremonial showed to be so important: 'Argument and emotional
appeal are equally necessary'.[135]

The same theme was expounded with much more enthusiasm in
loyal quarters. Bagehot in October 1874 wrote of the need to fund the
Prince of Wales munificently to carry out the ceremonial duties which
the Queen disliked: 'A monarchy which does not appear to be one of
the grandest things in the country is not doing one essential part of its
work – that of keeping itself always before the imagination of the
people'.[136] The Crown was a 'symbol of national unity. But to be . . .
an effective symbol, you must be vividly and often seen.' A *Letter to
the Queen on her retirement from Public Life*, published in 1875,
made the same points but stressed that only the Queen, still to resume

her duties on a regular basis, could adequately fill this symbolic ceremonial role.[137]

For the time being it was the Prince of Wales who was, as Bagehot had hoped, exciting the public imagination through striking presentations of royalty. Disraeli envisaged the Prince's tour of India in 1875–6 as a majestic way of symbolizing the strength of the ties of empire. Bagehot criticized the radical MPs who opposed the liberal grant for the Prince's expenses: 'If the Prince is to travel at all, especially in countries penetrated by traditions as to the significance of external symbols of power, he must travel in a manner becoming his position'.[138] Mundella said in the Commons: 'if they were to have a Monarchy at all it should not be a cotton velvet or a tinfoil one ... The Monarchy ought to represent the greatness and wealth of the Empire.'[139] The ceremonials of the tour received full pictorial coverage in the *Illustrated London News*[140] and delighted *The Times* which hailed the recognition that the empire consisted in more than good administration, and the overthrow of the narrow utilitarianism which had long pervaded government:

> Our government appears sometimes as if it had been cut down to the utilitarian level which was the ideal of some Radical philosophers some forty or fifty years ago ... Orderly administration is the essential condition of life ... But it does not make life. That which constitutes the characteristic life of a race lies in its passions, its ambitions, its imagination.[141]

Disraeli himself said of the Imperial Titles Act of 1876, 'It is only by the amplification of titles that you can often touch and satisfy the imagination of nations; and that is an element which Governments must not despise'. Even he was amazed by Lytton's plans for the Delhi Durbar to commemorate the new title in India: the first of the great imperial ceremonials of the late nineteenth century, they read, wrote Disraeli, 'like the thousand and one nights'.[142] As *The Times* observed on the Prince of Wales' return in May 1876, 'Invention is taxed to keep Royalty in the front of that stage of active and original life upon which all eyes are fixed.[143]

Henceforth royal events were marked with more magnificence and were occasions of an almost unanimous approval of state pageantry and calls for still more of it. The *Daily News* was pleased to see in the wedding of Prince Arthur in 1879 the most 'pomp and circumstance' since the Princess Royal's wedding[144] – that is the most since Albert's death.[145] However, the wedding, for all its lavish ceremonial, was of a private character, held at Windsor. *Lloyd's Weekly Newspaper* regretted 'The distance at which people are kept from all the festivities, or events, which closely concern the Royal Family'.[146] The *Observer* argued that 'For all great occasions in English history Westminster Abbey, or St

Paul's is the proper site'. This would afford the opportunity for great public celebrations in the capital: 'No doubt all gala making is what political economists would call "unproductive consumption"; but life cannot be carried on without cakes and ale'. The paper added that a 'more regular and magnificent court presence in London was desirable'.[147]

The wedding of the Queen's last son, Prince Leopold, in 1882 produced similar arguments from the *Observer*, which noted that putting on a fine pageant was a matter of 'national self-respect'.[148] The *Daily Telegraph,* hitherto lukewarm towards ceremonial, agreed that Britain, with 'unequalled resources in the way of ceremonial pomp, gorgeous pageantry and inestimable treasures', had confounded the commonplace that it did not excel in pageants.[149] *Lloyd's Weekly Newspaper*, which had always been eager to present the spectacular aspect of monarchy to its large readership,[150] wrote that those normally preoccupied with politics were fascinated by the 'high ceremonial' of the wedding.[151] Even the *Spectator* was now pleased to see royal pomp back in fashion: 'The ceremony ... was notable for a certain sustained and perfect stateliness and brilliancy, often absent from English Court festivities' – a reversal of the tendency since Albert's death to suppress 'the ornamental side of the Monarchy, which makes such pageants, when they do occur, much more attractive'. So long the mouthpiece of rational Benthamism, it acknowledged that the

> English people are exceedingly pleased with any ceremonial or pageant which is at once customary and splendid ... foreign to the orderliness of their own lives ... They like all that magnificence, just as they like descriptions of jewels or scenes in the "Arabian Nights".[152]

The *Illustrated London News* referred to the Chapel Royal as a 'theatre' and the royal children as its 'chief actors' in so many similar scenes. Royal events were seen as magical and polished performances.[153]

By the mid-1880s there was a consensus that royal pageantry should be splendid and public. A life of the Queen looked back at the wedding of 1840 and commented that 'the military was not a very prominent feature in the picture, and the State element was also to some extent wanting' – it was felt that 'the marriage of the sovereign was not so much a public ceremonial as a private event in her life'.[154] The Queen still tended to regard royal weddings in this way – the marriage of her youngest child, Princess Beatrice took place in the village of Whippingham in 1885. However, there was a determination in the press that the Queen's Jubilee would be marked by imposing ceremonial.[155] *The Times* wrote that it was an opportunity finally to dispel the myth 'that the English people do not care for shows and ceremonies'. The problem lay with the organizers of ceremonial in England – their 'excessive amount of "mauvaise honte"' and 'passion for privacy that is morbid'. They should recognize that 'Shows and ceremonies ... have their place in human nature, and ought accordingly to have their place in ordinances of wise rulers'.[156] The victory – albeit partial – of opinion orchestrated by the press over the Queen's minimalist inclinations in 1887 was to signal the beginning of a century in which every effort was made to gratify the popular taste for pageantry, and ceremonial became the forte of the British monarchy.

1887–1901: more substantial pageants

J.L. Lant and David Cannadine have described the improvements in the quality of royal ceremonial in the final years of the reign.[157] As can be expected from the foregoing analysis, press reaction to the Jubilees and the Queen's funeral was to applaud the efforts that had been made and to call for even more at a time when the significance of displaying national grandeur was seen as increasingly important. Criticism of ceremonial was confined to republicans, critics of the cost of the monarchy and opponents of the imperialism and militarism which the ceremonies celebrated – these criticisms were examined in chapters 3 and 6.

The *Spectator* remarked that 'the cultivated' felt that the ceremonial laid on for the Golden Jubilee was 'a little ridiculous' but that 'on the other hand, the interest and the pleasure felt by the body of people of all classes in the Jubilee as a show surpassed everything we can remember'.[158] Lant has shown how pressure from the newspapers induced the Queen to lengthen the intended route of the procession from the palace to Westminster Abbey and how there was widespread disappointment in the press that the ceremony was not to be in full state dress or coaches.[159] After the event there was some regret that it had not been even more splendid. The *Spectator* wrote, 'The people wished the procession longer and brighter ... the military display greater ... an infinitely larger Oriental element' – Londoners were 'as willing as Italians to organize a *festa*' and 'to witness a highly coloured moving scene'.[160]

The general feeling however was one of real, if somewhat surprised, admiration for the pageant which had been put on. The *Daily Telegraph* described it as 'the exception' to the rule that British ceremonial was drab.[161] *The Times* wrote of a pageant of 'unrivalled splendour'; the Jubilee had been a success 'beyond all expectation and hope'; Londoners had bedecked the streets with 'surprising splendour'.[162] The *Illustrated London News*, its pages packed with pictures of the event, described 'Pageantry such as this generation never saw'.[163] Such pageantry was a release from everyday life – the *Daily News* and *Spectator* both used the term 'fairyland'[164] and the *Pall Mall Gazette* wrote of 'magic'.

The deeper significance of the ceremony lay in its binding the nation together and displaying the strength of that united nation. *The Times* described the Jubilee as a 'festival of patriotism and loyalty', with the good relation between the crowd and the police being an example of the general consensus.[165] The *Daily Telegraph* wrote, 'It will enrich our national life with deeper sentiments of patriotism; it will link class together in closer bonds of good feeling; it will help England abroad and at home'. (We must note here, as shown in chapter 5, that statements of national unity in anti-Home Rule newspapers like *The Times* and *Telegraph* had a partisan purpose in 1887 and that Liberal newspapers like the *Daily News* regretted the lack of concord in Ireland as marring the celebrations.) As we saw in chapter 6, the Jubilee was seen as an opportunity to reinforce patriotism and show the might of the nation at a time of growing international rivalry – to quote the *Daily Telegraph*, 'national fetes . . . bring home to every Englishman the fact that he has a country'.[166]

The public appetite having been whetted for better ceremonial, there was much enthusiasm at the Duke of York's wedding event. *The Times* approved the longer processional route and was pleased to judge that 'we have improved somewhat in the art of popular rejoicing' since the groom's father's wedding 30 years earlier.[167] There were full diagrammatic details of the wedding day arrangements in the *Pall Mall Gazette*, which in 1889 at the time of the Royal grants debate had complained that there had not been enough pageantry in Victoria's reign.[168] The *Daily News* used the American term 'feel good' to describe the mood engendered, though it felt that for the wedding itself a venue five times the size of the Chapel Royal was needed.[169] Similarly the *Spectator* wrote of 'a splendid ceremonial' in a 'confined and rather dingy place'.[170]

Lant has described how, following the success of the Golden Jubilee, preparations for the Diamond were made with more confidence and much further in advance, with more careful planning and rehearsal and greater ambition – as seen in the use of St Paul's instead of Westminster Abbey for the main thanksgiving service. The result was a more imposing spectacle,[171] which certainly captured the imagination of the press. The *Pall Mall Gazette* wrote, 'The spectacle has lent colour to lives of drab monotony';[172] the *Daily Telegraph* pronounced it a 'pageant brilliant almost beyond imagination'[173] and *The Times* boasted of 'a Royal procession of unequalled grandeur'.[174] To critics of the militarism of the ceremony, the rejoinder was that marching troops and military bands made for the most pomp and spectacle – it was impossible to represent arts and industry effectively in a procession.[175]

A novel feature of the Diamond Jubilee was that the spectacle of the procession could be seen throughout the country as it was recorded on film by nearly all the recently formed British film companies. John Barnes has written that the Jubilee was 'an event upon which practically the whole of the British film industry directed its undivided attention'. One Bradford company succeeded in showing its film in the town on the very evening of the Jubilee. Barnes estimates that more films of the Jubilee were sold in Britain that year than of any other subject.[176]

As noted in chapter 6, display of imperial strength was the keynote of the Diamond Jubilee. The *Pall Mall Gazette* saw the importance of the presence of the imperial troops in bringing the reality of Empire home to the British public.[177] Moreover several newspapers remarked that the marching troops would, to quote the *Daily News*, 'remind our foreign critics of the existence of the British army' rated by some as inferior to the Belgian and Serbian but still in Napoleon's words, 'the best in the world' though 'there is very little of it'.[178] Such self-assertiveness may have betokened insecurity about Britain's continued greatness; Kipling's *Recessional* published in *The Times* on the morning of the Jubilee certainly struck a pessimistic note:

> Far-called our navies melt away:
>   On dune and headland sinks the fire:
> Lo, all our pomp of yesterday
>   Is one with Nineveh and Tyre.[179]

On the Queen's death, there was a general desire in the press for 'a stately and elaborate funeral'[180] and much approval of the ceremonial devised. As discussed in chapter 6, the predominantly military and imperial character of the ceremony caused some friction between supporters and opponents of the concurrent Boer War. The *Daily Telegraph* wrote approvingly that the funeral rites had 'an iron pomp'.[181] Even the pro-Boer *Daily News* wrote, 'No such impressive pageant has been seen before by anyone now living'.[182] The *Illustrated London News*, which contained magnificent pictures of the funeral, saluted the improvization of Prince Louis of Battenburg who (establishing a precedent in the process) ordered naval ratings to pull the gun carriage bearing the Queen's body when a horse snapped the traces: 'There imagination triumphed indeed in the most splendidly dramatic touch of the whole ceremony'.

One of the most important effects of the ceremony was held to be the way in which it brought the grandeur of the monarchy into people's lives with an impact which would be passed on through the generations. The *Illustrated London News* commented:

Many of the onlookers belonged to the poorer classes – men whose rough toil afforded little stimulus to the imagination. Few of them had ever looked on the Queen in life; but in her crowned death she touched them to a reverential awe that made a visible impression on their lives.[183]

For *The Times*:

Most priceless of all will be the memory . . . left in the minds of the little children, hundreds of thousands of whom will tell in the years to come that they were taken . . . to see the people's unspoken sorrow, to behold the coffin of the good Queen, with its pall of pure white and its insignia of Royalty . . . [184]

Conclusion

There was a fundamental continuity in attitudes to royal ceremonial during the years 1837–1901, and too strong a division should not be drawn between a 'utilitarian' early period and an 'irrational' later one. However, the circumstances surrounding this basic enthusiasm for pageantry were changing and imparting a greater significance to the ceremonial of the Crown. The blatant partisanship of the Crown was abandoned in the 1840s and this made royal events more consensual occasions – the party bickering of Whig and Tory newspapers over the coronation and wedding was not repeated at later celebrations. The perception of the diminution of the monarchy's political power increased the importance of its symbolic role as head of the nation. Though the *Examiner* equated the decline in the Crown's power with the decline of its pomp when compared with the Stuarts' elaborate rituals of power,[185] the general opinion was that the continued usefulness of the monarchy lay in making regular and striking ceremonial appearances. At the same time a greater self-conscious concern over Britain's place in the world dispelled the complacency which had marked earlier ceremonials: whereas imposing pomp had previously been considered the superficial vainglory of weaker nations, by the 1870s there was a feeling that British greatness had to be manifested in such pageants. By 1887 it was widely acknowledged by the rationalist, utilitarian and often republican critics of pageantry that spectacle had a considerable hold on the public imagination.

The underlying meaning of royal ceremonials was a more contentious matter. Most newspapers wrote of the deep-seated, popular loyalty to the Crown to which such events gave occasions for expression. William M. Kuhn has argued that there was a deep religiosity behind royal pageants: he points out that a service was the centre point of every royal celebration, and cites the role of the highly religious Gladstone in organizing the thanksgiving for the Prince of Wales' recovery.[186] There is some evidence of this in contemporary perceptions. The *Illustrated London News* wrote of the 'union of men's souls in the outpouring of a high religious feeling' in the Golden Jubilee service at Westminster Abbey[187]; *The Times* called the Diamond Jubilee a 'great national solemnity'.[188]

However, on the whole, as the *Examiner* observed of the 1872 thanksgiving, there was no doubt that it was 'the earthly not the heavenly sovereign who was worshipped' in the celebrations.[189] Though a greater ritualism in the established Church facilitated a greater royal ritual in the latter part of the century,[190] very little is found in newspaper editorials on royal ceremonial about the religious significance of the services – they are preoccupied with the devotion which they saw manifested to the sovereign in the popular reception of the attendant pageantry. The *Daily Telegraph* observed that comparatively few people would actually attend the service at Westminster Abbey in 1887 but that 'the public generally need not regret that they do not witness it. In the streets by day and by night will be constantly visible the best and most wonderful sights in the Jubilee celebrations'.[191]

The *Saturday Review*, one of the most consistent advocates of pageantry, argued that newspapers read too much into popular excitement – people, through loyal to the Crown, were not consciously thinking of the benefits of the monarchical system when they turned out in such large numbers; there was no deeper significance than the enjoyment of spectacle and of a holiday.[192] The *Spectator* agreed, seeing the only possible deeper meaning of such enjoyment as a desire to know, from royal example, what was 'right' in the conduct of weddings.[193] *The Times* suggested that the Golden Jubilee had various meanings:

> A solemn service of thanksgiving has been rendered in the sanctuary of the nation; its seriousness and importance has not been overlooked. Finally, the people have kept high festival, and have conspicuously and manifestly enjoyed a national holiday.[194]

In the previous chapter we saw how the appeal of the Royal Family consisted in its being like a typical middle-class family while at the same time inhabiting a remote, fairy-tale world. There was a certain contradiction in this – and some felt that the monarchy's ceremonial, which belonged to the realms of fairy-tale, of marked difference from the lives of the monarch's subjects, could only decline as the Royal Family became familiar to the public, through photography, as participants in a normal domestic life, wearing ordinary clothes.[195] However, for most the contradiction could be resolved and herein lay the secret of the

British monarchy's future success – to inspire a devoted interest in the Royal Family as a family with which the public could identify, and yet for that family to appear on great occasions with all the pomp of state to excite the public taste for the colourful and exotic.

Notes

1. J.L. Lant, *Insubstantial Pageant. Ceremony and Confusion at Queen Victoria's Court* (London, 1979).
2. William M. Kuhn, 'Ceremony and Politics: The British Monarchy, 1871 –1872', *Journal of British Studies*, vol. 26, no. 2 (April 1987), pp. 133– 62.
3. See above, chapter 7.
4. David Cannadine, 'The Context, Performance and Meaning of Ritual: the British Monarchy and the "Invention of Tradition" c. 1820–1977' in Eric Hobsbawm and Terence Ranger eds, *The Invention of Tradition* (Cambridge, 1983), pp. 101–64.
5. Walter L. Arnstein, 'Queen Victoria opens parliament: the Disinvention of Tradition', *Historical Research*, 43 (1990), pp. 178–94, does not look at contemporary comment on ceremonial but does make the point that there were for the first 24 years of the reign regular ceremonial appearances at the state opening of parliament before Albert's death.
6. See Philip Guedalla, *The Queen and Mr. Gladstone, vol. 1 (1845–1879)*, (London, 1933).
7. Lant, *Insubstantial Pageant*, pp. 216–17.
8. Elizabeth Longford, *Victoria R.I.* (London, 1983 edn), p. 402.
9. Lant, *Insubstantial Pageant*, p. 29.
10. *The Times*, 9 November 1837, p. 2.
11. Ibid., 1 February 1901, p. 7.
12. Linda Colley, 'The Apotheosis of George III: Loyalty, Royalty and the British Nation 1760–1820', *Past and Present*, no. 102 (1984), pp. 94– 129.
13. Christopher Hibbert, *George IV* (London, 1976 edn), pp. 597–604.
14. Ibid., p. 784.
15. Philip Ziegler, *King William IV* (London, 1971), p. 152.
16. See above, chapter 7.
17. Duke of Buckingham and Chandos, *Memoirs of the Courts and Cabinets of William IV and Victoria*, 2 vols (London, 1861), vol. 2, p. 336.
18. *Figaro in London*, March–May 1838, passim.
19. *Hansard*, vol. 43, cols 349–50.
20. Cannadine, 'The Context, Performance and Meaning of Ritual', p. 117; Longford, *Victoria R.I.*, pp. 99–104. For full contemporary accounts, see Agnes Strickland, *Queen Victoria. From Her Birth to Her Bridal*, 2 vols (London, 1840), vol. 1, p. 287–334, and *Anecdotes, Personal Traits and characteristic Sketches of Victoria the First. By A Lady* (London, 1840), pp. 571–683.
21. *John Bull*, 1 July 1838, p. 304.
22. *Globe*, 28 June 1838, p. 3.
23. *Sunday Times*, 24 June 1838, p. 4.

24. *Hansard*, vol. 43, col. 350.
25. *Spectator*, 30 June 1838, p. 609.
26. *Northern Star*, 30 June 1838, p. 4.
27. *Sunday Times*, 1 July 1838, p. 4.
28. Buckingham, *Memoirs*, vol. 2, p. 337.
29. *Record*, 29 June 1838, p. 4.
30. *Courier*, 28 June 1838, p. 3.
31. *Leeds Mercury*, 30 June 1838, p. 4.
32. Lant, *Insubstantial Pageant*, p. 24.
33. *Morning Chronicle*, 28 June 1838, p. 2.
34. *The Greville Memoirs*, (ed. Henry Reeve, 8 vols, London, 1888 edn), vol. 4, p. 113; *Anecdotes . . . of Victoria the First*, pp. 571–683
35. *Standard*, 29 June 1838, p. 2.
36. *Observer*, 10 February 1840, p. 3.
37. Lant, *Insubstantial Pageant*, pp. 17–18.
38. *The Times*, 11 February 1840, p. 4.
39. *The Greville Memoirs*, vol. 4, pp. 276–7.
40. Cecil Woodham-Smith, *Queen Victoria. Her Life and Times 1819–1861* (London, 1984 edn), p. 204.
41. *Morning Post*, 10 February 1840, p. 4.
42. See above, chapter 4.
43. *Standard*, 10 February 1840, p. 3.
44. *Morning Chronicle*, 11 February 1840, p. 1.
45. *English Republic*, vol. 1 (1851), p. 70.
46. Benjamin Disraeli, *Coningsby* (1st pub. 1844, Oxford, 1982 edn), p. 127.
47. *Morning Chronicle*, 1 May 1851, p. 4 .
48. *Illustrated London News*, 3 May 1851, pp. 343–51.
49. *Daily News*, 1 May 1851, p. 4 .
50. *Standard*, 2 May 1851, p. 2.
51. See above, chapter 7.
52. *Democratic Review*, vol. 1 (1849–50), p. 32.
53. *Reynolds's Political Instructor*, 24 November 1849, pp. 17–18.
54. *Red Republican*, 24 August 1850, p. 77.
55. Ibid., 2 November 1850, p. 160.
56. *Church Quarterly Review*, vol. 5 (October 1877–January 1878), p. 469.
57. See above, chapter 7.
58. *Punch*, vol. 11 (1846), p. 117.
59. Lant, *Insubstantial Pageant*, p. 18.
60. See above, chapters 4 and 7.
61. Robert Rhodes James, *Albert, Prince Consort. A Biography* (London, 1983), p. 102.
62. *The Times*, 22 June 1857, p. 8.
63. *Spectator*, 23 January 1858, p. 89. See for example *The Times*, 25 January 1858, p. 6; *Morning Chronicle*, 26 January 1858, p. 4.
64. *Illustrated London News*, 23 January 1858, pp. 73–4; 30 January 1858, p. 97.
65. *Daily Telegraph*, 26 January 1858, p. 3. The choice of the Chapel Royal was widely criticized: see *The Times*, 26 January 1858, p. 6. *The Morning Herald* declared that the wedding should have taken place at Westminster Abbey (26 January 1858, p. 4).
66. *Daily Telegraph*, 26 January 1858, p. 3.

67. *The Times*, 26 January 1858, p. 6.
68. *Daily Telegraph*, 26 January 1858, p. 3.
69. *Lloyd's Weekly Newspaper*, 3 January 1858, p. 6.
70. See above, chapter 4.
71. *The Times*, 24 December 1861, p. 6.
72. Paul S. Fritz, 'From "Public" to "Private": the Royal Funerals in England, 1500–1830' in Joachim Whaley, ed., *Mirrors of Mortality. Studies in the Social History of Death* (London, 1981), pp. 61–79.
73. *Daily Telegraph*, 24 December 1861, p. 2.
74. Norman St John-Stevas' introduction to *The Collected Works of Walter Bagehot, Vol. 5* (London, 1974), pp. 81–3.
75. Cannadine, 'The Context, Performance and Meaning of Ritual', pp. 118–19.
76. See above, chapter 5.
77. See above, chapter 3.
78. *The Times*, 2 July 1862, p. 8
79. Ibid., 2 July 1862, p. 8.
80. Ibid, 4 March 1863, p. 8; 9 March 1863, p. 7.
81. Jeremy Maas, *The Prince of Wales' Wedding. The Story of a Picture.* (London, 1977), pp. 25–39.
82. *Illustrated London News*, 7 March 1863, pp. 237–8.
83. *Saturday Review*, 28 February 1863, pp. 256–7.
84. Ibid., 9 February 1861, pp. 140–1.
85. Ibid., 8 February 1862, p. 153.
86. Ibid., 14 November 1863, pp. 633–4.
87. Ibid., 28 February 1863, pp. 256–7.
88. Ibid., 26 March 1864, pp. 367–8.
89. *The Times*, 12 October 1863, p. 8 .
90. Longford, *Victoria R.I.*, p. 401; *The Times*, 1 April 1864, p. 8.
91. *The Times*, 6 April 1864, p. 9.
92. Ibid., 30 August 1865, p. 8.
93. *The Collected Works of Walter Bagehot*, Vol. 5, p. 253.
94. Ibid., p. 234.
95. Ibid., p. 229.
96. Ibid., pp. 237–8.
97. Ibid., p. 226.
98. Ibid., pp. 230–4.
99. Ibid., pp. 239–40.
100. Ibid., pp. 240–1.
101. Ibid., pp. 238–9.
102. Ibid., pp. 418–20.
103. In 1866 because parliament would be asked to approve grants to Prince Alfred and Princess Helena, and in 1867 to show confidence in Derby's government as it launched the Reform Bill.
104. Freda Harcourt, 'The Queen, the Sultan and the Viceroy: A Victorian State Occasion', *London Journal*, vol. 5 (May 1979), pp. 35–56.
105. *The Collected Works of Walter Bagehot*, Vol. 5, pp. 411–13.
106. *The Times*, 12 August 1869, p. 6.
107. Guedalla, *The Queen and Mr. Gladstone, vol. 1*, pp. 156–304.
108. *The Times*, 8 November 1869, pp. 6–7.
109. Ibid., 21 October 1869, p. 6.

110. *Sunday Times*, 26 March 1871, p. 4.
111. *Spectator*, 25 March 1871, pp. 337, 346–7.
112. *Illustrated London News*, 25 March 1871.
113. *Daily News*, 21 March 1871, p. 4.
114. See above, chapter 3.
115. *The Collected Works of Walter Bagehot, Vol. 5*, pp. 431–4.
116. *Pall Mall Gazette*, 9 November 1871, p. 1; *Saturday Review*, 11 November 1871, pp. 608–9.
117. Cannadine, 'the Context, Performance and Meaning of Ritual', pp. 108, 123, 161; Lant, *Insubstantial Pagent*, p. 24.
118. Freda Harcourt, 'Gladstone, Monarchism and the "New Imperialism", 1868–74', *Journal of Imperial and Commonwealth History vol. 14* (October 1985), pp. 30–1; Kuhn, 'Ceremony and Politics', pp. 146–7.
119. Kuhn, 'Ceremony and Politics', p. 147.
120. Lant, *Insubstantial Pageant*, pp. 27–31.
121. *The Times*, 23 February 1871, p. 9.
122. *Pall Mall Gazette*, 27 Februaury 1872, p. 1.
123. *Daily News*, 27 February 1872, p. 4.
124. *Saturday Review*, 2 March 1872, pp. 259–60.
125. *Daily Telegraph*, 27 February 1872, p. 4.
126. *Daily News*, 27 February 1872, p. 4 .
127. Lant, *Insubstantial Pagent*, p. 81; *Daily News*, 27 February 1872, p. 4.
128. *Spectator*, 2 March 1872, p. 271; *Illustrated London News*, 2 March 1872, p. 203.
129. See above, chapter 6; *The Times*, 24 February 1872, p. 9; 26 February 1872, p. 9.
130. *Daily Telegraph*, 12 March 1874, p. 5 .
131. *Spectator*, 14 March 1874, pp. 331–2.
132. *Sunday Times*, 15 March 1874, p. 4.
133. *Daily Telegraph*, 15 March 1874, p. 4.
134. *Reynolds's Newspaper*, 15 March 1874, p. 4.
135. *National Reformer*, 22 March 1874, pp. 178–9.
136. *The Collected Works of Walter Bagehot, Vol 5*, pp. 418–20.
137. *Letter to the Queen on her retirement from Public Life.* By one of Her Majesty's Most Loyal Subjects (London, 1875), Preface and pp. 10–79.
138. *The Collected Works of Walter Bagehot, Vol. 5*, pp. 443–6.
139. *Hansard*, vol. 225, col. 1512.
140. *Illustrated London News*, February–May 1876, passim.
141. *The Times*, 6 March 1876, p. 9.
142. W.E. Monypenny and G.E. Buckle, *The Life of Benjamin Disraeli, Earl of Beaconsfield*, 6 vols (London, 1910–20), vol. 5, pp. 456–87.
143. *The Times*, 11 May 1876, p. 9.
144. *Daily News*, 14 March 1879, p. 4.
145. *The Times*, 14 March 1879, p. 9.
146. *Lloyd's Weekly Newspaper*, 16 March 1879, p. 6.
147. *Observer*, 16 March 1879, p. 5.
148. Ibid., 30 April 1882, p. 5.
149. *Daily Telegraph*, 27 April 1882, p. 6.
150. V.S. Berridge, 'Popular Journalism and Working Class Attitudes 1854–86: A study of *Reynolds's Newspaper, Lloyds Weekly Newspaper and the Weekly Times*' (unpub. PhD, London, 1976), p. 334.

151. *Lloyd's Weekly Newspaper*, 30 April 1882, p. 6.
152. *Spectator*, 29 April 1882, pp. 549, 556–7.
153. *Illustrated London News*, 29 April 1882, p. 398.
154. *The Life of her most gracious majesty the Queen*, by Sarah Tytler, 2 vols (London, 1885), vol. 1. p. 115.
155. See Lant, *Insubstantial Pageant*, pp. 150–76.
156. *The Times*, 24 March 1886, p. 9.
157. Lant, *Insubstantial Pageant*, passim, Cannadine, 'The Context, Meaning and Performance of Ritual', pp. 122–36.
158. *Spectator*, 25 June 1887, pp. 857–8.
159. Lant, *Insubstantial Pageant*, pp. 152–7, 167.
160. *Spectator*, 25 June 1887, pp. 857–8.
161. *Daily Telegraph*, 21 June 1887, pp. 4–5.
162. *The Times*, 22 June 1887, p. 5.
163. *Illustrated London News*, 25 June 1887, pp. 706–7.
164. *Daily News*, 21 June 1887, p. 4; *Spectator*, 25 June 1887, p. 852.
165. *The Times*, 22 June 1887, p. 5.
166. *Daily Telegraph*, 21 June 1887, pp. 4–5.
167. *The Times*, 7 July 1893, p. 9.
168. *Pall Mall Gazette*, 25 July 1889, p. 1, 6 July 1889, p. 7.
169. *Daily News*, 7 July 1893, pp. 4–5.
170. *Spectator*, 8 July 1893, p. 33.
171. Lant, *Insubstantial Pageant*, pp. 220–6, 244–6.
172. *Pall Mall Gazette*, 21 June 1897.
173. *Daily Telegraph*, 23 June 1897, pp. 8–9.
174. *The Times*, 23 June 1897, p. 9.
175. *Spectator*, 19 June 1897, pp. 856–7; *Daily News*, 21 June 1897, p. 6.
176. John Barnes, *The Rise of the Cinema in Great Britain, vol. 2 Jubilee Year 1897* (London, 1983), pp. 178–99. I am indebted to Dr Nick Hiley for drawing my attention to this aspect of the Jubilee.
177. *Pall Mall Gazette*, 21 June 1897.
178. *Daily News*, 23 June 1897. See also *Daily Telegraph*, 22 June 1897, p. 5, *Daily Mail*, 22 June 1897, p. 4, *The Times* 23 June 1897, p. 14.
179. *The Times*, 17 July 1897, p. 13.
180. *Daily Telegraph*, 24 January 1901, p. 8.
181. Ibid., 1 February 1901, p. 6.
182. *Daily News*, 4 February 1901, p. 6.
183. *Illustrated London News*, 2 February 1901, p. 186; 9 February 1901, pp. 187–91.
184. *The Times*, 4 February 1901, p. 5.
185. *Examiner*, no. 3711 (15 March 1879), p. 352.
186. Kuhn, 'Ceremony and Politics', pp. 161–2.
187. *Illustrated London News*, 25 June 1887, pp. 706–7.
188. *The Times*, 21 June 1897, p. 13.
189. *Examiner*, 2 March 1872, p. 221.
190. Cannadine, 'The Context, Meaning and Performance of Ritual', pp. 131–2.
191. *Daily Telegraph*, 20 June 1887, pp. 4 -5
192. *Saturday Review*, 14 March 1874, pp. 328–9. Similarly, the *Examiner* observed that a crowd would assemble to gape at anything [14 March 1874, pp. 250–1].

193. *Spectator*, 29 April 1882, pp. 556–7.
194. *The Times*, 22 June 1887, p. 5.
195. For example, *Daily News*, 21 March 1871, p. 4; *Daily Telegraph*, 13 March 1879, p. 4.

CHAPTER NINE

Conclusion

This book has shown that the Victorians were as preoccupied with the monarchy as our society is now. In uncovering and analysing the breadth and complexity of the public discussion to which the preoccupation gave rise, this study supersedes work which has touched on the aspects of the Victorian monarchy treated here. Previously there had been partial accounts of nineteenth-century republicanism, internal constitutional histories, schematic discussions of patriotism and of royal ceremonial, and references to reverence for the monarchy as part of late nineteenth-century social control. Here I shall draw together and summarize my findings and then demonstrate how they enhance our understanding both of the modern British monarchy and of the Victorian age.

I

The arguments advanced in this book can be summarized in three concluding statements. First, discussion of the monarchy throughout Victoria's reign was of a far greater volume, intensity and variety than has hitherto been realized. While those wanting the abolition of the monarchy were always in a minority – though a significant and organized minority in the early 1870s – there was always debate on the political and ceremonial functions of the institution, its cost and its patriotism; and on the way in which the Queen, Albert and the rest of the Royal Family fulfilled their roles.

Secondly, the old model of the linear rise in the standing of the monarchy – from unpopularity in the first half of the reign to popularity in the second – needs to be broken down and amended. A veneration for the monarchy, a devotion to the person of the sovereign and her family, existed from the outset of the reign and was not an offshoot of late-century imperialism or of a new form of social control. The transformation of the monarchy consisted in a stripping away of its most controversial characteristics, a process, by no means without abrupt checks, which gradually detracted from the force of the criticisms of the Crown which had existed alongside the veneration and which persisted in 1887–1901 – but now in self-acknowledged defeat.

Thirdly, the political power of the monarchy was its most controversial aspect and the fulcrum point of the other facets of this study. It was the rumour of political interference by the Crown which occasioned the greatest crisis of royal unpopularity in this period – in 1853–4. Conversely, it was the perception that the monarchy was a limited, constitutional one under which the people enjoyed self-government which was the chief stumbling block for English republicanism. As the power of the Crown was seen to decline, patriotic criticisms of the 'Germanism' of the Royal Family lost their bite, as the Crown could no longer be portrayed as influencing policy for unEnglish ends – as had been the explosive issue in 1853–4. The decline in the importance of the monarchy's political functions augmented that of its ceremonial and domestic ones. The Royal Family ceased to appear as controversial political actors but as the consensual cynosures of national pageants and of an ideal yet identifiable family life.

II

In what ways do these arguments illuminate the history of the modern British monarchy and of Britain in the nineteenth century? The circumstances which had coalesced by 1887 to give the monarchy its secure standing, which it enjoyed, apart from tremors in the First World War and at the time of the abdication crisis, for the next 100 years, are circumstances which no longer exist – a world role for the monarchy at the centre of an empire, an outwardly stable family life, mirroring those of its subjects, and an overwhelmingly deferential press. Today even Commonwealth ties are dissolving, there is a much-changed attitude in the press, particularly in those newspapers marked by the new, non-deferential Conservatism, and, were Bagehot alive, he would write that a princely divorce rather than a princely wedding was the 'brilliant edition of a universal fact'. The period 1887 to c.1987 now seems an exceptional period of stability in a generally turbulent history for the British monarchy since 1642. As noted in chapter 7, the admiration accorded to the monarchy at the time of the Jubilees and the Queen's death was conditional on the fulfilment by the Royal Family of the roles, public and domestic, expected of them. The *Spectator* wrote in 1901 that the British public would show 'in the future, as they have shown in the past, an attitude of free and vigilant watchfulness and criticism towards the Crown, as towards all other institutions'.[1]

David Cannadine argues that in some ways Victoria was less the founder of the twentieth-century British monarchy than the 'last Hanoverian monarch'.[2] Indeed, with regard to the Queen's actual conduct – Professor Cannadine's concern in that essay – this was in many ways true: she was an ardent political partisan and busybody, her court was very Germanic and the marriage ties of her children were as much contrived matches of state as had been those of her predecessors'. This is partly reflected in perceptions of the monarchy – my concern: Victoria had inherited a contentious crown from her uncles and her reign was to be characterized by periodic political controversies and criticisms of the Crown's 'Germanism'. Yet this was only part of the picture. The period 1837–1901 was a turning-point, a bridge between the Hanoverian and Windsor monarchies in that as political debate and slurs on the Crown's patriotism lessened, the consensual vision of the British monarchy came to predominate, with its less contentious ceremonial and domestic aspects to the fore.

But it was only from a very complex set of perceptions and attitudes that this vision emerged. In an article on advertising in the year of the Golden Jubilee, Thomas Richards wrote that by 1887, the advertising world 'had not yet settled on a systematic way of representing Queen Victoria ... there was no general agreement as to how to go about using Victoria's image'.[3] This was because Victorian England in general had not settled on one image of its ruler.

It is to Victorian England itself that we must look for the key to perceptions of the Crown. A rumbustious society of diverse political and social groups, it threw many different images up onto the monarchy, Queen and Royal Family – the Old Corruption, privileged incompetence, German parasites; the constitutional paragon, the symbol of nation and of empire, the faerie queen, the thrifty housewife, the perfect bourgeois matron. The monarchy had become a blank cheque on which to write one's own values – the completion of the process was visible at the end of the reign when, in their eulogies on the deceased Queen, the leaders of the two parties projected very different images, those of their respective political creeds, onto the reign's achievements. Balfour said 'We associate Queen Victoria with the great succession of events which has filled her reign, with the growth, material and moral, of the Empire over which she reigned'; while Campbell-Bannerman spoke of 'the Queen's personal and sincere devotion to the cause of peace and freedom and uprightness'.[4]

What happened around the monarchy was more important than what the monarch herself did. It could almost be said that Victoria did her utmost to subvert the standing of the monarchy, interfering partisanly and often in the interests of her German relatives and entirely abrogating her ceremonial duties after Albert's death. Yet she never induced a serious head-on clash with parliament and, for the rest, there was sufficient social cohesion and deference for a suspension of disbelief. Enthusiasm for ceremonial, the preoccupation of the press with the trivia of the Royal Family's day-to-day life showed, to the chagrin of republicans, that, for all its progress and rationality, nineteenth-century England was still rife with flunkeyism.

At the outset of this book I observed that nineteenth-century history has been written largely about the new working class and rising middle class and that the established hereditary elite had been comparatively neglected. Work on the aristocracy has begun in earnest but, while for her subjects the Queen was, in Lytton Strachey's words, 'an indissoluble part of their whole scheme of things',[5] the same has not been true for Victorian historians. Elizabeth Longford wrote that Victoria's role was 'to stamp a great age with the royal cypher. The nineteenth century would have been great without her. It would not have been "Victorian" as we understand it',[6] yet a curious gap in our understanding of the Victorian age and values has been the place in the Victorian mind of the Queen herself and the institution she represented. Until now someone wishing to learn of the nineteenth-century monarchy would have had recourse only to largely hagiographical biographies and to internal constitutional histories concerned with the minutiae of the Queen's correspondence, while comparatively little could be gleaned about the most important aspect of modern monarchy – its reputation. It is important that reputation should be studied, as I study it here, over a lengthy period of time, for it is only then that one can get a sense of continuity and change and of what are the important elements in influencing public perceptions. The work which I have initiated should be extended on both sides of its chronological limits and deepened in the Victorian period by local studies of popular attitudes. Modern British history can no longer be history with the monarchy left out.

Notes

1. *Spectator*, 26 January 1901, pp. 129–30.
2. David Cannadine, 'The Last Hanoverian Sovereign? The Victorian Monarchy in Historical Perspective 1688–1988' in A.L. Beier, David Cannadine and James M. Rosenheim eds, *The First Modern Society: Essays in English History in Honour of Lawrence Stone* (Cambridge, 1989).
3. Thomas Richards, 'The Image of Victoria in the Year of the Jubilee', *Victorian Studies*, vol. 31, no. 1 (Autumn 1987), pp. 14–16.
4. *Hansard*, 4th ser., vol. 89, cols 19–26.
5. Lytton Strachey, *Queen Victoria* (London, 1969 edn), pp. 253–4.
6. Elizabeth Longford, *Victoria R.I.* (London, 1983 edn), p. 17.

Index

Dixon, George 45, 119
Dunckley, Henry 130–1

Early Years of HRH the Prince Consort (Grey) 206–7
Economist 243
Edinburgh, Duke of *see* Alfred, Prince
Edinburgh (place) 52, 142
Edinburgh Review 4, 129
Edward VII *see* Albert Edward, Prince of Wales
Edward VIII 68
Edwards, John 71
Ellenborough, Edward, Lord 119, 167
Ellis, John E. 62
English Republic 21, 25, 155, 156, 162
Englishwoman's Review 145
Ernest, Duke of Cumberland, King of Hanover 90, 91, 181
Escott, T.E. 142
Esher, William, Viscount 95
Examiner 2, 4, 84, 118, 125, 206, 208, 255, 256
Eyck, Frank 92, 93, 95, 97

Fawcett, Henry 38, 44, 55
Fawcett, Milicent 145
Fife, Alexander, Earl of 216
Figaro 209
Figaro in London 233
Fisher, H.A.L. 51
Fitzwilliam, William, Lord 234
Fontane, Theodor 106, 164
Foote, G.W. 47, 50
Forster, William 54
Fortnightly Review 4, 40, 120, 243
Fox Bourne, W.R. 2
France, French 5, 21, 31, 32, 33, 36, 37–8, 39, 46, 48, 72, 100, 137, 175, 238, 244
Fraser's Magazine 38
Free Press 4, 103
Free Trade 23
Freedom 21
French, G.R. 195
Frere, Sir Bartle 133
Friend of the People 21
Frost, John 18

Fulford, Roger 95
funerals, royal 58, 177, 178, 239–40, 252

Garibaldi, Giuseppe 180
Gash, Norman 82, 89, 96, 200, 206
Gazettte de Lausanne 34
Geertz, Clifford 230
George III 5, 6, 63, 83, 90, 137, 154, 156, 160, 179, 190, 193, 201, 202, 232, 247
George IV 10, 34, 63, 83, 87, 157, 191, 193, 198, 200, 202, 204, 212, 213, 220, 232–3, 234, 238, 240
George, Prince of Denmark 102
George, Prince, Duke of York (*later* George V) 67–8, 178, 216, 217, 218
George, Prince Regent *see* George IV
George William, Prince, Duke of Cambridge 95, 159
Germanism 161–6
   see also Crown
Germany 175
Girls' Friendly Society 227 (154n)
Girls' Own Paper 212
Girouard, Mark 193
Gladstone, W.E. 34, 45, 50, 56–7, 61–2, 64, 98–9, 116, 122, 124, 127, 130, 133–8, 140–2, 146, 149 (88n), 153, 171, 209, 210, 217, 231, 237, 244, 247, 256
Glasgow 25
Globe 3, 88, 203, 233
Golden Jubilee 51, 57, 58–61, 137, 141, 153, 174, 175, 176, 180, 181, 182, 214–15, 231, 252, 253, 256, 265
   see also ceremonials; Diamond Jubilee; Thanksgiving celebration
Granville, George, Earl 34, 106
Great Exhibition (1851) 23, 25, 98, 162, 166, 198, 199, 202, 237
Greville, Charles C.F. 88, 90, 163, 193, 235
Grote, George 12

Halifax 52
Harcourt, Freda 157, 190, 209